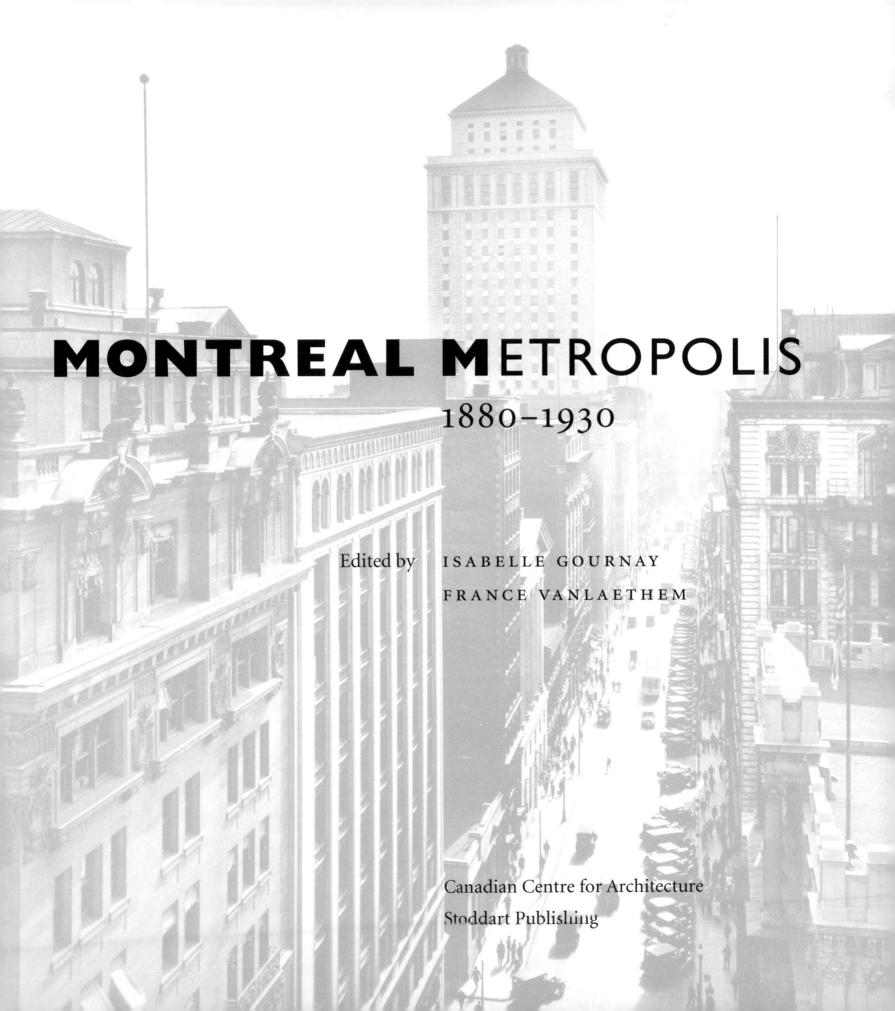

MONTREAL METROPOLIS

1880–1930

Edited by ISABELLE GOURNAY
FRANCE VANLAETHEM

Canadian Centre for Architecture
Stoddart Publishing

Copyright © 1998 by Centre Canadien d'Architecture/
Canadian Centre for Architecture

Published in 1998 by Stoddart Publishing Co. Limited in association with the Canadian Centre for Architecture.

Stoddart Publishing Co. Limited
34 Lesmill Road, Toronto, Canada M3B 2T6

02 01 00 99 98 1 2 3 4 5

ISBN 0-7737-5974-3

Printed and bound in Canada

Legal Deposit:
Bibliothèque nationale du Québec, 1998
National Library of Canada, 1998

Published in conjunction with the exhibition *Montréal Métropole, 1880–1930*, presented at the Canadian Centre for Architecture (CCA) in Montréal from 18 March to 24 May 1998, and at the National Gallery of Canada in Ottawa from 27 November to 24 January 1999. Guest curators of the exhibition are Isabelle Gournay, School of Architecture, University of Maryland, and France Vanlaethem, Département de design of the Université du Québec à Montréal.

Stoddart Publishing gratefully acknowledges the Canada Council for the Arts and the Ontario Arts Council for their support of its publishing program.

The CCA wishes to thank the Ville de Montréal for its generous support of the exhibition. The CCA also thanks the Department of Canadian Heritage, the Ministère de la Culture et des Communications du Québec, the Conseil des arts de la Communauté urbaine de Montréal, as well as the J.W. McConnell Family Foundation, Bank of Montreal, Bell Canada, Royal Bank, Teleglobe Canada Inc., Liberty Yogourt, and Omni, The Outdoor Company, for their support of the exhibition and the accompanying public programs.

Senior Editors: Christine Dufresne, Lesley Johnstone
Production Editor: Denis Hunter
Editing: Edward Tingley
Translation: Jill Corner, Helena Scheffer, Peter Smith, Judith Terry
Reproduction rights: Jocelyne Gervais
Design: Glenn Goluska

Photo Credits: Albertype Company/National Archives of Canada: fig. 67; AMS Imaging Inc.: fig. 122; Avery Architectural and Fine Arts Library: figs. 63, 101; François Bastien, Michel Boulet, CCA Photographic Services: figs. 9, 18, 19, 23, 24, 27, 31, 32, 35–40, 45, 46, 50–55, 65, 66, 80, 82, 85, 86, 87, 89, 92, 103, 106, 111, 112, 116, 118, 119, 123, 124; E.W. Bennett: fig. 120; William H. Carre: fig. 14; Kenneth Clark: fig. 115; J.(?) Bertram: back cover; Albert Dumas: fig. 4; Gordon, Montreal: fig. 42; Studio S.J. Hayward: figs. 47, 49, 104, 114; Reproduction Thierry Marcoux/Bibliothèque nationale du Québec: figs. 41, 97; The New York Historical Society: figs. 61, 62; William Notman: figs. 2, 6, 10, 30, 58, 64, 71, 93, 94; William Notman and Son: figs. 13, 25, 26, 28, 29, 33, 68, 69, 72, 79; Patent and Copyright Office/National Archives of Canada: fig. 109; Query Frères/National Archives of Canada: fig. 77.

We wish to thank the following institutions for granting permission for the use of their periodicals: Blackader-Lauterman Library of Art and Architecture, McGill University: figs. 10, 56, 78, 83, 84, 91, 96; library of the Faculté de l'aménagement de l'Université de Montréal: figs. 98, 99, 100, 107, 110; library of the École Polytechnique de l'Université de Montréal: figs. 102, 113.

Copyrights: © Bibliothèque nationale du Québec: fig. 41; © Canadian Architecture Collection, McGill University: figs. 31, 32, 35, 36, 80, 83, 85; © Centre Canadien d'Architecture/Canadian Centre for Architecture, Montréal: figs. 46, 50, 53, 65, 66, 116; © Notman Photographic Archives, McCord Museum of Canadian History, Montreal. All rights reserved: back cover and figs. 2, 6, 10, 13, 25, 26, 28, 29 (photo), 30, 33, 58, 64, 68, 69, 71, 72, 79, 93, 94, 120.

Every reasonable attempt has been made to identify owners of copyrights. Errors or omissions will be corrected in subsequent reprints.

Canadian Cataloguing in Publication Data

Montreal metropolis, 1880–1930

Issued also in French under title: Montréal métropole, 1880–1930.
Includes bibliographical references and index.
ISBN 0-7737-5974-3

1. Architecture–Quebec (Province)–Montréal–History. 2. Montréal (Quebec)–History. 3. City planning–Quebec (Province)–Montréal–History. I. Gournay, Isabelle, 1956– . II. Vanlaethem, France.

NA747.M65M6613 1998   720'.9714'28   C98-932034-0

Montréal in the era under study was a city whose streets and institutions often had names in both English and French. In the English edition of this book, the English forms in use in the period have been employed, and thus the spelling "Montreal."

CONTENTS

FOREWORD

BETWEEN TWO WORLDWIDE ECONOMIC CRISES, yet manifestly encompassing the greatest period of wealth the industrialized world had ever known, the fifty years between 1880 and 1930 were extraordinarily prosperous for Montreal, even in its North American context. The city was poised for development of a special nature. Its founding myth of 1642, a religiously inspired mission to Christianize and save the souls of the island's native peoples, was predicated on commerce – the fur trade. This dual destiny was expressed in the seventeenth and eighteenth centuries by the religious and commercial architecture of the French colonial town – notably its chapels and monasteries, and the commercially oriented vaulted basements of the stronghold stone houses within the town's fortifications.

The initial duality of religion and commerce continued, asserted by the British colonists who established Canada's first bank, the Bank of Montreal, at the edge of the old town's French Catholic centre, Place d'Armes. It was bordered on one side by the parish church of Notre Dame and the seminary of the Sulpicians (seigneurs of the island until the mid nineteenth century). The confrontation of commerce with religion was more aggressively stated with the elevation of Montreal to capital of the newly formed Union of Upper and Lower Canada in 1844; one year later the bank's imperially domed headquarters, with a six-column Corinthian portico based on the Commercial Bank of Scotland in Edinburgh, began to go up on Place d'Armes directly opposite the 1820s neo-Gothic parish church.

Within a generation, however, rivalry and accommodation between religion and commerce, francophone and anglophone, Catholic and Protestant again found a focus, in Montreal's new town centre, named in 1872 Dominion Square. Energized by unprecedented immigration during the 1850s and 1860s and by new rail access to markets in eastern Canada, the United States, and Europe, via the Victoria Bridge and Portland, Maine, the railways built their terminals to the south of the square. In 1855, the Catholic diocese itself moved westward to occupy the east side of what would become Dominion Square and the fast-developing heart of the emerging metropolis. Protestant churches would rise on the square's north and west sides in the 1860s.

In the last quarter of the century, architecturally, Dominion Square like Place d'Armes became emblematic of changing cultural values. In the 1860s the neo-Gothic, abandoned by Montreal's ultramontane Bishop, had become the preserve of Protestant churches inspired by British models. Built between 1870 and 1900, the new Cathedral of St. James the Great (now Mary Queen of the World), with its high dome and Corinthian portico crowned by statues of saints, was a scaled-down version of St. Peter's in Rome. By the late 1880s Windsor Station, a new, elaborate Richardsonian terminal for Canadian Pacific, designed by New York architect Bruce Price, exemplified the ever-growing importance of the United States to trade, commerce, and culture in Montreal. These important buildings achieved what David Hanna has termed an "architecture of a metropolitan stature."

The same signs were in full force at Place d'Armes as the old city became the financial capital of Canada. Clad in Scottish red sandstone rather than indigenous grey limestone and with a tower high enough to rise above those of Notre Dame, the New York Life Insurance Co. Building of 1887–89, by the New York architectural firm of Babb Cook and Willard, challenged the city's materiality and scale. Twenty years later, the Bank of Montreal radically changed in scale with the grandiose addition of a new banking hall to the designs of the pre-eminent New York architects McKim Mead and White. To contemporary critics Mammon had won the battle between commerce and religion.

But the battle was over, or rather the battleground relinquished, as the city – whose population had grown sevenfold between 1880 and 1930 – became differentiated. Commercial structures defined the new "downtown,"[1] while religious edifices were built at the heart of ethnically homogeneous new suburbs and new towns (French-speaking to the east, English-speaking to the west).

The architecture of eighteenth- and nineteenth-century Place d'Armes and nineteenth- and twentieth-century Dominion Square is paradigmatic of Montreal, a city accustomed to change and to accommodating opposing values, able both to absorb the shock of the new and to create the variety of urban structures and infrastructures called for by the twentieth century. This book, with the exhibition it accompanies, is an important new study of the forces forming the matrix that constitutes the early-twentieth-century metropolis. The authors examine the interrelated growth of population, culture, territory, and transportation as Montreal grows cosmopolitan and its professions and business practices mature to become more self-aware and self-reliant, finding expression in the highly crafted buildings that determine the quality of the city today.

Looking at the city as process is a way of linking the past with the future. The CCA holds with the eminent historian Eric Hobsbawm that "People cannot help trying to forecast the future by some form of reading the past. They have to. The ordinary processes of conscious human life, not to mention public policy, require it. And of course they do so on the justified assumption that, by and large, the future is systematically connected with the past, which in turn is not an arbitrary concatenation of circumstances and events,"[2] It follows that the past must be critically analyzed, brought into focus. This volume is one of a series of studies related to exhibitions devoted to the Canadian city,[3] undertaken by the CCA as part of its mandate to bring to consciousness, and to action, architecture as a public concern.

The CCA wishes to thank the Ville de Montréal for its generous support of the exhibition.

The CCA also thanks the Department of Canadian Heritage, the Ministère de la Culture et des Communications du Québec, the Conseil des arts de la Communauté urbaine de Montréal, as well as the J.W. McConnell Family Foundation, Bank of Montreal, Bell Canada, Royal Bank, Teleglobe Canada Inc., Liberty Yogurt, and Omni, The Outdoor Company, for their support of the exhibition and the accompanying public programs.

PHYLLIS LAMBERT
Director, Canadian Centre for Architecture

INTRODUCTION

THE CITY IS A LONG-TERM COLLECTIVE WORK. It cannot be reduced to the output of architects, for they have little impact on much of the built environment. In the nineteenth century, however, when societies throughout the Western world industrialized, investing substantial resources in the manufacture and distribution of goods, and as the city became a centre of economic administration and a place of residence for rising urban populations, architectural skills were in greater demand than ever before. Guided by ongoing debates over the utility and the ideals of architecture, architects shaped the city's facilities and designed the homes of its more prosperous citizens. In the public realm they gave form to reigning economic and political forces, to individual successes as well as to social solidarity, thus helping to attune urban form to contemporary values.

Turn-of-the-century Canada saw an unprecedented increase in the number of architects, who organized to found associations that would defend their professional interests and promote their skills. Most of Quebec's architects were based in Montreal, which had established itself as the metropolis of the nation. Architecture is an art whose realization involves many players, and the architect is the artist whose practice is most subject to economic and political change. As a result this study, which focuses on Montreal and explores the contribution of architects to the construction of this modern city, necessarily involves the adoption of a broader social perspective.

More than twenty years after its first appearance, Jean-Claude Marsan's *Montreal in Evolution* remains a standard reference in the fields of architectural and urban history, despite the considerable advances made on many fronts in historiography, and the amount of attention that has been paid to urban form within Quebec schools of architecture as well as in certain architectural firms. The 350th anniversary of the founding of Montreal, which was celebrated in 1992, fueled the first attempts to synthesize more recent research. In his *Histoire de Montréal depuis la Confédération*, for instance, Paul-André Linteau examined the various social forces that transformed Montreal into a modern metropolis, though without – as the author was the first to admit – granting architecture the attention it deserves. In the field of architecture, the design studios of artist and architect Melvin Charney had a profound effect on architects trained at the Université de Montréal during the 1970s and 1980s. The scholarship of urban form has not been marked by a comparable vitality, with the exception of the work accomplished by the Groupe de recherche sur Montréal set up in 1987 by the Canadian Centre for Architecture (CCA). The results of its investigations furnished the basis for the exhibition *Opening the Gates of Eighteenth-Century Montréal* in 1992.

Montreal's urban legacy has, of course, been the object of numerous monographs – some published, others not – undertaken in university, heritage, or museum contexts and focusing on particular building types or on the work and career of a specific architect, an approach favoured by architectural historians in Quebec. These studies have benefitted particularly from existing building inventories (established according to program or location) as well as from archives for which excellent research aids have been developed. But synthetic studies remain rare. This book is a response to that challenge. Written by several authors from a range of disciplines and published in conjunction with the CCA exhibition *Montréal Métropole, 1880–1930*, this study is a collaborative attempt to identify the agents, norms, and social values that gave Montreal at the turn of the century its urban form and a distinctively metropolitan architecture.

In the early nineteenth century Montreal was the largest North American city in the British Empire, and entered a new phase in its development from an eighteenth-century garrison town into a flourishing merchant city. However, the population explosion and the prosperity that marked the years between 1880 and 1930 were unprecedented in the city's history. As this period opened, the industrialized Western world was emerging from a serious economic depression; fifty years later, it ended with the stock market crash of October 1929, triggering a long period of severe recession. In the years between, as settlers moved into the Canadian West in ever-increasing numbers, Montreal took full advantage of its geographic position at the juncture of a major maritime route to Europe and a vast water and railway network branching out across North America. Most of the agricultural goods produced on the Prairies passed through Montreal Harbour, and the city's industrial development was stimulated by new markets opened up by the Dominion's rapidly expanding territories. These transformations took place at a time when the architect's position in society – his status as well as his role – was shifting. Montreal's turn-of-the-century architecture cannot be explained by the stylistic fluctuations that marked the Victorian era, since architectural historicism endured in Montreal long after 1901. Economic cycles rather than the reigns of monarchs thus become the key to understanding changes in the built environment.

The economic dynamism of the early twentieth century brought with it a steady increase in building, advancing in several surges between 1887 and 1931. The rationale behind construction activity underwent a change of its own as property and real-estate values became increasingly dominant factors. The territory of the city spread out and became more specialized, and the need for urban facilities and housing intensified with the growing population of Montreal and its suburbs, a population that quadrupled in forty years to reach a million by 1931. The boom in real-estate that immediately preceded the First World War pushed the development of Montreal well beyond the city's built-up areas. Architecturally, the period was marked by a change of scale and by an increasing functional diversification within the built environment. But modernization affected more than the city's building stock; it also influenced the practice of the architect, who now faced considerable competition in a swiftly burgeoning construction market. In 1890 architects organized themselves by founding the Province of Quebec Association of Architects (PQAA), and within a few years the first higher programs for architectural training were established.

Contemporary historiography identifies this period, especially the years just prior to the Great War, as Montreal's "Golden Age," a glorious era whose end came with the 1920s. Many of the buildings in the city's downtown area and adjacent neighbourhoods date from the years 1880 to 1930, and today, the urbanity of Montreal, a city with clearly configured streets and squares as well as beautifully realized historicist architecture, is particularly appreciated. Yet from the end of the nineteenth century the modernization of both society and architecture accelerated, resulting in changes that are of particular interest to the authors who have participated in this study.

Owing to its position at the heart of France's former colony, to its stature as the metropolis of British North America, and to its position as neighbour to the prosperous cities of the eastern United States, Montreal was a complex and unique crucible. To accurately assess Montreal's significance, it is necessary to gauge its position among the great cities of the Western world – a task undertaken by British historian Anthony Sutcliffe. In size and population, Montreal could not compare with either New York City or Chicago, and still less with the major cultural centres that were the great capitals of Europe. In those respects it was on par, rather, with cities like Detroit and Cleveland, though it surpassed both in economic importance. Montreal's position would be challenged after 1914 by Toronto, its closest rival. The city's development in the nineteenth century was closely linked to its role as Atlantic bridgehead, and Montreal strengthened its position as the centre of Canadian manufacturing after assuming the role of financial centre of the country. In his essay, the historian Paul-André Linteau examines the economic and social forces that have had an impact on the city's built form.

Between 1880 and 1930 the geography of international exchanges shifted as British domination weakened with Canada's growing economic dependence on the United States. While the lifestyle of the Anglo-Protestant bourgeoisie retained a distinctly British tenor, and the French-speaking elite looked increasingly to Paris, working-class culture became Americanized – much to the disapproval of the Catholic Church, which nevertheless succeeded in maintaining its ideological grip on French-Canadian society. Still, as sociologists Marcel Fournier and Véronique Rodriguez show, a gradual move towards modernity was now taking place. The founding of a handful of cultural institutions and a system of higher education by government and certain religious communities – powers that frequently clashed – led to the emergence of a learned culture in francophone Montreal, although one that lacked the resources of its anglophone counterpart, supported by rich merchants and industrialists. In addition, the autonomy that writers and artists achieved in the exercise of their art and in the dissemination and acceptance of their works sowed the early seeds of opposition to the clerical-nationalist tradition.

Architecture was not unaffected by these changes. Beginning in the early 1880s, the presence of the United States loomed increasingly larger. As Isabelle Gournay explains, the United States was an important source of architectural models, new building techniques, and architects whose impact on the transformation of the city was notable, and its ascendancy was a source of both fascination and anxiety. In Quebec and Ontario alike, American competition stimulated the development of professional associations and encouraged budding architects to go south in search of skills and prestige, New York and Boston being the favoured destinations.

That practice continued even after advanced architectural training, already established in Europe and the United States, became available in Montreal, first in English and later in French. Most of the architects working in the city early in the twentieth century, however, were formed through the apprenticeship system, and many were the sons of artisans working in the construction industry. Despite the continuation of that traditional form of training, access to both the profession itself and architectural commissions changed during this period, as explored in France Vanlaethem's essay on architects based in Montreal. The architectural community was enriched by immigrants, chiefly from Scotland and England but also several from the United States who settled in the metropolis during the 1910s, drawn by the local construction market and by the nation-wide entrepreneurial power of the major financial and communications companies headquartered in Montreal.

Strategic forces behind the country's economic advancement, these companies were major clients and the buildings they sponsored in Montreal were significant in modifying the scale, shape, and even the colour of the former merchant city, while also redirecting the development of its downtown core. At the turn of the century, when city planning was only starting to emerge as a discipline, and when the city's administration was still slowly organizing itself, the decision to build railway stations and hotels outside of Old Montreal and the relocation of major retail outlets along St. Catherine Street transformed Montreal into a bipolar city. The extension of the streetcar network also encouraged the creation of the new suburban neighbourhoods conceived by property developers. The geographer David B. Hanna focuses on the modernization of the interurban networks – the maritime and railway systems on which Montreal's metropolitan status depended – and explores the profound impact these had on the development of the city.

Compared to other North American cities, Montreal was quite densely built, especially in its working-class sectors, where multi-family housing had predominated since the mid nineteenth century. The architecture of the many neighbourhoods and municipalities that made up the metropolis was characterized by its contrasts, as linguistic and cultural divisions were superimposed upon spatial specialization and social segregation. Montreal was, as Walter van Nus explains, a "community of communities." The diversity that marked Greater Montreal, whose political unity was partially achieved during our period of study, relates to its natural topography, and stemmed from legal provisions that were formulated by certain developers as well as from decisions made by the first municipal administrations. The architect did not play a significant role in the design of urban spaces and housing, except in the more prosperous neighbourhoods, where architecture was a gauge of social success, and the stylistic palette of eclectic taste a means by which citizens proclaimed their cultural roots. At the same time, American ideals of a city beautified by nature and design, and the appealing model of the Garden City oriented the interventions of the land surveyor, who played a primary role in ordering the space of the city.

North American in its basic rationality, Montreal's urban plan bears the traces of the province's earlier political past. The grid of the city, composed of elongated blocks and narrow plots, has its origins in the cadastral division of the French seigneurial regime. But the grid is not uniform across the whole territory. In Old Montreal the divisions are irregular, and the new town that sprang up in the 1860s and 1870s at the foot of Mount Royal was a blend of row housing and large residential and religious estates. In addition, these newer areas were punctuated by a series of public squares much like those of Edinburgh and London. Created when the fortifications were destroyed and surrounding faubourgs were incorporated into the city, these squares brought order and unity but at the same time disturbed the existing layout. At the start of the twentieth century, when corporations held monopolies and workspace was at a premium, these irregularities encouraged the construction of buildings with an ever-larger footprint and height, both dimensions tending toward gigantism.

This growth in scale, whose beginnings can be traced to the late 1880s (with the construction of the first tall buildings and the heightening of existing structures), is examined by Isabelle Gournay, who gives special attention to the impact of municipal regulations. Throughout this period the grid outside the downtown area remained remarkably stable, for despite the beautification projects proposed by architects early in the century the layout of the city had not, as in certain American cities, been altered by the introduction of a system of parks and boulevards or by the creation of a monumental civic centre. Political tensions at the municipal level blocked such plans, which were proposed by both professionals and members of the upper classes. And although, subsequently, ideas advanced elsewhere concerning the improvement of working-class housing and urban sanitation and efficiency were well received, they left little mark on the built environment. With the proliferation of the automobile during the 1920s, the first master plans were developed for Montreal and its region, but gave clear precedence to the rationalization of infrastructural networks over aesthetic issues. City Hall also hired Montreal's first town-planning specialists, recruited from the engineering community which was then in competition with architects for this new professional territory.

The cultural diversity of Montreal's architectural milieu made the city a uniquely receptive locus for international debates on architecture. Its cosmopolitanism was the result of immigration and a cultural openness fostered by American competition and foreign training. Foreign experience is highly visible in Montreal; major players on the American scene built many of the city's prominent buildings, often collaborating with the city's best known architects. After the Richardsonian Romanesque, the Beaux-Arts movement became hugely popular, the ideal of superiority it embodied appealing as much to architects seeking to enhance their prestige as to clients concerned with making a distinguished mark on the urban landscape. Beaux-Arts interpretations varied, some focusing on formal rationalism, others exploring a more decorative approach. While Montreal boasted no official civic centre, the architecture on streets like Sherbrooke and St. Denis, chosen as sites for important cultural and educational institutions, became increasingly monumental. Although there was unanimity over the capacity of Beaux-Arts architecture to express civic grandeur, the universality of its language was challenged by supporters of the Arts and Crafts movement –

particularly Professor Percy Nobbs of McGill University, who was the first to elaborate a national, specifically Canadian architecture. Outside the residential sector, however, Nobbs's theory had little impact on the city's architecture, and in the 1920s it was reinterpreted by the advocates of regionalism. Meanwhile, Montreal's downtown had come under pressure from the growing rationalization of construction practices and techniques as its buildings became more complex, although a certain eclecticism remained.

It was in this half-century of prosperity that Montreal grew into Canada's undisputed metropolis. At the heart of the Dominion, the merchant town blossomed into a vibrant and populous industrial city with a burgeoning architectural community and a cosmopolitan elite preoccupied with professionalism and efficiency. But in a swiftly changing world, Montreal's position was precarious. Its fate was concomitantly linked to the decline of the British Empire and the rise of its great neighbour to the south, which was moving rapidly towards modernization. Artistically, however, New York City had not yet eclipsed the great capitals of Europe, home to the avant-garde movements whose achievements found little echo in Canada's metropolis. Was it the end of an era or the dawn of a new age? There is no clear and objective answer, for it was a period marked by the dynamic interweaving of several chronologies. But Montreal – heart of the Canadian economy and principal home of the Dominion's Anglo-Protestant ruling class – was undoubtedly in its heyday. From a cultural standpoint, although still clearly the capital of North American Catholicism, Montreal also showed signs of a growing identity as the centre of a French culture whose traditional attitudes prevailed at the same time as certain of its values were challenged. If Montreal's architecture bore witness to the city's economic strength, its functional and technological rationalism remained somewhat concealed beneath a decor inspired by the past, the relationship between modernization and modernism differed in the New World, where cultural production was only just beginning to achieve a certain autonomy. The urban and architectural diversity that marked turn-of-the-century Montreal reflected the cultural ambivalence and the social ambitions to which architects, as good professionals, sought to respond. This study therefore opens with an overview that situates Montreal in relation to the major cities of Europe and North America; continues with an account of the socio-economic and cultural context and of the territorial ambitions that gave rise to the urban development and architectural production of the period 1880–1930; and it concludes with an exploration of the major architectural projects of the period, both planned and built. It is illustrated by contemporary documents, many of which have never before been published, drawn chiefly from the archives of the CCA, but also from other depositories such as the Canadian Architecture Collection at McGill University.

This publication was developed in conjunction with the exhibition *Montréal Métropole, 1880–1930,* both of which have been made possible by the abiding interest in Montreal manifested by the Director of the CCA, Phyllis Lambert. Chief Curator Nicholas Olsberg has supported and defended the project from the outset, offering valuable constructive criticism. The assistance and dedication of the CCA staff have ensured the successful realization of this new research.

The editors wish to express their gratitude for the judicious advice received from the members of the scientific committee – Jean-Louis Cohen, Marcel Fournier, Phyllis Lambert, Paul-André Linteau, Nicholas Olsberg, and David Van Zanten – and wish to acknowledge the efforts of all those who worked on this pub-

lication and contributed to the research on which it depends. Thanks go, too, to all the archives, museums, and libraries who have so generously lent works and who have helped to identify important sources and documents used in both the exhibition and the publication.

FRANCE VANLAETHEM
ISABELLE GOURNAY

1 Bonaventure Station
2 Queen's Hotel
3 Windsor Station
4 Windsor Hotel
5 Sun Life Assurance Co. Building
6 Dominion Square Building
7 Mount Royal Hotel
8 Art Association Gallery
9 Le Château Apartments
10 Ritz-Carlton Hotel
11 McGill University Campus

12 École Technique de Montréal
13 Bibliothèque Saint-Sulpice
14 École Polytechnique
15 Viger Station-Hotel
16 City Hall
17 Grain Elevator no. 2
18 Grain Elevator no. 1
19 Court House Annex
20 Aldred Building
21 New York Life Insurance Co. Building

22 Bank of Montreal
23 London and Lancashire Life Assurance Co. Building
24 Board of Trade Building
25 Royal Bank of Canada Building
26 Read Building
27 Beaver Hall Building
28 Architects' Building
29 Canada Cement Building
30 Henry Birks and Sons Jeweller's
31 Jacobs Building

32 Henry Morgan and Co.
33 T. Eaton Co. Ltd.
34 CNR yards
A Chaboillez Square
B Dominion Square
C Phillips Square
D Victoria Square
E Place d'Armes
F Champ-de-Mars
G Jacques Cartier Square
H Viger Square

Schematic map of downtown Montreal, showing the location of prominent buildings, 1931. Cartography: Richard Bachand, for the CCA, 1998.

PART ONE **A CITY IN CONTEXT**

MONTREAL METROPOLIS

Anthony Sutcliffe

SINCE ITS ORIGINS SEVERAL THOUSAND YEARS AGO, the civilized world has been a world of great cities.[1] The ancient Greeks used the term "metropolis" to describe the leading city of a territory, one from which smaller cities had been founded as "colonies." These smaller cities reinforced the authority of a metropolis in outlying areas. At the height of its power and influence in the fifth century BC, Athens had a large number of these colony cities. Later, as the Romans extended their authority across Italy, they founded colonies in a similar way, Rome becoming the city to which all cities looked. Such colony cities virtually always reflected the form and character of the central metropolis.[2]

The metropolis of the Ancient world thus acquired two characteristics with which we still associate the term *metropolis* today: great size and a dominant position within a region or network of smaller places. The outstanding example was the city of Rome, which at its peak in the second century AD had an estimated population of around one million and an authority that extended over most of Western Europe, the Near East, and North Africa.[3] Nearly two millennia later, when the British Empire surpassed Rome as the largest empire the world had ever seen, its centre, London, had by the 1840s become the world's largest metropolis, and went on to accumulate a population of seven million by the time of the First World War.[4]

In English, literary use of the term "metropolis" began in the seventeenth century. In 1666 Dryden referred to London as "the Metropolis of Great Britain," and in the eighteenth century the English began to call London "*the* metropolis." By the nineteenth century the concepts of imperial capital and giant city would merge, but from the early eighteenth century it was common to describe quite small towns as the "metropolises"

1 St. Catherine Street looking east from the southwest corner of Stanley Street, 1930. Unknown photographer. National Archives of Canada PA-021279.

19

of their regions; the largest urban centres in their regions, these were looked to for services and the distribution of goods.

The concept of the metropolis altered in the nineteenth century with the proliferation of nation-states. Great Britain and France, as powerful, united kingdoms, had been dominated by a large capital city from as far back as the Middle Ages, as was Spain from 1561. With Berlin and Rome emerging in the mid nineteenth century as capitals of the united countries of Germany and Italy, the idea of the metropolis was seen more as a large, national capital than as the heart of an empire (though all these cities continued as or developed into imperial capitals as well). That change of perception gave metropolis status to some quite small capital cities, such as Brussels and Lisbon. By the mid twentieth century, the term was increasingly applied to large cities and their surrounding commuter regions, as in the American census unit of the SMSA (Standard Metropolitan Statistical Area) and in certain medium-sized cities like Birmingham and Manchester, with public-transport systems radiating around "Metros."[5] These dilutions of the concept must not be allowed to obscure Montreal's status as a true national metropolis.

Whatever their size, these national metropolises had certain features in common, and their characteristics came to be better understood from the end of the nineteenth century thanks to the scientific work of Adna F. Weber, Max Weber, the Chicago School of Sociologists, and Lewis Mumford, along with the creative thinking of Le Corbusier and many social scientists and planners. Among them figures the founder of modern town planning in Canada, Thomas Adams.[6]

As in Ancient times, many of these national metropolises had water access and so could prosper in long-distance trade while importing bulk requirements like food and fuel cheaply. Their average per capita incomes were generally higher than those of the surrounding regions and the country as a whole. High standards of living, the overall growth induced by industrialization, and the social opportunities of the metropolis, attracted influxes of immigrants mainly from the immediate hinterland, but also an important share of foreign immigrants. The result was a city with many young, ambitious people and a varied cultural life ranging from elite activities (such as the theatre and music) to a wide variety of newspapers to popular sports, gambling, and drinking. Religious institutions were generally well represented in these metropolises, as the churches used them to extend their influence across the country. The quality of architecture was generally the highest in the country, owing

to the presence of major institutions and the high incomes and sophisticated taste of the richer residents. However, great size generated poor, overcrowded districts worse than any in the provinces, and the presence of the headquarters of political parties and other movements could sometimes generate violence.

In North and South America the progress of former colonies towards national independence, which began with the formation of the United States of America, had by the end of the nineteenth century produced a pattern of nation states similar to that of Europe. Capitals in South and Central America were generally located in the largest cities, which tended to grow even larger as a result. In North America, on the other hand, the federal system of states adopted by the United States in 1787 prompted the choice of a very small city, Washington, D.C., as the new national capital. The intention was to prevent a very large city, and the state in which it stood, from dominating the nation if it were chosen as capital.

When Canada became a Dominion in 1867, the country was formed from the four colonies of British North America on lines reminiscent of the United States, the colonies becoming provinces under the new constitution.[7] Montreal had served as the capital of the newly created Canada Province from 1844 to 1849, but from 1867 the federal capital was located at the modest Upper Canadian city of Ottawa, 170 kilometres west of Montreal. Ottawa was an important lumber centre and canal port but as a communications centre, both actual and potential, it was far inferior to Montreal. None of Montreal's expanding industries and businesses moved to the federal capital. Instead, proximity to Ottawa encouraged the growth of the larger city's economy, with high-level legal services and political representation available just a short distance away. The foundation of the federal capital thus gave Montreal an advantage over both Quebec City downstream and the potentially well-located city of Toronto, 500 kilometres to the southwest on Lake Ontario.

With important, long-range railway developments in the 1850s and 1860s and major river and port improvements, Montreal overtook Quebec City in population and entered a sustained period of growth that strengthened its metropolitan status as the largest city in Canada, allowing it to progress from the small town of 16,000 that it had been in 1809 to a moderate-sized city of 48,207 in 1850, eventually to reach a million people in 1931. This extraordinary rate of growth, the fastest of any North American metropolis, was consequent upon three key conditions: Montreal's role as the head of a sweeping hinterland in Eastern Canada and the Great Lakes region; its emergence as Canada's main centre of banking, insurance, and business services; and its position as a terminus for North Atlantic trade.[8] These functions had arisen before 1850, but the main boost to Montreal's fortunes came around 1890, with the "closing of the Frontier" in the United States.

As the last agricultural land was settled in the States, investment and settlement turned towards Canada, a movement that coincided with a worldwide surge of urban growth born of an industrial economy based on cities.[9] The resulting "great Canadian boom," which lasted from about 1890 until about 1910, attracted a large flow of investment and immigration from both Europe and the United States.[10] With most of these new resources moving into the fertile strip that stretched right across southern Canada, Montreal's location at the eastern, seaward end helped make it the main junction between a Canada rich in raw materials and a Europe that consumed those materials and supplied the country with much of its manpower, capital, and manufactured goods. The twenty years of the "Canadian boom" created the modern metropolis of Montreal, which still bears the stamp of that exciting period.

Montreal could not hope to become a giant metropolis like New York City, Buenos Aires, or Rio de Janeiro — not to speak of London, Paris, and Berlin. There were two principal limitations on its growth. Firstly, the population density of Canada was very low. Secondly, with the great economic strength of Canada resting on agriculture and natural resources spread over a sprawling territory, making Canada the second-largest country in the world after Russia, great regional centres such as Winnipeg and Edmonton played a much more important economic role than did the provincial cities of Europe (except in Russia, where several huge regions were served by large, central cities, much as in Canada). Functions that in Britain were almost exclusively concentrated in London were much more dispersed in Canada and located far from Montreal.

When the population of Canada exceeded 10,400,000 in 1931, Montreal stood as a perfect instance of the world-wide phenomenon of the metropolis. Its population level, though outstanding in Canada and still well ahead of its rival, the expanding city of Toronto (population 673,000 in 1931), put Montreal on a par with some of the larger cities in the United States such as Detroit (1,570,000), Cleveland (900,000), Baltimore (805,000), and Pittsburgh (670,000) rather than with giant cities such as New York and Chicago. In Europe, the major provincial centres of Birmingham, Glasgow, Lyon, Hamburg, and Milan were all

much the same size as Montreal. In South and Central America, where national capitals could be very big, Montreal ranked with large provincial cities like São Paulo (880,000 in 1929) and some of the capitals of the smaller states.

Although Montreal could dominate Canada, its relatively small size meant that its cultural life could never rival that of New York, Chicago, or the big European capitals. Many of the cultural institutions of a national capital were located in Ottawa, where the National Museum of Man (now the Canadian Museum of Civilization) dated back to 1842 and other national museums were in place by 1930. The Montreal museum, theatre, music, and art worlds were comparable to those of a large European provincial city. Only in the cinema, which reached Montreal at the turn of the century, could the public enjoy the same entertainment as in New York and Los Angeles. Montreal was less a cultural metropolis like Paris and London and more a centre of employment and creation of wealth. That feature, which it shared with big provincial centres of Europe, like Birmingham and Hamburg, and the large industrial cities of the American Midwest, like St. Louis, was linked to the hardworking, sober mentality of English-speaking Montreal, with its Scottish-Presbyterian business class and its upwardly striving Roman Catholic communities (French-speaking workers from the province of Quebec and poor Irish labourers).

Also constraining everything but work was the climate. The long, icy winter kept people in their homes more than in any other metropolis outside Russia, and the humid summer heat, though fairly benign compared to the southern United States, also discouraged movement.

These limitations on leisure and culture were balanced by a high level of religious activity. By 1930 the Montreal skyline was pierced by the towers and spires of scores of churches. In the English-speaking western part of the city, the many Protestant churches of various denominations reflected the great wealth of the Montreal business community. In the east and north, the mainly twin spires of the Roman Catholic parish churches showed how successfully the Church had catered to the growing French-speaking and Irish communities. A number of great Roman Catholic seminaries, which drew their students mainly from rural Quebec, stood impressively at key points throughout the city, reinforcing the religious atmosphere of Montreal, almost a new Rome. Synagogues maintained a steady presence.

Montreal's division into two large Christian communities echoed Belfast, but there are other less obvious parallels among the world's largest cities. The linguistic division into French and English strengthened the unique character of Montreal, dividing the metropolis in two. The resulting physical division of the city into an English-speaking West End and a French-speaking East End minimized conflict between the two communities, while the aspects of Montreal culture shared between the communities made for a variety in public life that partly compensated for the relative lack of elite cultural activity. This dualistic character made Montreal unique in the world among cities of its size. Moreover, Montreal's way of handling the problems and opportunities that arose from this unprecedented situation would provide an example to divided cities in later years, such as Berlin, Vienna, Beirut, and the newly violent Belfast of the 1960s and later. Montreal would make a great contribution to the tolerant, internationalist image of Canada in the years after 1945.

Although a relatively small metropolis in world terms, Montreal in the years after its population boom, beginning in the 1850s, sought to achieve the highest standards in architecture, and looked to the example of the world's largest metropolises, especially London, Paris, and New York. The influences of these cities were numerous and complex, but a general survey can be made here.

While it lacked the grandeur of Paris, London made great advances in water distribution and sewerage under its Metropolitan Board of Works (1855–88). Montreal followed its example, transforming itself from an ill-equipped and unhealthy town before 1850 to a city built to modern health standards by 1930. Accelerated growth meant that Montreal housing was newer than in most other cities of its size, and the establishment of building regulations ensured that most new buildings were spacious and solidly constructed in brick or stone. The duplex and triplex apartments that have been characteristic of Montreal ever since the 1880s were a response to the suddenly increased demand for cheap accommodation, and proved a brilliant solution to the problem of metropolitan housing. Sometimes a little dark in their inner spaces, they were easy to run, comfortable, warm, and cheap.

That form of housing, unique to Montreal and the Quebec towns to which it would spread, was in part the product of the long blocks and narrow sites that had emerged from the *côtes* laid out on the Island of Montreal during the period of French settlement during the seventeenth and early eighteenth centuries.[11] The efficient division of farmland designed to attract settlers would later produce a pattern of straight streets running at right-angles to the main roads. When urban development spread

across most of the island in the nineteenth and early twentieth centuries, the long, rectangular blocks were ideal sites for the new housing, while the back lanes adopted over much of Montreal after the 1840s, for reasons of public health, provided useful space for refuse removal, children's play, and quiet strolls. In housing and street layout, therefore, Montreal managed to avoid the crowded tenement houses of New York City, the costly European apartment house as exemplified in Paris and Berlin, and London's pokey row houses.[12]

The duplex and the triplex, however, were neither grand nor romantic, especially when flat roofs became the norm around 1885. Montreal's rapid growth from a city of moderate size meant that by 1887 it still lacked the elegance of the great European metropolises. With little tradition of its own, it looked to Europe for examples of architecture and urban design. Until the later nineteenth century, its main source was London, supplemented by Edinburgh. Montreal public buildings adopted a sober classical style in the smoothly finished local grey stone. However, ever since the modernization program of Baron Haussmann (1853–70), Paris had become the world's leading example of urban planning and architecture. New developments in Paris were based on Baroque planning principles, with broad, straight boulevards and avenues, wide piazzas, and vistas terminated by tall monuments or striking buildings.[13] This approach could be traced back to the Italian Renaissance in the fifteenth and sixteenth centuries, and was associated with Roman Catholicism, as applied by popes such as Sixtus V in the reconstruction of Rome in the sixteenth century. With London increasingly influenced by the example of Paris at the end of the nineteenth century,[14] new building and urban design in Montreal began more and more to reflect the French capital.

New York City, the main American metropolis to influence Montreal, made a very different contribution. Tall buildings had begun to proliferate there in the 1880s with the development of the steel-frame skyscraper. The resulting cityscape had little to do with the European classical tradition, and new ways of planning and controlling a city with very tall buildings emerged. The main New York planning mechanism was the Zoning Resolution of 1916, which drew heavily on the German zoning system developed in the larger German cities beginning in the early 1890s. In New York, streets were zoned for a variety of uses, and maximum building heights were fixed as a multiple of the width of the street. The multiple was lowest on the residential streets and highest along a broad spine running up Broadway.[15] In the 1920s a great boom in skyscraper building occurred in New York, mainly along that axis, and a growing number of architects acquired experience in designing the new type of building. Montreal began to follow the New York example after the First World War. Relaxed building regulations allowing greater heights came into effect in 1924 and in the 1920s several tall buildings, though lower than their New York counterparts, began to generate a striking city of commerce along St. Catherine Street (fig. 1), continuing a commercial-development process that had begun in the 1890s. With Montreal now eyeing New York City as its chief model and commercial rival, that parallel became quite deliberate.

While the example of London had been somewhat eclipsed, its spreading suburbs, the most extensive in the world in 1930, remained a constant model for Montreal. The design and development of most of London's suburbs was mediocre and of poorer quality than that encountered in Montreal's duplex/triplex neighbourhoods. However, the middle- and upper-class suburbs that grew up chiefly in the west of London in the 1850s developed into an attractive swathe of villas, gardens, and often tree-lined streets interspersed with numerous parks and playing fields. When Ebenezer Howard published his book on the Garden City in 1898, there was new interest in greenery and villa and cottage layouts.[16] The English garden-suburb model, unique to England and the United States in not being the preserve of the rich but open to the whole of the middle class, was implicit in Britain's first Town Planning Act of 1909, which allowed local authorities to develop planning schemes for suburban areas that gave rise to "garden suburbs."[17]

One of the creators of the 1909 Act and a leading member of the state planning machinery thereafter was Thomas Adams, who came to work in Canada in 1914 at the invitation of the Canadian government.[18] Formerly the first secretary of the Garden City Association in London (1901–06), Adams was a strong advocate of garden suburb planning. He encouraged the creation of high-standard garden suburbs in Canada, including Montreal,[19] of which the Town of Mount Royal was an outstanding example.[20] More a feature of west Montreal than of the French-speaking sectors, these suburbs were modelled both in their layouts and in their details upon the British example, especially as seen in London. Thus the influence of London design and planning was revived in Montreal's western suburbs as it declined in the centre and the poorer eastern residential districts.

The result, in a spreading city of streetcar lines and soon cars and trucks, was a varied cityscape with distinct environ-ments, the combined product of influences from London, Paris, New York, and traditions of Montreal itself. In this way, Montreal took on something of the atmosphere of three very much larger metropolises without losing its unique residential character. Like many other cities of its day, especially in the United States, it strove to create the best of Paris in its centre while fostering a suburban paradise on English and American lines. But in Montreal the blend remained unique – a city of contrasts yet a city of strange harmony. With its historic network of broad, straight streets and its acropolis-like "royal mountain," Montreal's unique metropolitan character belied its relatively small size.

Its moderate size, however, meant that Montreal land values were not high enough to generate a large number of tall buildings in the downtown area, and by 1930 there was still no skyline of the type that now defined New York. Low rents, on the other hand, contributed to Montreal's high standard of living. The virtual absence of the large tenement blocks that typified New York City and most of the large centres of Europe was a great advantage in terms of health and general well-being. The streetcar system serving residential areas was on a par with the best in North America, and was superior to most in Europe. Rail links to Quebec City and Ottawa created a linear metropolis that tended to boost demand for Montreal goods and services, at the same time fostering family links along the St. Lawrence River valley. New York City lay only ten hours away by rail, not much further than Toronto.

With many of the advantages and few of the drawbacks of the big-city habitat, Montreal had graduated by 1930 to the status of a leading North American metropolis. In close touch with the metropolises of the United States and Europe, it was able to import the best in design and technology from cities much bigger than itself. These up-to-date facilities were combined with the improved quality of life that a smaller metropolis could offer. With its unique landscape and city-scape, Montreal had created a metropolitan experience without parallel in North America.

3172—PLACE D'ARMES, MONTREAL.

NOTMAN, MONTREAL

FACTORS IN THE DEVELOPMENT OF MONTREAL

Paul-André Linteau

THE YEARS BETWEEN 1880 AND 1930, WHEN Montreal stood at the height of its power as Canada's metropolis, are often seen as a golden age;[1] this was a period that left a lasting mark on the urban fabric of the city.[2] What were the forces and trends that shaped the Montreal landscape in these years? An answer to this question requires a look at the city's economic structures. The expansion of Montreal was fuelled by Canada's rapid development. With the city's control of transport networks, its strong manufacturing base, and its position as the country's financial centre came a surge of economic activity, mainly from private enterprise – the predominant influence on Montreal's urban development. Federal, provincial, and municipal governments, however, were also very active, and their contributions are to be seen across the island. The third major contributor to the building of the metropolis, and a powerful force in Quebec, was the Church, the provider of many of the city's social services. Business, State, and Church were thus the leading players in the shaping of Montreal. Other social and ethnic features of the city also influenced the course of events and the decision-making process, one such feature being the fundamental distinction between francophones and anglophones: clearly evident in this divided city, it was likewise reflected in decisions of urban development.

THE METROPOLIS OF CANADA

In 1894 an illustrated album devoted to the glories of Montreal began its description of the city with the words "The Metropolis of Canada, the largest, wealthiest, and most progressive city of the fair Dominion – the entrepot, par excellence, for the exports and imports of all her broad area."[3] Almost half a century later a Royal Commission report paints the city in almost identical

2 Place d'Armes with the New York Life Insurance Co. Building (1887–88, Babb Cook and Willard, architects) and the Church of Notre Dame (1824–29), c. 1895. Photograph: William Notman. Notman Photographic Archives, McCord Museum of Canadian History, Montreal.

tones: "Montreal, with its railway termini, shipping, manufactures, financial and distributive facilities, constitutes the entrepôt to the great exporting industries of the West which are the bases of the transcontinental economy."[4] The perception of Montreal as the hub of Canada's foreign trade, the country's gateway for the entry and exit of goods, was a long standing tradition.

Indeed, Montreal's entire history up to the opening of the twentieth century was marked by its role as the beachhead of the sea-link between Canada and Europe, a role that was strengthened from the 1830s on with the improvement of harbour facilities and the digging of a navigable channel in the St. Lawrence River. Canada forming part of the British Empire, the city's closest connections lay naturally with Great Britain. Indeed, this connection was fostered by that group of turn-of-the-century captains of industry in Montreal who were British by birth, men who were in touch with "the Old Country" and travelled back and forth frequently. Some of the city's leading financiers – George Stephen, Donald Smith, and Max Aitken – in fact returned home to end their working lives in Britain, and were rewarded with seats in the House of Lords. Not restricted to the economy and politics, the British influence in Montreal extended to social and cultural life as well, as the monied class copied the customs and behaviour of English upper-class society, with its deference towards royalty and respect for tradition, its nannies and attitude to schooling, its clubs and five-o'clock teas.[5] The pride felt in belonging to the greatest Empire of all time was very publicly expressed, as can be gauged by the monument to the fallen in the war in South Africa, erected in 1907 in Dominion Square. The attachment to Britain reached its height during the First World War, when great numbers of young English-speaking Montrealers cheerfully enlisted in answer to the call from the mother country.

Between 1880 and 1930, however, Montreal's connection with Great Britain underwent considerable change. Canadian raw materials, especially wheat, continued to be shipped out of Montreal Harbour bound for British ports, even increasing after the rapid colonization of Western Canada. For years, as well, Montreal had imported British finished goods, distributing them across the country, but Canadian industrialization and competition from the United States were reducing this volume. The demand for English china and luxury fabrics remained, but everyday items were now being manufactured in Canada and machinery was increasingly imported from the United States. At the start of this century, Britain's chief export to Canada was

mainly capital, which in the form of portfolio investments financed the construction of railroads, dams, factories, and urban infrastructures. The First World War caused a rupture in that process, obliging Canadians to turn increasingly to domestic savings, which Montreal's financial institutions were eager to collect, and enabling the United States to carve out a place in the market for capital, a realm it was soon to dominate.[6]

In the course of the 1920s Canada's economy fell increasingly within the sphere of the United States, now its main customer and supplier. Trade between the two countries had grown ever since the mid nineteenth century as railroads branched out over the continent, crossing the border at many points. Montreal was a junction for several such lines running out of the United States, and closer links with New York City and Boston were developed. Canada's largest city was now part of a new trade network, one in which it lacked the advantage – as the inevitable trans-shipment harbour for international trade – that had given it a special relationship with Great Britain. From now on every region of Canada could trade with the United States without going through Montreal, a condition that in the long run would pose a threat to Montreal's standing as a metropolis.

The city also lost another of its middle-man roles, as American companies tended far more than their British counterparts to invest directly in Canada by the establishment of branch-plants. In the nineteenth century, numerous American insurance companies opened their Canadian head offices in Montreal – for instance the New York Life Insurance Co., which built its headquarters on Place d'Armes in 1887 (fig. 2). But as the century drew to a close American business, especially in the manufacturing sector, opted increasingly for Ontario. In 1913 Montreal housed 12 percent of American manufacturers' Canadian branch-plants, Toronto 21 percent; by 1934 the Montreal share was only 13 percent (the entire province of Quebec, only 16 percent), compared to 32 percent for Toronto (66 percent for Ontario). This geographic concentration explains why one of the twentieth-century's most significant industries, automobile manufacture, failed to gain a foothold in Montreal.[7]

The nature and the extent of the links then existing between the Montreal business community and its American counterparts have not been studied extensively, but it is obvious that those links were strengthened with the increasing trade between the two countries – for instance, both the Grand Trunk Railway (later the Canadian National Railways) and the Canadian Pacific Railway had lines running south of the border; Sun Life sold insurance in the United States; the major Montreal banks opened American branches. As newspapers show, Montrealers were inundated with information about the United States. Early in the century, for example, Montreal members of urban-reform movements, both French- and English-speaking, were well aware of the progress made south of the border, especially in the fields of public health[8] and municipal government.[9] The Union of Canadian Municipalities, founded in 1901 at the suggestion of the mayor of Westmount, W.D. Lighthall, was inspired by the League of American Municipalities,[10] and in Montreal the Board of Commissioners (1910–18) and then the Administrative Commission (1918–21) were modelled on like organizations established in several American cities.[11]

Where American influence is most apparent is in technology and organization. Factory machinery was increasingly American-made or of American design.[12] Since at least the 1880s, railroads were built[13] and run in the American way, as demonstrated by the career of William C. Van Horne, who came from the United States to run Canadian Pacific. The impact on urban technology was equally noticeable: electrical equipment, streetcars, and also construction methods and materials began to follow the standards adopted south of the border[14] – a fact that may help to explain why it was American architects who were so often called upon to design major buildings.

Montreal was, then, a staging post in a network of international trade that it by no means dominated. At the same time it stood at the head of a domestic economic empire that it had helped to launch, build, and structure: the Dominion of Canada. With 4.3 million inhabitants in 1881, Canada grew to 10.4 million by 1931, all of them potential customers or consumers who could be reached from Montreal either by water or by rail. The city's importers and wholesalers had built up well-established networks of retailers even in far-flung villages and rural areas.[15] From the late nineteenth century on, Montreal banks had opened a series of branches in all provinces and territories from which local savings could be funnelled into nation-wide economic schemes. The city's ever-expanding factories were turning out a wide range of products aimed at a regional and national domestic market. Montreal's growth was thus linked to the growth of the country as a whole.

As the metropolis of Canada, Montreal stood at the centre of Canadian capitalism. Waves of mergers beginning at the turn

of the century and continuing through the 1920s only entrenched this role as the city collected the head offices of businesses whose operations were increasingly expanding. But it had a competitor. Toronto, at first just Ontario's regional capital, had also begun to build a Canadian empire which, with banks, industries, and businesses, entered more and more into competition with the larger city. Though Montreal held its lead it gradually lost ground, until by the start of the twentieth century Canada was a country with two economic capitals.[16]

Montreal was also important as a regional metropolis. Although some of its companies did business across the country, many others had a much more regional market, making the city the dominant centre of francophone Canada. Its French-Canadian banks and French-language mass-circulation newspapers had a clientele throughout Quebec as well as in the French-speaking areas of Ontario and New Brunswick. Other businesses concentrated on the Montreal region alone, which after all held half the population of the province. These companies, another element in the growth of Montreal, formed a vital component of the local economy.

This regional ascendancy had an impact on the development of Quebec's urban network. Whereas Ontario consisted of a large number of medium-sized towns within which Toronto only gradually rose to pre-eminence, in Quebec Montreal was dominant, drawing in the population and limiting the growth of towns and villages.[17] The situation was especially apparent in the vast plain around Montreal: even in 1931 the largest towns of the region – Joliette, Sorel, Saint-Hyacinthe, Valleyfield, Saint-Jean, Saint-Jérôme – had scarcely more than ten thousand inhabitants apiece.

BOOM YEARS

During the half century between 1880 and 1930, the population of the Montreal metropolitan area rose from 140,000 to a million. This rapid growth was marked by three demographic surges that corresponded to boom periods in city construction (fig. 3). The first spurt in construction took place in the second half of the 1880s, reaching its peak in 1887, following the completion of Canada's first transcontinental railway, the Canadian Pacific, in 1885. The second began at the start of the twentieth century and coincided with one of the greatest periods of expansion in the history of Canada and Montreal alike, a consequence of the rapid colonization of Western Canada. Montreal saw continuous growth from 1906 to 1912,

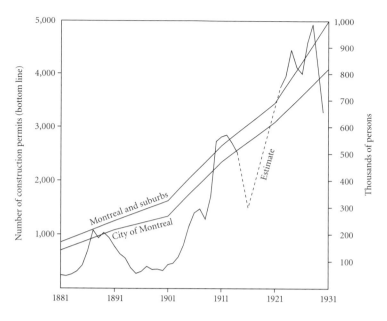

3 Population of Montreal and building cycles from 1881 to 1931.
Source: *Historical Atlas of Canada*, vol. 3, plate 14.

tapering somewhat by 1914. The third surge occurred from 1922 to 1930, peaking in 1928, a phase that reflected another period of expansion in the Canadian economy. The last two building leaps took place amid a frenzy of speculation that affected the property market.[18]

Montreal's population increase was due mostly to new arrivals. Throughout the half-century under consideration, a rural exodus brought substantial numbers to the city – French Canadians from across Quebec and English Canadians from all parts of Canada. Immigrants from abroad formed another part of the swell, especially during the two great waves of immigration that affected Canada in 1903–14 and 1923–30. Besides the very large numbers of English immigrants were many newcomers of other nationalities until then little represented in Montreal. Chief among these were the Ashkenazi Jews arriving from Eastern Europe, who would constitute 7 percent of Montreal's population in 1921, followed, in rather lesser numbers, by Italians and other groups of, mostly, European origin.[19]

This demographic growth was accompanied by an economic boom, though interrupted by sporadic depressions, in the first half of the 1890s, then in the period 1913–15, and again in the early 1920s. Montreal's strength in this period rested on its widely diversified economic structure and the establishment in the city of head offices of most of Canada's leading corporations.

Montreal's traditional involvement in commerce was reinvigorated by the opening up of the Canadian West, by the trend toward agricultural specialization, and by the wave of industrialization and urbanization that was underway in these years in Central Canada. Trade relied on an ever-expanding transportation network of which Montreal was the hub. Shipping tonnages in Montreal Harbour, both domestic and international, rose from about 1.5 million tons in the mid 1880s to almost 11 million by 1928, pushing the Harbour Commission to build new facilities to cope with the traffic increase.[20] As for railways, the Grand Trunk had established its Canadian head office and main workshops in Montreal in the 1850s. The Canadian Pacific did the same in the 1880s. Between 1918 and 1923, when the federal government amalgamated several railroad companies (including the Grand Trunk) under Canadian National, it too chose Montreal. These railways ranked among the biggest employers in the city.

The most significant phenomenon of the period, however, was the expansion of Canada's chief manufacturing centre. Modern industry in Montreal had become solidly established in the 1850s and 1860s; from the 1880s, the pace of development only increased. The turn of the century brought exponential growth, as many existing businesses extended their premises, sometimes relocating in the suburbs, and new factories sprang up. Montreal manufacturing embraced many sectors. Light industry was dominated by footwear, textiles, garments, tobacco, and food products (such as beer, meat-packing, sugar, flour, biscuits). Heavy industry began with the production of iron and steel products and rolling stock, and expanded in the twentieth century to include the petroleum industry and electrical products.[21]

Montreal was also Canada's financial capital. The wealth of Montreal banks stood at only 126 million dollars in 1896, but reached 2 billion by 1929, 59 percent of the country's bank assets. The trend to amalgamation reduced the number of players, so that by the end of our period only four major banks remained: the Bank of Montreal and the Royal Bank, under anglophone management, and the Banque Canadienne Nationale and the Banque Provinciale du Canada, francophone. Sun Life became the biggest insurance company in the country, and until the 1930s the Montreal Stock Exchange was the most important in Canada.[22]

Montreal's economy was thus ever more closely linked to that of Canada as a whole, a fact that was particularly evident during the Great Depression of the 1930s. The collapse of the economy of the West, too-greatly dependent on wheat alone, brought down with it many of Montreal's shipping and railroad industries, an event that had an indirect impact on both manufacturing and the financial sector, and the resulting unemployment was considerable.[23] Until this period, however, the development of Canada had enriched its metropolis.

This growth of both its population and its economy greatly altered Montreal's urban landscape, both vertically and horizontally.

In 1880 most Montreal residents still lived within the city limits established in 1792, although a movement toward the suburbs had already begun the decade before. The many new-comers who arrived in the early twentieth century accelerated that process, and Montreal was soon surrounded by a ring of smaller suburban municipalities. One of the largest of these was the Town of Maisonneuve, an industrial working-class neighbourhood in the island's East End that in 1910 began an ambitious beautification program. Montreal, for its part, wished to consolidate this urban expansion and between 1883 and 1918 absorbed more than twenty of these municipalities, increasing its territory five-fold. Large areas of land were available for construction, and the urban development of the 1920s took place mostly within the new city limits.[24]

The opening of an electric streetcar service in 1892 (horse-drawn public transport had been available since 1861) helped to widen the urbanized area.[25] In the 1920s the choice of residence for at least the wealthy was further extended by the automobile. These new means of transport not only permitted Montrealers to live further from their places of work but sparked the development of primarily residential neighbourhoods and municipalities. They also facilitated the expansion of administrative activities downtown.

Developments like these favoured territorial specialization and social segregation. The downtown core had long been limited to Old Montreal, a waterfront area bounded by McGill, Craig (now St. Antoine), and Berri streets and roughly corresponding to the perimeter of the old fortified town.[26] At the turn of the century, however, a second downtown core was beginning to emerge northwest of the first, in the area between Phillips and Dominion squares. Its backbone was St. Catherine Street, occupied at first by department stores in the 1890s, joined by office buildings after 1910.[27] These two centres were linked by the axis of McGill Street and Beaver Hall Hill.

Manufacturing in Montreal could be found close to downtown, especially printing ("Paper Hill" on St. Alexander Street),

the garment industry (spread along St. Lawrence Street), and furriers (concentrated around St. Alexander and Mayor streets). There were three main industrial districts outside the city centre. To the southwest along the Lachine Canal, where Montreal manufacturing began, lay the biggest concentration of factories in the metropolitan area, extending over several kilometres and through many municipalities. To the east lay a second industrial area, which began in the Sainte-Marie Ward and spread along the river and the railways across Hochelaga, Maisonneuve, Longue-Pointe, and Montréal-Est. From the early twentieth century a third zone grew up, forming a diagonal following the rail lines from Hochelaga to Outremont.[28]

Around these industrial zones clustered the main working-class neighbourhoods. North of Sherbrooke Street from the Plateau Mont-Royal to Notre Dame de Grâces and encircling the mountain, huge residential areas were built to house not only the new groups of service employees but also a substantial number of families from the middle and upper classes.[29]

At the same time the city grew vertically, especially downtown where buildings were becoming gradually taller, although true skyscrapers, arriving in the late 1920s, remained relatively rare. In the domestic sector, the first apartment buildings began to appear early in the century but were not built in any numbers until the 1920s. The most significant change occurred in working-class housing. From the 1860s on the duplex – a 2-storey house with one apartment above the other – reigned supreme, but in the 1890s entrepreneurs turned increasingly to the triplex, a 3-storey building initially comprising three flats.[30] For some forty years the triplex, especially the version with five apartments on three levels (also called a quintuplex), predominated, particularly in French-speaking neighbourhoods. Not only was Montreal expanding, it was also becoming denser as in the years between 1880 and 1930 its buildings grew in height.

A DIVIDED CITY

Everywhere, the birth of the industrial city accentuated divisions between social classes. Montreal was no exception. The living conditions of its new working class in the last decades of the nineteenth century were poor indeed; low and irregular wages, a high mortality rate, and inadequate housing were the lot of the majority.[31] Conditions improved in the new century with a strengthening economy and advances in public sanitation, but the city's large population of unskilled workers did not benefit from the general prosperity as much as did other groups, and a significant percentage of the population was poor.

Furthermore, as in all major North American cities where immigration played an important demographic role, distinct ethnic divisions were laid over the existing social strata.[32] In Montreal, a somewhat special case, new ethnic divisions were added to a centuries-old distinction between francophones and anglophones, more acute here than in other Canadian cities. Straddling the territory between the country's two main ethnolinguistic groups, Montreal was at one and the same time meeting point and zone of confrontation.

From the 1860s on, French Canadians were once again in the majority both in the city and in the metropolitan area, representing between 60 and 64 percent of the population. Yet the general appearance of the city did not much reflect this reality. The financial power of Montrealers of British origin had made English the principal language of the business world (thus its predominance in public signage) and also contributed a British look to the city's architecture. On the other hand, and despite their increased numbers, the demographic strength of English-speaking Montrealers gradually diminished. Their presence in the metropolitan area dropped from a third of the population at the end of the century to only a quarter by 1931, a fifth of the City of Montreal itself – a reflection of this group's increasing migration to suburbs in the western part of the island. The decline in strength of the English-speaking contingent is linked also to the rise in numbers of other ethnolinguistic groups, which grew from 2 to 14 percent of the population between 1881 and 1931.[33]

The city's linguistic divisions were reflected in its layout. The east of the city became massively French-speaking and the west increasingly English-speaking, while the southwest constituted a mixed area with large concentrations of francophones. Other groups settled mainly in the "immigrants' corridor" running along St. Lawrence Street, Jews to the south, Italians to the north.

Social class sometimes forges links that transcend ethnic solidarities, but it is important to note the relatively impervious compartmentalization in Montreal of ethnolinguistic and religious groups, each with its own extensive network of social and cultural institutions. The Anglo-Scottish group formed the dominant core of the upper class, extended by individuals of Irish, French, and Jewish origin. In the more populous upper-middle class there was greater diversity, but ethnic affinities prevailed. A considerable number of French-speaking businessmen gravi-

tated toward their own institutions, such as French Canadian banks. Similar divisions extended through the middle classes, which ranged from the traditional small businessman or professional to the emerging class of the salaried manager. Powerful players in French-speaking Montreal, the Catholic clergy held control of social, cultural, and educational institutions.[34]

Within these upper strata of Montreal society, power struggles were frequent – between anglophones and francophones, certainly, but also between traders, industrialists, financiers, and businessmen at various levels. Among French Canadians, special tensions existed between some members of the secular elite and the clergy. The leading voice representing Montreal's business community was the Board of Trade, but its domination by anglophones led French-speaking businessmen to found their own Chambre de commerce de la cité et du district de Montréal in 1887.[35] The two boards disagreed on matters such as expanding East End port facilities, but they often united to promote civic interests with the provincial and the federal governments.

Where power struggles were most apparent was in the city council. Francophones achieved a majority there only in 1882. For about fifteen years Raymond Préfontaine headed a political group that undertook a wide program of public works aimed at encouraging development in the city's East End, a French-speaking enclave. The policy of favouritism he established at City Hall was challenged by a group of English-speaking reformers headed by Herbert Brown Ames. Ames succeeded in attracting a number of francophone businessmen to the cause, and so the struggle between populists and reformers, initially ethnic, took on a more social character: the interests of the average citizen versus those of the rich and powerful. This development was clearly demonstrated by the election of Médéric Martin as mayor in 1914. After a partial victory in 1900, the reformers took hold of city government between 1910 and 1914, especially through their domination of the Board of Commissioners. Concerned mainly with reforming the administration, the Board proved unable to work out an urban-development policy at a time of frantic city growth. Requests for the adoption of a city improvement plan went unanswered. Some public buildings, among them the City Hall Annex, were constructed and more streets were paved, but the only major project of the time (a wide boulevard along the Montreal Aqueduct) was never carried out.[36]

The turn-of-the-century debate over the establishment of a Municipal Library gives a clear indication of the tensions of the time. On-hold for some ten years, the very validity of the project was questioned – on moral grounds by the archbishop of Montreal, Monsignor Bruchési, who succeeded in having the project postponed, and on grounds of need by certain English-speaking councillors, who felt their constituencies were already well served by the libraries of various local institutions. The library was finally approved in 1910, but it would take another four years to agree on where to build it, anglophones proposing the west part of the city, most francophones the East End. The latter eventually won the day (see fig. 37).[37]

Another powerful force on Montreal's political scene was the government of Quebec. With exclusive authority over municipal institutions, the province frequently intervened to impose policies on the city administration and to define or limit its powers. The Montreal business community increasingly turned to Quebec City to counteract what it viewed as certain negative consequences of democracy, an effect of the growing political power of the masses. While it was able to win voters' approval for the creation of a Board of Commissioners (1910–18) and to have business-supported reformers elected to the Board, when these lost power the business community pressured Quebec to assume government control over the City, which was achieved through the Administrative Commission (1918–21). The protests of local politicians at this seizure of "municipal autonomy" brought about a return to democracy, with an executive committee, in 1921.[38]

For its part, the federal government had no direct authority in municipal matters. However, the control it exercised over the railway companies, Bell Telephone, and the Harbour Commission, along with the government departments located in Montreal, gave it a considerable role in the development of the city.

THE AGENTS OF URBAN DEVELOPMENT

The groups and institutions active on the political front were also those that largely shaped the city's pattern of growth. Already established in the nineteenth century as a distinct industry with its own specialized entrepreneurs, urban development took on new life in the early 1900s.[39] The thrust was led by property developers who were especially active in the suburbs, where they shaped the subdivision and urbanization of the farmlands surrounding the city. Until 1914 these entrepreneurs were typically businessmen who had made their money in other sectors of the economy and had the resources needed to invest

in real estate. Extending their operations in the years prior to the First World War, they created joint-stock companies for the raising of extra capital, touching off a frenzy of speculation that induced thousands of Montrealers to invest in real estate – money that went up in smoke with the collapse of the market in 1913 and the World War that followed.

Besides the developers there also were real-estate agents, whose numbers rose with the turn-of-the-century euphoria, and building contractors, economic players whose vital role in the history of urban development has yet to be chronicled. Of two basic types, contractors either operated in the residential sector (usually these were small individual entrepreneurs) or specialized in major projects, such as public works and the construction of buildings. The larger firms competed with their American counterparts for major contracts, especially those offered by private enterprise. Another force was the manufacturer of building materials, some of which were newly powerful corporations like the Dominion Bridge Co. and Canada Cement.

Of interest here, however, are the three groups that were pre-eminent in influencing architects' commissions and undertaking the construction of the important buildings studied in part three of this book: private enterprise, government, and the Catholic Church.

The economic transformations outlined above generated a considerable amount of building in Montreal. In the last decades of the nineteenth century, importers and wholesalers had built numerous warehouses in the city, especially in the west of Old Montreal and in Griffintown. The boom in the retail trade had its effect, too, leading to the appearance of department stores on St. Catherine Street in the 1890s, to be expanded and modernized in the 1920s. But an even greater impact on the city was due to growth in manufacturing. This brought about the construction of entire industrial zones and huge factories, many of them expanded more than once. The most impressive of these were the Angus Shops, the Canadian Pacific Railway workshops in the East End, but other industries – textiles, tobacco, transportation, electrical hardware, breweries, sugar refineries, flour mills – also demanded considerable space and required substantial investment. Just prior to the First World War the large loft-style building sprang up in Montreal, making room for a variety of commercial tenants that included print shops and garment-trade workshops. The Jacobs Building (fig. 98), completed in 1910, was the prototype of these.[40]

It was big business that increased the building stock in the city's downtown core. Large corporations with factory and branch-office networks, employers of thousands across the country and in some cases outside Canada as well, required premises to house the steadily growing staff needed to run their head offices. For instance, head-office employees of the Sun Life Assurance Co. of Canada increased from 20 in 1890 to 2,856 in 1930, a staggering rate of increase that prompted the decision in 1918 to erect a new building on Dominion Square (fig. 117) and that well explains its two later expansions (fig. 118).[41] The increasing number of professionals and service-providers – lawyers, notaries, accountants, engineers, and advertisers – created a serious need for office space, and thus led to the appearance in Montreal of the multi-tenant commercial building.

In 1880 Montreal's economy was still dominated by businesses built from the ground up by their owners – men inclined to control all the important decisions in their company's construction projects. In the large corporations that were to come, power of this sort would be diluted, but in the early twentieth century big businesses were still headed by great financiers and entrepreneurs who commanded considerable authority, men like Herbert Holt at the Royal Bank or William Van Horne and Thomas Shaughnessy at Canadian Pacific. The distinction between owners and professional managers would emerge more slowly in Canadian companies than in American ones. It is reasonable to suppose, then, that the key decisions in the choice of architecture during this period were made by leading businessmen, most of them, as we have seen, English-speaking. The French-speaking businessman, who headed mostly smaller companies, rarely needed to construct tall buildings.

In the public sector, the federal government commissioned buildings for some of its departments, notably Post and Customs. In addition, the power it exercised over the Harbour Commission made it indirectly responsible for the extensive work carried out in Montreal Harbour, plans to which it gave pre-construction approval. Government ownership of railway installations came with the creation of the Canadian National Railways. In addition, the federal Board of Railway Commissioners had the power to accept or reject projects for railway lines in Montreal as well as elsewhere in Canada.

The government of Quebec also had a number of public buildings erected in Montreal. In the judicial domain, the Court House was expanded, the Court House Annex was erected (fig. 47), and a new provincial prison was built in the Bordeaux

Ward. The provincial government was also responsible for the construction of major institutions of learning: the École Polytechnique (figs. 12 and 27), the École des Hautes Études Commerciales (figs. 4 and 34), the École Technique de Montréal (figs. 35 and 36), and the École des Beaux-Arts.

The City's investments in building concentrated mainly on public infrastructures: streets and sidewalks, waterworks and sewers, and the creation of parks. City council also exercised considerable influence over private construction through by-law legislation. Both Bonsecours Market and City Hall were built prior to our period, but between 1880 and 1930 the City undertook the construction of many new buildings including the City Hall Annex, the Municipal Library (fig. 37), the water-treatment plant, police and fire stations, public markets, and public baths. City Hall itself had to be rebuilt and enlarged after the fire of 1922. The smaller suburban towns and cities generally confined themselves to a single multi-purpose building housing all municipal services, the exceptions being Maisonneuve (which built four large public buildings between 1910 and 1916) and Westmount. At the local level, an important role was also played by school boards, which were responsible for the construction of many schools.

As three quarters of the population of Montreal was Catholic, it is hardly surprising that the presence of the Church was widely reflected in the cityscape, chiefly but not solely through Montreal's large churches, which were built as the growing population generated new parishes. While the archbishop had some say here, decisions regarding church building were made locally by the parish priest and churchwardens, with the financing underwritten by parishioners. Other major building projects were initiated by the religious orders – priests, brothers, and above all nuns – whose vocation was service to the community. Along with their motherhouses, religious communities built and expanded a large number of classical colleges, convents, hospitals, homes for the aged, orphanages, and other specialized institutions.[42] Moreover, the archbishop had commissioned a new cathedral for Montreal and in 1895 the Church-governed Université Laval in Montreal opened its new building (fig. 17), later entrusting Ernest Cormier with the design of an entire campus (fig. 48) when it outgrew those premises in the 1920s.[43] Within the Catholic Church in Montreal, decision-making with regard to architecture thus seems to have been relatively decentralized, each parish and religious community coming to its own conclusions.

The situation was much the same in Protestant communities. Here the various denominations built churches, though these were not usually so large as the Catholic ones. Public-service institutions, typically not run by the Church, were also established for these communities – examples being McGill University and Anglo-Protestant hospitals and social services, all of which needed new buildings. It is likely that the leading businessmen who often sat on the boards of these institutions, and who helped to fund them, carried some weight in the decision-making process. Other ethnolinguistic and religious groups, arriving later, had yet to leave their mark with the construction of major buildings.

IT WAS IN THIS CONTEXT THAT A NEW MONTREAL arose between 1880 and 1930. First a colonial city of the British Empire, then a North American metropolis, Montreal took advantage of its international connections, attracting men, capital, and ideas from elsewhere that would contribute to the creation of a new cityscape. But Montrealers did not just borrow and skilfully adapt foreign ideas to the local setting; Montreal was also shaped by internal forces that gave the city's development its own special dynamic. The financial power of the corporate elite had a great impact upon the planning of the city's centre and industrial zones. Then came the complexities of the political system, with a three-tiered government leading to an uncoordinated decision-making process. Montreal was also distinct because of the powerful Catholic Church, which here managed services that elsewhere were often State-run.

The development of the city was affected as well by the great divide between anglophones and francophones, involved in power struggles of their own. Each group occupied its own territory, its city-within-the-city – divisions commonly exacerbated by social disparities as well. French-speakers relied chiefly on the provincial government, the municipality, and the Church, whereas English-speakers dominated the world of business and the federal government. The building and the planning of Montreal the metropolis are thus the product and the reflection of tensions that were internal as well as external.

AN AGE RICH IN MIRACLES

Marcel Fournier and Véronique Rodriguez

IN THE EARLY TWENTIETH CENTURY MONTREAL prospered as never before: huge construction projects were underway, the telephone arrived, and the city gained a fast, regular streetcar service, street lighting, water-treatment plants, and many new public buildings. These improvements made Montreal Canada's metropolis, not just an enterprising commercial city but an "intellectual centre and seat of learning."[1]

A new urban culture sprang up as immigrants flocked into the city, making Montreal more cosmopolitan, and as new generations of writers and artists expressed their francophone identity, which necessarily embodied a political dimension. These phenomena accelerated the move towards modernity, at the same time forming the basis for a more vibrant and independent intellectual and artistic life.

There were many constraints upon the burgeoning of such a community: the linguistic divide; the fact that both political-administrative centres – Quebec City and Ottawa – lay outside Montreal; the limited educational level of the French-speaking population; and the city's dependence on Europe and the United States. Montreal was a somewhat different case from other North American cities. The English-speaking well-to-do class of the Square Mile constituted a kind of British aristocracy still enjoying its day in the sun.[2] The Catholic Church, too, had remained both powerful and prominent in this city where French and English language and culture rubbed shoulders uneasily.

Industrialization and urbanization in Quebec meant a confrontation between traditional and modern values[3] but also involved a class struggle, as well as a clash between clerical-nationalist and liberal ideologies and the growing Americanization of life-styles and culture. Some groups saw films and stage shows from the United States as a threat to French Canada's

4 École des Hautes Études Commerciales (1908–10, Gauthier and Daoust, architects); view of the Musée industriel et commercial, 1916. Photograph: Albert Dumas, Archives H É C

religious and cultural identity.[4] French Canadians "streamed into the city" and Montreal would from now on play a central role in their future.

A NEW URBAN CULTURE

Urban culture in this period was already based on information and communications, spread not only by rapid-transit systems (railways and streetcars), a wide-circulation press, and the telephone but also by films, gramophone records,[5] and radio.

The appearance of broadly distributed, inexpensive newspapers (one cent a copy) created what has been called an everyday modernity. The *Montreal Daily Star* was first published in 1877, *The Gazette* the following year. The French-language papers *La Patrie* and *La Presse*, founded respectively by Honoré Beaugrand and William-Edmond Blumhart, launched their first issues on 23 February 1879 and 20 October 1884. Several foreign-language publications followed, such as the Italian weekly *Corriere del Canada* (1900), the Yiddish *Keneder Odler* (1907, founded by H. Wolofsky and appearing first as a daily then as a weekly until 1980), and the Russian paper *Russkoye Slovo* (1910, published by Victor Shinkin). The evening paper became "the book of the people."[6] In 1891 the average Quebec family bought almost three (2.98) newspapers on a regular basis.[7] People had never read so much.

In fact journalism, the "cradle of Quebec letters," opened up a new kind of access to intellectual life.[8] The importance of the profession in the development of Montreal's literary scene is evident from the names of its luminaries: Olivar Asselin, Henri Bourassa, Hector Fabre, and Jules Fournier – all of them newspapermen.[9]

The world of the arts, theatre, and entertainment was not immune to linguistic divisions: "We have in reality become two cities, somewhat unequal in size," wrote B.K. Sandwell in 1915.[10] Montreal's principal theatres – the Royal (1852), the Academy of Music (1875), the Français (1893), and Her Majesty's (1898–99) – were controlled by John Bolingbroke Sparrow, a Montreal impresario and member of the Syndicate, a big New York management company, who had a virtual monopoly on Montreal's larger halls. The Academy of Music, whose recital hall included three balconies, could accommodate over 2,000 people and was home to the Montreal Symphony Orchestra from 1903 until the building was demolished in 1910. On Guy Street, Her Majesty's (later His Majesty's) opened its doors with 1,700 seats.[11] The

majority of the shows produced in these theatres featured professional American companies on tour; between 1893 and 1914, the United States provided more than sixty percent of the shows presented, most of them musical comedies and the rest (in decreasing numbers) operettas and comic operas.[12] Montrealers had to wait until the late 1920s to see the city's first English-language theatre company, the Montreal Repertory Theatre founded by Martha Allen.

The francophone newspapers attacked the frivolity and mediocrity of the American shows and chided theatre-goers for deserting their own theatres to go and listen to rubbish. Montreal, they complained, had been "invaded by barbarians."[13] At the instigation of the Société Saint-Jean-Baptiste and with the explicit aim of presenting entertainment in French, the Monument National theatre on St. Lawrence Boulevard opened to the public in 1893 with seating for 1,550 spectators. After initial difficulties, its multi-purpose auditorium (shows, concerts, and political meetings) held regular *Soirées de famille* on which, between 1898 and 1901, almost 70 plays and over a hundred shows were staged under the direction of Elzéar Roy. The local actors, singers, and musicians who performed there were thus able to evade the American monopolies governing the playbills of other theatres. The first professional theatre in the French language, however, was the Théâtre des Variétés, established in 1898 by Léon Petitjean at the corner of St. Catherine Street and Papineau Avenue. Later came the Théâtre national (1900), founded by the playwright-actor who also directed the company, Julien Daoust, and the Théâtre des nouveautés (1902), which presented shows mounted by professional companies from France.[14]

The impact of the cinema, the new art of the people, on cultural life was even more profound, as seats cost four times less than at the theatre.[15] The first public screening of a film in Montreal was held on 27 June 1896, presented to an audience of journalists and prominent citizens at the Palace Theatre at 78 St. Lawrence Boulevard in a new downtown neighbourhood already home to several theatres. In the early days, films were shown by travelling projectionists, and were always accompanied by live stage-shows to offset the new medium's technical limitations (reel-changing, the shortness of the films, and so on). Until the arrival of talking pictures, most kinescopes and cinemas had therefore a dual function. Many of the traditional theatres that kept films out – like the Queen's, the Français, and the Royal – were eventually faced with bankruptcy and were forced to turn themselves into cinemas offering film screenings and variety shows.

The Ouimetoscope – from the name of its founder Léo-Ernest Ouimet – opened in January 1906 in the Salle Poiré on the corner of St. Catherine and Montcalm streets, in the heart of a French-speaking district. With its 450 seats, it was the first establishment in all of North America designed specifically for films. Ouimet's example was soon followed by other entrepreneurs, so that by April 1910 there were already 36 cinemas in the city, most of them in the new downtown area. St. Catherine Street, especially in the east between Bleury and Papineau, became Montreal's cinema row.[16] A few cinemas also sprang up on the main streets of municipalities and suburbs such as Outremont, St. Henri, and Maisonneuve, and moviegoers there could now frequent the Papineau, the Rialto, the Outremont (fig. 53), the Monkland, the Granada, etc.

The growing popularity of films was not without opposition. In 1905 the religious authorities, in their battle against a form of entertainment they perceived as a new threat to public morals, succeeded in having Sunday screenings declared illegal.[17] Theatre owners, however, preferred to pay the fines from their Sunday receipts, and in 1911 the Supreme Court of Canada finally decided in their favour. One year later a board of censors was established in Montreal.

Like the theatre, the cinema business was almost completely under American control. The distributed films came from the United States[18] and independent distributors found themselves excluded. From around 1916 until the early 1920s, cinema architecture reflected the overwhelming influence of the American companies that built super-palaces like the Imperial (1916) and Loew's (1917; fig. 63) for the exclusive presentation of their new releases. Though also on St. Catherine Street, these newer cinemas were built farther west, between Phillips Square and Dominion Square, and the older theatre nucleus gradually disappeared as the kinescopes closed down and almost no new construction replaced them.

Despite the huge enthusiasm for movies, there was scarcely any film production in Montreal before the early 1940s. Ouimet's short newsreels made him Quebec's first film director, but in documentaries it was English-language firms such as Associated Screen News and Patricia Photoplays that led the way, first copying American films before going on to make their own. A film pioneer in the French-speaking community was Father Albert Tessier, who in the 1920s employed a movie-camera

"to help man become aware of his surroundings, to show the value of work carried out in harmony with nature, and to glorify God, man's creator."[19] Later Joseph-Arthur Homier made the first fiction film in Quebec, *Oh! Oh! Jean* (1922) and then *La drogue fatale* (1924). Other directors followed his lead, but the momentum of production slowed when talking pictures arrived in Montreal in 1928. As distribution remained under American control and many small independent theatres closed down as a result of the stringent new safety regulations imposed after a fire at the Laurier Palace cinema,[20] the few films produced in Quebec could find no distribution outlets.

In Montreal the talking-film industry got off the ground slowly, its birth coinciding with the start of the Depression. The first theatres to bring in the new sound technology were the Capitol and the Palace in 1928; two years later most cinemas were screening talkies. The advent of sound effectively raised a linguistic barrier against American films, opening Montreal to French cinema, and the first French talkie (*Les trois masques*) premiered on 31 May 1930 at the St. Denis Theatre, one of the last cinemas to adapt. That same year saw the founding of the Compagnie cinématographique canadienne, later to become France Film. This new leading distributor of French films, previously almost impossible to obtain in Montreal, countered American domination and a few years later would be instrumental in reviving Quebec-made feature films.

A CHANGING INTELLECTUAL CLIMATE: SOME "DANGEROUS THINKERS"

The notion of a "republic" of letters[21] had its tentative beginnings in the Quebec City journal *Les Nouvelles Soirées canadiennes* (1882).[22] The province had as yet few French-language writers, or men of letters as they were called at the time, and still fewer French publications. During the first decade of the twentieth century no more than three novels were published in French in an average year,[23] many of them serialized novels originally issued in various newspapers – for instance Rodolphe Girard's *Florence*, first published in 1900, and Louis Hémon's *Maria Chapdelaine*, which appeared in *Le Temps* in 1914, both of which were bound into volumes in 1916. The journalist Rodolphe Girard was unusually prolific, publishing four novels in the ten years before 1910.[24]

Indicative of the times was the case of the poet Louis Fréchette, who, defeated at the polls in 1878, left his longtime home in Quebec City for Montreal. In 1880 – a memorable year for Fréchette – his *Retour de l'exilé* was performed (1 June), his *Papineau* was acclaimed by Montrealers (7 June), and Fréchette was awarded the Prix Montyon by the Académie française (5 August). It was not until the turn of the century, however, that Montreal's French literary community became truly energetic and independent, establishing its own outlets and networks. Literary societies sprang up – the Spaslac,[25] the Encéphale, the Soc, and so on – as did gathering places such as the Cénacle, where luminaries including the economist Édouard Montpetit, the architect Ernest Cormier, and the financier Gérard Parizeau met at the Librairie Déom.[26] There were also new magazines and bookshops with publishing operations of their own, the two most important of these being Granger and Beauchemin.

The 1890s were characterized by a ferment of new ideas, a change in the intellectual climate, and the arrival of a new and highly creative generation. More than 25 French periodicals were founded in the course of the decade.[27] Cultural leadership had clearly passed from Quebec City to Montreal: 15 June 1889 saw the publication of the first issue of the weekly *Le Samedi*;[28] 1895, the establishment of the École littéraire de Montréal, a group modelled after literary academies; 1900, the launch of the periodical *Les Débats*; and 1904, the publication of the works of Émile Nelligan – sufficient proof that Canada was no longer a "*terre de sauvagerie*"?[29]

The École littéraire de Montréal, founded by Louvigny de Montigny and Jean Charbonneau, united young writers who called for nothing less than a revolution in both aesthetics and symbols.[30] The École's first public meeting took place on 29 December 1898 in a room in the Château Ramezay in Old Montreal, recently turned into a museum of history under the management of the Antiquarian and Numismatic Society – hence the title of the École's first collective work, *Les Soirées du Château de Ramezay* (1900). Nine years later a second collection of essays was published in the form of a monthly review with the earthy, and hence somewhat misleading, title *Le Terroir*, for despite the regionalism of their approach its contributors were determined that "art shall be our master."[31] Indeed, Louis Dantin has observed that the writing of Émile Nelligan, who joined the group in February 1897, demonstrates "the love of art and of pure thought only."[32]

The years leading up to the outbreak of war in 1914 were a watershed, "an age rich in miracles" according to Marcel Dugas,

who nonetheless remained far from uncritical of his "village" of Montreal.[33] In 1910 the newspaper *Le Devoir* was launched by the nationalist leader Henri Bourassa. Around the same time, several collections of poetry were published that raised the "regionalist debate." Led by Father Camille Roy, professor of French literature at the Université Laval, the adherents of regionalism wanted a literature of local colour that captured the picturesque qualities of the culture, and were sometimes labelled "profiteers of the past, monopolizers of history …, grabbers at success."[34] Supported by the ruling French-Canadian elite, they believed that the survival of the French-Canadian people was tied to religion and agriculture. Given their opposition to the industrialization of cities and to French republican ideas, Montreal seemed to them a monster that devoured its inhabitants.[35]

On the other side, grouped around the poet and critic Marcel Dugas, were the "exotics," the first defenders in Montreal of "art for art's sake." Prominent among Montreal's bohemians were Paul Morin, René Chopin, and Guy Delahaye, writers whose early work appeared in the newspaper *Le Nationaliste* published by Olivar Asselin. This was a group that refused to limit its inspiration by geographical boundaries, and was prepared to reject everything that might distance its literature from that of France. These upholders of universalism were considered by some to be "Parisified," and indeed were inclined to picture themselves at home in the City of Light winning the recognition of the French.

In an attempt to counter the excesses of regionalism, Dugas assembled a few "dangerous thinkers"[36] newly returned from the war in France; in 1918, Dugas and the novelist Robert de Roquebrune, the architect Fernand Préfontaine, and the musician Léo-Pol Morin founded *Le Nigog*. This short-lived "review of art in action"[37] was intended to "establish, in opposition to the *Devoir* School, the rationale of French modernity, to create a taste for it in contemporary art, literature, and music." Its contributors defended the idea that a grain elevator, "despite being a mass of cement, despite being designed by an engineer, could be considered in the end to be a work of art."[38] Indeed the journal published a sketch of such an elevator by Adrien Hébert, a painter whose work was closely involved with modernity through Hébert's chosen subject matter: the city and its infrastructures – bridges, harbour, elevators.[39] Hébert was in fact one of the first artists in Montreal whose work directly addressed the industrialized city. Unlike Marc-Aurèle Fortin, who depicted the city as either invaded by greenery (*Landscape in Hochelaga*, 1931) or else crushing humankind beneath its giant constructions (*Fire in Montreal Harbour*, c. 1928), Hébert celebrated it, showing the harbour machinery that made the dockers' work easier (*Montreal Harbour*, 1925).

It was not easy to "work for artists and not in order to please the public,"[40] as the painter Marc-Aurèle de Foy Suzor-Côté remarked to Rodolphe Duguay. Sculptor Alfred Laliberté, as well, complained of the dearth of encouragement he received: money was spent "on war, sports, mechanics, travelling, theatre, and films, but not on the fine arts. Such is modern progress."[41] In Montreal students could study drawing, painting, and sculpture under Father Joseph Chabert, Edmond Dyonnet, William Brymner, Maurice Cullen, and other artists in the classes of the Conseil des Arts et Manufactures (1869–1928), the Institut national des Beaux-Arts (1874–95), the Montreal Art Association, and in studios run like medieval workshops. The creation of the École des Beaux-Arts in 1922 was to change substantially the teaching of art in Montreal; nevertheless, many architects, painters, sculptors, and musicians preferred to complete their education abroad, in France, Britain, or the United States. On returning to Montreal these young artists brought with them new influences, such as the Impressionism that marked the works of Maurice Cullen and James Wilson Morrice. They opened studios and taught classes in the city, making regular trips to the countryside in search of inspiration.

The example of the Canadian Group of Painters in Toronto provoked Montreal artists to unite. Some, like the English-speaking students of William Brymner, got together under the name of the Beaver Hall Hill Group in the 1920s; other groups were the painters of the Montée Saint-Michel[42] and the circle that formed around John Lyman after his return from Paris in 1931. However, most found little occasion to meet other than at meetings of the Montreal Art Association, exhibitions at the Bibliothèque Saint-Sulpice (after 1915), and the presentation of student works at the École des Beaux-Arts (after 1924). As for commercial galleries, it was not until the mid 1910s that William Watson began to sell Canadian paintings and bronzes in his Peel Street shop, not just the French, British, and Dutch Romantic and Neoclassical works that his predecessor John Ogilvy had sold on St. François Xavier Street in Old Montreal.[43]

THE ASSERTION OF A FRENCH CULTURE

At the end of the nineteenth century Montreal's major cultural institutions were anglophone, and all situated in the west end of the city north of Old Montreal: the Montreal Art Association (founded in 1879, it moved in 1912 from Phillips Square to Sherbrooke Street), the Redpath Museum (opened in 1882), the Mechanics' Institute, the Fraser Institute library (1885),[44] and the Westmount Public Library (1899).[45] The city's great art collections were in the hands of the transcontinental railway barons – men like Sir William Van Horne, Sir George Drummond, Charles Hosmer, James Ross, R.B. Angus, and Lord Strathcona.[46]

As far as universities were concerned, the most distinguished institution in the city was McGill University, which had been richly endowed with a library, a museum, lecture halls, and green spaces.[47] At the turn of the century, under the leadership of Principals John William Dawson and his successor William Peterson, the university underwent considerable expansion thanks to generous donations from Montreal's wealthy English-speaking families, and between 1890 and 1910 many new buildings rose on the campus (fig. 25). McGill was also the first university in Montreal to offer music classes: in 1905 the McGill Conservatorium of Music was opened, due to the efforts of Clara Lichtenstein. Harry Crane Perrin, the British organist who founded the university's first symphony orchestra, taught there from 1908 to 1929. McGill also established its own system of music examinations, and in 1920 opened a faculty of music.

Until late in the nineteenth century there was little music teaching outside institutions for girls run by the religious orders; considered essential to a young girl's education, music was granted an important place in their curricula. It was not until the urban population explosion and the rise in living standards of the late 1880s that conservatories began to appear.[48] In 1890, when Ernest Lavigne established a symphony orchestra in Sohmer Park, he was still obliged to bring in professionals from Belgium, France, and Italy, though Lavigne harboured the hope that once in Montreal his imported musicians would train a future generation of local orchestra members. In fact his initiative had a substantial effect on the history of music in Montreal, since it was his group that formed the core of the first Montreal Symphony Orchestra, organized as a cooperative venture by J.-J. Goulet. Its director for the first two seasons, from 1894 to 1896, was Guillaume Couture. Goulet took over two years after that, and the orchestra reappeared in 1927 with J.-J. Gagnier, its artistic director until 1929.[49]

There were few francophones among the city's ruling elite: the names that stand out are Louis-Joseph Forget, Frédéric-Liguori Béique, the Rolland family, and the brothers Oscar and Marius Dufresne.[50] The French-speaking community was intent on changing this situation. For men like Athanase David, Victor Doré, and Édouard Montpetit, the rallying cry was "Nothing is possible without schooling. With schooling everything is possible."[51] The destiny of French Canada was considered dependent on the development of the education system: from 1851 onwards pleas were made for a French-speaking university in Montreal.[52] The only francophone campus in the city was a branch of Quebec City's Université Laval, established in 1876. The provincial government under Liberal premier Lomer Gouin undertook to correct the obvious deficiencies of the educational system and adapt it to the new needs of the economy, founding the École des Hautes Études Commerciales (figs. 4 and 34) and the École Technique de Montréal (figs. 35 and 36), both of which opened in new premises in the student quarter in 1908 and 1909 respectively. It was there, in 1893–95, that the Université Laval's new building had been built on St. Denis Street (fig. 17). A lively francophone intellectual milieu thus began to develop around St. Denis between Viger and St. Louis squares. Two new libraries were under construction: the Bibliothèque Saint-Sulpice (1911–15) on St. Denis, near these institutions, and the Bibliothèque municipale de Montréal (1914–17; fig. 37) on Sherbrooke Street East.

The most ambitious project was undoubtedly the construction of a modern university on the slopes of Mount Royal to make up for the chronic lack of space in the various buildings of the Université Laval in Montreal. In 1919 and in 1922 this situation had been aggravated by fires in the building on St. Denis Street. Meanwhile the initiatives for change had borne fruit: a document signed in Rome on 8 May 1919 ratified a change in status for the Montreal branch of the Université Laval, which, now independent, became the Université de Montréal. A major fund-raising campaign brought in over 4 million dollars, while the City of Montreal donated land on the mountain. The planning of the campus was entrusted to the architect Ernest Cormier, who was asked to begin construction with wings for the faculties of science and medicine and to incorporate an observatory at the top of a centrally located tower. In May 1928 construction began (fig. 48), only to halt a few years

later in the fall of 1932, stopped by the Depression. Some called the new university an "unfinished symphony," others a white elephant. When it opened finally in June 1943, the university hailed as a future "seat of learning" and a "storehouse of knowledge" bore the motto *Fide splendet et scientia.*[53]

The creation of the Université de Montréal's faculty of science in 1920 marked the beginning of a scientific revolution in the francophone community: the first team of professors brought together Brother Marie-Victorin, Dr. Georges-H. Baril, Dr. Joseph-Ernest Gendreau, Father Joseph Morin, and Louis-J. Dalbis. New learned societies were formed – for instance, the Association canadienne-française pour l'avancement des sciences (1923), the Institut scientifique franco-canadien (1926), and the Cercle des jeunes naturalistes (in the early 1930s)[54] – and well-attended public lectures were also held.

Schools, libraries, university departments, learned societies: all were looked upon as Quebec's own. The old slogan "Let us take over the land" was to be replaced by "Let us take our place at the top." The well-being of French Canada, dependent on economic control, was henceforth linked to the education and training of an intellectual elite. "Let us train men; let us foster abilities.... That is the price of our future," wrote Édouard Montpetit in the first issue of the periodical *L'Action française*, published in 1917 under the editorship of Father Lionel Groulx. Citizens not only had to take some distance from their traditional habits and strike out in new directions – commerce, the natural sciences, the social sciences – they also had to "unite in order to grow," as expressed in the *Revue moderne* in 1919. All of these concerns were expressed in the pages of *Le Devoir*, the *Revue trimestrielle canadienne* (1915, published by the École Polytechnique), and the *Revue nationale* (1919, published by the Société Saint-Jean-Baptiste).

The crash of 1929 brought unemployment and poverty. Some looked to *La Relève* (a journal launched in 1934 aimed at young people) or dreamed of a *Renaissance* (the title of a newspaper founded in 1935 by Olivar Asselin). Others saw the survival of the French Canadian people in a return to the land. In 1933 Clarence Gagnon, one of the best-known and most-esteemed painters of his generation – virtually its guiding star[55] – illustrated the deluxe edition of *Maria Chapdelaine*. In his mildly Impressionist paintings and prints he sought to capture the landscapes of the Laurentians and the Charlevoix region and the enduring values of Quebec's rural life.

IN THE YEARS BETWEEN 1880 AND 1930 MONTREAL seemed torn between the United States and Europe. The many influences it absorbed from both sides of the Atlantic tended to obscure the qualities that made it distinctive, unless perhaps that distinctiveness lay in this divided allegiance itself. It was because Montreal during this period stood at a crossroads between two worlds that gallery-owners could find no market for local art works before the mid 1910s, that there was almost no film production until the 1930s, and that the first English-speaking theatre company was founded only in 1929. Yet this fact, along with the steady influence of modern life on traditional values, brought about a thriving cosmopolitan culture that made the metropolis of Montreal different from the rest of Canada.

Was turn-of-the-century Montreal marked by any defining characteristic?[56] Was there a "generation of 1900" that represented this transitional period? Figures such as Ernest Cormier, Marcel Dugas, John Lyman, Édouard Montpetit, and Émile Nelligan did not strictly speaking constitute a generation: their language, culture, goals, and approaches varied too much for that. Indeed, the commitment to modernism of Montreal's intellectuals and artists was expressed differently by the city's various cultural groups and took root at different moments. Moreover, resistance to things modern was strong and setbacks were frequent, and in some fields it was not until the mid 1930s or even during the Second World War that modernity would leave its mark.[57]

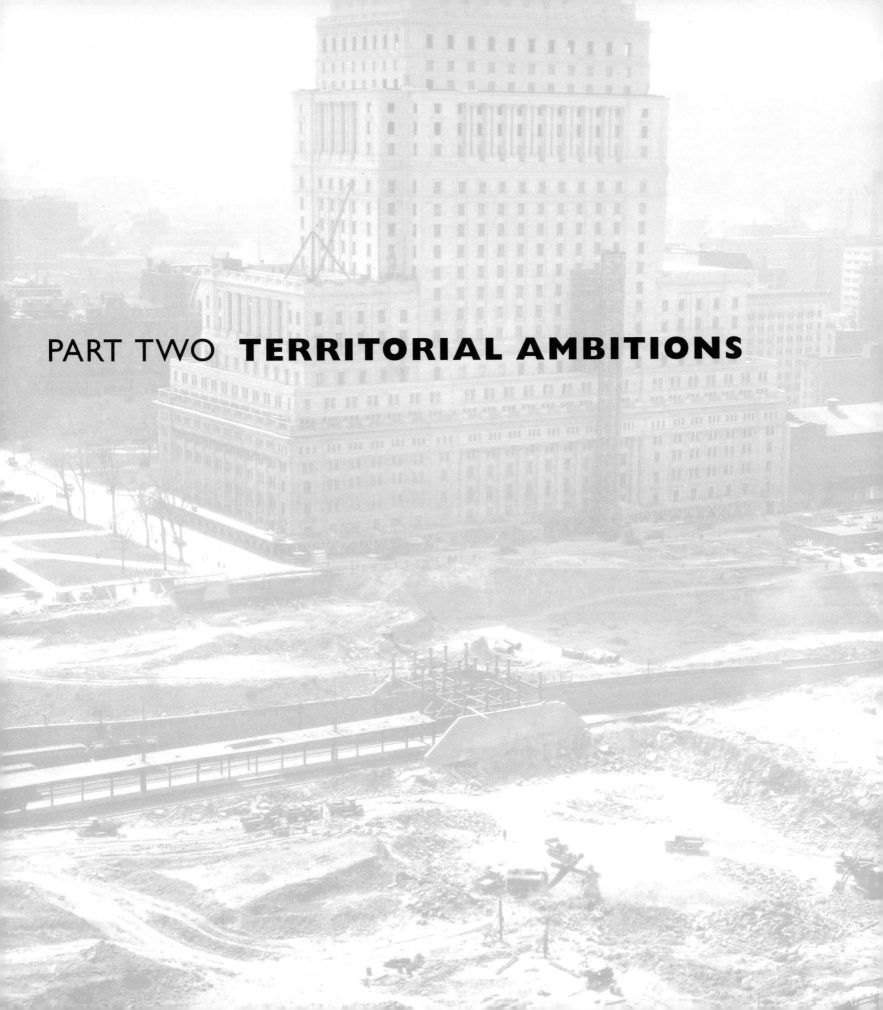

PART TWO **TERRITORIAL AMBITIONS**

THE IMPORTANCE OF TRANSPORTATION INFRASTRUCTURE

David B. Hanna

BETWEEN 1880 AND 1930 MONTREAL CLEARLY positioned itself as an industrial metropolis, the North American centre for the administration of Canadian and British capital. The city dominated transatlantic trade between Europe and Canada, advertised itself as the "Imperial bridge" between Great Britain, Canada, and the Asian possessions, and harboured further ambitions regarding the lucrative traffic of the American Midwest. It stood in direct competition with the much larger Atlantic Seaboard metropolises, from Boston to Baltimore, all of whom were in turn feeling fairly keen competition from the newer metropolitan centres then on the rise inside the continent. Though smaller than its American competitors, Montreal had visions of grandeur, planning and often accomplishing ambitious projects. The role that it had opted for, however, could not be carried off without the creation of outwardly oriented infrastructures on a highly substantial scale. An investigation of the characteristics and stature of these projects sheds considerable light on the questions of how and to what extent the City of Montreal won the status of a continental and even an international metropolis.

BUILDING FOR A CONTINENT, 1840–80

Starting in 1840, Montreal set itself on a course of important infrastructural investments that betrayed its metropolitan ambitions, as the old colonial city was completely rebuilt as a new and "modern" business district.[1] Two major projects from this period merit particular attention on account of both their scale and their impact on the era to come. The first was the St. Lawrence Canal System circumventing navigational impediments along the St. Lawrence River. While Montreal had witnessed the opening of the Lachine Canal in 1825, allowing

5 CNR Central Station excavation project with Dorchester Street Bridge under construction, also showing the Sun Life Assurance Co. Building in the final phase of construction (1929–31, Darling and Pearson, architects), 1931. Unknown photographer. National Archives of Canada/PA-182360.

marine traffic to bypass the Lachine Rapids for the first time, that Canal had only a shallow draught of 5 feet (1.5 m) and single locks. Between 1842 and 1848, however, the Canadian government created a twin-lock canal system 9 feet deep (2.7 m), allowing full marine access to Lake Ontario, Lake Erie, and beyond. The locks were further enlarged in 1875–78.[2] The dredging of the St. Lawrence River downstream from Montreal, undertaken by the government in 1850, created an 11-foot depth (3.3 m), gradually deepened to 22.5 feet (6.9 m) by 1880. The number of ocean-going vessels passing through the system in this period surged from 211 to 710. Montreal was racing to keep up with its seaboard competitors. Baltimore had dredged its sea channel in 1873 in order to keep pace with New York. In 1863 New York had enlarged, twin-locked, and deepened its 370-mile (595 km) Erie Canal, giving New York City access to Lake Erie.[3]

While the public purse was being used to enhance access to the Port of Montreal, private capital was behind the city's other great continental infrastructural project. The Victoria Bridge represented one of the era's most audacious undertakings. Spanning a huge river that had never been bridged, a nearly 3-kilometre long square tube of iron plates was laid across 24 massive stone piers (designed to withstand the enormous shock of the huge ice sheets loosed each year in the spring thaw), sheltering two iron rails that carried the trains of the Grand Trunk Railway Co. (GTR). Designed by the famous British master engineer Robert Stephenson and built under tremendous hardship between 1854 and 1859, the gigantic project attracted visitors from both sides of the Atlantic and was hailed as the "Eighth Wonder of the World."[4]

The bridge was part of an overall continental strategy launched in 1853 by a company of British investors seeking to run an Imperial rail line from the coast to the heart of the continent. Starting at Portland, Maine – the closest ice-free port to Montreal, whose own harbour facilities had to shut down for four to five months of the year due to freeze-up – the trunk line reached Sherbrooke and Saint-Hyacinthe in the prosperous agricultural and industrial hinterland of southern Quebec. Another line was built to Lévis opposite Quebec City and further to Rivière-du-Loup, thereby controlling the lower St. Lawrence hinterland as well. The GTR also purchased two older railways that stretched from the South Shore opposite Montreal to the United States border, where connections were made for Boston and New York City. West of Montreal, the trunk line reached the upper St. Lawrence and the rich Great Lakes hinterland, linking Kingston, Toronto, London, Sarnia, and finally Detroit by 1859.

Extended across the Victoria Bridge in 1859, this network now used Montreal as its managerial and maintenance hub. Ambitious though it was, there were drawbacks to this new continental system: it was built to superior British standards and featured a distinct, Imperial, broad gauge of 5 feet 6 inches incompatible with just about every other railway in North America.[5] But once the GTR corrected its fruitless isolationism by converting to standard gauge in 1873 and 1874, it expanded aggressively to meet further competition from New York and other cities, entering Buffalo in 1873 and at last reaching a grateful Chicago in 1880, breaking the stranglehold over eastern freight rates held by the New York Central.[6]

At the opening of the new era in 1880, Montreal, through the agency of the now well-connected GTR, offered fast passenger-train service to most key American cities. New York could be reached in 14 hours by day train and 17-and-a-half hours by night train over its subsidiary, the Central Vermont Railway. An American railway, the Delaware & Hudson, offered a competing 13-and-a-half-hour day train and a 15-and-a-half-hour night train, but had to pay high fees for use of the Victoria Bridge and the GTR terminal. The GTR benefitted either way, and business, professional, and pleasure traffic flowed year-long over the two lines. A similar situation prevailed between Montreal and Boston, except that the GTR controlled most of the mileage of the two Boston routes, offering a 10-and-a-half-hour day train and a 14-hour night train over its Central Vermont route, and a 19-and-a-half-hour night train over its Portland route. Finally, the Grand Trunk offered 24-hour service to Detroit and 35-hour service to Chicago over its own lines by day or night.[7]

By 1860 the city of 100,000 people was already in control of some very impressive outside links. Montreal was serving notice that it intended to control its Canadian hinterland in Quebec and Ontario, while invading the American Midwest and New England, this at a time when Greater Boston had more than twice its population, Philadelphia nearly six times, and New York and Brooklyn had already reached the million mark. Twenty years later in 1880, when the GTR broke up the New York Central's monopoly on eastern traffic from Chicago, Montreal, with a mere 171,000 people, was fighting a giant network based in New York City. Matching its giant competitors move for move, it had indeed accomplished much.

MONTREAL: RAILWAY CAPITAL OF CANADA

Few phenomena are so inextricably interlinked as industrialism, the growth of cities, and railways. The sometimes epic battles that have been fought by railways to gain privileged access to the core of metropolises have resulted in more than a few grand transportation infrastructure schemes and have left behind some splendid architecture. It was thanks to such struggles that Chicago accumulated six major downtown terminals by the 1920s, while Toronto gained its monumental Union Station. The two major contenders in the eastern United States battled it out for rail supremacy on Manhattan Island, which thus gained two spectacular terminals: Pennsylvania Station (1906–11, McKim Mead and White) and Grand Central Terminal (1903–13, Reed and Stem, Warren and Wetmore).[8] Montreal, Canada's premier industrial and financial capital and the country's most important port of entry, was something of a similar case, and was likewise caught in an ongoing struggle between two national railway giants.

The battle lines were drawn during the 1880s between the old established Canadian giant, the Grand Trunk Railway, and the new transcontinental giant, the Canadian Pacific Railway (CPR). Founded in 1881 by Montreal capitalists, with the full backing of the government of Canada and the Bank of Montreal, to build a railway from North Bay, Ontario, to Vancouver on the Pacific Coast, the CPR launched a series of lightning strikes to secure access to Montreal and Toronto through the purchase of existing railways.

Coming in on the northern and eastern outskirts of Montreal, the CPR immediately extended its purchased railway to the northeastern edge of the business district, building Dalhousie Square Station (1882–83, architect unknown), also known as the Gare du Faubourg Québec, at the corner of Notre Dame and Berri streets.[9] The company quickly added the DeLorimier Shops or New Shops at Notre Dame Street and DeLorimier Avenue in 1883, where locomotive and railway-car construction could now commence. Two huge iron-clad grain elevators were built in 1885 and 1887 along the waterfront near Dalhousie Station. The GTR fought furiously, buying up railways in an attempt to block the CPR, but to no avail.[10]

Despite the intense development of the railways since 1847, no company had what might be termed a prestige terminal in Montreal. The GTR owned the original Bonaventure Station (1847, architect unknown) built by the Montreal & Lachine Railway on Chaboillez Square – little more than a shed – and

constructed its own Point St. Charles station on St. Etienne Street (c. 1880–81, probably by Edmund P. Hannaford), designed to accommodate company offices. But neither it nor the CPR's new Dalhousie Square Station approached what might be termed architecture of metropolitan stature. This would all change by 1889, by which time Montreal had gained two prestigious new terminals located a mere block apart on Windsor Street (now rue Peel), much in the way Euston Station, St. Pancras Station, and King's Cross Station are clustered together in London, or like the Gare du Nord and the Gare de l'Est in Paris.

The new GTR terminal was built on the site of the old Bonaventure Station (retaining the name), but this was no longer the peripheral location it had been in 1847. Only a step from Montreal's prestigious retail thoroughfare, Notre Dame Street, it was now a strategic downtown location. The new brick Bonaventure Station (fig. 13) that went up in 1888–89 was designed by Thomas S. Scott and Edmund P. Hannaford. It followed in the grand tradition of elegant Second Empire public buildings established by Henri-Maurice Perrault and Alexander C. Hutchison with Montreal's City Hall (1876–78).[11] But by 1887, the station was very dated compared to the much grander and more modern designs of contemporary terminals such as Union Station in Indianapolis (1886–89, Thomas Rodd) or Chicago's Dearborn Station (1883–85, Cyrus Eidlitz). The eight-track stub terminal behind it, though comparable in size to important stations of the time, was without the usual glazed shed of contemporary railway terminals.[12]

The CPR completed its transcontinental line to Vancouver in 1885, and now focused on improving its eastern accesses. Between 1885 and 1889 a new line was built proceeding east to Sherbrooke and then striking out across the wilds of northern Maine to the ice-free port of Saint John, New Brunswick. Branching off the existing main line in north-end Montreal, it crossed the St. Lawrence River at its narrowest point, upstream from the Lachine Rapids at Kahnawake, on a bridge built by the Dominion Bridge Co. (1885–87, C. Shaler Smith and P.A. Peterson, engineers).[13] Further acquisitions brought the CPR deep into Vermont with connections to Boston.

During the same years, the CPR branched off from its Ontario acquisitions and entered Montreal directly from the west, paralleling the GTR main line into the city. The lines diverged at Lachine, however, where the CPR chose to carve out a new right-of-way higher up along an ancient glacial sea ledge, travelling past the mansions of the wealthy to Windsor Street opposite Dominion Square, where the railway placed its jewel, Windsor Station (fig. 68). The railway's American-born president William C. Van Horne called in New York architect Bruce Price to draw up plans for a modern terminal that would outclass his rival's new station down the street. Even though it could handle only a limited number of trains, the Richardsonian-Romanesque station and office complex that was built in 1888–89 gave an impression of grandeur partly due to the steeply sloping land and the effect of its heavy rustication.[14] It was a building in keeping with the newest terminals being built in the United States, such as Detroit's Union Station (1889, Isaac S. Taylor) and the Chicago & North Western Railroad Terminal in Milwaukee (1889, Charles S. Frost).[15] The combined draw of the new GTR and CPR terminals would have a powerful effect on the Central Business District, till then centred in Old Montreal but soon to shift northward. For the moment, however, the powerful Grand Trunk line had been outflanked by its new rival almost everywhere across its system, including Montreal.

The turn of the century brought a second burst of railway activity. The CPR started the ball rolling with another building by Bruce Price. Built to replace Dalhousie Station, Viger Station (fig. 69) combined a railway station and a luxury hotel of the sort popular in London (such as the St. Pancras, Victoria, Paddington, and King's Cross stations, among others). As evocative of the picturesque aesthetic as St. Pancras Station (1865–76, G. Gilbert Scott), the building was executed in 1897–98 in the Loire Valley château style in recognition of its location in the heartland of the French-Canadian elite, a site-choice much fought for by Montreal's mayor Raymond Préfontaine.[16] With its nine tracks, though without a glazed shed, Viger Station would see a great deal of activity in years to come.

The GTR devoted its energies to solving a major traffic bottle-neck: the single-track Victoria Bridge was carefully dismantled in 1897–98 while a double-track steel-truss bridge was erected around it, using the same stone piers. Two extra roadways added to each side with government funding made the new Victoria Jubilee Bridge the first road and footpath to cross the St. Lawrence River at any point.[17] In 1899–1902, the building of a new head office on McGill Street in the traditional business district, designed by Richard Waite, conferred a new-found prestige upon the GTR (fig. 67); the media of the time called it a "Palatial New Home."[18] The CPR, on the other hand, kept expanding its office space at Windsor Station. In 1900 and 1906 it added a substantial wing along Osborne Street (now rue de La Gauchetière) complete with a new entrance to the train shed, all conceived to harmonize with the Romanesque lines and

massive rustication of the existing structure. Its designer was Edward Maxwell, William C. Van Horne's newest protégé.[19] Three new tracks were added in 1900 under an adjoining train shed, bringing the total to seven.

No doubt feeling that its terminal was now hopelessly out-classed by its rival, the GTR set out to change its dowdy image, and around 1905 commissioned designs for a new Montreal terminal complex from Frost and Granger of Chicago (fig. 122). Three ambitious Beaux-Arts-inspired designs were furnished, featuring a U-shaped office building of either 3, 6, or 8 storeys that incorporated a glass-roofed waiting room linked to a glass-and-steel concourse and an immense steel-arched train shed.[20] The 6-storey design was not unlike a lower-rise version of Daniel H. Burnham's Pennsylvania Station in Pittsburgh, following the architectural program of its building and train shed. The 3-storey version featured a monumental triple-arch classical entrance similar to that of Burnham's famous Union Station (1903–07) in Washington, D.C.[21]

There can be little doubt that Charles M. Hays, the American general manager of the GTR, had every intention of rendering the CPR's Romanesque Windsor Station quaint and dated. That the Bonaventure Station project never got off the drawing board, however, is probably eloquent testimony to the vast sums of money drained off since 1903 by the construction of his western folly, the Grand Trunk Pacific – an unneeded trans-continental railway built to the highest standards, running from Winnipeg, Manitoba, to the wilderness town of Prince Rupert, B.C., the whole completely disconnected from the rest of the GTR network.[22] But possibly Hays was merely distract-ed by what he saw as more urgent building projects elsewhere, for in the years 1906–12 he embarked upon very opulent and ambitious hotel and railway-station projects in both Ottawa and Winnipeg.[23] Curiously the GTR heartland in Montreal was ignored, though the drawings produced remain a testimony to the company's vision.

The railway project that most clearly defined Montreal's stature and ambitions was the CPR's Angus Shops complex. Designed by company engineer Henry Goldmark and built in 1903–04, the gigantic complex can be described only in super-latives. Occupying 22 acres (9 hectares), this was a massive complex for the manufacturing and rebuilding of locomotives, freight cars, and passenger cars. In addition to three shops and many ancillary buildings, it contained its own water supply system, fire station, library, and mess halls. Devoting an almost unprecedented 14 pages to the complex, the respected Chicago journal *The Railway Age* called it "one of the largest and most thoroughly equipped locomotive and car shop plants in America."[24] It was a model application of Taylorism and the rapid delivery of parts, employed 3,000 people at the outset, rising rapidly to 5,000, and launched the neighbouring Rosemount district – a whole new section of the city.[25]

Unlike the Grand Trunk, the CPR had no need to devote vast resources to westward expansion, as its transcontinental line and infrastructure were secure and already very profitable. The CPR's plan was to refocus on its huge Montreal infrastructure with another major round of investments throughout the 1910s. In 1912 the railway-station function was removed from the Viger Station-Hotel into a new, plain passenger terminal built to the rear, on Berri Street.[26] In 1913–14 the Angus Shops complex was expanded, practically doubling its capacity.[27] And in 1910–13 a new trussed-arch bridge with a double-tracked steel deck was built over the Lachine Rapids (by Dominion Bridge Co. again) at Kahnawake.[28]

The most prestigious project of all was the CPR's expansion and complete revamping of Windsor Station. In 1909 Walter S. Painter, an American architect employed by the railway to design many stations across the system, was given the commission for an extension that would double the building's ground area while increasing its floor space dramatically, exploiting a downward slope on the site that would allow for 8 floors plus a massive 15-storey tower. The whole design was faithful to the Romanesque character of the original building of 1888–89, despite the wave of classicism sweeping North America since the late 1890s. The overall effect was harmonious and powerful and in-keeping with Canadian Pacific's trademark châteauesque architecture.

Behind this fortress-like building stood a very modern railway terminal, the classical interior contrasting with the Romanesque exterior. All passenger areas were redesigned for greater efficiency following the latest techniques in passenger management. Also, a new steel-and-glass-roofed concourse reached nearly the entire width of the block and the old train shed was demolished to make way for a new Bush-type shed.[29] Replacing the huge, expensive, and corrosion-prone train sheds of yore, the new system consisted of a reinforced-concrete roof rising a mere 16 feet (5 m) above the rails and supported by steel piers, pierced by slots for the smokestacks and skylights above the passenger platforms. Below the innovative roof structure were 11 tracks, each serviced by a platform for passengers and another, on the other side, for baggage and express. First

introduced in the Frankfurt-am-Main Station in Germany (1879–88, Georg P. H. Eggert),[30] this separation of platform traffic was relatively new in North America. It is indicative of the mores of the day that the building included separate waiting rooms for men and women off the concourse, while below there were waiting rooms both for third-class passengers and for the Chinese.

The enlargement of Windsor Station lasted from 1910 to 1913.[31] At the same time, a study was commissioned with an eye to electrifying the entire terminal trackage all the way to Glen Yard (Westmount), so that the steep grade out of the station could be better negotiated while eliminating the smoke problem for the 52 trains passing both ways through the station each day. The plan was never implemented.[32] The CPR achieved a clear triumph over the Grand Trunk, whose dynamic president, Charles M. Hays, was lost with the *Titanic* in 1912 and whose Bonaventure Station down the hill was gutted by a fire in 1916.[33] Now suffering from acute financial strain, all the GTR could do was rebuild the interior and replace the ornate pavilion roof with a simple flat roof. There was nothing grand about the Grand Trunk anymore.

Although access to major American cities had always been a preoccupation of the aspiring metropolis, a certain measure of Montreal's status may be derived from the fact that at least two important American railways made concerted efforts during this period to enter the city. The first was the powerful New York Central (NYC) system. Building a new line leaving the main New York–Chicago route at Utica, New York, it reached Valleyfield and ultimately Kahnawake on the South Shore in 1898. In another attempt in 1900, the railway took over the Rutland Railroad connecting the NYC near Albany, New York, to the Quebec border via Vermont, less than 100 kilometres from Montreal. Both efforts were fundamentally stalled by the high cost of crossing the river, and the NYC decided instead to seek a strategic alliance with the CPR using its Montreal bridge and terminals. As of 1901, the NYC was offering new inter-metropolitan services with a Montreal–New York day train and night train (the "Green Mountain Flyer" and the "Mount Royal") over its Rutland Railroad subsidiary and a Montreal–Utica day train and night train with connections for Buffalo, Cleveland, and Chicago, all departing from Windsor Station.[34]

In 1900 a second railway, the Delaware & Hudson (D & H) pursued the same course. No longer content with transferring its trains to the Grand Trunk at the border, it launched a major invasion of Quebec with the goal of reaching Montreal and

Quebec City directly. At stake was the sale of coal from its Pennsylvania coal fields, the gathering of newsprint for its eastern United States markets, and of course direct access for its lucrative Montreal–New York passenger trains. While the D & H did manage to reach the South Shore opposite both Quebec City and Montreal, the collapse of the Quebec bridge in 1907 and the high cost and low revenues of the company's entire Quebec system brought it to a stop. It would abandon most of the region in 1929.[35]

Perhaps the greatest coup in Montreal's railway history took place suddenly in 1911, taking CPR and GTR magnates rather by surprise. Since the 1890s Canada's second transcontinental railway, the Canadian Northern, had established an impressive network throughout the Prairies. In 1903, failing to hammer out a logical merger with the GTR, the Canadian Northern began buying up regional railways to secure access of its own to important eastern cities. Its link with Montreal was poor, however, as the line bypassed the city to the north via Saint-Jérôme and Joliette, then doubled back, entering the island from its northeasternmost point, at Bout-de-l'Île, thence to Hochelaga where it erected a very modest 2-storey brick terminal at Moreau Street in East End Montreal near the CPR's Hochelaga Yard, a solid obstacle to any further progress.[36] The line was an orphan, totally disconnected from the rest of its growing empire, and the station, very cheaply built, was unable to serve downtown customers and shippers alike.[37] The Canadian Northern was hardly a threat to its well-established rivals.

By 1910 the railway had secured entry into Toronto and Quebec City and had begun to build the rest of its all-important western route to Vancouver. All that remained, apart from a missing Lake Superior and Ottawa River link, was the Montreal problem. Then in 1911 the Canadian Northern dropped a bombshell that would have lasting consequences for the very structure of the city of Montreal. William Mackenzie and Donald Mann, the Toronto financiers who controlled the railway, had worked out a bold new entryway into the downtown core, completely outflanking the GTR and the CPR, who thought they had all approaches sewn up. The Canadian Northern announced that it would serve the metropolis by way of Saint-Eustache. Drawing a straight line to the business district and tunnelling directly under Mount Royal, the railway would reach the downtown area (fig. 6) and build its own terminal just two blocks east of Windsor Station. A long viaduct running out of the station would carry the line right across the old town to the harbour.

The plan was far-reaching, easily the most ambitious railway project yet seen in Montreal. Mackenzie and Mann obtained an initial million-dollar loan from a private bank in London and prior to their announcement had secretly purchased choice properties in downtown Montreal and a roughly 5-kilometre-square section of agricultural land on the far side of Mount Royal, with additional tracts beyond. These properties were placed under the control of a subsidiary, the Canadian Northern Montreal Land Co. Another company, the Canadian Northern Montreal Tunnel and Terminal Co., was formed to build a 5-kilometre-long railway tunnel beneath Mount Royal for two electrified tracks.[38] One could almost hear the corporate jaws drop in the boardrooms of the CPR and the GTR.

As a means of financing the tunnel project, a real-estate venture was launched in 1912 with the selling of lots northwest of the mountain. Indeed, the initial loan was nearly made up on the first day of sales, when almost one million dollars worth of building lots were sold off. The "Model City," soon incorporated as the Town of Mount Royal (fig. 8), was a garden suburb planned on a grid with two radial boulevards, winding drives, crescents, and parks, all focused on the railway station. The whole plan was developed by Frederick Todd, Canada's first professional landscape architect.[39]

The real-estate venture underway downtown was made public in greater detail in 1913 under the signature of famous New York architects Warren and Wetmore (the Canadian Northern's and Grand Trunk Pacific's choice of architect for Winnipeg's huge Union Station, 1908–09), then collaborating with Henry K. Wicksteed, Canadian Northern's chief engineer. The downtown scheme called for a series of massive U-shaped Beaux-Arts-inspired buildings for offices, a luxury hotel, and the railway station (fig. 101). The project was to cover four city blocks along the east side of Mansfield Street, from Cathcart to St. Antoine, comprising four 10-storey buildings cradling a 2-storey railway terminal.[40] As with the "Model City," the income from renting or selling the office buildings was meant to pay for the railway tunnel and terminal.

The scale and scope of the project was almost without precedent. No Eastern Seaboard station approached it in comprehensiveness, with the exception of New York City's two

6 Aerial view of the southern end of the Mount Royal Tunnel in the new downtown core of Montreal near the Cathedral of St. James the Great (1870–94), c. 1923. Photograph: William Notman. Notman Photographic Archives, McCord Museum of Canadian History, Montreal.

massive terminals, Grand Central Terminal and Pennsylvania Station, which included vast tunnels and viaducts but no multi-functional building complex. The only hint of the building program envisaged for Montreal comes from Detroit, where a beautiful Beaux-Arts station built for the Michigan Central line (owned by NYC) was cradled by a 17-storey office tower. It is no coincidence that this project was designed by Warren and Wetmore and Reed and Stem in 1913.[41] The entire system called for a railyard at Val Royal near Cartierville, where incoming trains would exchange their steam locomotive for a 2,400 volt electric locomotive that would continue to the downtown station. In the north of the island, a special connecting line was to veer off to link with the old 1903 line at the Moreau Street station in Hochelaga.[42] The entire project was both innovative and audacious.

By 1916 the tunnel, the yard, the electrification of the tracks, and the plotting of the Model City were all basically ready, but the downtown terminal-and-building project, the viaduct to the port, and the connection to the Hochelaga line had not yet been begun. Now in the midst of a war and with ever-tightening money markets, the Canadian Northern was in serious financial trouble. The ambitious transcontinental railway was finally open for traffic from Quebec City to Vancouver, except for the little unfinished business in downtown Montreal, but the railway could no longer meet its payments and the government had no more money to offer. The Tunnel Terminal, the temporary downtown station that Mackenzie and Mann had asked Warren and Wetmore to design in 1914, was finally built and opened to traffic in 1917–18. Despite its modest size, with two storeys above ground, one below, and five tracks, it was a model of efficiency and good design executed in a restrained Neoclassical style.[43] But the Canadian Northern's day was over. In 1919 the government moved to nationalize the Canadian Northern, calling in the many railway properties it already owned to create the Canadian National Railways (CNR).

In 1923, the Grand Trunk finally ended its years of trouble by declaring bankruptcy, and it too was absorbed by the Canadian National. The merger that should have been was finally consummated. Railway infrastructure was at a standstill until 1929, when activity suddenly broke out on all fronts. The new CNR wished to implement the former Canadian Northern's gigantic downtown terminal-and-viaduct plan, but with a difference. Instead of running down to reach the port, the viaduct would curve southwesterly to meet up with the old GTR mainline at Point St. Charles. The CNR would thus create a unified system in Montreal. After trying vainly to involve the CPR in its plans for a true Union Station, it announced its own plans in 1929, which included several major linkage lines on Montreal Island and regrading proposals to raise tracks above street level in St. Henri and Point St. Charles. The keystone of the CNR's sweeping review of its terminal problems was a new Central Station. The whole project was estimated at $50 million.[44]

CNR president Henry Thornton was a driving force behind the plan, and despite the stock market crash in October work began on this massive undertaking in November. Hugh G. Jones, the company architect, produced drawings for several schemes of the new Central Station (fig. 89) that all reflected the spirit of Mackenzie and Mann's gigantic project of 1913: a grand station south of Dorchester Street with trains underground, surrounded by office buildings running from 8 to 18 storeys, straddling Dorchester Street.[45] In 1930, with demolition and excavation continuing apace, the CNR publicized new drawings with a decidedly more modern cast (fig. 123). This time a taller single tower rivalling the adjacent Sun Life Building in height was planned for the railway's offices, with a terminal below on the south side of Dorchester Street, while similar but lower office buildings were to cover the tracks both south and north of the railway tower.[46]

In 1929 the CPR, no doubt feeling the heat of the competition, quietly commissioned Fellheimer and Wagner of New York – famous for their just completed, monumental and modernistic New York Central Railway terminal in Buffalo (1927–29) – to produce a study for a new Windsor Station (fig. 124). Each of their six proposals, compiled in a document prepared in 1930, called for a huge terminal located at the foot of Dominion Square opposite Windsor Station, which would disappear to make way for a viaduct surmounted by a massive Art Deco tower and a surrounding complex of offices, hotel, convention centre, and, potentially, a sports arena.[47] Although it borrowed freely from the multi-functional concept advanced by the CNR project, its architectural program more closely resembled the architects' own Buffalo Central Station, notably through its massing and its exploitation of the site to create monumental perspectives.[48] It was the most ambitious real-estate venture ever contemplated for Montreal.

These vast infrastructural projects were being planned at a time when the construction of railway stations elsewhere in America had come to a virtual standstill. As the Depression wore on and the railways shed more and more trains and employees, Canadian Pacific quietly shelved its big terminal redevelopment plans with no damage done: the project was dead, and Windsor Station, saved from demolition, would go on to become one of the oldest of North America's great terminals. The only remaining trace of the CPR's grand vision for Montreal in 1929–30 was a sumptuous, if overbuilt, Park Avenue Station on Jean Talon Street, located in the North End five kilometres from the Central Business District. This orphan, built in 1931 to plans by company architect Colin Drewitt,[49] never assumed the dual function it was slated for: an interchange station, with shuttles connecting trains serving either Windsor Station or Viger Station, and at the same time a major passenger-distribution centre for the expanding North End.

The Canadian National, on the other hand, was caught in an impossible predicament. With virtually its entire infrastructure dismantled and only some construction completed (mainly grade-elimination projects), it had no choice but to keep work going. The government, which was footing the bills, finally put a stop to all work late in 1931. The project would have to wait for the brighter economic conditions of the postwar period before reaching completion.

A WORLD-CLASS PORT SYSTEM

The development of major metropolitan centres is almost always closely tied to the development of its port, since world trade, via water, is usually a key factor in obtaining such status. In Montreal, the harbour function was an element in its very founding, as ocean-going vessels were stopped here, unable to pass its rapids on their way into the interior. Between 1830 and 1850, the government of Canada and private corporations had gradually built up a complete system of wharves stretching the full width of the business district,[50] and between 1859 and 1872 the GTR built a long, linear grain-storage facility along the Lachine Canal near Lock no. 1 (Mill Street).[51] To make up for the inadequate wharfage capacity, Montreal introduced a unique technology in 1857: the steam-powered "floating elevator." Piloted out to meet transatlantic freighters, it removed grain from the holds of lake vessels and deposited it simultaneously into ocean-bound vessels without so much as touching a wharf. By the end of the century, 17 of these floating machines were in use in the harbour.[52] With developments such as these, Montreal was ready to do large-scale business.

The development of the port in the nineteenth century is a chronicle of battles against incredible odds. For example, the Montreal Harbour actively advertised and promoted its proximi-

ty to European ports, compared with its Seaboard rivals in the United States (4,445 km to Liverpool as opposed to 4,800 from Boston, 4,947 from New York City, 5,156 from Philadelphia, and 5,243 from Baltimore), yet it could be accessed only by long and tortuous navigation up the St. Lawrence River, which was closed to navigation for five months of the year.[53]

While shipping traffic to Montreal was always healthy and expanded steadily, it was no match for the Atlantic coast's ice-free ports and far-reaching railway links. Montreal Harbour probably became a serious rival in 1880–82, when it became the first port in the world to outfit its facilities completely with electric lighting.[54] Proof of the Harbour's importance came with the arrival of the CPR. Consistent with its program to build on a grand scale in Montreal, the company put up two gigantic grain elevators (A and B, in 1885 and 1887) alongside the wharf near its Dalhousie Square Station.[55] These two structures were huge wooden elevators clad and roofed in corrugated iron and designed much like the many smaller elevators scattered across the Prairies today. Each had a capacity of about 800,000 bushels (29,094 kl). Two railway tracks penetrated the buildings to allow box cars to dump their load inside, while the lifting, weighing, and sorting machinery, powered by a nearby steam plant, was located in the huge clerestory at the top, called the "cupola." The steam plant also powered a system of aerial conveyors leading to the wharf.[56] While hardly revolutionary in world terms, the first such structure having long before been erected in Buffalo, New York (the Evans Elevator, invented by Joseph Dart and Robert Dunbar in 1847),[57] the sheer bulk of the 133-foot-high (41 m) Montreal elevators made them the first structures to alter its old skyline of church steeples and towers.

In 1893, John Kennedy, Montreal Harbour's chief engineer, drew up a proposal for a massive redesign of the entire fixed plant. The plan called for a long guard-pier stretching two kilometres northward from Victoria Bridge to ward off ice floes, a whole new set of high-level wharves next to the Lachine Canal and opposite the business district, and another set of high-level wharves opposite the industrial area in the East End. Shipping tonnage was soaring, going from 50,000 tons (50,802 tonnes) in 1850, to 2,220,585 tons (2,256,225 tonnes) in 1896 (a volume surpassed only by New York City),[58] yet the wharves opposite the business district were still essentially those of 1850.[59] Something drastic had to be done to accommodate this soaring growth.

The new Liberal government of 1896 took the initiative as J. Israël Tarte, federal Minister of Public Works, approved Kennedy's plan.[60] The work proceeded apace and none too soon, as gross tonnage would reach 9,044,457 tons (9,189,620 tonnes) by 1914.[61] The long guard pier (named Mackay Pier) protecting the harbour from ice during the spring break-up, was built first. Then followed the new high-level piers, Jacques Cartier, Alexandra, and King Edward, all completed between 1899 and 1902, with Victoria Pier added in 1910, all replacing the now obsolete wharf structures dating back to the early nineteenth century. During the same period, a much larger pier, Bickerdike Pier, was created along the mouth of the Lachine Canal, and three new high-level piers, Laurier, Tarte, and Sutherland, were built at the boundary between Hochelaga Ward and the Town of Maisonneuve four kilometres down river. All of these wharves were constructed of heavy wooden caissons encased in concrete. On top of them, the Harbour erected a total of 21 steel-and-concrete warehouses between 1904 and 1914.[62]

The real measure of gigantism came with the new generation of grain elevators planned during 1899. The Harbour's first contract was won by the Steel Storage Elevator Construction Co. of Buffalo, employing a new steel technology taken up in the 1890s to replace the old and dangerously flammable wooden elevator. Resting on deep concrete piles, a gigantic steel-tube structure known as Grain Elevator no. 1 was erected at the foot of St. Sulpice Street in 1902–05 to plans signed M. Weber.[63] Built to hold 1 million bushels (36,368 kl) of grain it rose to the height of a 12-storey office building.[64] Almost simultaneously, under great pressure from the federal government, a 1-million-bushel (36,368 kl) steel-box elevator of colossal dimensions was built in 1903–06 by the Grand Trunk Railway, nearby on the south side of the Lachine Canal entrance.[65] The contract was entrusted to the John S. Metcalf Co. of Chicago. Up to that point the GTR had refused to invest in any elevator capacity in Montreal, preferring instead to pour money into its year-round port at Portland, Maine.[66]

The construction of an even larger elevator in 1910–12, Grain Elevator no. 2, also built by the Metcalf Co., led to the application of still-newer technology.[67] Located opposite Bonsecours Market, the immense structure was about the height of a 15-storey building and offered a capacity of 2,622,000 bushels of grain (95,357 kl). Unhampered by City of Montreal building restrictions, which limited heights to 10 storeys, this was then truly the tallest building in Montreal. It was constructed entirely of reinforced concrete, the new wonder material of elevator construction – it neither burned nor burst, nor was it subject to water condensation or rusting, all problems that had plagued previous technologies.[68] Though Elevator no. 2 was

not the world's first such structure in concrete – that title belonged to the Frank Peavy Elevator in Minneapolis, of 1899 – it was certainly the largest.[69] Inside, a huge set of mechanical clamps rotated the box cars, emptying them of grain and eliminating the need to shovel them out by hand.

In 1913–16, the Harbour Commissioners went on to expand nearby Elevator no. 1 with concrete annexes on each side, increasing its capacity to 2,500,000 bushels (90,920 kl).[70] The GTR simultaneously extended the capacity of Elevator B, by building a concrete-tube extension of 1,000,000-bushels capacity (36,368 kl), once in 1913–14 and again in 1922–23.[71] Only then, around 1915, were the CPR's two obsolescent wooden elevators demolished. When the GTR went bankrupt in 1923, the Elevator B complex was bought by Montreal Harbour. The Metcalf firm also furnished the Harbour with an integrated aerial-conveyor system joining these three elevators with all the various wharves, creating a truly integrated transportation system. From 1900, when Montreal offered 1,600,000 bushels (58,189 kl) of grain-elevator capacity, to 1916, when that capacity had jumped to 7,122,000 bushels (259,013 kl), the City had managed to capture the lion's share of the North American grain traffic. Western Canadian grain production had increased dramatically and Montreal controlled its main outlet. It is no surprise, then, that the city also held the head office of the country's largest inland shipping conglomerate, Canada Steamship Lines, with close to 100 lake vessels afloat in the 1930s.[72]

With the 1920s came a few more mega-projects further east in the Harbour, such as the huge Refrigerator Warehouse next to the CPR installations at the Viger terminal, and the equally massive Grain Elevator no. 3 complex located opposite the Hochelaga piers. Both structures were designed and built in the period 1922–24 again by the Metcalf Co.; the elevator was further expanded in 1927–28 to reach a total capacity of 5,000,000 bushels (181,840 kl).[73] Between 1924 and 1926, the Harbour Commission electrified its entire port railway system, ordering nine locomotives from Great Britain.[74] By this time, Montreal's harbour was world famous. Its grain traffic had finally surpassed even that of New York City, making Montreal the largest grain port in North America.[75] When Le Corbusier wrote his well-known manifesto on modern architecture *Vers une architecture* in 1923, he extolled the virtues of the modern grain elevator using Montreal's Elevator no. 2 as one of his examples.[76]

By 1931 when Montreal and its suburbs had finally reached the million mark, its population remained substantially smaller than that of North America's other major metropolitan centres. Yet through an extraordinary concentration of effort that fuelled an extensive development of national railway, canal, and port infrastructure, the city was able to surpass all. With its gigantic and technologically sophisticated port installations, Montreal achieved world status and emerged as one of the North American centres best connected with the rest of the continent.

MONTREAL, IMPERIAL PORT OF CALL

Having extended its operations to the transatlantic trade in 1903, by 1929 Canadian Pacific operated 14 first-class and cabin-class passenger liners out of Montreal and Quebec City destined for ports in Great Britain, Ireland, and France. Its 131 Atlantic crossings that year established a new company record. In 1930 it launched the *Empress of Britain,* the largest and fastest ocean-liner serving the British Empire, carrying a passenger list of 1,095 and a crew of 700. Featuring a squash court, tennis court, Turkish baths, the largest on-board swimming pool in the world, and the first ship-to-shore radio telephone service anywhere, CP Steamships was not ceding any ground to the New York ocean-liner trade.[77] In fact Montreal ranked second after New York in North American passenger traffic overseas. Cunard and White Star, basically New York oriented British companies, also offered many additional sailings from Montreal.

On the landward side, the railways competed vigorously to offer modernized and faster train service, especially to New York, Boston, and Chicago. The 1920s had put a whole new generation of prestige trains on the international runs. Three companies competed for business in the Montreal–New York corridor. The Delaware & Hudson introduced the "Montreal Limited," a new night train, in 1924 and the "Laurentian," a new day train, in 1929, giving 12-hour and 10-hour service, respectively. The Rutland, now independent of the New York Central, accelerated its night and day service to make 10- and 11-hour times. And in 1924 Canadian National introduced the "Washingtonian/ Montrealer" with night service to New York City in 11 hours and to Washington in 15, with sleeping cars through to Florida during the winter, by an arrangement made with American railways. A new 11-hour day train to New York City, the "Ambassador," complete with a radio lounge, was launched in 1927.[78] Competition was stiff.

The Montreal–Boston corridor, while slightly less prestigious, saw as much service as the New York one. Here the CNR and the CPR, with the Boston & Maine at the other end, were the main

players. Canadian National offered a revamped 8-and-a-half-hour day train and a 10-hour night train branching off from its New York trains, while Canadian Pacific offered direct competition with the 10-and-a-half-hour day "Alouette" and 10-hour night "Red Wing" trains. The Rutland also served Boston at competitive speeds with its "Mount Royal" and "Green Mountain Flyer" New York trains.[79]

The most travelled corridor, however, was the Montreal–Toronto–Detroit–Chicago one, hotly contested by the CNR and the CPR, with trains running between 20 and 22 hours. The CNR offered the "La Salle," the "Inter-City," and the "International Limited," the latter billed as the fastest long-distance service on the continent in 1930. The CPR offered the "Royal York," the "Canadian," and the "Overseas," the latter timed to make Montreal steamship connections for Europe.[80] In business volume, Montreal was second only to New York City thanks to the CPR's highly competitive transatlantic "bridge" concept, by which the company's transcontinental trains were scheduled to link up with CPR ocean-liners bound for Europe and Asia. One third of its European route, moreover, was along the scenic St. Lawrence River, giving Montreal a decisive edge in the tourist trade from the Midwest and the West. This role in transport was a defining aspect of Montreal's metropolitan status in 1930.

THE END OF AN ERA

As the 1930s began and all attention was focused on the economic crisis, no one had quite recognized that an era had closed. Only time would reveal the profound nature of the change. Montreal's harbour infrastructure, the most magnificent expression of the City's metropolitan ambitions, was essentially complete. Much the same could be said of the City's railway infrastructure, excepting only the huge Thornton plan of the CNR. Cut short in mid-construction by the Depression, the project would ultimately be brought to completion, first with a railway terminal opened in 1943 (Central Station),[81] and then with a much-admired ground-breaking office, hotel, and shopping-mall complex opened in 1962 (Place Ville-Marie and the Queen Elizabeth Hotel).[82]

In the 1920s, Montreal had carried out two major infrastructural projects designed for the future. The Canadian aviation industry had then got underway with the opening of several routes to the North, where neither roads nor railways existed. Meanwhile Great Britain and Germany were at work on dirigible technology for transatlantic crossings, and given Montreal's pre-eminent role in transportation it was no surprise that the Canadian government chose it as the site of a major airport facility, with the construction in 1927–30 of St. Hubert Airport on the South Shore across the river from the metropolis.[83] Although the new technology seemed promising, its dirigible mast was used but once, when the British *R-100* arrived on its inaugural run in 1930. The subsequent fatal crash of its sister ship terminated the British Imperial airship program, and the spectacular explosion of a German zeppelin at New York's Lakehurst facility a few years later ended the era for good. It was small airplanes that held the most promise, and in 1931 regular flights departed year round from St. Hubert Airport bound for Toronto, Detroit, Albany, and Saint John.[84]

The other major achievement was the Harbour Bridge (renamed Jacques Cartier Bridge in 1934; fig. 7), which was the crowning achievement of some twenty years of road development and an integral part of the automobile revolution. To enhance American tourist access to Montreal and to facilitate the growing flow of trucking between Montreal and the eastern United States, not to mention coping with the surge of automobile commuters from the South Shore, something had to be done to relieve the totally inadequate, narrow, two-lane automobile passage on Victoria Bridge.[85] In 1925 Montreal engineers Montserrat and Pratley, with J.B. Strauss of Chicago, drew up plans for the Harbour Bridge, the Dominion Bridge Co. acting as contractor.[86] About 3 kilometres long and a breathtaking 120 metres high, it surpassed all the city's industrial-age structures, being longer than the Victoria Bridge and taller than the grain elevators and the city's new office towers. Opened to traffic in 1930, the bridge was Montreal's last gigantic infrastructural creation before the city slipped into a quarter-century slumber.

Montreal had nursed an ambition in 1850 that it would compete with the emerging North American urban metropolises. The infrastructure that aim demanded was supplied first by the Grand Trunk Railway, but it was only from the 1880s, thanks especially to huge investments by the Canadian Pacific Railway, that the metropolitan ambition really took shape. With the infrastructural projects initiated by the Canadian Northern Railway and by the Montreal Harbour Commission in the 1900s and 1910s, Montreal could rightfully take a place, even despite its smaller population, in the pantheon of North America's metropolitan giants, also claiming for itself the title of Imperial port of call in the great network of the British Empire. It achieved this status for a brief time only, however, for by the

1920s a new pattern of continental and world trade was emerging, as industrial and commercial activity shifted to the centre of the continent and as north–south trade between Canada and the United States dominated the economy. No longer strategically positioned to dominate in these markets, Montreal lost the very geographic advantage that had won for it a true metropolitan stature. But both the freight- and passenger-traffic statistics and the infrastructural projects stand as unassailable testimony to a single-minded ambition maintained by Montreal for over three-quarters of a century.

7 Photomontage of Jacques Cartier Bridge, with dirigible, ship, and railway tracks, c. 1930.
Unknown photographer. Bibliothèque nationale du Québec.

A COMMUNITY OF COMMUNITIES

Suburbs in the Development of "Greater Montreal"

Walter van Nus

THERE WAS MARKED VARIETY AMONG THE communities that grew up around Montreal between 1880 and the Great Depression of the 1930s. Evident in the quality of the built environment, so different from one suburb to the next, that diversity deepened the rifts that already existed within the City of Montreal itself. Suburban expansion reinforced the city's serious linguistic, religious, and class divisions, though not to the extent portrayed in popular caricatures. Moreover, locally specialized development ensured that architects and urban planners could contribute to the design of some suburbs far more than they could to others.

The 1880s began fifty years of enormous urban development beyond the City of Montreal's old boundaries, unchanged from 1792 until 1883 except for the acquisition of land for Mount Royal Park in 1874. For ninety years, Montreal had extended north from the St. Lawrence River to the southern flank of the mountain, and from about Atwater Avenue in the west to the area of Frontenac Street in the east. It was within these ample borders, extending over two kilometres west, north, and east of the old fortified town, that most of the urban development on the Island of Montreal continued to occur even into the 1880s. After 1890, however, the population within the 1792 city limits grew little, while it increased phenomenally outside them. Whereas in 1891 the Island of Montreal beyond those limits had housed only 94,830 people (34 percent of the Island's 277,525 residents), by 1911 it contained 329,629 (almost 60 percent of the Island's population of 554,761).[1]

Between 1871 and 1914, 43 new municipalities were incorporated on the Island of Montreal, not including those of the "West Island."[2] Montreal would annex 24 suburbs between 1883 and 1918 and in the process more than quintuple its own geographic size.[3] As a result, by 1921 only 14.6 percent of the Island's

8 Canadian Northern Montreal Land Co. Ltd. *Mount Royal, The Model City* (Montreal: The Federated Press, c. 1911). Cover, 22 x 15 cm. Collection Canadian Centre for Architecture, Montréal.

residents lived beyond Montreal's new city boundaries.[4] Yet in many cases the governments and elite classes of the annexed towns had already determined both the ultimate land use and the eventual economic level of the local population. Annexation agreements often included the guaranteed continuation of certain development policies. Local councils could bargain hard, because until 1907 Montreal's charter stipulated that both a suburb's council and its ratepayers approve the terms of union, and after 1907 a suburban referendum would still be required to ratify such deals.[5] Hence, it is necessary to examine not only municipalities that remained independent but also important ones that did not.

DIVERSITY IN MAINLY WORKING-CLASS SUBURBS

The earliest suburbs to undergo rapid growth lay along the Lachine Canal west of the Montreal city line and along the St. Lawrence River just east of the City. All attracted heavy industry and housed chiefly working-class populations. To the west lay the contiguous towns of St. Gabriel, St. Cunégonde, and St. Henri. As early as 1881 the three had a combined population of 16,000, a figure that would triple in the twenty years to follow.[6] Logically, the advantages of the site suggested that this area form an extension of the industrialized Lachine Canal waterfront in southwestern Montreal. But the government of St. Henri held out the promise of larger and cheaper industrial sites by offering tax exemptions and (until 1900) cash bonuses even to types of industry judged noxious in the town's own by-laws. In 1890 St. Henri actually set aside an area for abattoirs, a use banned by most suburbs. Small industrial cities, however, did attract some professionals. St. Henri, for instance, zoned a few areas as residential, and dignified middle-class housing did emerge, for example around St. Henri Park.[7] Just as industrialization proceeded west of the City by placing factories near the waterfront, it also extended along the St. Lawrence east of Montreal. The adjacent town of Hochelaga granted tax exemptions to lure industries looking for large sites.[8] Montreal annexed all of these industrial areas between 1883 (the developed western part of Hochelaga) and 1905 (St. Henri and St. Cunégonde).

The most extreme case of a waterfront suburb welcoming dirty industry arose early in the twentieth century. The Town of Montréal-Est, located on the western edge of Pointe-aux-Trembles, was the brain-child of realtor Joseph Versailles, who in 1910 induced the Quebec legislature to create a town where virtually no one yet lived. Gripped by the Garden City ideal,

Versailles planned to build an imaginatively designed residential haven even more green and peaceful than Westmount, a well-to-do suburb nestled on the south slope of Mount Royal. The collapse of the real-estate boom in 1913 and the outbreak of the First World War ended that dream. At the same time, the Queen Oil Co. was seeking port and refinery sites downwind. In 1916, as mayor of Montréal-Est, Versailles welcomed Queen Oil to the town's many unwanted building lots, determined to create a major industrial suburb. By the time of his retirement in 1931, Mayor Versailles had welcomed ten companies in all, including four refineries and two metals plants, some occupying huge sites. By 1960 that policy would make Montréal-Est, covering only 12 square kilometres, the fourth-most-productive industrial municipality in Canada and the foulest smelling spot on the Island of Montreal. After more territory was annexed in 1914 and 1916, the town's residential sector was reduced to its southeastern corner: a standard prosaic, rectilinear grid of streets downwind from all those reeking plants.[9]

The East End industrial suburbs would indeed remain predominantly working-class and French-speaking, but they were not exclusively so. Montréal-Est, like other Island suburbs with heavy industry (such as Rosemount), also housed lower-level managerial personnel and skilled workers, who in this period were often English-speaking. Thus, as early as 1920, 50 Protestant families in Montréal-Est built a community church. (Almost forty years later, 21 percent of the town's 5,730 inhabitants would be anglophone, 75 percent of them Protestant.)[10] By 1931, the town's housing stock consisted not only of duplexes but also of modest "cottages," although neither type held much interest for architects.

The governments of other working-class suburbs created more pleasant residential environments by banning heavy industry. Several of the towns that saw rapid growth after 1900, like Ville Émard, fit this description, but the most important was Verdun – by 1931 the most populous independent suburb on the Island of Montreal, with over 60,000 residents. Although it lay next to the industrialized southwest corner of Montreal, Verdun could expect no tide of workers' families much before 1900, as springtime flooding often covered the low land in its eastern end. The town council turned to engineers to upset the verdict of geography, and between 1895 and 1900 constructed a protective dike complete with steam-powered water-pumps.[11] As a result, the Montreal Street Railway Co. agreed to serve the area in 1899, and within a decade a sleepy village became the fastest growing town in Quebec.

The delay in Verdun's growth allowed it to benefit from two technological advances. First, newly available electricity permitted modern plants with electrical production machinery, thus providing some local factory employment without increasing pollution. Second, the duplexes that mushroomed there after 1900 shared the improved quality of the duplex type that spread across the Island in the new century. New "plexes" boasted indoor toilets and running water, and coal replaced wood as a heating fuel (although central heating remained a largely middle-class luxury even as late as the 1920s). Gas for cooking and electricity for domestic lighting became standard features in new buildings by 1920.[12] It is little wonder that workers from the grimy southwest of Montreal regarded their move to Verdun as a step up.

Whether in heavily industrialized suburbs or not, most working-class housing was designed by the small builders who constructed it, not by architects.[13] Architects did plan town halls as well as some bank, commercial, and factory structures. And, of course, Catholic and Protestant churches and school boards provided commissions. For example, in St. Henri the architectural firm of Perrault and Mesnard created the imposing new façade of the parish church in 1887, and provided a major project in the dignified Pensionnat de l'Ange-Gardien in 1897.[14] These opportunities continued to benefit architects as late as 1925, when Ludger Lemieux and René Charbonneau oversaw the completion of their impressive St. Zotique Church. The fact remained, however, that the poorer the local population, the fewer opportunities there were for professional design of the cityscape.

Several suburbs with large working-class populations adopted a sustained policy of creating bourgeois residential areas as well. Immediately to the east of Outremont lay St. Louis du Mile End, the third-largest city in Quebec (with 37,000 people) when annexed by Montreal in 1909. By that date several clothing manufacturers had established their shops on St. Lawrence Boulevard and a few factories had appeared along the Canadian Pacific Railway (CPR) tracks in the north end of the town, but there was little industrial activity to be found. Around 1900, developers and local parish priests stressed rather the purity of the air north of the steep hill (easily climbed by the new electric streetcars) that descended south from Sherbrooke Street to the older, overcrowded district below. Many working-class families heeded the call, but so did many from the middle-class, attracted by such distinguished addresses as St. Joseph Boulevard, which townsfolk hailed as the first "boulevard planté" on the Island. The luxuriously appointed triplexes along this street, as well as

the elite schools that served them, remind us that living in a "plex" did not necessarily mean proletarian status.[15]

Perhaps the most strenuous attempt to add more affluent districts to a basically working-class suburb was made by the Town of Maisonneuve (located along the St. Lawrence just east of Hochelaga Ward), though the effort was not part of the town's original strategy. Soon after the creation of Maisonneuve in 1883, its municipal council launched a drive to attract industry, and with it the workers who would become local tenants. Location made the goal realistic: the waterfront provided excellent sites for harbour development and the Canadian Northern Railway ran across the town. Through advertising, tax exemptions, and cash grants it attracted so many major industries that by 1910 Maisonneuve ranked fifth in Canada for value of manufactured products. To encourage population growth, its bonussing agreements with companies obliged them to hire 80 percent of their employees from within Maisonneuve. By 1911, almost half its working population laboured in factories, and 90 percent of household heads rented rather than owned. Fewer than 10 percent were proprietors, professionals, managers, or foremen.[16]

To a limited extent, the town's small comfortable minority segregated themselves, some in the stone-faced homes of the "Viauville" district at the eastern edge of town, others on nearby stretches of Adam and Lafontaine streets, where single-family homes sported large covered porches and exuberant turrets.[17] In 1910, a new administration in Maisonneuve decided that a few clusters of superior homes were not enough, and between 1910 and 1915 endeavoured to transform the northern part of town (still largely unoccupied) into the "Garden of Montreal" by means of City Beautiful projects: magnificent public buildings, boulevards, and a large park. In this setting, along such tree-lined routes as Pius IX Boulevard, the wealthy would build homes on large lots. Marius Dufresne, architect and Town Engineer, whose rich brother sat on council, tried to set the tone with his magnificent château, begun in 1915 at the corner of Pius IX and Sherbrooke Street. The cost of four splendid public buildings (all but one designed by Dufresne) and the acquisition of the town's parkland from speculators at scandalously inflated prices provoked the Quebec government to compel Montreal to annex its nearly bankrupt neighbour in 1918. At the time of its demise, the overly ambitious town left behind a rich heritage: the City Hall (1910–12), the Public Market (1912–14) that served as the vista for Morgan Boulevard, the Public Baths and Gymnasium (1914–16; fig. 38), and the Wright-inspired Police and Fire Station (1914–15; fig. 39).[18]

THE PROMOTION OF PRIVILEGED SUBURBS

Other suburbs largely excluded the two-thirds of the work-force then living at or below the poverty line.[19] Some of these catered neither to the working poor nor to the rich. For instance, Notre Dame de Grâces (NDG), which was subdivided largely between 1905 and 1912, housed economically stable craftsmen and white-collar workers, most of whom commuted. Located just west of Westmount, the bulk of NDG shared Westmount's ideal location for homes on the western slope of the mountain, separated from the smoky industrial area along the Lachine Canal by a cliff running for several kilometres along the suburb's southern edge. Annexed by Montreal in 1910, the population of this cozy district, with its Arts and Crafts cottages, grew to 46,850 by 1931.[20] NDG's exceptional economic position within the city by that date is revealed by Montreal welfare statistics for the Depression era, during which NDG had fewer poor than any other ward in the city.[21] Compared to predominantly working-class suburbs, the significant middle-class populations of suburbs like NDG provided substantially more work for architects.

There existed, however, a still-more-privileged type of suburb where architects helped design most of the built environ-ment: residential havens for upper-middle-class families. Not coincidentally, the principal examples have retained their inde-pendence from Montreal: Westmount, Outremont, Montreal West, Hampstead, and the Town of Mount Royal. But what are the factors that explain the concentration of architects' suburban work in these neighbourhoods?

The role of private developers

Developers had ways to encourage the selection of certain suburbs for costlier homes, understanding the attraction of the affluent to life at higher altitudes, where they could enjoy magni-ficent views, fresher air, a greater sense of privacy, and quiet. No one missed how perfectly the slopes of "the mountain" (which really consists of three peaks) served that desire: all of the above-named suburbs ringed the mountain. Height, indeed, deter-mined gradations of prestige even within a single suburb. In Westmount, for example, the most elegant district lay north of The Boulevard, on the steepest part of the slope above 120 metres in altitude (fig. 85).[22] Similarly, in Outremont, the toniest streets developed just next to the mountainside; exclusive Maplewood Avenue, for instance, rose to 101 metres, and the town sloped downward in both altitude and socio-economic status to the

industrial fringe along its northern border, at 68 metres.[23] Realtors' advertisements trumpeted the advantages of elevated "Homes for the Higher Classes – Full of Light, Pure Air, and Sunshine." [24]

But advertising the advantages of elevation was not enough. By the late nineteenth century developers had learned hard lessons from the deterioration of once-fashionable areas in downtown Montreal, where distinguished homes had been subdivided into flats or converted into warehouses.[25] As well, shack-towns had arisen in some of the city's outlying districts. Developers in new areas destined for the "respectable classes" began to use restrictive covenants to prevent cheap methods of building and mixed land-use; that is, deeds of sale set con-struction standards and often also restricted the type of building that a buyer might erect on his lot. In 1893, for example, a speculator bought building-lots on Columbia Avenue in lower Westmount on condition that only First Class buildings of brick or stone, set back 10 feet (3 m) from the street, be erected there – a condition that would extend to all future buyers.[26]

By the turn of the century Westmount's developers, then focused on the mid-level area north and south of Sherbrooke, had become stricter. In 1903, for instance, the vendors of the area north of Westmount Park not only imposed minimum construction standards but also limited buyers to the building of detached and semi-detached homes (more exclusive than the terraced housing typical of lower Westmount).[27] In the Town of Mount Royal (TMR) and in Hampstead, each dominat-ed, as discussed below, by a single developer, restrictive agree-ments blanketed whole municipalities. Deeds of sale that were issued in both these suburbs during the 1910s and 1920s not only regulated land use but also established minimum home values. In Hampstead, the clauses stipulating the construction of only single-family houses proved so airtight that only a special act of legislature permitted the building of churches, schools, and municipal buildings! [28] The cost of homes built within these privately imposed but legally enforceable constraints excluded much of the working class.

The role of local governments

Like developers, municipal governments could also promote the exclusion of the working poor. The most effective way to keep the lower orders out was to impose construction standards that generated housing which they could not afford. Even a modest set of restrictions had some exclusionary effect, as in the case of the town of NDG. Here in 1906, in the pure air of Mount Royal's western slope, stood dozens of cheap, wooden cabins rented by the working poor, who had come to exurbia to escape the slums and supplement their diets with vegetables grown on nearby vacant lots. Beginning in 1908, they benefitted from the new streetcar service running along nearby Sherbrooke Street. But the local developers, such as Georges Marcil, had intended that service to attract middle-class buyers who would be disinclined to live near shacks. Thus the town council passed a building by-law in 1909 reserving the prime district – the area within walking distance of Sherbrooke – for 2-storey homes veneered in brick or stone and with full basements. The outside staircase, considered a badge of proletarian status, was outlawed.[29] The council regularly refused to grant exemptions from the ban on further wooden cabins.[30] The by-law's screening effect emerges clearly in a comparison of the value of a typical worker's cabin ($400) with that of a brick-veneered 2-storey cottage ($3,000): the new standards raised the cost of a home in NDG eightfold.[31] Only the highly skilled worker with steady employment would become numerous in NDG Ward.

Some suburbs went much further than NDG in trying to lure the rich. Westmount set the pace, as its competitors often copied Westmount's latest upgraded construction standards soon after they had been adopted by "Canada's model city."[32] Westmount's extraordinarily detailed and highly technical building by-laws of 1909 and 1911 set a new benchmark for Island suburbs. By 1911, Westmount had banned new wooden buildings and even those of plank frames and brick veneer (the NDG standard). All construction had to be either "First Class" (up to 100 feet high [30.5 m] and built of incombustible material throughout, except for finished floors, doors, window frames, and so on) or "Second Class" (up to 60 feet high [18.3 m], with external and party walls of incombustible materials). Moreover, the by-laws laid out page after page of technical specifications outlining the minimum quality of materials, load-bearing and stress capacities, gas and electrical installations, etc.[33] These requirements raised costs yet higher.

As home buyers flocked to Westmount between 1909 and 1912, the per capita assessment of taxable property rose 19.4 percent.[34] Imposing strict building standards seemed to pay. In the long run, these by-laws helped preserve Westmount's architectural heritage. More immediately, they encouraged imitation by other towns keen to repeat Westmount's success. In 1910, Outremont plagiarized Westmount's 1909 building by-law, and in 1911 restricted its more exclusive southern and western areas to First and Second Class construction.[35] When the new municipality of

Hampstead established its building by-law in 1921, it simply adopted the entire Westmount building code.[36] The Mayor of Montreal West was merely more candid than the heads of other affluent suburbs when he declared in 1912 that his town "had established Westmount as its ideal and was copying her example in many methods of civic improvement."[37]

Zoning by-laws were another tool of exclusivity. Here, too, Westmount led the way. In 1897 the Town reserved its entire upper portion (north of and along Montrose Avenue) for detached or semi-detached single-family homes.[38] In 1908, new apartment buildings and even duplexes became illegal in all of Westmount, except for the fringe area adjacent to St. Henri.[39] A year later commercial development was confined to a short list of specified streets.[40] Westmount never offered special concessions to lure industry, never allowed heavily polluting factories, and in 1913 restricted light industry, workshops, and warehouses to a small district on the town's southern edge.[41] Thus by 1913 Westmount had developed a comprehensive system of building and zoning regulations that severely restricted factory employment, made rental accommodation scarce, and established a residential area on most of the town's property containing houses that few could afford to buy.

Outremont never made so high a proportion of its territory exclusive, since sociologically it was two towns: a working-class district to the northeast (where the CPR had a marshalling yard) and an increasingly upper-class area as one walked south or west. Outremont's town council restricted the political power of poorer citizens by hiving them off in a single "North Ward," while the affluent controlled the other two wards of "South" and "West." By 1907, however, half the population lived in North Ward. The town refused its demand to be split so as to create an extra ward, which would give the two communities equal representation on council. Influenced by powerful developers who were promoting the construction of flats in North Ward,[42] the town council permitted development trends there, but prevented their infiltration into the more desirable areas located at higher altitudes. Outremont's massive building by-law of 1910 restricted industry to the northern fringe of town and reserved the more elevated streets for detached and semi-detached homes. The outside staircase, that symbol of the working class, was banned altogether in the South and West. Finally, commercial streets, a source of noise, were kept well away from the exclusive areas.[43] When in June 1928 Westmount restricted its most prestigious area (north of The Boulevard) to detached houses (henceforth excluding semi-detached ones), Outremont followed four months later with the same restriction for its finest streets.[44] Gradually, detached homes came to dominate the part of Outremont above 84 metres in altitude, and semi-detached homes the part between 76 and 84 metres. During the 1920s Outremont finally surpassed Westmount in population (28,641 compared to 24,235 in 1931),[45] but not in the proportion of the Island's elite. In 1930, in any case, Westmount and Outremont were the two large, well-populated suburbs where the Island's most rigorous construction standards and zoning restrictions were applied.

The affluent desired to live in technologically advanced homes, but also longed to locate their houses amidst an elegantly tamed version of nature. English-speaking Montrealers, especially, shared the British ideal of a home in a park-like setting.[46] Suburbs on the Island that tried to attract such residents provided more green space. The deeper the front lawn, the more one's home felt like a haven – and so, by 1914, Westmount and Outremont had imposed deep setbacks on their more prestigious streets, with a range of more modest setbacks covering the rest of town, varied according to the planned dignity of the neighbourhood.[47] Substantial side-yards also fostered privacy. Outremont encouraged them indirectly, by setting substantial minimum widths for various house-types and thus discouraging subdivision into smaller lots.[48] Westmount did so by insisting that no home cover more than 60 percent of the lot. In addition, in its exclusive upper district Westmount normally insisted on a frontage of 50 feet (15.2 m) for detached homes and 75 feet (22.9 m) for semi-detached pairs, with a side-yard at least 10 feet (3 m) wide in all cases.[49] Large and expensive lots naturally promoted commissions for architects.

Some suburbs benefitted the profession even more directly, by appointing architectural boards. Once again, Westmount set the regional precedent. Its Architectural Commission, established in 1916, consisted of the mayor, the city manager, the city engineer (*ex officio*), and four local architects named by the city council. The Commission's task was to approve the plans and specifications of every new building, statue, arch, fountain, and even fence before construction could start.[50] In 1921, the fledgling Town of Mount Royal invested these powers on its own Architectural Commission, soon to be headed by E.W. Barnes, an architect partial to Arts and Crafts cottages.[51] Five years later Hampstead gave similar authority to its Architectural Advisory Board.[52] Outremont did not follow suit, but helped architects in 1928 by banning the same exterior design on more than two buildings in the same block, within the exclusive areas restricted to detached and semi-detached homes.[53] By the 1920s, in short,

the exclusive suburbs wanted their built environments to be professionally designed.

But ample lawns for well-designed homes were not sufficient to make of a suburb "the original garden of Eden,"[54] and the most affluent suburbs spent much on developing municipal parks. By 1911, Westmount had sunk over $600,000 (a huge sum for the time) into acquiring land for parks, and by 1931 boasted more park acreage per capita than any other municipality in Quebec.[55] Outremont too developed a network of neighbourhood parks, especially between 1918 and 1928 when its total park area more than doubled, going from 4.92 to 10.85 hectares.[56] Sadly, the greatest difference in the level of public amenities between elite and workers' suburbs was in the creation of parks.[57]

Among the measures deemed necessary for the creation of a respected community of respectable people was a ban on the sale of alcohol. At the turn of the century, most Protestants in Canada favoured the prohibition of alcoholic drink, while a majority of French-speaking Catholics opposed it, as the 1898 national referendum on the issue showed. This was more a difference of religion than of class: Verdun, which housed many Protestants, "went dry" in 1875, and in 1919 its populace voted two to one against permitting the sale of even beer.[58] Contrast the equally proletarian but heavily Catholic suburbs of St. Henri and Maisonneuve, which never ceased to issue liquor permits, the number of which continued to grow. In Maisonneuve, for example, the number of licensed establishments multiplied from 2 in 1887 to 24 in 1905 when a by-law authorized an increase scaled to population growth.[59]

Since Protestants occupied a disproportionately large share of the best jobs in Montreal during this era, localities catering to the affluent generally banned taverns. Soon after the heavily French and Catholic western part of Westmount seceded in 1876, the largely Protestant remainder prohibited the sale of liquor.[60] For decades thereafter, local politicians scorned the ready access to liquor licences in Montreal.[61] Imperialistic Westmount remained fanatical about the question – in 1912 even refusing the Victoria Rifles permission to build an armoury, because wine was served in the officers' mess![62] For most of the period between 1880 and 1930, the majority of Outremont's residents were of British rather than French origin; the two groups equalled each other only in the late 1920s.[63] After 1910, Mayor Beaubien, a prohibitionist whose mother was English-Canadian, ignored the sentiments of North Ward and preserved the ban on liquor licences imposed in 1888.[64]

The exclusion of liquor outlets was only one of the many differences that existed between these suburbs and Montreal. Elite neighbourhoods sought to restrict street-life generally, and encouraged domesticity. Westmounters in particular distrusted the City's raucous night-life, with its dance-halls and other "vulgar entertainments ... that call for the wild excitement that is productive of a nature that is devoid of higher thinking."[65] Instead of seeking adventure downtown, earnest suburbanites might improve themselves through serious reading or participation in municipal affairs. Westmount, especially, promoted both. In 1898 the town built the first free municipal library in Quebec (fig. 23). Nearby in 1899 it built Victoria Hall, which housed along with athletic facilities a large auditorium (seating 500) for public meetings on crucial questions,[66] and citizens indeed filled the room to cross-examine mayor and councillors.[67] Westmount advertised itself as a refuge not only from Montreal's "coarse, noisy, Bohemian" street-life but also from the "obscene political character" of a corrupt government chosen by uneducated "masses."[68]

And what if undesirables from those coarse, Bohemian parts of Montreal invaded the sanctuary of the elect? Westmount reassured affluent home-buyers with a series of exclusionary measures. Only residents might use public playgrounds; pawn-brokers and pool-hall operators were effectively banned by an extremely high annual licence-fee; and rag-picking was prohibited outright.[69] Westmount Police Court dealt sternly with beggars, drunks, and loiterers, most of whom, had they an address to give, gave one in Montreal. The Salvation Army's plan to open a maternity hospital for the destitute provoked petitions from angry neighbours and a flat "no" from town council.[70] Whatever it took, Westmount would remain "the home of sterling businessmen."[71]

But in the end, neither Westmount nor Outremont could resist one challenge to the desires of their elite residents: apartment buildings. Westmounters loved to call their town "a city of homes," while Mayor Beaubien cherished the vision of Outremont as "une ville de cottages."[72] Many home-owners feared a decrease in amenity and property-value from an apartment building next door. And should children be cooped up in apartments? Were most tenants not transients showing little interest in their town's welfare? In 1908, Westmount banned apartment construction in almost the entire town (the area north of the CPR tracks).[73] Yet the demand for apartments with modern conveniences grew rapidly between 1910 and 1930, especially in districts with heavily English-speaking populations.[74] Moreover, the cost of high-quality construction and the ban on duplexes

and apartments in Westmount were by 1913 forcing Westmount's own young couples to rent elsewhere. By then, the quality of the Island's best apartment buildings could attract the finest tenants – for instance, the Mount Royal and Mountain View Apartments at the eastern edge of Outremont, completed in 1911. Five storeys high, they offered suites provided with open fireplaces, refrigerators, and gas ranges; each floor, concrete and soundproof, could be reached by electric elevator.[75] Outremont and Westmount both arrived at the same compromise on the issue, in 1910 and 1913 respectively: insist on high-quality construction and keep the buildings away from the districts reserved for detached and semi-detached homes.[76]

THE ROLE OF RELIGION IN PROMOTING SEGREGATION

With language groups concentrated in different suburbs, linguistic polarization on the Island (with St. Lawrence Boulevard acting as the popularly recognized "boundary")[77] encouraged stronger local loyalties. The concentration of people by religion, in part a result of linguistic segregation, had the same effect. It also resulted in larger religious buildings and schools, another source of major projects for architects. Outside the banning of liquor outlets, most municipal governments did not clearly discourage specific religious groups. The Town of Mount Royal was an exception. In 1926, its town council refused to give a sports club run by the Young Men's Hebrew Association the same tax exemption it would grant to the Young Men's Christian Association only two months later.[78] While such action was rare at the municipal level, developers, realtors, and landlords often tried to influence the cultural composition of neighbourhoods, most visibly by advertising building lots and apartments as "Restricted," a widely understood euphemism for Jewish exclusion. To some extent, however, Jews segregated themselves. Orthodox Jews needed to live within walking distance of their synagogue, as they were not permitted to use any means of transport on the Sabbath. And between 1900 and 1914, many traditional Jews from eastern Europe moved into the "immigrant corridor" between St. Lawrence Boulevard and Park Avenue, helping to make St. Louis du Mile End the Island's first multi-ethnic suburb. That confluence permitted the Jewish community to finance a major project there: the St. Urbain Street Synagogue (1905).

Even among the Island's Catholic majority, religious concentration helped fund some particularly impressive church and school buildings. Catholic landowners in some suburbs donated land to the Church at the outset of development, thus giving it a head start in the area. Charles-Théodore Viau, for instance, offered land in eastern Maisonneuve provided that a new parish arise there, and then gave $5,000 to help build Saint-Clément Church (1899), one of the most delightful church designs of the period.[79]

Several Catholic religious orders also acted as developers, helping to direct the religious makeup of a suburb. The Clercs de Saint-Viateur began to speculate in Outremont property in the 1880s as a source of additional funds for their charity work, and by the 1890s had become the town's biggest developer. In part by creating a separate parish matching Outremont's boundaries in 1902, the clerics strove to increase the town's French-Catholic population, going so far as to build some north-end flats themselves. Another step was the erection in 1896 of their new provincial headquarters, a decisive move in establishing Outremont as a home to major Catholic institutional buildings.[80] Elite Catholic schools, in particular, would help attract French-speaking business leaders from the best streets on the Plateau (increasingly noisy, like St. Denis Street) to the posher districts of Outremont.[81]

Had the Island's Protestant minority been evenly distributed, its contribution to church architecture would have been modest indeed. Not all anglophones were Protestant, of course, but almost all Protestants were anglophone. The percentage of the Island's English-speaking population living outside the City of Montreal grew from 13.8 percent in 1881 to 32.4 percent in 1931.[82] As more and more anglophones moved to neighbourhoods north and west of the city, suburbs like Westmount and Montreal West grew substantially, yet retained large Protestant majorities. In 1911, for example, 78 percent of Westmounters were Protestant.[83] Their numbers and wealth meant that Westmount's Protestants funded a church architecture that was far more imposing than the little Protestant chapels in the Island's East End. Many Protestants of this era had a romantic sensibility, and medieval architecture symbolized their more heroic aspirations, their ambition to become leaders in social and moral uplift rather than conform to the modern routine of the workplace.[84] Thus the Anglicans' St. Matthias Church (1912), seating 700, recalled the Gothic, and the Stanley Presbyterian Church (1913), whose main auditorium housed 800, resembled a Byzantine basilica. Towering above them on The Boulevard stood the neo-Gothic complex of Dominion-Douglas United Church (1927). All three, needless to say, were designed by architectural firms.[85] Further work came to architects in the form of the impressively expensive Protestant school buildings erected in Westmount.[86] These imposing churches and schools visibly reinforced Westmount's self-image as a bastion of "Protestant and cultured Christendom."[87]

BEYOND THE GRID: STREET PLANNING IN ELITE SUBURBS

Landscape architects, too, found their suburban opportunities mainly in privileged districts. True, Westmount and Outremont had, apart from some key streets, been planned piecemeal by developers,[88] and only a few of their subdivisions boasted imaginatively planned street patterns.[89] However, corporations later planned two entire towns reserved for the affluent from the very outset. The Town of Mount Royal (TMR, established in 1912) and Hampstead (created in 1914) gave early town planners the chance they had wanted to design street layouts more imaginative than the standard grid. To the northwest of Outremont, TMR was created directly out of farmland by a subsidiary of the Canadian Northern Railway Co., which needed to blast a tunnel through the mountain to gain access to Montreal Harbour. It hoped to recoup part of the enormous cost of the work by developing a prestigious, planned suburb linked to the downtown by commuter trains using the same tunnel (fig. 6).

Streets in TMR conformed to an advanced design by landscape architect Frederick G. Todd (fig. 8). Diagonal arteries divided the town into four quadrants and met at the commuter railway station in the centre. To increase exposure to sunlight, Todd placed the long sides of blocks northeast to southwest – not the usual Montreal pattern. An elliptical driveway system, linking 13 neighbourhood parks, wove its way through each quadrant. Todd provided amply sized building lots, typically with frontages of 50 feet (15.2 m).[90] As already demonstrated by subdivisions built elsewhere in Canada (like Rosedale in Toronto), curving streets appealed to English Canadians, who wanted homes in more "natural" settings. Despite both a recession (1913–15) and the war, the population of TMR numbered over 2,000 by 1929. When catering to the affluent, developers and town planners need not conflict.

The other "corporate suburb" designed at the time was Hampstead, carved out of the eastern part of Côte St. Luke. A syndicate led by utilities magnate Herbert Holt owned the entire district and hired landscape architect Leonard Schlemm to plan its streets, most of which curved to varying degrees.[91]

Schlemm's plan shared with TMR's (and with the rectangular plan of Montreal West) another tool of exclusivity: a limited number of entry-points that discouraged through traffic. The corporate development of large, professionally planned projects would become more common after 1945.

CIVIC PRIDE IN THE SUBURBS

The political will to keep the suburbs of the elite independent from Montreal was sustained not only by an aversion to sharing tax revenues; a degree of civic patriotism was involved. As we have seen with regard to the liquor question, some of these residents felt morally superior to Montreal. The rich suburbs also believed themselves more competent and technologically advanced. Did Montrealers pay excessive hydro rates to Montreal Light Heat and Power? Westmount, from 1906, got cheaper power from its own electric generating station, which a prominent expert dubbed "a triumph of electrical Engineering."[92] For decades thereafter, Westmount encouraged domestic modernization by the sale of electrical appliances in the basement of City Hall.[93] Was the beauty of Montreal's architecture compromised by utility poles and wires? From the start of the 1910s, both Westmount and Outremont were placing their wires in underground conduits.[94] Did financially irresponsible demagogues like Médéric Martin dominate Montreal's government? During the 1910s, Westmount and Outremont appointed tight-fisted City Managers.[95] Montreal's attempt in late 1910 to annex Westmount and Outremont against their will provoked an angry outcry in both suburbs, and when in 1917 Montreal asked the Quebec legislature to add these municipalities (along with Verdun) to the City as compensation for having to swallow indebted Maisonneuve, public fury in all three suburbs boiled over.[96] The fact that most of the residents of these towns earned their living in Montreal did not prevent them from developing an identity of their own.

That civic pride found symbolic expression in architecture. Westmount chose Tudor Gothic, associated with the English Reformation, for both its new City Hall (1922) and the rebuilt Victoria Hall (1925), a choice that contrasted with the French-inspired designs for town halls in more-French-speaking suburbs like St. Cunégonde (Second Empire) and St. Louis du Mile End (Château style). In Outremont, however, architectural grandeur found its chief expression in Catholic religious and educational buildings, such as the Pensionnat du Saint-Nom-de-Marie, opened in 1905 (fig. 19), the Académie Querbes

(an exuberant Beaux-Arts essay of 1916), and the enormous Mother House of the Sœurs des Saints Noms de Jésus et de Marie (fig. 45), completed in 1925. Such projects helped make at least the richest suburbs seem something more than dormitories for Montreal.

CONCLUSION

By 1930, the metropolitan region of Montreal consisted of many specialized districts varying enormously in economic function, population density, class and ethnic composition, environmental quality, and the extent of their input from architects and urban planners. The geographic attributes of different sites, great differences in personal income, developers' tactics, the policies of suburban governments, and linguistic and religious ties all fostered these striking variances. While creating disparities, the economic and, to a lesser extent, the cultural segregation of the Island's residents helped promote municipal amenities and impressive architectural and planning work in certain favoured communities. And despite the *laisser-faire* doctrine that prevailed among the affluent, the privileged suburbs imposed restrictions on individual property rights, for collective environmental improvement, to a greater extent than did other municipalities. It was the residents of the poor suburbs, the citizens who most needed governmental and professional help to improve their home environments, who received it least.

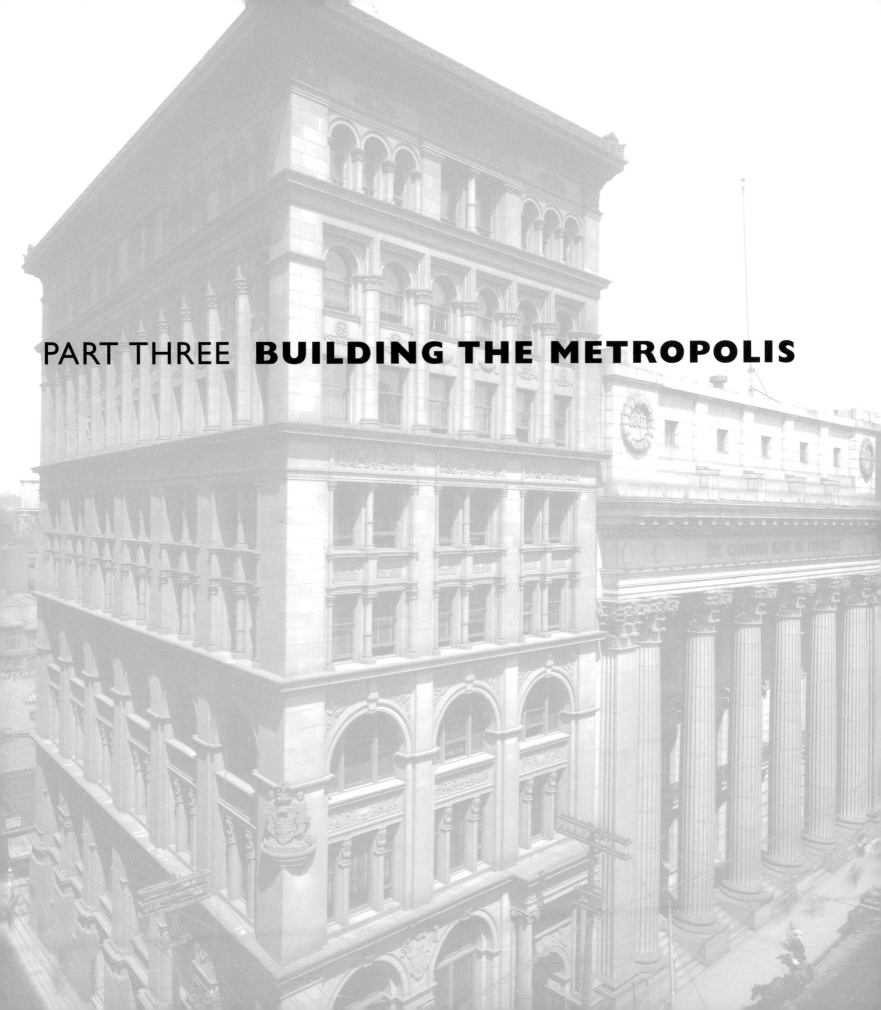

PART THREE **BUILDING THE METROPOLIS**

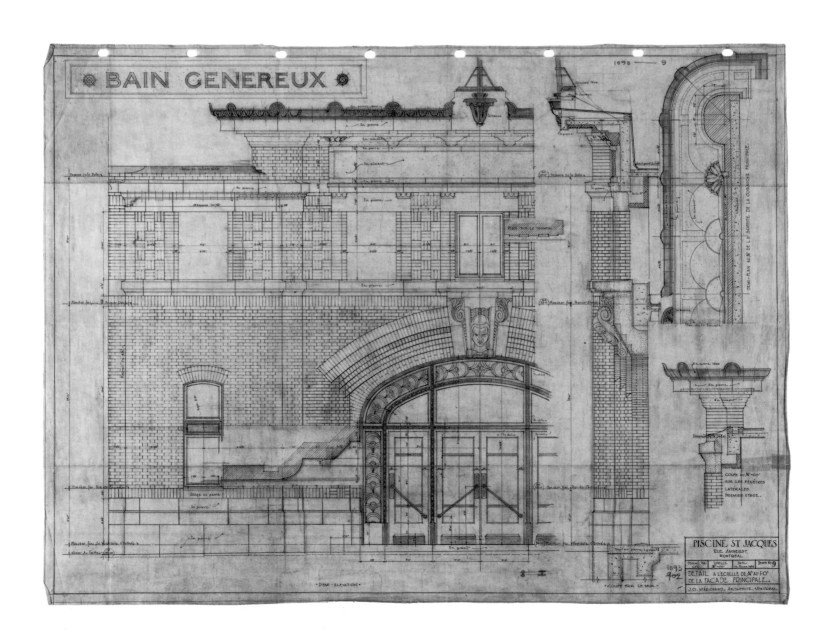

BAIN GENEREUX

PISCINE ST JACQUES
RUE AMHERST
MONTREAL

DETAIL A L'ECHELLE DE ¾ AU PD
DE LA FACADE PRINCIPALE.

J.O. MARCHAND, ARCHITECTE, MONTREAL

MONTREAL ARCHITECTS
AND THE CHALLENGE OF COMMISSIONS

France Vanlaethem

IN 1888 THE NEW YORK LIFE INSURANCE CO. BUILDING on Montreal's Place d'Armes (fig. 2), designed by the New York firm Babb Cook and Willard, attracted the attention of the new Toronto journal *Canadian Architect and Builder* (1888–1908).[1] The tower of this 8-storey building was higher than any structure in the city excepting a few church spires, and its façade of Scottish red sandstone stood out in a cityscape dominated by the local grey limestone. That same year marked the death of architect Victor Bourgeau, who on 3 March died at the age of 78 after some forty years of loyal service provided mainly to the parishes and religious communities of the diocese of Montreal. A craftsman by training and a city-dweller by choice, he had received his first major commission in 1851 from the Bishop of Montreal, Monsignor Ignace Bourget, for the Church of Saint-Pierre-Apotre in the Sainte-Marie district. It was the first of hundreds of commissions to follow for churches and convents.[2] These two events show the direction in which Quebec architecture was moving in the late 1880s. The passing of Victor Bourgeau marked the end of an era in which success as an architect was a matter of basic practical knowledge and the right social connections. The construction of Montreal's first tall commercial building ushered in an age of transformations driven by unprecedented urban growth and a collateral boom in the construction industry.

In the late nineteenth century, architecture in Canada became a profession as architects organized to protect their field by establishing standards of competence and ethical norms. Most architects in Quebec being located in Montreal, that city was home also to the organizations that represented them. As their number steadily increased, architects played an important part in the building of Montreal, even with the competition they faced from American colleagues and, despite their collective

9 Généreux Baths (1926–27, Jean-Omer Marchand, architect); details of the main façade, 1926. Pen and black ink on linen, 75 x 100 cm. Ville de Montréal, Service des immeubles.

claim, though they held no monopoly over construction. Indeed, this new solidarity notwithstanding, architects were not evenly matched in the commissions they received. Moreover, the hierarchical logic of this specific community continued to change as professional, collective, and personal strategies adapted to shifting economic and political conditions. Our examination of the building of the metropolis during this era of change opens with the initial steps taken to establish architecture as an autonomous *champ,* and turns to an examination of the institutions by which access to the profession would be controlled. It continues with a look at the careers of Montreal's most prominent architects during this period, with particular attention paid to the conditions of their success. The years 1880–1930, a period marked by two severe economic slumps, saw three great cycles of construction that will serve to structure our account.[3]

THE DEVELOPMENT OF A CONSTRUCTION MARKET

Economic growth, waves of immigration, and the urbanization of rural populations are three defining features of the period between 1880 and 1930. By 1915 the Quebec populace was predominantly urban-dwelling, with Montreal – the nerve centre of Canada's economy – by far the province's largest and busiest city. These events stimulated a gradual if not continuous growth in the construction industry, halted only by the stock market crash of 1929, which slowed building for many years. Records of the number of construction permits issued in Montreal indicate three main building cycles during the period (see fig. 3): 1887 (like 1864 and 1880) was a year of strong growth during which about 1,000 permits were granted; that number was practically tripled in 1911, and in 1928 the figure rose to almost 5,000. Not only did numbers increase, but construction activity became more complex with the growing economic diversification, the densification of the downtown core, and the arrival of suburban sprawl. New building types arose and new architectural demands were formulated – more sophisticated culturally and more rigorous in their response to public health and safety – resulting in railway stations and large hotels, office and apartment buildings, factories, educational institutions, hospitals, and public baths. In addition, the exchange value of land and buildings increasingly outstripped their use value with no decrease in the buildings' symbolic significance. Architects were in demand not only by government, at all levels, and by the Church, but also by financiers, industrialists, and real-estate developers. These multiplying commissions, however, also attracted American architects, creating a competition that pushed Montreal architects to protect their market and to increase their own prestige and authority.

THE PROFESSIONALIZATION OF ARCHITECTURE

It is in this context of economic growth and the competition it generated that the establishment in Canada of professional associations and schools of architecture must be considered. Few architects were affiliated with the Royal Canadian Academy of Arts, founded in 1882 with a somewhat vague program for "the encouragement of Design as applied to Painting, Sculpture, Architecture, Engraving, and the Industrial Arts, and the promotion and support of education leading to the production of beautiful and excellent work in manufactures."[4] Membership, moreover, was elitist, generated by co-optation and subject to final approval by the Governor General of Canada. The establishment of the Province of Quebec Association of Architects (PQAA) in October 1890 (fig. 10) came ten months after the founding of the Ontario Association of Architects. These professional organizations came relatively late to Canada by comparison with those countries with which Canada had close cultural or economic ties. In Great Britain architects had been represented for over half a century by the Royal Institute of British Architects, founded in London in 1834. For those whose interests were not served by that distinguished society, a group of young London draftsmen established the Architectural Association in 1847. Three years later Scottish architects followed by creating the Architectural Institute of Scotland.[5] In France the Société Centrale des Architectes had been in existence since 1840, and in the United States the American Institute of Architects was established in New York City in 1857.[6] The first attempt in Quebec at the association of architects was made around 1865, as the province underwent its first wave of industrialization, but this effort came to nothing.[7] One fact is noteworthy in the Canadian context: the organization of architects at the end of the nineteenth century was not, as elsewhere, a response to competition from other players in the construction industry, such as engineers and contractors, but rather a response to the preference shown by Canadian patrons of building for architects from south of the border.

In an account of the events leading up to the founding of Canada's first architectural associations, Kelly Crossman makes clear the sense of inferiority that Canadian architects felt with respect to their American counterparts, in particular the

Reproduction of Group Photograph of Montreal Members of Province of Quebec Association of Architects presented to the Quebec Members, October, 1894.

1 C. CLIFT.
2 A. PRÉFONTAINE.
3 M. PERRAULT.
4 J. SMITH.
5 J. W. HOPKINS, R.C.A.
6 J. PERRAULT.
7 A. VINCENT.
8 S. LESAGE.

9 VICTOR ROY.
10 GEO. W. WOOD.
11 JAS. WRIGHT.
12 A. MESNARD.
13 G. DE G. LANGUEDOC.
14 JAS. NELSON, A.R.C.A.
15 A. DUBREUIL.

16 A. GENDRON.
17 O. MAILLOUX.
18 A. BOILEAU.
19 ERIC MANN.
20 L. Z. GAUTHIER.
21 JOS. VENNE.
22 T. DAOUST.

23 R. FINDLAY.
24 A. T. TAYLOR, F.R.I.B.A.
25 J. F. MONTBRIAND.
26 A. FLOCKTON.
27 J. Z. RESTHER.
28 G. A. MONETTE.
29 J. B. RESTHER.

30 A. C. HUTCHISON, R.C.A.
31 A. LEVESQUE.
32 A. H. LAPIERRE.
33 H. C. NELSON.
34 A. F. DUNLOP, R.C.A.
35 J. R. RHIND.
36 A. RAZA.

37 A. G. FOWLER.
38 JOS. HAYNES.
39 C. CHAUSSÉ.
40 E. C. HOPKINS.
41 W. E. DORAN.
42 C. ST. JEAN.
43 W. MCLEA WALBANK, B.A.S.

10 Montreal members of the PQAA in 1894. Reproduction of a photograph by William Notman. From *The Canadian Architect and Builder* (January 1895).

humiliation they experienced in failed attempts to leave their mark at major competitions in Canada. In Ontario the competition announced in 1880 for the design of the new legislative building came to its conclusion six years later with the appointment of its juror – Richard Waite, of Buffalo – as architect. A similar situation occurred in 1888, when after a dubious decision an American team was commissioned to design the head office of the Toronto Board of Trade. Architects in Quebec and Ontario were galvanized by this series of snubs, and largely boycotted the competition launched in August 1890 by the Montreal Board of Trade, protesting the appointment of the renowned American architect Richard Morris Hunt as juror and the remunerated participation of five other Americans.[8] That incident, however, was not the main trigger of the events soon to unfold in Quebec.

In 1889, when construction began on Montreal's Young Men's Christian Association (YMCA), directed by Fuller and Wheeler of Albany, on Dominion Square opposite the cathedral (fig. 71),

Montreal architects felt they had been expressly passed over by local clients in favour of firms from across the border, irrespective of the Americans' qualifications.[9] In January 1890, the plan to establish a professional body arose not in Montreal but in Quebec City, provoked by yet another controversial competition. In the March issue of *Canadian Architect and Builder*, a news item from the provincial capital announced the formation of a committee to establish a local association of architects, and at the same time criticized the competition for the new city hall, the program of which had been issued in English only.[10] Quebec City architects, the vast majority of them French-speaking, felt at a disadvantage in having to face so many professional rivals, the competition having been opened to the whole of North America. Encouraged by the passing of the bill constituting the Ontario Association of Architects in April of 1890, Quebec's architectural community pushed ahead with its own mobilization. In May a committee in Montreal was struck to formulate a charter,[11] tabled in October before 35 architects from across the province assembled at the Mechanics' Institute in Montreal.[12] On 30 December 1890 the provincial government passed the bill constituting the PQAA. The new organization, seated in Montreal, had won a mandate "for the better protection of the public interest in the erection of public and private buildings" and for the "furtherance and advancement of the art of architecture."[13]

One of the priorities emerging from the speeches given at the lunch that inaugurated the PQAA on 11 October 1890 was the need to establish courses of higher education in architecture – the dual aim of this measure: to improve the architect's professional competence and, implicitly, to bring his social standing in line with that of other professionals, even with his clients, so as to enable Quebec architects to stand up to their competition. Until then young architects had received their training on construction sites or in architects' offices, having sometimes been given a slight exposure to architecture in high school. Certain colleges were already noted for their teaching of drafting, notably Mont-Saint-Louis in Montreal, run by the Frères des Écoles Chrétiennes,[14] and in the 1890s the religious institutions affiliated with McGill University, which offered classes in architectural history and drafting.[15] By the end of the century apprentices could also complement their on-the-job experience with drafting courses offered by several other institutions.

Without a more thorough study of the teaching of drafting in Quebec, it will remain difficult to assess the prospects for professional advancement then available to an apprentice or other member of the construction industry. In Montreal the best-known institutions for the study of drafting were the Mechanics' Institute and the École du Conseil des Arts et Manufactures. The oldest of these was the Mechanics' Institute; established in 1828 with the support of the political elite and the city's business community, it was closely modelled on similar institutes created in Scotland and England: independent bodies dedicated to workers' education, primarily in the sciences and secondarily in the arts.[16] The École grew out of the Conseil des Arts et Manufactures, a government-sponsored venture launched in 1869 to develop industrial training across the province, in which drafting classes were seen as the best way to improve the skill of the workforce.[17] In Europe, the same concern had led to the opening of drawing schools for factory workers in France, as far back as the seventeenth century. In nineteenth-century Great Britain, similar convictions brought about the famous state-sponsored Normal School of Design, with branches all across Britain.[18]

In the 1890s, among the dozen or so evening classes offered at the École du Conseil des Arts et Manufactures, several were tailored to craftsmen and construction workers and gave instruction in modelling and wood carving, stair building and building construction, decorative painting, and plumbing. An architectural course taught by a practising architect focused on the teaching of descriptive geometry and orthographic projection, although this teaching was not designed for architects. As the École's regulations stipulate, the school was founded to train carpenters, tinsmiths, joiners, and cabinetmakers who, concerned with efficiency or aesthetics, wanted to understand architectural plans and learn how to put down on paper their own ideas for a cornice or a piece of furniture.[19] Young men seeking a solid training in architecture had little choice but to go to the United States, where eight technical institutes and universities offered them programs.[20] Not everyone, of course, could simply leave the country in pursuit of a profession, and the need was felt for a Chair of Architecture at McGill University, and equally for the establishment of architectural courses in French in collaboration with the Université Laval, as proposed by several guests at the PQAA inaugural dinner.

Six years later, in 1896, one of these wishes was granted with the founding of the Department of Architecture at McGill University (fig. 11). The precise reasons for the delay, despite the numerous approaches made to university authorities by architects and their association,[21] are still not clear – lack of funding,[22] or a disinterest in architectural training? The latter seems more likely, as money appears to have been no object. At the start of the decade two new chairs in engineering had been created and two new buildings erected. After remaining empty for two years, the post of Principal was at last filled in 1895. The Scotsman William Peterson, a classics scholar with degrees from Edinburgh and Oxford, was doubtless better disposed towards architecture than had been his predecessor, the geologist William Dawson, who in a somewhat Calvinist fashion saw the Arts Faculty as too humanistic.[23] During Peterson's tenure, tobacco magnate William C. Macdonald – the largest single shareholder in the Bank of Montreal and one of the richest men in the city – became a great benefactor of the sciences at the university. One of his gestures was to finance the development of the Department of Architecture in 1898.[24]

It took ten years more and a strong comeback in the building trade for a specialized division to be created within Montreal's École Polytechnique (fig. 12), at the instigation

11 Macdonald-Workman Engineering Building (1907–08, Percy E. Nobbs, architect), McGill University; drawing studio, c. 1910. Unknown photographer. Canadian Architecture Collection, McGill University.

12 École Polytechnique (1903–04, Joseph-Émile Vanier, architect); architecture studio, c. 1910. Unknown photographer. Archives de l'École Polytechnique.

of Honoré Gervais, a federal Member of Parliament with a seat on the École's board as a delegate from the Université Laval's Bureau des examinateurs.[25] As in Great Britain and the United States, the programs created at both McGill and the École Polytechnique were a subdivision of departments devoted to engineering. These had been established in Quebec in the 1860s and 1870s, part of the general movement favouring science and technology, crucial suppliers of knowledge for a society anxious to take up the challenge of industrialization. In English-speaking Montreal these institutions were founded with the support of the business community, while the French-speaking ones were government-funded. Both schools, however, "imported" their educators from Europe.

The pre-eminent role of Scottish immigrants in the development of Canada is well known. Leading players in Montreal's economy, these men also contributed to the establishment of colleges and universities. A superior commitment to education had made Scotland unique in Europe ever since the eighteenth century.[26] At McGill, the first incumbents of the Chair of architecture – Stewart Henbest Capper, Percy Erskine Nobbs, and Ramsay Traquair – had all three studied and practised in Edinburgh, though their activities had extended to Lisbon, Paris, London, and Constantinople. All had been hired on the recommendation of Gerald Baldwin Brown, Professor of

Fine Arts at the University of Edinburgh and a close friend of McGill principal William Peterson.[27]

Stewart H. Capper, who had also studied at the École des Beaux-Arts in Paris, arrived in Montreal in 1896 and at the behest of the University devoted himself wholeheartedly to the direction of the McGill school. He also took part in the activities of the PQAA, of which he became President in 1900.[28] Capper was experienced as both a teacher and a practitioner of architecture, having been a professor at the Edinburgh School of Applied Art, where his one-time apprentice Ramsay Traquair had also taught.[29] Traquair, who became director in 1913, also complied with university requirements by devoting himself entirely to teaching and to research, studying early Quebec architecture. His friend and predecessor Percy C. Nobbs, however, had been unwilling to accept those conditions.[30] Trained by the Scot Robert Lorimer, a notable Arts and Crafts architect, Nobbs had travelled in Italy with Traquair and another young architect, Cecil Burgess, and worked for the London County Council, a body known for its social commitment.

France was the main source of educators for the École Polytechnique, a connection dating back to 1873, when the teaching of engineering began at the Académie commerciale catholique de Montréal.[32] In a French-Canadian society dominated by an ultramontane Church, however, the land of the Revolution was popular only in certain economic and cultural circles.[33] In 1903, in the enthusiasm over their new building, the directors of the École Polytechnique began a search for professors to strengthen architectural training, which from the beginning had been a component of the civil construction course under Professor Joseph Haynes. Ernest Michel Hébrard, a French architect and *Prix de Rome* laureate, was approached but declined the offer.[34] However, the first student of architecture from Quebec at the École des Beaux-Arts had recently returned from Paris after studies in the *atelier* of Gaston Redon. A young Montrealer named Jean-Omer Marchand was thus offered the École Polytechnique's course in perspective. The school created an independent architectural section finally in 1907, appointing as head the French diocesan architect Max Doumic, who left in dissatisfaction after only a single term.[35] His replacement was Jules Poivert. In 1923 that division and its teaching staff were transferred to the newly established École des Beaux-Arts in Montréal, one of several measures taken by the Quebec government to develop higher professional education. It now formed part of a cultural network including a museum, a commission of historic monuments, and archives created to assist the development of an elite French-Canadian workforce.[36]

Beside the PQAA's efforts to encourage institutions of higher learning to incorporate the teaching of architecture, it is interesting to note that the Association did little to help graduates enter the practice. While it demanded only one year of articling, that, added to four previous years of study, made for a training period a year longer than was required of apprentices in architectural offices. In addition, the PQAA fought to retain its control over licensing, with all aspiring architects being obliged to pass its examinations.[37] The Association was fiercely protective of the title of "Architect" and from 1898 acquired complete control over its bestowal. After 1929, indeed, any architect from abroad wanting to practice in Quebec would be required to work in association with a PQAA member.[38] Quebec architects may have been late in organizing themselves, but did so rapidly, and they preceded not only their colleagues in Ontario but also the Americans, British, and French in obtaining legal protection for architectural practice.[39] Though these measures did not secure them a monopoly over the construction market, they guaranteed Quebec architects a substantial share in it, especially in the urban centres – Montreal above all, where most members of the PQAA had established their practices.

THE MODERNIZATION OF THE CITY, 1887–1900

Montreal had been expanding and changing ever since the mid nineteenth century. The original city, now known as Old Montreal, whose boundaries corresponded to the dismantled fortifications, became more and more unifunctional, a home to the service sector; manufacturing grew up elsewhere, mainly along the Lachine Canal, with residential neighbourhoods situated on the outskirts. In a creeping expansion, buildings spread over the adjacent countryside, densely to both west and east and in a lighter development to the north, creating the first ring of suburbs. The popular "plex"-type housing built here, with buildings accommodating several families each, differed from dwellings in the bourgeois residential area (known as the Square Mile) that grew up between 1850 and 1860 to the northwest at the foot of Mount Royal. There row-housing, sometimes architect-designed, was the norm, while large and luxurious single-family homes covered the upper part of Beaver Hall Hill and the slope of the mountain.[40] Ravenscrag (1861–64), the sumptuous villa in the Italian style commissioned by Sir Hugh Allan from the firm of William Spier and Sons,[41] overlooked the whole city and surrounding area, a symbol of the power acquired by the Anglo-Protestant bourgeoisie that had made its money in trade, finance, and transport. It was in this district, on the east corner of Phillips Square at St. Catherine Street, that in 1879 one of the city's major cultural institutions, the Art Association of Montreal, established itself in a building designed by John William Hopkins.

In the 1870s the city centre near the port had acquired some imposing new buildings: at the top of Jacques Cartier Square a stately City Hall was built (1876–78) along the Champ de Mars, while an equally majestic Post Office (1874–76), also in Second Empire style, flanked the Bank of Montreal on St. James Street. On De la Commune Street the Harbour Commissioners building (1875–78), designed by Hopkins and Wily, proudly reared its tower in the McGill Street area – the tower being a symbol common to edifices with a claim to civic value. St. James Street increasingly became the main business thoroughfare.

During the 1890s Montreal modernized. Stone or brick façades became the norm, streets were paved, and both street lighting and the streetcar system were electrified. The reconstruction of buildings along St. James Street continued apace, changing in scale considerably. Existing structures were raised as the city saw its first tall buildings, a new type that benefitted from technological innovations such as the invention of the

13 Bonaventure Station, Grand Trunk Railway Co. (1888–89, Thomas S. Scott, architect), at the corner of Peel and St. Antoine streets, c. 1895. Photograph: William Notman and Son. Notman Photographic Archives, McCord Museum of Canadian History, Montreal.

elevator and the use of steel-frame construction. At the corner of St. Pierre Street, the Canada Life Insurance Co. built an 8-storey office building (1894–96; fig. 58) – yet another commission given to an American, Richard Waite. At the west end of the centre, Victoria Square, strategically sited beside the St. Anne industrial area, continued to be a commercial venue. But the old city centre was facing rivalry from recent development to the north, along St. Catherine Street. The Henry Morgan & Co. department store, which had resettled on Victoria Square in 1866 after leaving its earlier premises on Notre Dame Street, moved further north in 1890 to Phillips Square (fig. 28), initiating a trend that would attract not only retail trade but also cultural facilities.

Other major buildings were the two railway stations constructed by the Canadian Pacific Railway (CPR), run by the American-born Sir William Van Horne. Since its creation in 1880 the CPR had become the main competitor of the established Grand Trunk Railway, which situated its Second Empire designed Bonaventure Station (1888–89; fig. 13) to the east of Chaboillez Square.[42] The

first of the CPR's terminals, Windsor Station (1888–89; fig. 68) erected its medieval-looking tower at the foot of Dominion Square, near the Windsor Hotel (fig. 72), which had opened in January 1878. The station also held company offices, previously located at Place d'Armes. The second station was built some ten years later, further east near the middle-class French-Canadian district around St. Denis Street. Located on the edge of the broad and elegant Viger Square, for which it was named, this French-château-inspired building also incorporated a hotel (1896–98; fig. 69). Both were the work of Bruce Price, another American who challenged Montreal's architects.

By 1890, 47 architects listed practices in Montreal in *Lovell's Directory,* many describing themselves as both architects and surveyors.[43] The latter speciality had its heyday as properties were appropriated by the city administration, involved in the widening of various streets.[44] Of these architects 36 were affiliated with the PQAA, which in December 1890 numbered 39 members across the province.[45] Three-quarters of the

14 Montreal Street Railway Co. Building (1893–95, J.W. and E.C. Hopkins, architects; George B. Post, consulting architect). Photograph: William H. Carre. From Arthur Weir, *Art Work on Montreal, Canada* (1898). Collection Canadian Centre for Architecture, Montréal.

"registered" architects, to use the term now protected by law, were therefore established in Montreal. Others speedily joined the new organization, which only a year later boasted twice as many members, a number that held until mid decade and doubled again. The explanation for these two jumps in membership lies with the special conditions that were in force in the months following the introduction of the *Act to Incorporate the Province of Quebec Association of Architects* in December 1890 and the later amendment made to it in 1898, aimed at further protection of the title of architect. On both occasions, a 6-month transition period was declared during which practising architects could join the association with no other formality than the payment of dues.[46]

The first president elected by the PQAA was the senior figure among the founding members, John William Hopkins, a native of Liverpool and the veteran of a long and productive career nourished by the city's economic boom. Hopkins was much favoured by the business community, and in the 1890s, working

with his son Edward C. Hopkins, was still transforming the cityscape with new buildings: the John Murphy department store (1894) at St. Catherine Street and Metcalfe, and, at the foot of the slope a short distance from Place d'Armes, the Montreal Street Railway Co. Building (1893–95; fig. 14), for a dynamic and ambitious company chaired by Louis-Joseph Forget that controlled urban passenger transport. The Romanesque façade of the Railway Co. Building was somewhat weaker than its precedents, Montreal's Windsor Station and the Marshall Field Wholesale Store in Chicago, the overall composition lacking amplitude and the decor wanting in simplicity. The metal frame used was a technological advance for Montreal, but in this case also an unfortunate experiment, as the building collapsed before completion.[47] Another highly esteemed member of the PQAA was Alexander Cowper Hutchison, the second architect in Quebec (after his senior and rival Hopkins) to be elected to the Royal Canadian Academy of Arts and the head of one of the city's busiest firms.[48] Hutchison chaired the inaugural meeting of the PQAA in October 1890 and was an ardent defender of formal architectural training. He refused to accept apprentices in his firm, since work made it impossible to give them the attention they needed.[49] The son of a Scottish immigrant, a mason-turned-contractor, Hutchison trained as a stone mason in his father's company and gained solid experience on the construction sites of Montreal's Christ Church Cathedral (1857–59) and the Parliament Buildings in Ottawa (1859–66). He rounded off this practical training by following classes chiefly at the Mechanics' Institute in Montreal, where he later taught.[50]

A practising architect from 1865, Hutchison was trusted by the Anglo-Protestant bourgeoisie, as demonstrated by the houses he built for leaders of the English-speaking community and likewise by the elegant Greek-revival building of the Peter Redpath Museum (1880–82) designed for the McGill University campus – one of the major projects Hutchison carried out with his first partner, British-born Alexander Denton Steele, who had come to Canada to oversee construction of Montreal's first YMCA building on Victoria Square (1872–73). Besides the industrial commissions he worked on during the 1890s, Hutchison received the commission for the Erskine and American United Church on Sherbrooke Street (1891–94; fig. 15), a brilliant exercise in Richardsonian Romanesque and a powerful and original building in both its proportions and its materials. The Watson Foster wallpaper factory (1896–97) that he built in Maisonneuve was by contrast completely stark, save for the architectural elements emphasizing base, cornice, and entrance.

15 Hugh Allen Inglis Valentine, draftsman. Erskine and American United Church (1891–94, Alexander C. Hutchison, architect), 1894. From *One Hundred Years of Erskine Church, Montreal: 1833–1933* (1934).

16 Canadian Express Co. Building (1900, Hutchison and Wood, architects), c. 1900. From *Montreal, the Imperial City of Canada, the Metropolis of the Dominion* (c. 1909). Collection Canadian Centre for Architecture, Montréal.

As the new century opened Hutchison teamed up with son-in-law and one-time apprentice George W. Wood and son William Burnet Hutchison. Hutchison and Wood became the first Montreal firm to construct tall buildings. In the heart of the city they built the sober and imposing Telegraph Chambers (1900–01) for Canadian Pacific, and on McGill Street, opposite the head office of the Grand Trunk Railway, the Canadian Express Co. Building (1900; fig. 16). This 10-storey structure, built for a transport company specializing in international financial transfers,[51] was given an elaborate Baroque ornamentation emphasizing, although in a somewhat confused manner, the triple register of its elevation. From the 1870s on, Hutchison's intimate knowledge of materials and wide familiarity with

architectural styles enabled him to respond with great competence to current notions of decorum and fashion as the architect of many new commercial and civic buildings in Montreal. In the commission for Montreal's first City Hall, Hutchison had collaborated with the most distinguished French-Canadian architect of his generation, Henri-Maurice Perrault, the son of a joiner and the nephew of the great Montreal architect John Ostell. Perrault's skill and reputation would help to found one of Quebec's great architectural dynasties.[52]

Successor of Henri-Maurice, the firm of Perrault and Mesnard, established in 1880, virtually monopolized commissions from the French-speaking community for institutions and ecclesiastical buildings. In 1890 it was asked to design the

17 Université Laval in Montréal (1893–95, Perrault Mesnard and Venne, architects); main façade, c. 1905. Unknown photographer. Collection Canadian Centre for Architecture, Montréal.

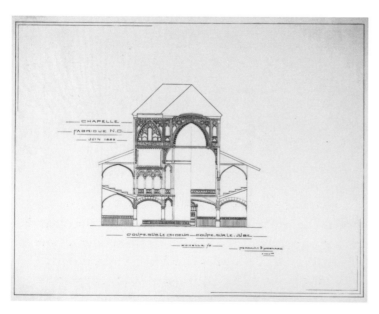

18 Notre-Dame-du-Sacré-Cœur Chapel (1888–91, Perrault and Mesnard, architects), annex to Notre Dame Church; section of the choir and the choir-screen, c. 1889. Pen and ink on drafting cloth, 68 x 93 cm. Collection of La Fabrique de la paroisse Notre-Dame de Montréal.

Monument National (1891–93) on St. Lawrence Boulevard south of St. Catherine Street, the headquarters of the patriotic Société Saint-Jean-Baptiste. Combining multiple functions, this building, whose rhythmic façade recalled great Romanesque secular structures, would become the major cultural and educational centre for French-speaking, working-class Montrealers. Shortly thereafter the firm obtained the commission for the Montreal branch of the Université Laval (1893–95; fig. 17), which would regroup the university's then-scattered departments. The site first proposed was a lot along St. Denis Street adjacent to the Collège Mont-Saint-Louis on Sherbrooke Street, but the new building finally arose further down, on a smaller plot offered by the Sulpicians beside the university chapel of Notre-Dame-de-Lourdes (1873–76).[53] Renaissance in inspiration, the decoration of this palatial edifice was more restrained than that of the Monument National, emphasizing the solemnity of a seat of higher learning. Its relationship to the street was also different: whereas the St. Lawrence Street building was flush with the street, the Université Laval featured an open entrance court with a horseshoe staircase leading to the second-floor lobby.

A founding member of the PQAA, Maurice Perrault, the son of Henri-Maurice and brother of Joseph, also an architect, had good connections in the political world, while Albert Mesnard, an architect and sculptor and previously chief designer in the firm of Henri-Maurice, was a master of eclecticism. The firm's projects drew on many sources for their building types and ornamentation, their approach to decoration becoming even more exuberant after the team was joined by Joseph Venne around 1892.[54] Venne's rich approach to sculpted and painted surfaces was much to the taste of the increasingly triumphant clergy. Perrault and Mesnard built several churches and convents in Montreal and the surrounding area, also enlarging Notre Dame Church by adding Notre-Dame-du-Sacré-Cœur Chapel (1888–91; fig. 18) and rebuilding the south transept of St. James Cathedral (1891; fig. 6). The firm had nevertheless to contend with competition from the Resthers. Father and son, Jean-Baptiste Resther (himself the son of a building contractor) and Jean-Zéphyrin Resther had been the first architects approached – around 1884, when land near the Champ-de-Mars was acquired – by the Société Saint-Jean-Baptiste for the design of their headquarters.[55]

The Resthers were popular with the clergy and the city's numerous religious communities, who were good clients with growing resources and a need of new buildings. The Sœurs

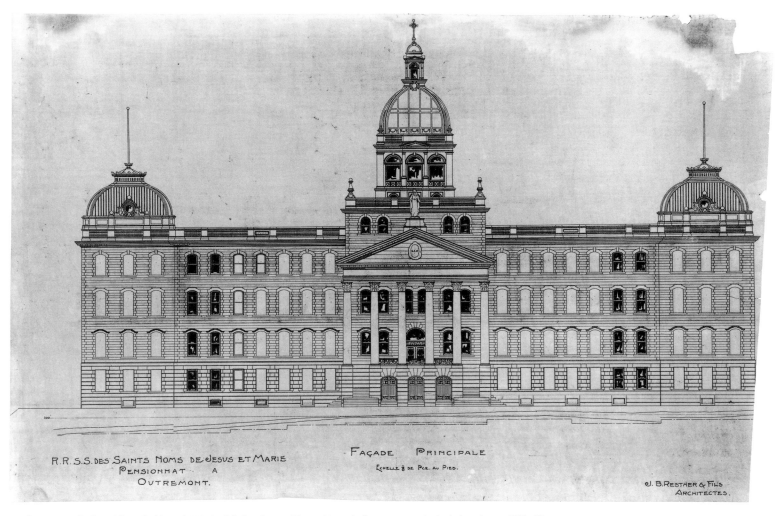

19 Pensionnat du Saint-Nom-de-Marie (1903–05, J.B. Resther et Fils, architects), Outremont; principal elevation, c. 1902–03. Blueline print, 60.2 x 91 cm. Congrégation des Sœurs des Saints Noms de Jésus et de Marie, Service central des archives.

des Saints Noms de Jésus et de Marie, who were establishing their boarding-school (1903–05; fig. 19) in quiet Outremont, turned to the son Jean-Zéphyrin for the building.[56] The Resthers had already built Mont-Saint-Louis college (1887–1913) for the Frères des Écoles Chrétiennes, the convent of the Pères du Très-Saint-Sacrement (1892–94), and the Saint-Basile boarding-school (1895–96) opposite it on Mount Royal Avenue. These buildings have a Spartan simplicity typical of Quebec convent architecture, save for the entrances and the spatial arrangement and decoration of the chapels. As the Catholic clergy consolidated its partitioning of land and control over the community, ecclesiastical architecture became an increasingly important field – dominated, unlike the commercial sector, mostly by French-Canadian architects.

Commercial building was also on the rise. While the Hutchison firm was still active in the 1890s, Alexander Francis Dunlop, a recognized expert in "designing sturdy structures of the highest quality and large residential developments," had won equal if not greater prestige.[57] The Montreal-born Dunlop[58] had worked in Detroit before returning home in 1874 to set up practice in the metropolis, where immediate success was not forthcoming. His first major commission was for "Canada's Methodist cathedral" St. James Methodist (1887–89), a huge Gothic-Revival structure built on the former site of Sir Hugh Allan's luxurious residence on St. Catherine Street, near Phillips Square. But one commission brought in another. Having been unable to sell the St. James Street lot, where its previous church had stood, the Methodist

20 Alexander Francis Dunlop, draftsman and architect, Temple Building (1889–90); detail of the entrance, 1890. Pen and black ink, watercolour, and graphite on vellum, 48.7 x 36.7 cm. National Gallery of Canada, Ottawa. Reception piece for the Royal Canadian Academy of Arts, submitted by the architect, Montreal, 1890.

congregation commissioned Dunlop to redevelop the property – for which he designed the Temple Building (1889–90; fig. 20), a 6-storey structure that was considered among the finest of its kind in North America. In this little Montreal "Rookery Building" a number of his colleagues opened their offices.

Dunlop also designed many commercial and industrial buildings, including the Queen's Hotel (1891–93; fig. 21) near Bonaventure Station (built partly of steel and hailed at the time for its fire-resistant qualities), a brewery on St. Lawrence Boulevard (1893–94) for his father-in-law Henry A. Ekers, and a building for *The Star* newspaper on St. James Street (1899–1900). In addition, he built a number of houses in the Square

Mile, his residential clients often being those with whom he had done business in the commercial sector (such as the journalist and founder of *The Star* Hugh Graham). As official architect of the Montreal Protestant School Board, Dunlop designed several schools as well. Among the many young architects that articled at his firm were Edward Maxwell, Théodose Daoust, David R. Brown, Georges Alphonse Monette, and Kenneth Guscotte Rea. Another who found a job with Dunlop, upon arriving in Montreal in 1885,[59] was Robert Findlay – with Edward Maxwell and David R. Brown, one of the most promising architects of the new generation.

Having already worked with the country's best architects, Findlay left Scotland at the age of 26, headed for Mexico in the hope of work. He had got as far as Montreal when his plans fell through, and it was there he decided to stay. A few years later in 1889 Findlay won the competition for the head office of the Sun Life Assurance Co. (1890; fig. 22), his entry triumphing over 15 others on account of the building's richly decorated façades and the high quality of design.[60] This project for a fast-growing Canadian company brought Findlay the approval of his new milieu, in particular that of Sun Life president Robertson Macaulay, a fellow Scot whose family would commission more than one residence from him.[61] Indeed, Findlay's work was mostly residential, and he built many houses for the Anglo-Protestant elite in the Square Mile and in Westmount. In a sense, Findlay was the architect of that green and patrician western suburb, designing the Westmount Public Library (1898; fig. 23), a red-brick Queen-Anne-style building at the edge of Murray Park, and, much later in 1922, the Tudor city hall, in partnership with son Francis R. Findlay. Whether public or private, Findlay's Westmount architecture assumed a domestic scale suited to the suburban environment into which it blended. Aiming beyond stylistic change, his work referred repeatedly to British sources, in keeping with the background of its clients. While Findlay's career benefitted from both his Scottish origins and his early success in a competition reserved for architects practising in Canada – still a rare event[62] – Edward Maxwell followed in the footsteps of his patron Alexander Dunlop, who advised him to continue his training in the United States.[63]

Maxwell made his debut in Montreal while still employed by the American firm Shepley Rutan and Coolidge, as site supervisor during construction of the head office of the powerful Montreal Board of Trade (fig. 59). This afforded him a unique opportunity to become known to members of the wealthy class, many of whom were also of Scottish descent. While his initial

Queen's Hotel, Montreal

21 Queen's Hotel (1891–93, Alexander Francis Dunlop, architect). Unknown photographer. Collection Canadian Centre for Architecture, Montréal.

commissions – mainly alterations and extensions – were not always prestigious, they would come from influential members of Montreal society.

Research shows the importance to Maxwell's career of his earliest clients and the special relationships he built up among families and businesses linked with the Bank of Montreal and the Canadian Pacific Railway, two important financial powers in Montreal.[64] In 1892 Maxwell obtained the commission to build a house for the newly married Henry Vincent Meredith and Isobel Brenda Allan – a present from businessman Andrew Allan to his daughter and her husband, "a rising star in the firmament of Montreal business." The red-brick residence was magnificently situated on the slope of Mount Royal opposite Ravenscrag. In both plan and elevation, the Bostonian sources

of the design were unmistakable, especially the influence of Richardson, whom the young Maxwell greatly admired.[65] The following spring, his first major commission made it possible for him to leave Shepley Rutan and Coolidge. The prosperous jeweller Henry Birks, hitherto established on St. James Street, had asked him to design the new store slated for a prime site Birks had acquired on St. Catherine Street, at the corner of Phillips Square (figs. 24 and 43) opposite the Henry Morgan & Co. department store.[66] Like Morgan, Birks was moving closer to his clients in the upper part of town. Maxwell responded with an elegant variation on the "part Roman, part Italian Renaissance"[67] conception of the Board of Trade, expressing the purpose of an edifice housing a company specializing in luxury goods.

22 Sun Life Assurance Co. Building (1890, Robert Findlay, architect), c. 1889. Lithograph: Toronto Lithograph Company, 68.6 × 53.3 cm (framed). Sun Life of Canada Corporate Archives.

Further private houses were followed by branches of the Merchants' Bank of Halifax, two schools in Westmount, buildings for the Bell Telephone Co. (whose architect he became), and, after 1897, several stations for the CPR's transcontinental line, as well as the extension to its Windsor Station (1900–06). On St. James Street, Maxwell extended the home office of the Merchants' Bank of Canada (1899–1900) and built the new offices of the British insurance company London and Lancashire Life (1898–99; fig. 92), the latter a commission of considerable prestige given both the location of the building and the client's reputation. While spending some time in Montreal, Maxwell's younger brother William Sutherland Maxwell, also an archi-

tect, made a major contribution to the design of this building, which avoided the familiar hackneyed models in favour of Beaux-Arts precedents;[68] it stands out as a stylistic exercise of some exuberance, unusual in the Montreal cityscape. In 1902 Edward and William became partners, the younger brother's cultural background complementing the elder's solid professional reputation. But as the century drew to a close, the architect with the most prestige among Montreal's elite was, without a doubt, the Scot Andrew Thomas Taylor, one of the PQAA's most active and influential members.

Taylor was born in Edinburgh, and after practising for some years in London moved to Montreal in 1883 to join his uncle, the financier Sir George Drummond.[69] His professional qualifications were then outstanding in Canada, as Taylor had followed a thorough apprenticeship with brilliant work at London's Royal Academy under the tutelage of Richard Phené Spiers.[70] Both his Scottish origin and the reputation he had earned explain the trust in his ability shown by major institutions such as the Bank of Montreal, McGill University, and the Art Association, whose premises he extended (1892–93). Taylor's success made his name known from England to British Columbia.[71] On the McGill campus, undergoing expansion thanks to funds donated by prosperous industrialists,[72] Taylor and his associates built in only a few years all the facilities for the Faculty of Science (fig. 25): the Macdonald Physics Building (1890–93), the Macdonald Chemistry and Mining Building (1896–98), the Macdonald-Workman Engineering Building (1890–93; fig. 26), the Redpath Library (1892–93), and the successive extensions to the medical faculty buildings.[73] In the area around University and McTavish streets he gave the campus its urban face, providing an architectural unity in scale and materials rather than in style. Some pavilions have a classic dignity while others are more picturesque; all of them, in greystone like John Ostell's central pavilion (1839–43), embody a strong and simple tectonic presence, Taylor being much opposed to any form of sham.[74] As architect-in-chief for the Bank of Montreal, he refitted and redecorated the interior of the Head Office on Place d'Armes in 1889, also designing bank branches for various districts of the growing city – small picturesque buildings that contrasted with their settings.

The confidence vested in Taylor by Montreal's most prestigious institutions, from bank to university, together with the commissions granted to American architects, both indicate the low prestige accorded local practitioners. Montreal architects had all trained through apprenticeship, and often followed in

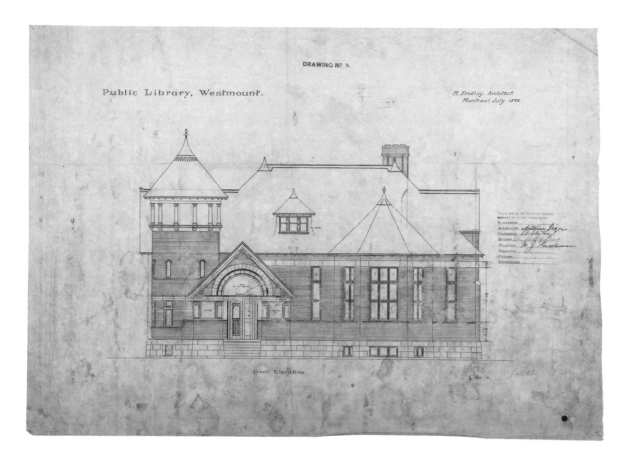

23 Westmount Public Library (1898, Robert Findlay, architect), 1898. Pen and ink on drafting cloth, 54 x 76 cm. City of Westmount Archives.

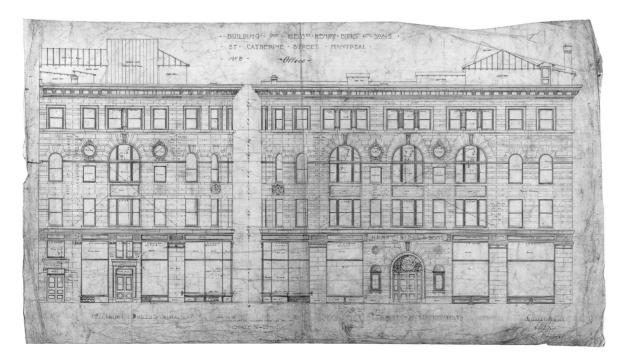

24 Henry Birks and Sons Jeweller's (1893–94, Edward Maxwell, architect); elevations. Pen and black ink on drafting cloth, 59 x 105 cm. Canadian Architecture Collection, McGill University.

25 Campus of McGill University showing, from left to right, the Macdonald-Workman Engineering Building (1890–93), the Macdonald Chemistry and Mining Building (1896–98), and the Macdonald Physics Building (1890–93, Taylor and Gordon, architects), c. 1904. Photograph: William Notman and Son. Notman Photographic Archives, McCord Museum of Canadian History, Montreal.

26 Macdonald-Workman Engineering Building (1890–93, Taylor and Gordon, architects), McGill University; staircase. Photograph: William Notman and Son. Notman Photographic Archives, McCord Museum of Canadian History, Montreal.

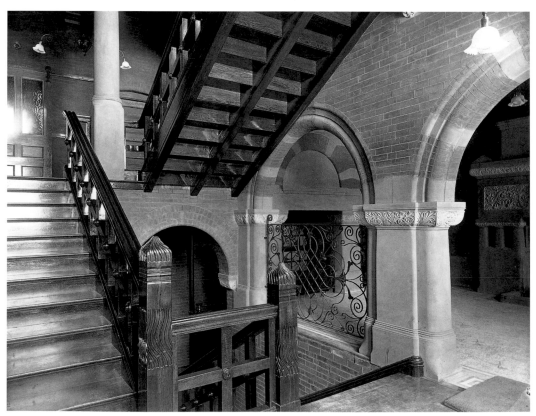

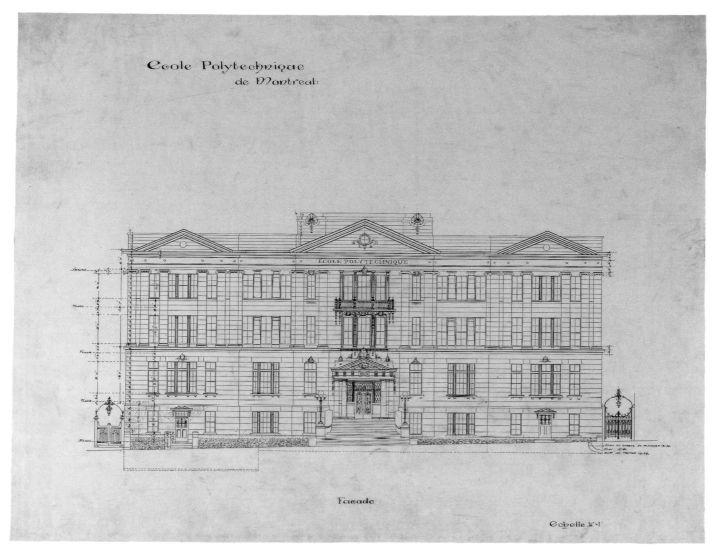

27 École Polytechnique (1903–04, Joseph-Émile Vanier, architect); principal elevation.
Pen and black ink on vellum, 54 x 70 cm. Service des archives et de gestion des documents de l'Université du Québec à Montréal.

the footsteps of fathers who had worked in the building industry. Many were first-generation immigrants, the English-speakers being largely from Scotland. Is it wise to stress these sociocultural distinctions? With regard to the awarding of commissions, both the English- and the French-speaking communities had a flourishing practice in residential architecture – a shared market even if much was to escape both groups. In number of commissions, breadth of clientèle, and range of building programs (mostly commercial for anglophones and usually institutional and ecclesiastical for francophones), work was also shared. Within the PQAA, positions of responsibility were more or less equally distributed between the two linguistic groups, and official documents were generally bilingual.

A few Montreal architects at the turn of the century followed unusual career paths. One such was the engineer, architect, and surveyor Joseph-Émile Vanier, who registered as an architect in 1898 and became an active member of the PQAA.[75] A one-time associate of the Resthers, Vanier worked chiefly as a hydraulics engineer and surveyor – rare and much-sought-after skills in this period of suburban development and urban modernization. His architectural ventures were perhaps less numerous than his engineering projects, and included townhouses, Saint-Jean-Baptiste Church (1898–1903), the town halls of St. Louis du Mile End (1905) and Côte St. Paul (1910), and the new building of his *alma mater*, the École Polytechnique on St. Denis Street (1903–04; fig. 27). Like all his colleagues, he could vary his style to suit his clients' budgets and sense of decorum. His success as an engineer was the greater for the little competition he faced, as Quebec had as yet very few engineers, and Vanier would become head of the public works company Montreal Water and Power. He was also one of the few members of the construction industry who could claim experience in the United States. That was true also of Alexander Dunlop, and of two of Dunlop's former apprentices who both began their careers in the 1890s: Edward Maxwell and David R. Brown. Experience gained in the great nation to the south was increasingly in demand with the younger generation and was much valued by patrons.

THE CONSTRUCTION BOOM OF 1900–18

Following a slow but steady increase in the number of new worksites, construction once again surged ahead in 1906, reaching a peak in 1911 (see fig. 3). The boom in building and in the real-estate market accelerated the centripetal tendency of urban development. In the heart of Montreal's upper-town bourgeois residential district, demolition and rebuilding continued as St. Catherine Street between Berri and Peel streets increasingly became the main commercial and cultural thoroughfare. A number of theatres had opened only a few blocks from Morgan's department store (fig. 28) and the Art Association Gallery. On Phillips Square behind the Birks store (extended in 1902 by Hutchison and Wood, who respected the existing architecture), the construction of the New Birks Building (1911–12, Nobbs and Hyde; fig. 43), the first tall structure to arise in this part of town, was quite an event. A short distance away, opposite St. James Methodist Church, the Jacobs Building (1909–10; fig. 98), by architects Mitchell and Creighton, was another novelty for Montreal. This new horizontally extended, concrete-frame, loft-type building, whose vast floors could house commercial, manufacturing, and service industries at the same time, was a type much used in the redevelopment of Paper Hill just prior to the First World War. The Jacobs Building was famous for its modernity, the speed of its construction, its practical design, and its broad expanse of windows ornamented in the Renaissance-Revival style.[76] One of the very first buildings in Montreal to employ the Kahn construction system, it was then the largest reinforced-concrete structure in Canada, exploiting a new material in use in the metropolis since the turn of the century.[77]

Between 1910 and 1920, with the appearance of many new public, educational, and cultural buildings designed along

Beaux-Arts lines, Sherbrooke Street in the Square Mile and St. Denis Street, which since the turn of the century had developed into the city's *Quartier Latin*, began to take on a "monumental" character. In 1915 a large French-language public library was opened by the Sulpicians, an order very active in the city's intellectual life that maintained close links with France. A fortunate replacement for the old parish Cabinet de lecture on Notre Dame Street, which had been demolished to make way for the imposing new Transportation Building (1911–12), the library became "a lively and much-frequented centre of culture."[78]

On the outskirts of the city, urbanization was proceeding at a faster pace, helped by the expansion of the streetcar network. In the north of Montreal east of Mount Royal, neighbourhoods were becoming more heavily populated. To the west the suburban municipality of Westmount, where construction was booming, was a district providing numerous opportunities for architects. Many architects indeed lived there. In 1916 Westmount's town council, concerned to preserve the status of the area, established an architectural committee that included Robert Findlay, John Smith Archibald, David H. MacFarlane, and Donald Norman MacVicar.[79] To the east, along the shore of the St. Lawrence, the industrial suburb of Maisonneuve embarked upon an extensive program of urban renewal.

The PQAA numbered 124 architects in 1911, 90 of them Montrealers.[80] Only some headed their own firms; there were only 60 architects advertised in *Lovell's Directory*.[81] Few then held degrees, most having been trained as apprentices. By 1911, McGill University's Deparment of Architecture had graduated 26 students[82] and the École Polytechnique had awarded its first five architectural degrees. At the turn of the century, the quarter preferred by architects for setting up shop was no longer the St. James Street area but the new city centre around Phillips Square, and in 1898 the PQAA, housed since 1894 in the New York Life Insurance Co. Building (fig. 2), moved there itself.[83] Painters and sculptors were likewise drawn to the area by the nearby Art Association Gallery, with its exhibitions and classes. Edward and William Maxwell and a number of artist friends all set up their studios in a building on Beaver Hall Hill.[84]

In the first fifteen years of the new century, the Maxwell brothers were at the peak of their careers. Their personalities and talents were an ideal combination, Edward's gregariousness and organizational ability complementing the creative gifts and friendships in artistic circles of his younger brother, who was a brilliant draughtsman and a passionate book lover. The faith shown in them by their major clients had been amply

28 Phillips Square and the Henry Morgan & Co. Ltd. Department Store (1890–91, John Pearce Hill, architect), 1915–16. Photograph: William Notman and Son. Notman Photographic Archives, McCord Museum of Canadian History, Montreal.

warranted by the many residential and commercial projects the two had executed across Canada. The CPR commissioned work from the Maxwells in Winnipeg and Calgary, and the two major national competitions they won in 1907 increased their renown.[85] In Montreal the brothers built their largest office building, the head office of the Dominion Express Co. (1910–12; fig. 93), a 10-storey structure at the corner of St. James and St. François Xavier streets. Following this, after a closed competition organized by the Boston architect Edmund Wheelwright, they designed one of the city's major buildings, the Montreal Art Association's new museum on Sherbrooke Street (1911–12; figs. 32 and 33).[86] Whereas the building designed for the London and Lancashire Life Assurance Co. at the turn of the century, with its traditional mansard roof, was still derived from the traditional palace type, the glazed, white-ceramic façades of the Dominion Express Co. Building showed that the architects had assimilated the American approach to tall building while retaining a high degree of ornamentation. In that field, Montreal architects had succeeded in making their mark, although their demands for

a protectionist policy continued to appear in the press; many of the service-industry buildings constructed in and near the downtown core were now being designed by local firms.

One notable example was the commissioning in 1903 of a Montreal architect, David R. Brown, to rebuild the Board of Trade headquarters, destroyed in a fierce fire that had devastated the neighbourhood. Brown, however, was undoubtedly keen to acknowledge his experience in the United States and his tenure with Shepley Rutan and Coolidge of Boston, designers of the previous Board of Trade building (figs. 59 and 60). This commission – like Brown's winning entry in the competition to design McGill University's Strathcona Medical Building (1908–11; fig. 29) – effectively launched a career that had in fact begun in 1892. Brown collaborated with various colleagues and in 1907 formed a partnership with the Ontario architect Hugh Vallance that would prove especially productive for both men. The reputation of Brown and Vallance spread as far afield as Saskatoon and Calgary.[87] Their work in Montreal included the print-shop of *The Montreal Herald* on St. Antoine Street (1911–12) and the

29 Herbert Raine, draftsman. Strathcona Medical Building (1908–11, Brown and Vallance, architects), McGill University, 1908. Notman Photographic Archives, McCord Museum of Canadian History, Montreal.

30 Belgo Building (1911–12, Finley and Spence, architects), 1916. Photograph: William Notman. Notman Photographic Archives, McCord Museum of Canadian History, Montreal.

Southam Press Building on Bleury Street (1913–14; fig. 97), both innovative designs in the Tudor style in contrast with the Beaux-Arts character of the Board of Trade.[88]

One of the architectural firms most in demand early in the century when the building boom was at its height was the long-lived firm of Alexander C. Hutchison. With his partners, Hutchison designed the premises of the haberdashery wholesaler John Greenshields on Victoria Square (1903) and the Shaughnessy Building for the CPR (1912) further down McGill Street opposite the Canadian Express Co. That tall building reflected the trend towards the plainer style appropriate to this type of construction. To the west on Sherbrooke Street, two architects with degrees from the Massachusetts Institute of Technology (MIT) in Boston, Samuel Arnold Finley and David Jerome Spence, built the first large apartment building in the metropolis, the Linton (1906–07; fig. 96). The rich ornamentation of this residential edifice provided a contrast to the plain look of two concrete structures based on American models, the industrial and commercial Belgo Building designed by Finley and Spence on St. Catherine Street (1911–12; fig. 30) and the Unity Building (1912–13; fig. 97) erected below St. Catherine Street in the Paper Hill district, designed by Spence, who had gone into business on his own.

In the French-Canadian community Maurice Perrault was still very active on both the architectural and the political fronts. His commitment to the Liberal Party, then in power in both Quebec and Ottawa, may have had an impact on his career, depriving him of some ecclesiastical commissions but bringing him more work in the public sector. For the federal government he built post offices and expanded the post office on St. James Street near Place d'Armes. He also entered the invited competition organized by the provincial government for the École Technique de Montréal in 1908, on which work he was succeeded by Perrault's closest colleague Louis-Alphonse Venne. From 1903 Venne served as both designer-in-chief and head of the office, and when his employer died he inherited many of his clients. He designed the building of the Artisans canadiens-français in 1910–12 in partnership with Dalbé Viau, with whom he had been teamed following Venne's involvement in the preparation of ceremonies for the Eucharistic Congress in Montreal in 1910.[89] Architects were needed for this gathering of international significance, which included a grand procession through the city demonstrating the power of the Catholic Church. Joseph Venne, a favourite with the clergy, designed the impressive temporary altars on Mount Royal, while Louis-Alphonse Venne and Joseph-

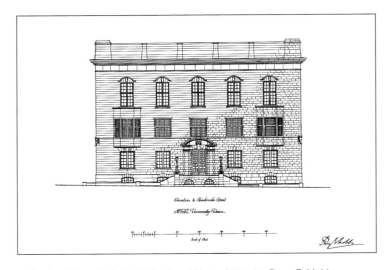

31 Student Union Hall, McGill Students' Union (1904–06, Percy E. Nobbs, architect); principal elevation. Ink on paper, 54 x 79 cm. Canadian Architecture Collection, McGill University.

Arthur Godin, both competition-winners, planned the accompanying structures.

Dalbé Viau, who in scarcely ten years of practice had acquired sound experience in the fields of residential, educational, and ecclesiastical building, completed his training with the intensive course offered at McGill University and by joining the PQAA's Sketching Club in 1905. A detailed study by André Laberge has made it possible to follow the early career of an architect from a modest background, and shows how connections in a Church-dominated neighbourhood like Mile End helped Viau get his career underway.[90] Viau and Venne were a solid team well-connected with potential clients in their social milieu; among their commissions were many churches and several schools. In 1910 they were employed by the Pères de Sainte-Croix to undertake the design for St. Joseph's Oratory (fig. 44), Montreal's largest church project, which was to continue until 1967. This impressive building, showing influences from many sources,[91] was conceived by Venne as Quebec's own basilica, a classical monument. It is noteworthy that from 1902 to 1909 he had served as a teacher at the École du Conseil des Arts et Manufactures.

Percy E. Nobbs, who arrived in Montreal from Britain in 1903, was both a practitioner and an educator, and soon made his mark as a prolific author, a very active member of the PQAA, and a competent architect. Nobbs's conviction that an architectural practice was essential to the valid teaching of architecture led him to offer his resignation at McGill in 1909. But the

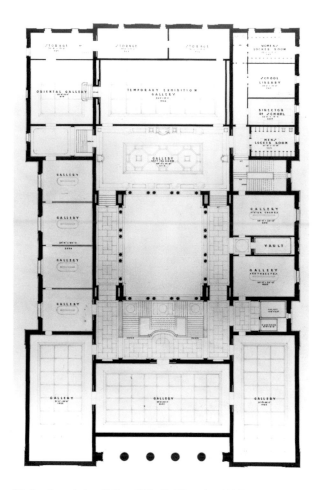

32 Art Association Gallery (1911–12, Edward and W.S. Maxwell, architects); first-floor plan, 1910. Ink and wash on paper, 93.7 x 62.2 cm. Blackader-Lauterman Library of Architecture and Art, McGill University.

33 Art Association Gallery (1911–12, Edward and W.S. Maxwell, architects); detail of the entrance colonnade, 1913. Photograph: William Notman and Son. Notman Photographic Archives, McCord Museum of Canadian History, Montreal.

university wanted his services and refused Nobbs's request, reducing his teaching obligations to studio work.[92] In 1910, after a few casual business associations, Nobbs linked his professional future to that of George Taylor Hyde, a graduate of McGill who had done further studies at MIT. Nobbs and Taylor would design many homes and schools, and their expertise in the design of schools and universities in particular would win them Canada-wide recognition.[93] Nobbs had received his first commission, the Student Union Hall at McGill (1904–06; fig. 31), barely a year after his arrival in Montreal, and based his design on the *palazzo* type, a model then fashionable in England for clubs. The resulting building was of a great simplicity, and very original for Montreal, freely mixing architectural elements drawn from a variety of sources, classical and medieval. Nobbs

was convinced that "style" is as much an expression of an artist's individuality as an expression of national character.[94] It was a new and unusual stance for Canada, and Nobbs would become its tireless exponent.

When McGill's trusted architect Andrew T. Taylor left Montreal for London, Nobbs not only designed a number of buildings for the university – including the Macdonald Engineering Building (1907–08; fig. 11), which had been destroyed by fire in April 1907 – but also advised on the physical layout of the campus. Nobbs's English-inspired buildings presented a strong contrast with the Beaux-Arts structures that, commissioned by both public- and private-sector organizations, were then flooding the city. One example was the Mount Royal Club (1904–06; fig. 62), designed by the best interpreters of

34 École des Hautes Études Commerciales (1908–10, Gauthier and Daoust, architects). Unknown photographer. Archives H.É.C.

the "American Renaissance," the celebrated firm of McKim Mead and White. Another was the Montreal Art Association Gallery (1911–12; figs. 32 and 33) by the Maxwell brothers.

As the twentieth century dawned, governments were intervening more and more in economic and social life. The City of Montreal, for example, addressed problems of public security and hygiene by studding the town with public facilities like fire stations and baths – designed in various styles, though classicism seems to have been favoured for the most prestigious buildings. The provincial government affirmed its presence in metropolitan Montreal primarily through the construction of institutions of higher learning. The decision to build the École des Hautes Études Commerciales (1908–10; figs. 4 and 34) on Viger Square came shortly before the federal election of 1908. Rumilly's

account of the decision-making process reveals what the École (and the concurrent modernization of urban infrastructure) meant politically in a riding (St. James) where the Liberal incumbent was in difficulty, and allows us to see the interplay of forces converging on the selection of an architect,[95] here Louis-Zéphirin Gauthier.

The architecture of the École des Hautes Études Commerciales contrasts with that of the École Technique (1909–11; figs. 35 and 36), which is more restrained from the standpoint of massing and decoration and more ordinary in its construction materials (yellow brick being used in conjunction with stone). The commision for the École Technique was awarded after a competition that set Maurice Perrault against John Smith Archibald, an associate of Charles Jewett Saxe.[96] Both Archibald

35 École Technique de Montréal (1909–11, John S. Archibald and Maurice Perrault, associate architects); details of the entrance elevation and section, c. 1910. Pen and ink on drafting cloth, 76.5 x 100.5 cm. Canadian Architecture Collection, McGill University.

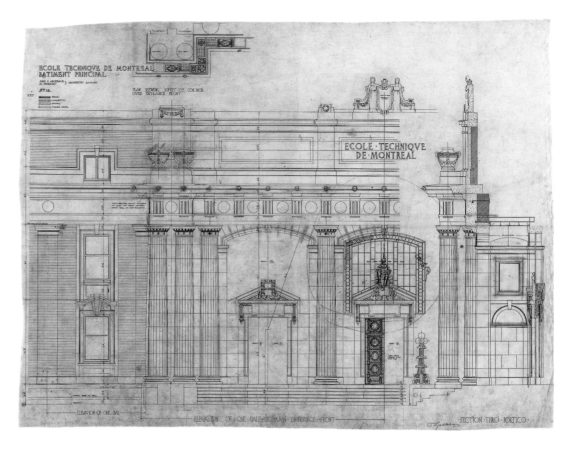

36 École Technique de Montréal (1909–11, John S. Archibald and Maurice Perrault, associate architects); ground-floor plan, 1910. Pen and ink on drafting cloth, 77.2 x 105 cm. Canadian Architecture Collection, McGill University.

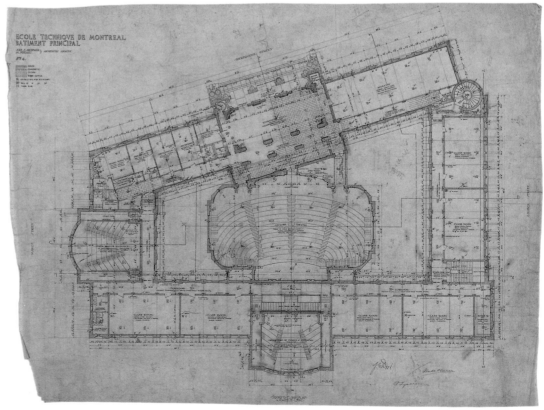

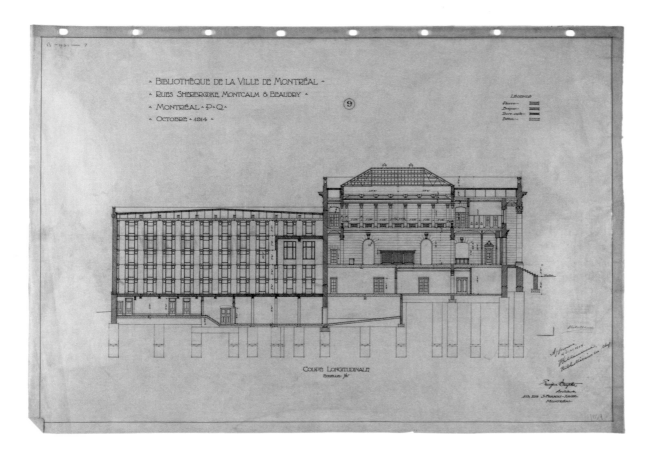

37 Montreal Municipal Library (1914–17, Eugène Payette, architect); longitudinal section, 1914. Ink and graphite on oilcloth, 69 × 99 cm. Ville de Montréal, Service des immeubles.

and Saxe had worked as draftsmen for Edward Maxwell, and in 1897 formed a partnership known for its concern for budgets, its reliable organization, and its diverse practice: single- and multi-family dwellings, office buildings, and public baths for the City of Montreal.[97] Equally Beaux-Arts in manner was the Bibliothèque Saint-Sulpice (1911–15), built on St. Denis Street in the *Quartier Latin*. In a competition organized by the Sulpicians in 1911 and open to all Roman Catholic members of the PQAA, the winning design was by Eugène Payette, selected primarily for its functionality.[98] Payette was shortly thereafter awarded the contract for the Municipal Library (1914–17; fig. 37). All these buildings were in the area of Sherbrooke and St. Denis streets and attested to the rise of the classical ideal in Montreal, though interpretation varied from architect to architect. If the Maxwell brothers had especially well assimilated classical principles prevalent in the United States, their French-speaking colleagues demonstrated a sensitivity to the more grandiloquent French tradition. The Art Association Gallery – with its compact massing, its broad smooth wall surfaces, and its neat and simple decorative motifs – was comparable to its American counterparts, although it was more modest in scale and more discreet in its urban presence.

Similar architectural qualities may be found in the buildings of Maisonneuve, a satellite of Greater Montreal. Founded in 1883, Maisonneuve had been developed by a small group of French-Canadian real-estate promoters. They were initially assisted by civil engineer and surveyor Joseph-Émile Vanier, who subdivided the land and provided the infrastructures required by the many industries attracted to the town by its especially favourable fiscal climate. But after the election of 1909, and despite the many contracts he had negotiated, Vanier fell from grace with the newly elected administration, in which Oscar Dufresne, brother of Marius Dufresne, a young engineer from the École Polytechnique de Montréal, held the important post of chairman of the finance committee.[99] Marius Dufresne became the town's municipal engineer, and from then on an ambitious program of urban beautification went forward in Maisonneuve. Plans were made for the "boulevardization" of certain streets and for the creation of a large public park, and in five short years four public buildings were erected.

The first of these was Maisonneuve City Hall (1910–12), designed by the architect Cajetan Dufort, who had completed his training through night courses at MIT in the 1890s. The other

38 Maisonneuve Public Baths (1914–16, Marius Dufresne, architect); principal elevation, 1914. Pen and ink on drafting cloth, 75 x 105 cm. Ville de Montréal, Service des immeubles.

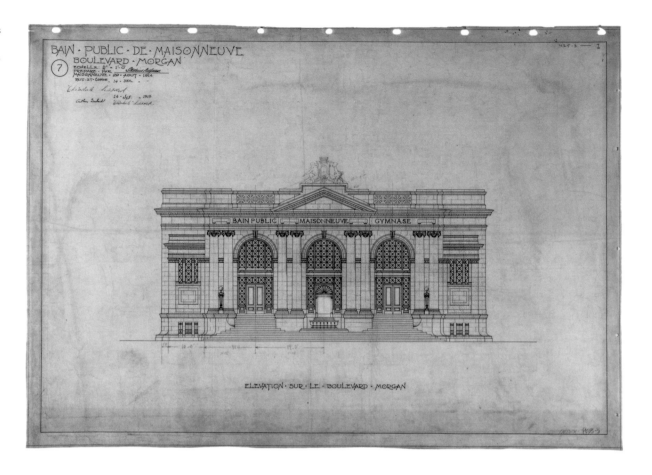

39 Police and Fire Station (1914–15, Marius Dufresne, architect), Maisonneuve; Letourneux Avenue elevation, 1914. Pen and ink on drafting cloth, 77 x 127 cm. Ville de Montréal, Service des immeubles.

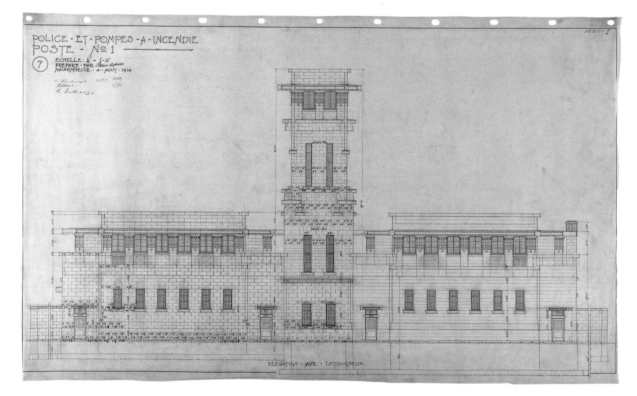

three buildings were designed by Marius Dufresne himself: the Public Market (1912–14), in the French Second Empire manner; the Public Baths (1914–16; fig. 38), whose architectural affinity with New York's Grand Central Terminal has often been remarked; and the Police and Fire Station (1914–15; fig. 39), reminiscent of Frank Lloyd Wright's Unity Temple. Dufresne doubtless knew Wright's work through Francis Sullivan, an Ontario colleague who worked for the federal government and was Wright's Canadian partner, and through publications like *The Architectural Record*. But Dufresne imitated Wright's manner without understanding its revolutionary feature, spatial continuity. Dufresne shared this eclectic approach with most of his colleagues. The double house (1915–18) that he designed for himself and his brother's family at the corner of Sherbrooke Street and Pius IX Boulevard shows the range and diversity of his universe of reference, with its allusions to the Petit Trianon and every room with a style matched to its function. An item from Dufresne's library – *The Petit Trianon*,[100] yearbook of the Boston Architectural Club – suggests the important role the United States played in the diffusion of the Beaux-Arts tradition.

Certain architects went directly to the source, one such being Jean-Omer Marchand. Only the second Canadian to study at the École des Beaux-Arts in Paris,[101] Marchand entered the École in 1893 after an apprenticeship with the firm of Perrault and Mesnard and a night course at the École du Conseil des Arts et Manufactures.[102] After a brilliant academic career he spent the next ten years in Paris,[103] returning to Montreal in 1902 at the age of thirty, secure in the possession of a *diplôme* from the French government (the first granted to a Canadian) but also in the experience he had gained at the Exposition Universelle in Paris in 1900, for which Marchand had designed the Canadian exhibit (a commission received from J. Israël Tarte, Minister of Public Works in the Liberal government of Wilfrid Laurier).[104] In partnership with the American Samuel Stevens Haskell, a former fellow-student in Paris, Marchand opened two offices, one in Montreal and one in New York City. Their first commissions came from the Sulpicians: the book repository for the libraries of the Grand Séminaire and the Collège de Montréal, where Marchand had studied, and the expansion of the Grand Séminaire's chapel. Well connected in Canadian society, Marchand was an architect of unrivalled prestige in early twentieth-century Montreal. Numbered among his clients were the Roman Catholic hierarchy and religious orders, but also governments, for whom he designed court houses, prisons, and schools.

On the advice of both the archbishop of Montreal, Monsignor Bruchési, and the superior of the Sulpicians, the Sisters of the Congregation of Notre Dame hired Marchand and Haskell to design their new mother house on Sherbrooke Street (1904–08; fig. 40). It was an astonishing choice, given the absence to date of tangible proof of the firm's competence, but it was a felicitous one for the young architects, as the Congregation became a faithful client. Though the mother house was Marchand and Haskell's first large-scale project, it was a master-stroke, outstanding among the conventual buildings designed by these architects' contemporaries in Montreal. Large and isolated, the Congregation's mother house rose majestically on its Westmount site, not far from the Sulpicians' Grand Séminaire. Its composition, with an ample and hierarchical comb-like plan, is dominated by a lofty chapel that is not, however, the major feature of the building, preceded as it is by a domed entrance, a feature as effective visually as it is functionally. Rationalist in design, in the French academic tradition, it is also technically innovative. The building's framework of reinforced concrete was clad in yellow brick of American origin, a material that would be much used for institutional architecture in Montreal.[105] Marchand also collaborated on a number of projects with local colleagues: St. Paul Hospital (1903–05) and Notre Dame Hospital (1903–11), with his former employer Maurice Perrault; the Chalet on Mount Royal (1904–06), with the Maxwell brothers; Bordeaux Prison (1907–12), with R. Adolphe Brassard; the Crédit Foncier Franco-Canadien office building (1907–09), with Alfred Arthur Cox and Louis A. Amos; the École Gabriel-Souart (1915–16), with Emmanuel Arthur Doucet and Morrissette; and the Church of St. Peter Claver (1915–18), with Joseph Venne. In 1911 Marchand barely missed out on the commission for the Bibliothèque Saint-Sulpice. His entry to the competition (fig. 41) had been inspired, as he explained, by fifteenth-century Italian architecture, and placed second with a special mention. The Sulpicians highly valued the Gothic style associated with the great teaching institutions of Europe, and deplored the overly commercial appeal of the winning entry for the Bibliothèque by Eugène Payette.[106] On the eve of the First World War, after ten solid years of work in Montreal, the Marchand-Haskell job book was completely full. To the important projects already mentioned one must add many private homes, including one for Senator Rodolphe Forget (1912–15), as well as the Académie Marchand (1909), the Académie Garneau (1910), and the City Hall Annex (1912–13).

If, in the context of closer relations between Quebec and France, Marchand began a trend that would lead future

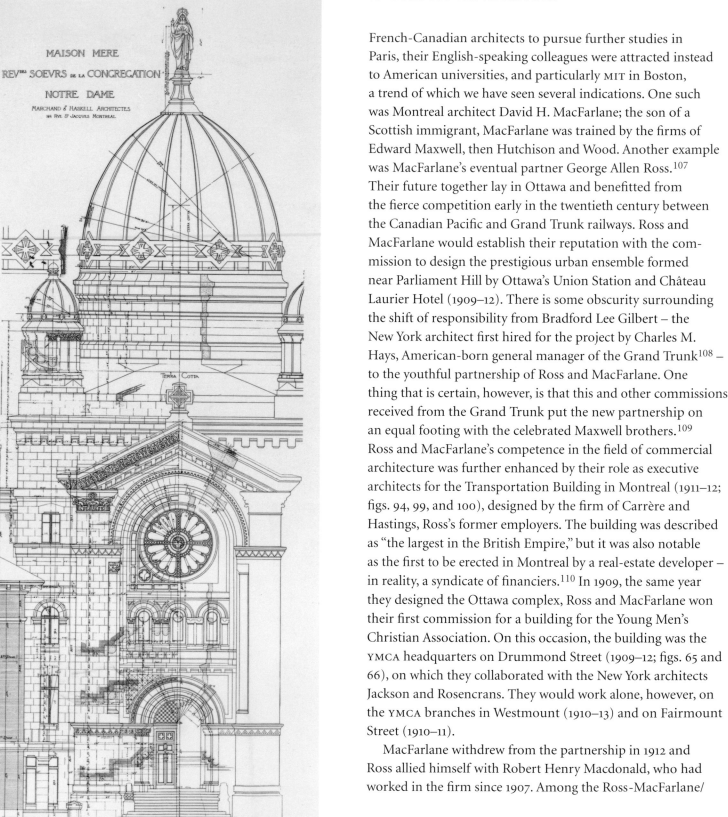

French-Canadian architects to pursue further studies in Paris, their English-speaking colleagues were attracted instead to American universities, and particularly MIT in Boston, a trend of which we have seen several indications. One such was Montreal architect David H. MacFarlane; the son of a Scottish immigrant, MacFarlane was trained by the firms of Edward Maxwell, then Hutchison and Wood. Another example was MacFarlane's eventual partner George Allen Ross.[107] Their future together lay in Ottawa and benefitted from the fierce competition early in the twentieth century between the Canadian Pacific and Grand Trunk railways. Ross and MacFarlane would establish their reputation with the commission to design the prestigious urban ensemble formed near Parliament Hill by Ottawa's Union Station and Château Laurier Hotel (1909–12). There is some obscurity surrounding the shift of responsibility from Bradford Lee Gilbert – the New York architect first hired for the project by Charles M. Hays, American-born general manager of the Grand Trunk[108] – to the youthful partnership of Ross and MacFarlane. One thing that is certain, however, is that this and other commissions received from the Grand Trunk put the new partnership on an equal footing with the celebrated Maxwell brothers.[109] Ross and MacFarlane's competence in the field of commercial architecture was further enhanced by their role as executive architects for the Transportation Building in Montreal (1911–12; figs. 94, 99, and 100), designed by the firm of Carrère and Hastings, Ross's former employers. The building was described as "the largest in the British Empire," but it was also notable as the first to be erected in Montreal by a real-estate developer – in reality, a syndicate of financiers.[110] In 1909, the same year they designed the Ottawa complex, Ross and MacFarlane won their first commission for a building for the Young Men's Christian Association. On this occasion, the building was the YMCA headquarters on Drummond Street (1909–12; figs. 65 and 66), on which they collaborated with the New York architects Jackson and Rosencrans. They would work alone, however, on the YMCA branches in Westmount (1910–13) and on Fairmount Street (1910–11).

MacFarlane withdrew from the partnership in 1912 and Ross allied himself with Robert Henry Macdonald, who had worked in the firm since 1907. Among the Ross-MacFarlane/

40 Mother house of the Sisters of the Congregation of Notre Dame (1904–08, Marchand and Haskell, architects); elevation of central bay showing main entrance and dome, 1905. Pen and ink on drafting cloth, 287 x 103 cm. Dawson College.

Ross-Macdonald projects conceived before the First World War, a notable example is the Read Building (1912–13; fig. 97), a loft building erected by a group of promoters that included Ross himself. Ross's participation was an indication of changing attitudes among architects: as professionals, they no longer held any interest in the construction process proper, while as businessmen they took an active role in commissioning designs and sharing the profits of real-estate speculation.[111] The firm's local projects, compared to those on which it was engaged outside Quebec, were fairly limited prior to 1920,[112] as was the case for another, equally promising firm: Barott Blackader and Webster.

The firm of Barott Blackader and Webster, which executed projects in Vancouver, Winnipeg, and Saint John, New Brunswick,[113] was founded in 1912 by three former employees of the prestigious New York firm McKim Mead and White: Montrealer Gordon H. Blackader, from an established local family, and two Americans, Ernest Isbell Barott and Daniel T. Webster. Blackader had obtained his b.a. in architecture from McGill, then studied at the École des Beaux-Arts in Paris. In 1912 Webster was in Montreal to supervise construction of the Royal Trust Building (1912–13; fig. 95), which had been designed by McKim Mead and White. Barott had just come to town to work for the Canadian Pacific Railway,[114] and it was from the CPR that the new architectural partnership obtained its first commissions. The firm also designed the headquarters of the Bank of British North America (1912–14; fig. 42) on St. James Street, a building notable for its references to the work of McKim Mead and White, and the St. Denis Theatre (1914–15), which were then their most substantial projects in Montreal. Large Canada-wide companies like banks and railways were precious clients for architects, as well as interesting employers. Many of the worksites then underway across Canada were controlled from Montreal.

It was as a result of his appointment as assistant chief architect for the CPR that Hugh Griffith Jones arrived in Montreal in 1908; Jones would open a private practice three years later, a case that was not unique in early twentieth-century Canada. While several American-based architectural firms were at work in Montreal, many individual American architects chose to live there as well, doubtless hoping to turn their expertise to profit due to the disproportion between Montreal's fairly small architectural community and its flourishing construction market. The United States thus displaced Britain as a talent-pool, except in the case of academic appointments, where traditional ties to Scotland and France continued to hold. Not only did it capture

41 Jean-Omer Marchand, renderer. Project for the Bibliothèque Saint-Sulpice competition, June 1911. Watercolour on paper mounted on paperboard, 38 x 30.5 cm. Bibliothèque nationale du Québec, fonds bibliothèque Saint-Sulpice.

the attention of major clients on the lookout for architectural experience, it also continued to serve as a source for architectural models – a condition that Percy Nobbs, among others, combatted in the name of a Canadian national identity. The United States became a more and more fashionable destination for Canadian students who had a special liking for the Department of Architecture at MIT. Other students chose the more distant France, whether they were well off, like Gordon H. Blackader and Harold Lea Fetherstonhaugh, or culturally predisposed to France, like Ernest Cormier, Wilford Arthur Gagnon (brother of painter Clarence Gagnon), and Lucien F. Keroack. While not all the architects who studied abroad would be able to pride themselves on great professional success in the 1920s, the vast majority of those then most prominent on the Montreal scene had completed their education outside Canada.

42 Bank of British North America (1912–14, Barott Blackader and Webster, architects), 1914. Photograph: Gordon, Montreal. Collection Canadian Centre for Architecture, Montréal. Ernest Isbell Barott Archive.

THE RETURN OF PROSPERITY, 1919–31

The First World War only exacerbated the weakening in the construction sector that had begun in 1912. The market hit its lowest point in 1918, but rebounded very rapidly at the outset of the 1920s to reach a new peak in 1928. Throughout the decade, when the scale of the old city was once again transformed – this time by the erection of the first skyscrapers – the development of the new commercial downtown intensified and reached westward. Imposing new buildings arose around Phillips Square (fig. 43) and along St. Catherine Street, where the Toronto-based T. Eaton Co. (1925–27) was enlarged into a department store to rival Morgan's and Ogilvy's, and where the Dominion Square Building (1928–30; figs. 111–13), with its innovative indoor shopping gallery, was built. Both projects were designed by Ross

and Macdonald. A little to the north, the Mount Royal Hotel (1920–22; fig. 106) had already opened its doors. Some of these new buildings were highly specialized, purpose-built for specific professional tenants. At the corner of Sherbrooke and Guy streets, the Medical Arts Building (1922–23; fig. 104), also designed by Ross and Macdonald, was devoted to medical practices and with its 10 storeys established a new limit in the downtown area, where tall buildings were dispersed rather than concentrated into a single area. The increasingly popular automobile telescoped distances and required indoor parking lots, the first appearing in the basement of the new Canada Cement Co. head office (1921–22; fig. 43), another arising behind the Drummond Medical Building (1929–30; fig. 105), since city by-laws did not permit the downtown construction of a straight-forward multi-storey parking facility.[115] The face of Montreal was being altered not only by commercial buildings, which emerged without rhyme or reason in the cityscape, but also by the wide swath cut through the very heart of the city by the Canadian Northern Railway for the building of its terminus near Dominion Square and St. Catherine Street (fig. 6). Construction also picked up in the suburbs. Westmount, whose growth had slowed, completed its array of public buildings with, among other things, a new City Hall (1922) designed by the Findlays, senior and junior. Outremont grew by leaps and bounds. There, apartment buildings and multi-family dwellings were as popular as single-family dwellings and duplexes, at least in the north end. Several architects were particularly active in Outremont during this building boom.

The PQAA in 1928 now numbered 218 members, 167 of whom were Montrealers.[116] Many were newcomers, and the number of architectural graduates was on the increase. Montreal's own schools of architecture had been active: since 1912 McGill had graduated 67 people, while the École Polytechnique and the École des Beaux-Arts had between them graduated 65.[117] Though not all architects belonged to the PQAA or worked in Montreal, the number of local practitioners had nonetheless almost doubled in a little over fifteen years, a growth matching the increase in the number of building permits issued.

Certain firms and individuals indisputably dominated the market, monopolizing a great portion of the available commissions and giving each other stiff competition: Ross and Macdonald, then the largest architectural firm in Canada; Barott and Blackader, a name retained by the firm after Blackader's death in the field in the First World War; and J.-Omer Marchand, who at the beginning of the 1920s was for a time associated with

43 Phillips Square showing, from centre to right, the Dubrule Building (1919–21, Ernest Cormier and Jean-Omer Marchand, architects), the Canada Cement Building (1921–22, Barott and Blackader, architects), and the New Birks Building (1911–12, Nobbs and Hyde, architects), c. 1930. Unknown photographer. National Archives of Canada / PA-049852.

his young and ambitious colleague Ernest Cormier. But while Ross and Macdonald and Barott and Blackader worked chiefly in the commercial sector, as did Harold Lea Fetherstonhaugh, Marchand's principal clients were various levels of state government and the Roman Catholic Church – a client with whom Joseph-Dalbé Viau and Louis-Alphonse Venne had as much success as before, if not even more.

Judging by the number of their projects, other professionals were also much in demand, though they may have lacked the prestige of some of the above-mentioned names. Several of these had been active since the beginning of the century: the American-born D. Jerome Spence and his one-time associate Hugh Vallance, both of whom built up diverse practices; the Nobbs and Hyde firm, which was kept busy with the building of the McGill campus and with many residential commissions; the architect Alphonse Piché, in business since 1903, who worked on governmental, commercial, and religious projects, particularly for the religious communities; and Ludger Lemieux and Kenneth Guscotte Rea. Still others were new to the scene. The

firm created by Alfred Leslie Perry and Morley Corbus Luke was especially active in the field of domestic architecture and executed an interesting cluster of houses in Westmount in the Garden City spirit.[118] The firm formed by the young Jean-Julien Perrault and J.-Roméo Gadbois, along with the firm of René Charbonneau, played a major role in the construction of Outremont, where architects were kept very busy indeed.

At the end of August 1924 the grandly ceremonial blessing of the cornerstone of the future basilica of St. Joseph's Oratory (fig. 44) was a glorious moment for the firm of Viau and Venne. They had won their spurs in the service of religious communities, for whom they built a great deal in Montreal and the surrounding region. Although their business did not increase after the First World War, some of their later commissions involved budgets that were extraordinarily large for their time.[119] Viau and Venne designed the largest conventual building ever to be built in Montreal. The mother house of the Sœurs des Saints Noms de Jésus et de Marie in upper Outremont (1923–25; fig. 45) resembled an Italian *palazzo*[120] in its compact massing and the

44 St. Joseph's Oratory under construction (1910–30, Viau and Venne, architects); phase I, 1927. Unknown photographer. National Archives of Canada/PA-87830.

interior courtyards of its plan. The convent had a total of 52,036 square metres of floor space, more than the great downtown towers erected shortly thereafter.[121] That comparison also affords some idea of the importance of the commission received by Ernest Cormier in 1924 to plan and build the new campus of the Université de Montréal. A prestigious assignment, in that university authorities wished to establish a "centre for Christian higher learning in the midst of a society avid for science,"[122] it was still more remarkable for its scale. The main pavilion had nearly 100,000 square metres of floor space. Montreal buildings of the 1920s tended toward gigantism.

In 1918, at the age of 33, Ernest Cormier had returned to Montreal after ten years in Paris. He had been enrolled at the École des Beaux-Arts, where he was a student in the *atelier* of Pascal, and then worked in the engineering office of Considère Pelnard and Caquot, spending some time also in Rome. Cormier's training permitted him the double title of Engineer-Architect. Cormier undertook his first important commission in Montreal working with Marchand on the Dubrule Building on Phillips Square (1919–21; figs. 43 and 46), a highly rationalist design whose stripped-down brick façade clearly expressed its concrete

post-and-beam frame.[123] Soon after, Cormier turned to the building for the newly founded École des Beaux-Arts (1922–23) on St. Urbain Street. This was Cormier's second and last collaboration with Marchand, both of whom were *diplômés* by the French government. Each would now pursue an independent career working in similar areas, as both were instilled with the French professional ideal of the architect as a designer of great civic and religious monuments – an ideal that Cormier would pursue with the greater zeal.

In 1922, Marchand and Cormier joined Louis A. Amos, D.J. Spence, and Viau and Venne on the committee of experts supervising the reconstruction of Montreal's City Hall, destroyed by fire. Marchand, who was a generation older than Cormier, had something of an advantage over him, having already gained the favour of governments, his long-time clients. In 1924 Marchand's appointment to the position of chairman of the Conseil supérieur des beaux-arts du Québec, which sponsored the province's art schools, gave evidence of his cultural prestige and credibility among politicians. Cormier was equally successful in obtaining some of the most prestigious commissions of the 1920s, designing the Court House Annex (1920–26; fig. 47),

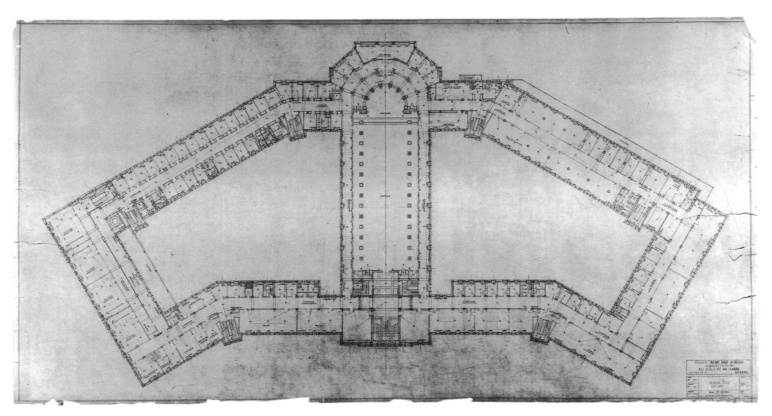

45 Mother house of the Sœurs des Saints Noms de Jésus et de Marie (1923–25, Viau and Venne, architects), Outremont; second-floor plan, 1924. Blueline print, 107 x 204 cm. Congrégation des sœurs des Saints Noms de Jésus et de Marie, Service central des archives.

in collaboration with L.A. Amos and Charles J. Saxe, and, above all, receiving the commission for the Université de Montréal in 1924.[124]

If the Court House Annex was from a formal point of view not very innovative, it nonetheless reveals its young architect's great artistic mastery – in the monumental composition of its façade, in the well-proportioned hemicycle of the entrance and the large entrance hall, in the magnificent sequences of spaces, and in the refined choice of materials. Much more daring was the main pavilion of the Université de Montréal. Its construction finally got underway in 1928 (fig. 48), on the basis of plans resulting from protracted negotiations between the architect and his client, which had surrounded itself with a committee of experts.[125] The delay involved had, however, occasioned a fruitful artistic maturation in the plans. The main pavilion of the university is considered "the first institutional appearance of a style free of historicism,"[126] and the building indeed represents an essential step in the advent of architectural modernity in Quebec, even if it finally owes more to classicism than to modernism, thanks to its overall axial composition and its very simple and restrained ornamentation.

The small hydroplane hanger (1928) that Cormier designed for Pointe-aux-Trembles, with its thin-shell concrete roof and reinforced-concrete frame, was a more radical departure. Here architectural form, building program, and construction techniques were freely articulated, as the novelty of such a commission and the site's distance from the city were both factors favouring experimentation. Cormier also designed two parish churches in the 1920s, along with a monastery and some schools for the Commission des écoles catholiques de Montréal (CECM). Marchand, for his part, also won many commissions from the CECM and, in collaboration with his colleague L.A. Amos, designed the Institut pédagogique in Westmount (1925) for the Sisters of the Congregation of Notre Dame. For the City of Montreal, Marchand designed the Généreux Baths (1926–27; fig. 9), whose swimming pool he roofed over with an interesting structure in exposed concrete. If the Institut pédagogique, very Beaux-Arts in conception, showed a tendency to formal simplicity, the Généreux Baths marked a step toward the redefinition of the status of ornament, whose figurative character was strongly affirmed here. Like the house Marchand designed for Léopold

46 Dubrule Building (1919–21, Ernest Cormier and Jean-Omer Marchand, architects); longitudinal section, c. 1920. Ink and graphite on tracing paper, 64.5 × 100.4 cm. Collection Canadian Centre for Architecture, Montréal. Ernest Cormier Archive.

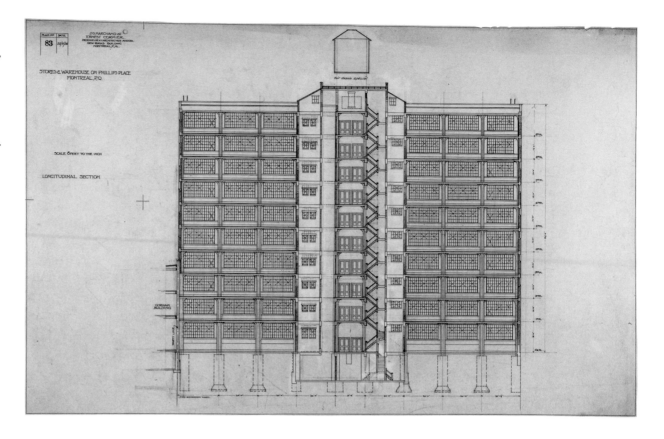

Fortier (1930) in Westmount, the Généreux Baths is evidence of an artistic enterprise that frees itself from convention not so much to embrace the rigours of technical rationalism as to orient itself to a more formal originality.

Marchand's and Cormier's commissions were thus similar in nature, and formed a contrast with the work given to Ross and Macdonald and to Barott and Blackader, which included office buildings, department stores, hotels, and residential developments. But the architectural solutions advanced by the latter two firms were of a different nature. Ross and Macdonald designed office buildings that resembled the loft type in their plan and restrained decoration – the Castle Building (1926; fig. 49) and the Hermes Building (1927) – while Barott designed two of the first skyscrapers in Montreal, the Bell Telephone Co. of Canada Head Office on Beaver Hall Hill (1927–29; fig. 116) and the Aldred Building (1929–31; fig. 50) on Place d'Armes. The two latter buildings were remarkable for their profiles and for the care devoted to their ornamentation, inside as well as out. The difference in approach between Ross and Macdonald on the one hand and Barott on the other was closely tied to the particulars of given commissions. Ross and Macdonald were exclusively commercial-speculative in approach, while Barott

was more specifically client-oriented. Barott's important buildings were associated with dynamic and prosperous companies, first Canada Cement, then Bell Telephone, and finally Aldred and Co. All of these were enterprises directed with an iron hand by their respective chairmen: rich financier Max Aitken, engineer Charles Fleetwood Sise, Jr., and businessman John Edward Aldred, the latter two American in origin.

Barott's rapport with his client is especially evident in the architecture of the Canada Cement Co. Building (1921–22; fig. 43), where the use of reinforced concrete, whether in the frame or in the partially bearing walls of artificial stone,[127] does not compromise the recourse to a dignified and severe classicism. While the Canada Cement Building, like the Bell Telephone skyscraper, was a corporate headquarters, the Aldred Building displayed the name of its individual owner, proprietor of the brokerage firm Aldred and Co. The latter had to its credit the many deals that had led to its monopoly over the production and distribution of electricity in Quebec by the Shawinigan Water and Power Co., a world-class firm that Aldred had directed since its foundation.[128] In 1929 Aldred asked Barott to design an office building for a choice location on Place d'Armes, beside the New York Life Insurance Co. Building. Two perspective drawings

47 Court House Annex (1920–26, Ernest Cormier with L.A. Amos and C.J. Saxe, architects); entrance hall, c. 1927. Photograph: S.J. Hayward Studio. Collection Canadian Centre for Architecture, Montréal. Ernest Cormier Archive.

48 Main pavilion of the Université de Montréal (1928–43, Ernest Cormier, architect); phase 1 of construction, 1930. Unknown photographer. Collection Canadian Centre for Architecture, Montréal. Ernest Cormier Archive.

49 Castle Building (1926, Ross and Macdonald, architects), c. 1928. Photograph: S.J. Hayward Studio. Collection Canadian Centre for Architecture, Montréal. Ross and Macdonald Archive.

raise a question about the role played by Barott's dynamic client in the subsequent development of the project. The first shows a tower of classical proportions, rather similar to the Bell Telephone Building, while the second (fig. 50) shows a building closer in its assertive verticality and non-historicist ornamentation to the latest Art Deco skyscrapers of New York City.[129]

Also among Montreal's earliest skyscrapers was University Tower (1929–30; fig. 119), a rental property stripped of "every architectural detail" and built by the Montreal promoter McRitchie and Black Ltd. Its concrete frame was poured in record time just ahead of the onset of winter in 1930, thanks to the efficient use of forms.[130] University Tower was designed by Harold Lea Fetherstonhaugh, a graduate of McGill who had studied and worked in Europe before going into partnership with his former fellow student James Cecil MacDougall. In the 1920s, under Fetherstonhaugh's direction, the firm received

many commissions in the commercial, religious, educational, and residential sectors.

Two fairly prolific figures in domestic architecture were Perrault and Gadbois. Jean-Julien Perrault was the son of Joseph Perrault and the nephew of Maurice Perrault, and thus belonged to a dynasty of Quebec architects that went back to the beginning of the nineteenth century. He was the first in his line to receive a higher education, first at McGill then in the United States, where he attended Columbia University, and before his return to Montreal worked in various American offices acquiring an experience in residential design – the field in which the partnership he formed with J.-Roméo Gadbois, a former collaborator with Joseph Perrault, would excel. Besides several commercial buildings erected in the city – like the imposing Thémis Building (1928) at the east end of St. James Street and the elegant Crescent Building (1931) on St. Catherine Street, one of the finest examples of Art Deco in Montreal – Perrault and Gadbois designed many residential buildings of all types and sizes, mostly in Outremont. The firm sprinted ahead as construction activity peaked in Outremont, and its accumulated experience must have been much in demand. But its success was also assured by a legal document working in its favour. In 1921 the young J.-J. Perrault married the daughter of Joseph Beaubien, mayor of Outremont. The deeds of sale for the vast property belonging to her grandfather Louis stipulated that all future plans for the land were to be approved by an architect – a task for which it named J.-J. Perrault.[131] It is no surprise, therefore, that Perrault and Gadbois became the most active firm in Outremont construction.[132]

While Perrault and Gadbois designed a great number of single-family dwellings along with some duplexes and triplexes, their main contribution was community housing, mostly in the form of apartment buildings (figs. 51 and 52). Several of the latter were located on Bernard Street, like the luxurious Royal York (1928–29), built on land purchased from the brothers of Saint-Viateur by the contractor-developer Pierre Guidazio, who with Joseph Besozzi was one of Perrault and Gadbois's main clients. Opposite the Royal York was the largest building devoted to automobile parking in Canada, the Bernard Garage (1924), opened at the initiative of a contractor turned real-estate developer[133] – a very common occurence when demand for new construction was strong. With a growing number of construction sites throughout the 1920s (more than a hundred each year),[134] Outremont was a place where architects prospered. The alliances that a small number of architects were able

50 Aldred Building, final version (1929–31, Barott and Blackader, architects), 1934. Watercolour and graphite on paperboard, 77 x 53 cm. Collection Canadian Centre for Architecture, Montréal. Ernest Isbell Barott Archive.

51 Apartment building for Bernard Street (1922–23, Perrault and Gadbois, architects), Outremont; principal elevation, 1922. Blueline print, 58 x 70 cm. Archives de la Ville d'Outremont.

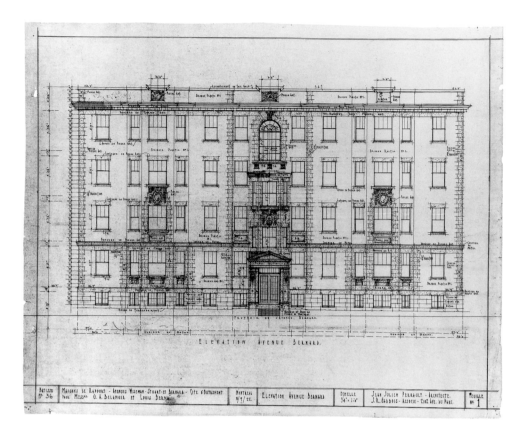

52 Apartment building for Bernard Street (1922–23, Perrault and Gadbois, architects), Outremont; second-floor plan, 1922. Blueline print, 58 x 70 cm. Archives de la Ville d'Outremont.

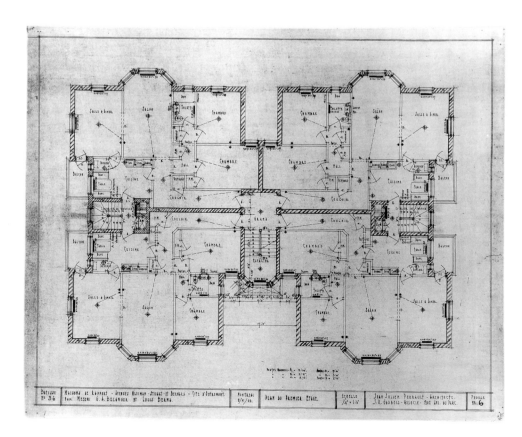

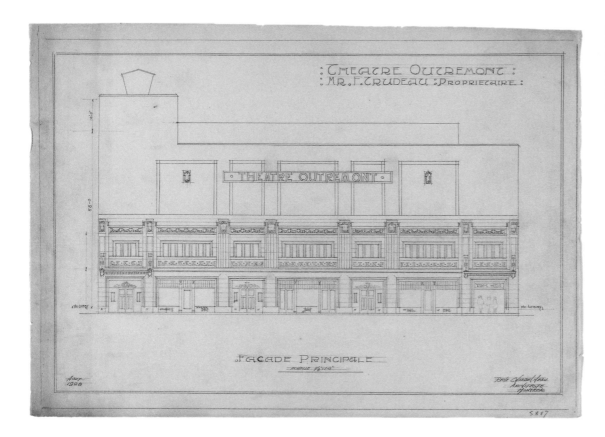

53 Outremont Theatre (1928–29, René Charbonneau, architect); principal elevation, 1928. Graphite on tracing paper, 38.2 x 54.4 cm. Collection Canadian Centre for Architecture, Montréal. Charbonneau et Charbonneau Archive.

to form with the most important of the city's developers and the common cultural reference of classicism reinforced the architectural unity of the built environment, which was also predetermined by Outremont's by-laws and regulations and the standardization of construction methods.[135]

Like his colleagues Perrault and Gadbois, René Charbonneau, in practice since 1909, accumulated an impressive number of building permits in Outremont.[136] An associate of Louis-Napoléon Audet, Charbonneau designed the Montcalm (1914), one of the first of the Bernard Street apartment buildings. In the 1920s he cooperated with two of the most important developers in Outremont in the construction of many single- and multi-family units. And in collaboration with the great interior decorator Emmanuel Biffra, Charbonneau designed the town's most significant cultural building, the Outremont Theatre (1928–29; fig. 53).

This intense building activity, both downtown and in the suburbs, was endangered by the stock market crash of 1929. Within a few months, the bottom fell out of the construction market too, startling architects still buoyed up by the euphoria of the 1920s. One instance of this was the Architects' Building

(1930–32), designed by Ross and Macdonald, a real-estate venture financed by a group headed by George Allen Ross hiself.[137] The top three storeys of the 16-storey tower were reserved for the firm of Ross and Macdonald itself (figs. 54 and 55), which was run according to the example of R.H. Macdonald's former employer George Post, who had updated the model created by Richard Morris Hunt, rationalizing, fragmenting, and specializing it.[138] The partnership thus completely epitomized the ideal of the American Beaux-Arts-trained architect, who combined architectual erudition with technical and administrative expertise. There was a great disparity between the roughly one hundred employees of Ross and Macdonald and the ten or so people who had worked for Perrault Mesnard and Venne, one of the most productive firms at the end of the nineteenth century, located in the Banque du Peuple in St. James Street. The floor plan for the offices of Perrault Mesnard and Venne (fig. 56), still very small, suggests the work of a multi-disciplinary, hierarchical team of a practical size that some were reluctant to renounce. Ernest Cormier, for one, though burdened with the largest construction job in metropolitan Montreal, made do throughout his long career with a small, all purpose, and loyal work-force.[139]

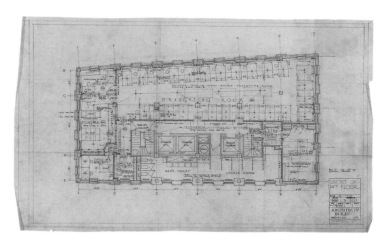

54 Architects' Building (1930–32, Ross and Macdonald, architects); plan of the 14th floor with offices for Ross and Macdonald, 1931. Graphite on tracing paper, 45 × 67 cm. Collection Canadian Centre for Architecture, Montréal. Ross and Macdonald Archive.

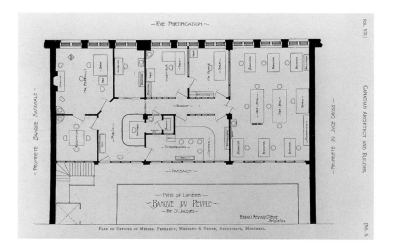

56 Banque du Peuple Building (1893, Perrault Mesnard and Venne, architects); plan of offices for Perrault Mesnard and Venne, c. 1895. From *The Canadian Architect and Builder* (August 1895).

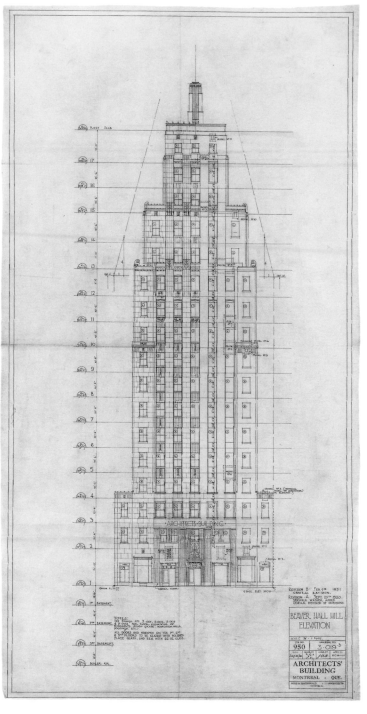

55 Architects' Building (1930–32, Ross and Macdonald, architects); Beaver Hall Hill elevation, 1930. Pen and ink on drafting cloth, 92.6 × 47.7 cm. Collection Canadian Centre for Architecture, Montréal. Ross and Macdonald Archive.

Cormier and Marchand were without question Montreal's, if not Canada's, most innovative architects in the early twentieth century. That said, their contributions were not of the same order as those by the period's European or American "pioneers." The cultural milieu in which Cormier and Marchand evolved was still rather amorphous and, above all, conservative, and in a sense the interruption of construction of the main pavilion of the Université de Montréal in 1931 and the erection of the Architects' Building at a net loss symbolize the fragile success of early twentieth-century Montreal architects. Only a limited number of firms would survive the economic crisis of the 1930s.

OVER THE HALF-CENTURY OF MONTREAL'S HISTORY covered here, not only did the built environment of the city grow taller and spread out, the city redefined itself as certain functions migrated to the margins of the old city core, while others, often of a more specialized nature, were housed in new buildings that took the place of old ones torn down with little hesitation. The vitality of the construction sector derived as much from the vigour of industry and commerce, stimulated by transatlantic and transcontinental trade, as from the religious fervour fanned by an all-powerful Roman Catholic Church. By the end of the period architecture had become a profession whose Quebec practitioners had quintupled thanks to the transformation of the mode of education: higher education more and more replaced apprenticeship, and the transmission of the trade within families was no longer a common factor subtending practice.

Montreal architects formed a diversified community within which the traditional British influence was displaced by Americans drawn north by the construction boom and by opportunities to build for nation-wide railway and financial institutions. In spite of this foreign presence, which continued through 1930, it must be noted that Montreal architects were widely successful in reclaiming architectural commissions for themselves, turning to France and more often to the United States for the knowledge they needed to establish their command of the market. For the first time, they exported their expertise on a national scale. If their architectural output showed a formal assimilation of new design programs and technical advances, the decorative schemes they proposed were still largely retrospective and showed the dead hand of stylistic programs that had been worked out elsewhere in the world, more in the United States than in Britain, at least in the area of commercial architecture. It seems clear that eclecticism was a characteristic feature of an architectural practice subordinated to a real-estate

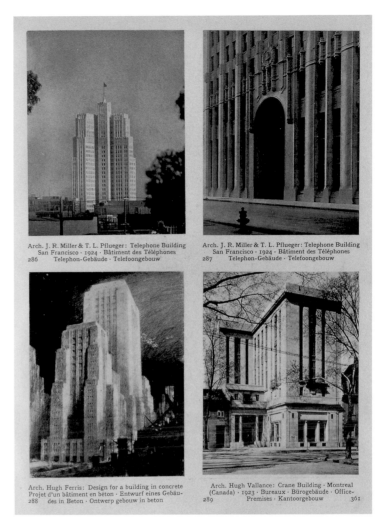

Arch. J. R. Miller & T. L. Pflueger: Telephone Building
San Francisco · 1924 · Bâtiment des Téléphones
286   Telephon-Gebäude · Telefoongebouw

Arch. J. R. Miller & T. L. Pflueger: Telephone Building
San Francisco · 1924 · Bâtiment des Téléphones
287   Telephon-Gebäude · Telefoongebouw

Arch. Hugh Ferris: Design for a building in concrete
Projet d'un bâtiment en béton · Entwurf eines Gebäu-
288   des in Beton · Ontwerp gebouw in beton

Arch. Hugh Vallance: Crane Building · Montreal
(Canada) · 1923 · Bureaux · Bürogebäude · Office-
289   Premises · Kantoorgebouw   361

57 Clockwise from upper left, Telephone Building in San Francisco (1924, J.R. Miller and T.L. Pflueger, architects); Telephone Building in San Francisco, entrance detail; Crane Building in Montreal (1921–22, Hugh Vallance, architect), and project for a building in concrete (Hugh Ferriss, architect). Page 361 in *Moderne Architectuur* (Amsterdam, c. 1927). Collection Canadian Centre for Architecture, Montréal.

market in which architects affirmed their competence by the attention they paid their clients and by their capacity to express the new diversity of urban functions. In that regard, it is startling to note that for European observers dazzled by artistic avant-gardes, the symbol of architectural modernism in Montreal was the Crane Building (1921–22), a "stripped classical" edifice on Phillips Square that was reproduced in J.G. Wattje's *Moderne Architectuur* (1927; fig. 57),[140] one of many works published in Europe in the 1930s to promote the new architecture.

PRESTIGE AND PROFESSIONALISM:
THE CONTRIBUTION OF AMERICAN ARCHITECTS

Isabelle Gournay

IN 1870 WHEN THE PRESIDENT AND THE SECRETARY of the Montreal Board of Trade returned from a study tour of the United States, they returned to Montreal "quite convinced" that the organization's headquarters could not be designed by a Canadian architect.[1] What, we might ask, convinced them? Why also, risking charges of a lack of "patriotism,"[2] did the Board engage the American architect Richard Morris Hunt (1827–1895) as the sole judge of a competition that would openly favour American entries, eventually retaining the services of Shepley Rutan and Coolidge over any local or even Canadian entrant?[3] The heads of the Board of Trade, which was the major representative of the Montreal business community, had various motivations, some personal, some related to wider issues. On the one hand, the kind of economy and society then developing in the United States held a tremendous appeal, and was becoming increasingly attractive to an Anglo-Protestant upper class for whom recourse to American expertise had become the norm. On the other, the reputation and the competence of the American architects in question had been established beyond any doubt.

Hunt was, in a sense, the dean of American architects. The first American to train at the École des Beaux-Arts in Paris and the first to adapt French academic methods in his New York studio, he was also a founding member and later president of the American Institute of Architects and the man who designed for the Vanderbilts. He had done a great deal to advance architectural institutions in the United States well beyond the state of those in Canada, and his achievements had been recognized by many architectural associations in Europe.[4] In short, Hunt brought to the Board of Trade competition an international prestige to which no Canadian architect could lay claim

58 Canada Life Insurance Co. Building (1894–96, Richard Waite, architect) and Canadian Bank of Commerce Building (1907, Darling and Pearson, architects), 1914. Photograph: William Notman. Notman Photographic Archives, McCord Museum of Canadian History, Montreal.

59 Board of Trade Building (1891–93, Shepley Rutan and Coolidge, architects; Edward Maxwell, supervising architect). Photogravure: Sabiston phot. eng. From *The Montreal Board of Trade: A Souvenir* (1893). Collection Canadian Centre for Architecture, Montréal.

The professional standing of George Forter Shepley, Charles Hercules Rutan, and Charles Allerton Coolidge was based on several things. The three architects took over the established practice of Henry Hobson Richardson upon the latter's death in 1886, completing several of his unfinished projects, notably the impressive Chamber of Commerce in Cincinnati.[5] A Chamber of Commerce of their own design followed in 1892 for the firm's home city, Boston, a major architectural centre at the time. Shepley Rutan and Coolidge was a transcontinental practice, with projects that stretched from the Stanford University campus in California to the New Orleans central library. In addition, the "Richardsonian Romanesque," of which the firm was in a sense the heir, was popular beyond the United States; appreciated in Montreal, its influence was also beginning to be felt in Europe and as far off as Australia.[6]

Shepley Rutan and Coolidge could not, however, rest on its laurels, as its work-load declined with the completion of Richardson's projects.[7] Montreal offered new opportunities. Although it was not one of the firm's most original buildings,[8] the "Florentine Palace" of St. Sacrament Street[9] (completed in 1893 under the supervision of Edward Maxwell, then an employee in the Boston firm; figs. 59 and 60), with its flat roof,

expansive arched windows, and efficient interior design provided a dynamic and cosmopolitan image of the Montreal business community – in a word, a "modern" image, far ahead of, for instance, the competing entry by J. Rawson Gardiner published in the *Canadian Architect and Builder*.[10]

The Board of Trade competition represents one of the earliest and most significant indications of the direct and massive importation of American architecture, a trend first observed in Montreal and Toronto. The steady flow of American architects to Montreal, from the 1880s until the Depression, is a phenomenon that has been studied only summarily, the emphasis falling on the negative reactions of local architects. That controversy should be seen as a kind of distorted reflection of the cultural, intellectual, and even moral prejudices of neighbouring countries. Clearly, convictions on both sides were deeply rooted. Americans chose to think of Quebec residents (and French Canadians in particular) as backward,[11] and American architects, whose work in Montreal represented only a fraction of their practice (except in the case of Bruce Price and Richard Waite), made little effort to establish personal contacts in the city.[12] Their Canadian colleagues would not have spoken of "humiliation" nor complained about the (very few) designs that

60 Board of Trade Building (1891–93, Shepley Rutan and Coolidge, architects; Edward Maxwell, supervising architect); entrance. From *The Montreal Board of Trade: A Souvenir* (1893). Collection Canadian Centre for Architecture, Montréal.

passed illegally through customs had they not felt injured by the lack of reciprocity in the face of rampant American protectionism.[13] In fact, commissions were more often offered to American architects than sought by them. The few architectural firms aiming at a truly trans-Canadian practice – Richard Waite, Carrère and Hastings, Thomas Lamb, Stevens and Lee – chose to establish their offices in Toronto, where the Ontario Association of Architects required them to maintain a branch and where they had more business than in Montreal. The controversy, however, was more often fuelled by financial frustration[14] or by personal friction between client and architect, or colleagues of different nationalities and cultures, than it was a systematic rejection of American architecture. Proof to the contrary can be seen in

the number of American architects who chose to settle permanently in Montreal, where they were both accepted and successful – men like Howard C. Stone (who arrived in 1896), David Jerome Spence (1901), Hugh Jones (1908), and Ernest Barott (1911). After the real-estate panic of 1913 they, along with their Montreal-born and American-trained colleagues, would be the main purveyors of Americanism in architecture.[15]

Despite a few jarring lapses in the technical and design skills the Americans brought with them, their presence seems to have been largely beneficial, and thus warrants a study unto itself, focusing, as in the preceding essay, on the mechanics of patronage and the architect's role in creating a metropolitan image. By examining the complementary notions of prestige and professionalism and by exploring the relationships between socio-economic conditions and personal contacts, the predominance of Montreal's Anglo-Protestant elite among clients and of the major New York firms among commissioned architects becomes even clearer.[16] Architecturally speaking, Montreal stood within the sphere of New York City; no designs came out of Chicago and the influence of Daniel Burnham, his partner John Welborn Root, and his successors Graham Anderson Probst and White, so apparent in Toronto, was negligible in Quebec. An instructive look at the process by which Americans were awarded commissions between 1880 and 1930 will be followed by a closer examination of a few of the buildings they built in Montreal prior to the First World War.[17]

AT THE SERVICE OF BIG BUSINESS

In the late nineteenth century commissions in Montreal went not only to leading architects from New York City but also to distinguished practitioners from Boston and lesser-known architects from Albany, Buffalo, and Cleveland. Subsequently the New Yorkers took the lion's share, their direct influence reaching its peak between 1901, when work started on the Bank of Montreal on Place d'Armes (figs. 76 and 77), and 1913, the year its neighbour, the Royal Trust Building (fig. 95), was completed – both projects by McKim Mead and White. While his Wall Street Stock Exchange was under construction, George B. Post was given the commission for the Montreal Stock Exchange on St. François Xavier Street (1903–04, Edward and William Maxwell supervising architects; fig. 61).[18] Similarly, the two cities' Ritz-Carlton hotels were entrusted to Warren and Wetmore (figs. 78 and 79). In a country where their profession seems to have been held in higher esteem than it was in Canada,

the New York architects we have just mentioned moved in the highest circles and were on terms of equality with their millionaire clients. In Great Britain and France too the reputation of New York firms was growing, especially those whose partners had been trained in France.[19] New York's pre-eminence was yet again demonstrated by the hiring of York and Sawyer to build Montreal's first skyscraper, the Royal Bank of Canada Building on St. James Street (1927–28; figs. 114 and 115).

The Americans were competing with local architects in very particular arenas. Their best clients were members of Montreal's Anglo-Protestant elite. These included the heads of railway companies, especially if American-born like Sir William Van Horne and Charles M. Hays, inclined to commission American architects so as to bolster their credibility in the eyes of their powerful competitors to the south. The heads of local insurance companies and banks, however, generally hired architects from Montreal or Toronto, perhaps counting on the patriotism of less cosmopolitan shareholders lower on the social scale. Such reservations did not apply, however, to "supra-national" commissions such as the head offices of the Bank of Montreal and the Royal Bank. The English-speaking business community also hired Americans for the Transportation Building (1911–12, by

Carrère and Hastings with the Toronto architect Eustace Godfrey Bird, Ross and MacFarlane acting as supervising architect; figs. 94, 99, and 100),[20] the Ritz-Carlton Hotel (1911–12; fig. 79), and several commissions outside the commercial sector. The latter included Bruce Price's Royal Victoria College on Sherbrooke Street (1895–99), financed by Lord Strathcona, and the Mount Royal Club (1904–06; fig. 62), designed by McKim Mead and White.

Since Americanization also affected the entertainment industry, many upscale theatres were designed by architects from the United States. Among this group were several New York specialists in the genre: for instance John Bailey McElfatrick, who designed Her Majesty's Theatre (1898–99),[21] and Thomas W. Lamb, whose world-wide practice began with Canadian commissions that included Montreal's Loew's (1917; fig. 63) and Capitol (1921, now demolished) and the renovation of the Français (1920).[22] A favourite architect of the American movie-theatre chain Keith-Albee was Albert Westover of Philadelphia, who designed the Imperial (1913; Ulric Asselin, associate architect, Ross and MacDonald, supervising architects).[23] Thomas Lamb's major rival, Howard Crane, who was to build over two hundred theatres in the United

·MOVNT ROYAL CLVB · MONTREAL CANADA ·
· SHERBROOKE STREET ELEVATION · SCALE ONE INCH EQVALS FOVR FEET ·

MSKIM MEAD & WHITE NEW YORK ASSOCIATED
HVTCHINSON & WOOD MONTREAL ARCHITECTS

62 Mount Royal Club (1904–06, McKim Mead and White, architects; Hutchison and Wood, associate architects); principal elevation, 1904. Pen and ink on drafting cloth, 49.7 x 92.7 cm. Collection of The New York Historical Society.

States and Canada, constructed the Palace (1921)[24] and, in partnership with Charles D. Goodman, the cinema in the Amherst Building (1926).[25]

Other areas of American activity in Montreal were less dominated by New Yorkers. In the Square Mile, Rotch and Tilden of Boston built the residences of both Andrew Alexander Allan on Stanley Street (1890–91, Edward Maxwell, supervising architect) and J.S. Allan on Sherbrooke Street (1889–90; now demolished),[26] Bruce Price designed the James Ross house on Peel Street (1890–92; fig. 64),[27] and Richard Waite remodelled the home of Reid Wilson on Sherbrooke Street (1900–02).[28] Ecclesiastical commissions were few. Around 1890 two Methodist churches were built in the working-class district of southwest Montreal by Sidney Rose Badgley, an Ontarian established in Cleveland.[29] The 1920s brought the Ascension of Our Lord Church on Sherbrooke Street in Westmount, designed by Maginnis and Walsh of Boston, the favourite architects of the American Catholic hierarchy,[30] in collaboration with Edward J. Turcotte.

With regard to loft-style buildings and factories, few designs were imported from the United States even though a large number of American industries had established branches in Montreal. The Boston engineering firm Lockwood Greene and Co., reputed for reinforced-concrete construction, and the architectural firm of Densmore and Leclear built structures for two American companies, Gillette on St. Alexander Street (1911; fig. 97)[31] and Salada on St. Lawrence Boulevard (1921–22, in collaboration with Alphonse Piché).[32] In 1916 Albert Kahn of Detroit was responsible for the Ford assembly plant in Montreal.[33]

There were some "targeted" sectors in which American experts provided "reliable" buildings: Jackson and Rosencrans of New York designed the Central Branch of the YMCA on Drummond Street (1909–12, Ross and MacFarlane, associate architects; figs. 65 and 66),[34] while Stevens and Lee of Boston and Toronto were entrusted with the Royal Victoria Hospital's Ross Memorial Pavilion (1915–16; with Kenneth G. Rea) and its Women's Pavilion (1925–26), as well as Notre Dame Hospital (1922–24, in collaboration with Alfred Hector Lapierre; 1930, with Louis-Auguste and Pierre-Charles Amos).[35] No public commission went to American architects. Their low profile in non-commercial sectors was due to political considerations, socio-cultural attitudes, and tastes. In addition, hiring an architect with a practice in the United States to design a private house was an expensive luxury when the "American look" could be achieved at home by local architects and contractors.

63 Loew's Theatre (1917, Thomas Lamb, architect); longitudinal section, 1916. Graphite on tracing paper, 105 x 137.5 cm.
Avery Architectural and Fine Arts Library, Columbia University in the City of New York.

64 James Ross house (1890–92, Bruce Price, architect), c. 1900. Photograph: William Notman. Notman Photographic Archives, McCord Museum of Canadian History, Montreal.

THE ENIGMA OF RICHARD WAITE

Before construction began on the New York Life Insurance Co. Building in 1887 (figs. 2 and 73) and on Windsor Station early in 1888 (fig. 68), buildings by Americans were the exception in Montreal. There had nevertheless been two significant precedents: Notre Dame Church on Place d'Armes (1824–29; fig. 2), designed by James O'Donnell, an Irish immigrant established in New York City, and the Windsor Hotel on Dominion Square (1876–78; fig. 72), the work of William W. Boyington.[36] The first sign of the "popular demand and craze of the day for Americanism" denounced in the *Canadian Architect and Builder*[37] came with the Standard Life Assurance Co. Building on St. James Street (1883–85; demolished in 1929 after a fire in 1922), designed by Buffalo architect Richard Waite.[38] Waite enraged not only the Province of Quebec Association of Architects,[39] which refused him registration, but also local contractors and suppliers, whom the architect had passed over in favour of fellow Americans.[40] Such strong reactions make the case of Waite worthy of investigation.

The London-born Richard Waite set up practice in Buffalo after an apprenticeship with New York architect John Kellum, a specialist in cast-iron commercial design. From there he

mounted a campaign of penetration into eastern Canada, starting in nearby Toronto,[41] and in 1880 was chosen as a judge in the competition for Ontario's parliament buildings at Queen's Park, Toronto. Five years later when the Ontario government asked him to decide between the submissions of two local firms, Waite judged both designs too costly and awarded himself the commission. He completed it in 1892, at an enormous deficit. This scandal did not, however, prevent him from receiving further commissions in Montreal for the Canada Life Insurance Co. Building on St. James Street (1894–96; fig. 58)[42] and for the Grand Trunk Railway Head Office on McGill Street (1899–1902; fig. 67).

The success of this "provincial" architect is harder to justify than that of Shepley Rutan and Coolidge. Waite's clients in Montreal were companies that were not locally based. Moreover, it was probably not by chance that the owners of Standard Life and the Grand Trunk Railroad were, like Waite, of British origin. His presentation drawings impressed clients, and according to the *Canadian Architect and Builder* this was the true explanation for the commission from Canada Life:

It is another proof of how an interior design can be made to look well.... I hear that designs much superior in composition were submitted by Montreal architects in private competition, but unfortunately their authors overlooked the absolute necessity of rendering their drawings brilliantly and effectively in order to be successful under the circumstances.[43]

Waite certainly possessed a keener flair for public relations than most of his Canadian colleagues, as may be sensed from the rhetoric he employed in introducing the Grand Trunk building to the readers of *The Railway and Shipping World*:

The elevations are treated Neo-Greco [sic], that is a modern adaptation of Greek & Roman architecture, not a servile copy, but from the spring whence marvellously simple and logical inspirations of the art of the Greek are obtained, for architecture is required to modify its forms in accordance with the conditions of life, of temperature, & plan of required arrangement. The sculptural parts are concentrated upon features supported by dignified and quiet masses of walls; and while Greek will have the French phase.[44]

Waite's output did not conform to any specific trend, and it is difficult to define the course of its evolution. Atypical though it was, it did demonstrate that "bigness of ideas" that Percy

65 Central Branch of the YMCA (1909–12, Jackson and Rosencrans, architects; Ross and MacFarlane, associate architects); principal elevation, 1912. Pen and ink on drafting cloth, 89 x 121 cm. Collection Canadian Centre for Architecture, Montréal. Ross and Macdonald Archive.

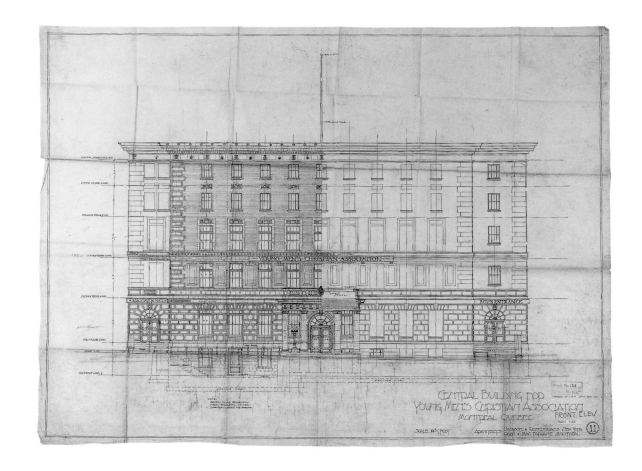

66 Central Branch of the YMCA (1909–12, Jackson and Rosencrans architects; Ross and MacFarlane, associate architects); lateral section A–B through the entrance hall, 1910, revised 1926. Pen and ink on drafting cloth, 84.4 x 139 cm. Collection Canadian Centre for Architecture, Montréal. Ross and Macdonald Archive.

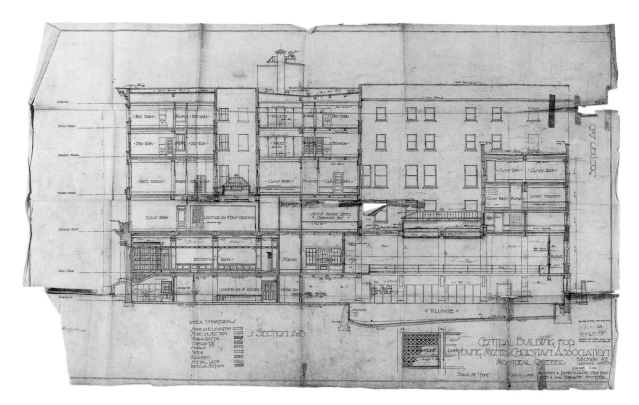

67 Grand Trunk Railway Head Office (1899–1902, Richard Waite, architect), c. 1900–25. Photograph: Albertype Company. Albertype Company/ National Archives of Canada/ PA-032051.

Nobbs, normally reluctant to pay tribute to Canada's southern neighbours, praised in the work of McKim Mead and White.[45] Waite was not afraid to behave arrogantly and upset the established order of things. In Toronto, Hamilton, and Montreal he offered insurance companies a monumental and flamboyant architecture. The imposing high-relief decoration of Montreal's Standard Life building is closer to that of the latest public buildings in Old Montreal – like the nearby Post Office on St. James Street and City Hall – than it is to the district's plainer, simpler office buildings. Indeed, Waite's extant buildings still show a high quality of workmanship, doubtless because "he himself oversaw the work,"[46] as *Le Prix Courant* assured its readers regarding the Grand Trunk Head Office. The interiors of these buildings have an elegant, luxurious look that was to characterize the best of American construction in Montreal.

BRUCE PRICE AND THE PICTURESQUE

Bruce Price is the American architect whose career was most greatly affected by his work in Quebec, which proved to be very different from his production in the United States.[47] Price's initial popularity among Montreal's wealthiest business leaders was based mainly on his designs for houses and hotels, while his work for railway companies was limited to the design of "parlour cars" for two railroads, the Pennsylvania and the Boston & Albany. Harold Kalman emphasizes the close but sometimes antagonistic relationship that existed between Price and Sir William Van Horne, a self-made man who was clearly happy to have a self-taught architect as his designer. Price, the outsider, brought an apparently novel ethno-cultural approach to Montreal's debate over architecture.[48] A francophile, he attempted to convey the French origins of the city in the design of both Windsor and Viger stations, while in his plans for Royal Victoria College he invoked the Scottish background of McGill University.[49]

68 Windsor Station (1888–89, Bruce Price, architect) from the corner of Peel and La Gauchetière, 1889. Photograph: William Notman and Son. Notman Photographic Archives, McCord Museum of Canadian History, Montreal.

69 Viger Station-Hotel (1896–98, Bruce Price, architect), c. 1901. Photograph: William Notman and Son. Notman Photographic Archives, McCord Museum of Canadian History, Montreal.

Windsor Station (fig. 68), which opened early in 1889, does not reflect Price's true ambitions. To increase the impact of a building with a fairly limited footprint, he first used the picturesque and monumental style that was becoming the predominant approach in the design of city railway stations in the United States, a combination of Richardsonian Romanesque and Renaissance Revival.[50] Based on his entry to the Cincinnati Chamber of Commerce competition (1885), Price's first proposal of 1886 was for a brick and elaborately sculpted terracotta building topped by a clock tower (fig. 70).[51] According to Price, "Whatever is picturesque in design should be accomplished by the exigencies of the site rather than deliberately made."[52] In the mid 1880s, picturesqueness was therefore justifiable in the relatively unbuilt area at the southwest corner of Dominion Square, where small houses rubbed shoulders with the Gothic-Revival Church of St. George. In the built design, the tower became lower and Price de-emphasized pitched roofs and dormer windows: "After the building had been raised to the cornice I was required to completely change my roof. It had been designed with a high sloping roof with great dormer windows which would have given the building a character it now lacks."[53] He also employed the local grey limestone, rough-hewn in massive blocks. As Kalman points out, the style followed here was not the lively, abstract Romanesque Revival of Richardson's later work, but the more hesitant approach of his previous decade.[54] In holding Price to a milder course of action than he

was used to, the Canadian Pacific Railway, beside its concern to get an affordable building that was suited to the climate, appears to have sensed that the initial design clashed with the modernization and monumentalization underway in Montreal. A more generic, more "modular" station would lend itself much better to expansion.

For the Viger Station-Hotel (1896–98; fig. 69), Van Horne and Price eventually reached a consensus: the client welcoming the architect's picturesque ethno-culturalism, the architect giving more consideration to the client's budget. Price seems to have been pleased with his design:

There is no detail in this building, which depends for its effect wholly upon masses of the design, the breadth of wall, and the sequence of the windows. The lower part serves as a railroad station, the upper as a hotel. It seems to me that here is a common-sense picturesque handling of the subject. The situation of the building calls for more than simple treatment, and its purpose forbids anything that might appear incongruous.[55]

The Viger Station-Hotel, like the Château Frontenac Hotel in Quebec City (1892–94), represents "another example of the same application of the early French chateau to modern requirements."[56] Both hotels legitimized the Château Style in an urban setting and ensured its success in other major Canadian cities. The two buildings had an obvious impact on Montreal

70 Windsor Station (Bruce Price, architect); proposed Windsor Street elevation, 1886.
Photolithograph: Robert A. Welke. From *Building* (March 1888).

71 Dominion Square with the YMCA Building (1889–91, Fuller and Wheeler, architects) and St. James's Cathedral, c. 1894. Photograph: William Notman. Notman Photographic Archives, McCord Museum of Canadian History, Montreal.

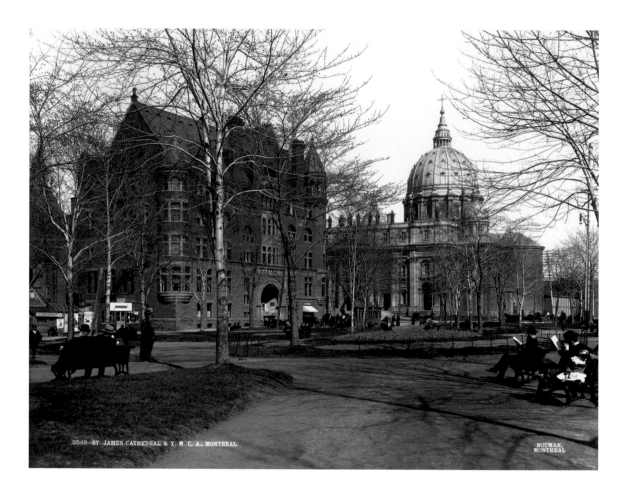

architects – the Maxwell brothers, Ross, MacFarlane, and John S. Archibald all built hotels in this style. However, they appeared too late to have much influence on later construction in Montreal, and had little impact on what Price himself would build in the United States, both of which took a more classical line.

AMERICAN EXPERTISE IN QUESTION

In theory, the advantage of hiring an American architectural firm was that it would offer solutions still new to Canada but already tested at home, while providing a level of experience that would permit the construction of sturdy, fireproof buildings with multiple functions on time and within budget. The importing of "ready-made" solutions, however, was at times problematic, and local architects were not slow to point out the occasional slip.

In 1889 *American Architect and Building News* reported that the YMCA's construction committee, which included Henry Birks and the chief engineer of the Harbour Commission, intended

"with praiseworthy and Christian humility ... to surpass all other similar associations in the splendor of their new building and the perfection of its arrangement."[57] The High Victorian Gothic building that had opened in 1873 on Victoria Square, and was already out of date, would be abandoned and a new building erected on Dominion Square (fig. 71). The new YMCA was to measure up, both literally and figuratively, to the almost completed St. James's Cathedral, and would include shop and office space for lease on the ground floor in order to make the venture profitable.[58]

Having just completed its home-town YMCA building, the Albany firm of Fuller and Wheeler, which was slightly better known in the United States than Waite, was called in. The Richardsonian character of Albany's YMCA, with its hint of Queen Anne Revival, was emulated in Montreal, especially in the treatment of elevations. Certainly Albert W. Fuller, who published illustrations of his major buildings in several portfolios entitled *Artistic Homes in City and Country*[59] (a kind of self-advertisement not yet practised by Montreal architects),

72 Windsor Hotel (1876–78, William W. Boyington; annex, 1905–07, Bradford Lee Gilbert and Henry Janeway Hardenbergh, architects), c. 1906. Photograph: William Notman and Son. Notman Photographic Archives, McCord Museum of Canadian History, Montreal.

produced pleasing façades that confirm his reputation as a residential architect.[60] But in the course of the YMCA's construction, "the whole centre portion of the interior" collapsed.[61] According to *American Architect and Building News*, the architects had scrimped on the walls and overused cast-iron columns unable to withstand the extremes of Montreal's climate, and whose weight, especially given their off-centre placement, could not be supported by the masonry below.[62] Equal blame seems to attach to both architects, who had not supervised the construction site stringently enough, and contractor, a Syracuse firm that had replaced another firm from this city whose bid had come in well below those from local builders but who had gone bankrupt in the interim. To avoid further fiascos of this nature, local architects were increasingly called in to supervise construction sites.

With the extension to the Windsor Hotel (1905–07; fig. 72) – a collaboration between renowned New York architects Henry Janeway Hardenbergh, builder of the Waldorf-Astoria (1891–93, 1895–97) and the New York Plaza Hotel,[63] and Bradford Lee Gilbert – Montreal was again a 'fashion victim.' The perpendicu-

lar wing overshadowing the original building respects neither its proportions nor its ornamentation, and it is conceivable that the person in charge of the project had never set foot in Montreal.[64] The extension employed the already outdated steep-pitched roof in the Parisian manner popularized by Hardenbergh in the Martinique Hotel in New York (1897) and the Willard Hotel in Washington (1901). This choice came as something of a surprise to the anonymous columnist of the *Canadian Architect and Builder* – none other than Percy Nobbs – who wrote that it was of "a type which our reading of the building act had led us to believe was prohibited in Montreal owing to danger to the public from ice falling from the eaves." Nobbs went on to say that

In the matter of design the elevations do not aspire to much....
Not unnaturally the placing of this work has re-awakened to some extent the old question of whether United States architects should be excluded from practicing in Canada till such time as this amiable republic shall see fit to permit Canadians to practice in their free and enlightened reservations.[65]

THREE GREAT ACHIEVEMENTS
STAND THE TEST OF TIME

There were nonetheless many American-designed buildings, resulting from harmonious architect-client relationships, that were well-built and suited to their sites and programs. Three of them still standing on prime sites bear a distinctive architectural and historical significance. The first was commissioned by the New York Life Insurance Co., then launching its new policy of expansion and real-estate investment on a transatlantic scale.[66] Company management realized that architectural excellence attracts both tenants and policy holders and hired the Babb Cook and Willard office of New York to design its branches in Montreal (1887–89), St. Paul, and Minneapolis (both completed in 1890).[67] At that time the firm was closely linked to McKim Mead and White, the architects that New York Life chose to design its branches in Omaha and Kansas City (these identical buildings were both built between 1887 and 1890).[68] George Fletcher Babb had a great reputation as a teacher, and had been approached by the Massachusetts Institute of Technology (MIT) to help create the first school of architecture in the United States.[69] Walter Cook was an active and respected member of his profession both locally and nationally, and had been one of the first American architects to study in Paris, training, like Richardson, in the *atelier* of the "rationalist" Émile Vaudremer. The firm's technical expertise was provided by Daniel Wheelock Willard, an MIT-trained mechanical engineer.

This team of client and architects had few scruples about designing a building that stood out from its surroundings, competing with Notre Dame Church (fig. 2). They favoured red sandstone imported from Scotland (the base, of the same colour, was of Thousand Islands granite) over the local limestone.[70] The exterior of the New York Life Building embodied "no distinctive style,"[71] and presented the challenge that faced every architect of the period: the design of an unusually tall façade (fig. 73). Openings were as high and wide as the load-bearing masonry permitted, and the windows of the upper three storeys were grouped in impressive arcades similar to those of the warehouses for which Babb Cook and Willard were already well known.[72] The high-relief decoration (horizontal bands, lions' heads, shields, and corner turrets), executed in a colour to match the sandstone, were of American-made terracotta, a material new to Montreal. Decorative notes of great elegance were provided by the porch sculptures executed by Henri Beaumont, and by the mosaic floors in the hall, by Herter Brothers of New York City.

Although the structural design was not unusual for such a tall building (metal was used only to reinforce the floors and the roof), the New York Life Building nevertheless set new standards for technical excellence and comfort in Montreal workplaces. American-made hollow bricks, which offered protection against fire, were used for the partitions and flooring. The building contained several hydraulic elevators and a combination of gas and electrical lighting with its own basement generator. Though imported from the United States, the plumbing and mechanical fittings were installed by local construction companies. Two large water tanks were housed in the observatory tower, which also held "the finest and most extensive law library in Canada, owned by the company, which has been placed there for the use of its tenants, who are for the most part leading lawyers."[73]

Nearby on Place d'Armes, the Bank of Montreal, one of North America's financial giants, was finding itself short of space in the building designed half a century earlier (1845–47) by John Wells, and made the decision to expand northwards towards Craig Street. The board of directors asked architect Andrew Taylor, a nephew of the bank's vice-president and the designer of its first renovations in 1885[74] (fig. 74), to bring in a major American firm. Taylor recommended McKim Mead and White, whose Bowery Savings Bank in New York City, completed in 1895, had marked a turning-point in bank architecture.[75] A commission of such magnitude was flattering for the New York architects and opened up new markets.

After a visit to Montreal in 1900, Charles McKim seems to have assumed responsibility for the spatial arrangements and the decorative scheme[76] (figs. 75 and 76): the old banking hall was partly refashioned as a foyer and entrance hall; a passageway spanning Fortification Lane led to the new banking hall – an enormous space, at the time the largest in North America, whose clerestory windows and coffered ceiling recalled the early Christian basilicas of Rome. This T-shaped public area was articulated by colonnades using the same intercolumniation and Corinthian orders as Wells had employed on Place d'Armes. The severity of the volumes is softened by the natural lighting and the choice of materials – dark-green polished granite for the pillars and bronze for the capitals. The impression of "dignified simplicity,"[77] so suitable to the image the bank wished to project, is equally apparent on the Craig Street façade (fig. 77), with its flattened ornamentation using Neo-Grec roundels as metopes. McKim Mead and White also renovated the original building, reconstructing the collapsed dome using the Guastavino method[78] and rearranging the workspace around

THE MONTREAL BUILDING NEW YORK LIFE INSURANCE CO

73 New York Life Insurance Co. Building (1887–88, Babb Cook and Willard, architects). Engraving, c. 1890. Collection Louis Melzack, Université de Montréal.

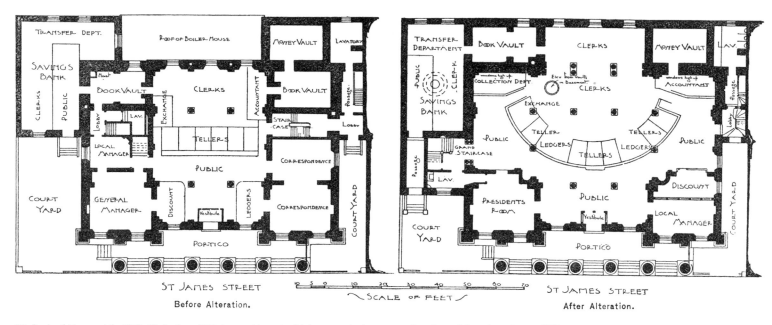

ST JAMES STREET
Before Alteration.

SCALE OF FEET

ST JAMES STREET
After Alteration.

74 Bank of Montreal (c. 1885–89, Andrew T. Taylor, architect in chief, renovation); comparative plans of first alteration, c. 1885.
From *The American Architect and Building News* (April 1887).

75 Bank of Montreal (1901–05, McKim Mead and White, architects;
Andrew T. Taylor, associate architect); ground-floor plan of second alteration
and annex, 1904. Pen and ink on drafting cloth, 80 x 68.75 cm.
Collection of The New York Historical Society.

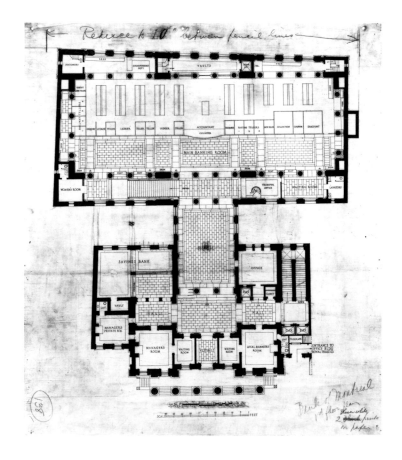

76 Bank of Montreal (1901–05, McKim Mead and White, architects;
Andrew T. Taylor, associate architect); vestibule. Unknown photographer.
Collection of The New York Historical Society.

77 Bank of Montreal Building (1901–05, annex, McKim Mead and White, architects; Andrew T. Taylor, associate architect); Craig Street façade, 1906. Photograph: Query Frères. Query Frères/National Archives of Canada/PA-053139.

the dome. As Howard Shubert notes, "the monumental entrance portico that remained from John Wells's earlier bank was justified, in a sense, as never before by the addition of McKim Mead and White's four-storey banking hall."[79] Not only were the main decorative elements imported from the United States, but, to achieve the standard of workmanship the architects were noted for, McKim Mead and White brought in the Boston general contractor Norcross, with whom they had often worked.

Despite some friction on the worksite[80] the New York firm emerged from this experiment in triumph, and in 1904 received commissions for another bank-extension from the National City Bank of New York and to design new buildings for the New England Trust Company in Boston and the Girard Trust Company in Philadelphia. It was also rehired by the Bank of Montreal to design its Winnipeg branch (completed in 1911), and soon after returned to Place d'Armes to produce the Royal Trust Building (1912–13, supervising architect Daniel T. Webster of Barott Blackader and Webster; fig. 95). A perfect example of a "semi-public" building,[81] the Bank of Montreal Annex introduced a new scale for bank architecture in North America.[82] According to the *Architectural Record*, it was the type of building that helped to "establish a higher standard of popular taste."[83] In its first issue, the avant-garde review *Le Nigog* devoted to it an overall laudatory article that ended with the assessment "No twisted lines or superfluous ornamentation. This is an elegant

and sumptuous building in which the principles of art are nowhere contravened."[84] Perceived as being "a great success with the Montreal public,"[85] this edifice introduced and legitimized what Percy Nobbs called "rarefied classic ... with all the Beaux Arts claptrap chastely omitted."[86] That trend was seen also in the Maxwell brothers' Montreal Art Association Gallery (fig. 33), in Eugène Payette's Bibliothèque Saint-Sulpice, and in the Court House Annex designed by Ernest Cormier (fig. 47). In Canada's metropolis, the popularity of the Bank of Montreal Building opened the way to prestigious commissions for former employees of the firm, not only the New Yorkers Carrère, Hastings, Warren, York, and Sawyer but also Ernest Barott and his early associates.

The construction of the Ritz-Carlton Hotel came about through the desire of Montreal business leaders such as Sir Herbert Holt and Charles Hosmer to build a luxury hotel on a more intimate scale than the Windsor. The Ritz-Carlton Development Company of London recommended Warren and Wetmore, who had just completed the Manhattan Ritz-Carlton at the corner of Madison Avenue and 46th Street (fig. 78).[87] That firm was then at the peak of its success, largely due to the social contacts of Whitney Warren, who was related to the Vanderbilts, and the business acumen of Charles Wetmore, a lawyer by training. Collaborating with Reed and Stem on the Grand Central Terminal project, Warren and Wetmore transformed the area around it by erecting large hotels like the Belmont (the first-completed, in 1906).

A comparison of Montreal's Ritz-Carlton on Sherbrooke Street (1911–12, in collaboration with Fred Garfield Robb; fig. 79) with its "big brother" in Manhattan demonstrates how Warren and Wetmore succeeded in preserving the best of the earlier design, while imaginatively adapting it to a different setting.[88] The European-style marquee and the arcaded top storey were retained. The Montreal façade, however, was not as high and was less grandiose, with the omission of the *piano nobile* colonnade. Its tripartite composition was better-balanced (as in New York, the mezzanine floor, clearly expressed in the elevation, included two hairdressing parlours and staff areas). The cladding of grey limestone accented with matching terracotta gave a more luxurious and refined look than the New York stone-brick-stone "sandwich." The L-shaped plan and the quieter character of the neighbourhood made it possible to add a terrace and a Dutch garden to the restaurant. The formula introduced in New York of a deliberately modest entrance hall was repeated on a smaller scale. It entailed elevators and a reception desk that were not

78 Ritz-Carlton Hotel (1910, Warren and Wetmore, architects), New York City; main façade. Photogravure. From *The American Architect* (February 1911).

79 Ritz-Carlton Hotel (1911–12, Warren and Wetmore, architects), Montreal; main façade, 1915. Photograph: William Notman and Son. Notman Photographic Archives, McCord Museum of Canadian History, Montreal.

overly prominent; a vestibule used as a tea-room and adorned with potted palms, opening onto a beautifully shaped elliptical diningroom; a ballroom with balcony and mezzanine; and an oak-panelled bar and café. Along Sherbrooke Street as on Madison Avenue, "gilding and gaudy marble" were yielding ground to a more intimate use of the pale colours that Charles Wetmore believed lent "simplicity and dignity."[89] The hotel offered 180 rooms with bathrooms that were more spacious than those in the New York Ritz-Carlton – half the bathrooms had windows providing daylight and fresh air, in keeping with the architects' notions of cleanliness and hygiene – as well as 27 suites with a sitting-room fireplace. Employing local contractors and local materials, Warren and Wetmore brought a new standard of elegance, comfort, and cosmopolitanism to Montreal hotels.

The new Bank of Montreal Building and the Ritz-Carlton Hotel afford ample proof that the more accomplished American

architects had nothing more to learn from their European counterparts. The prestige and professional reputations of McKim Mead and White and of Warren and Wetmore were strengthened by their Montreal projects. In the years preceding the First World War Canada's metropolis served as the testing-ground for a new, purer monumentality that would spread to Great Britain and throughout the Empire. Although the established American architects who contributed to Montreal's cityscape took no personal part in the debate discussed in the following essay, their work nevertheless stimulated it and often dictated its direction. American designs, numerically only a small part of the local construction market, had nonetheless a considerable impact upon Montreal's image as a metropolis. Their importance will be further explored in the essay on commercial gigantism.

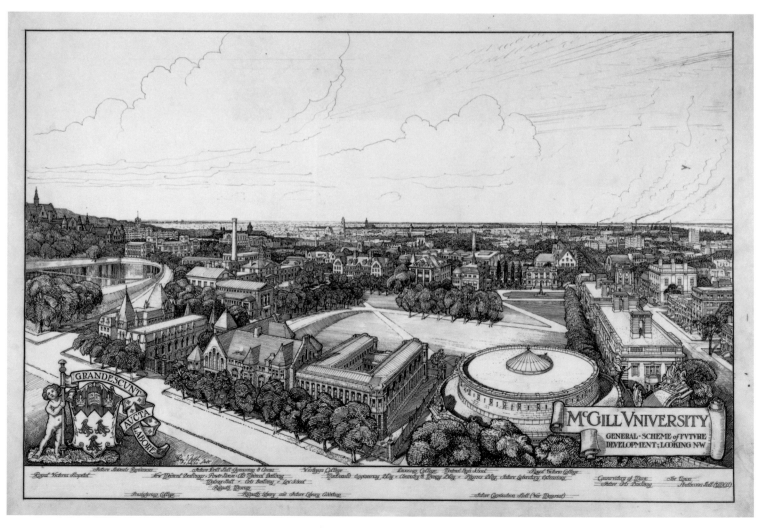

80 Percy E. Nobbs, draftsman, Project for the development of McGill University campus (Nobbs and Hyde, architects), 1920.
Ink on tracing paper, 84 x 123 cm. Canadian Architecture Collection, McGill University.

BEAUTIFICATION VERSUS MODERNIZATION

France Vanlaethem

France Vanlaethem

AS THE TWENTIETH CENTURY APPROACHED, architecture in Montreal underwent profound changes as new building types and modern construction techniques were introduced into a booming construction market. It was during this period, moreover, that architects united to form a professional organization that boasted a growing and increasingly educated membership. Despite the modernization of the practice, however, architectural culture was slow to free itself from inherited models, as the stylistic eclecticism of the buildings of the period illustrates. That attachment to tradition was evident also in the architectural debate of the time, intensified by the appearance of specialized journals, although less so in Canada given the few Canadian periodicals in the field.[1] The press, however, was not the only forum in which architects could conduct the discussion that enabled them to adjust their ideals and principles as the practice of architecture was transformed by political and economic change. The professional association afforded another means, both in facilitating the exchange of ideas and in generating a new solidarity among the architects. Architectural schools likewise played a major role, for behind every training program lay a particular definition of architecture. Discussion of the issues of the utility or the ideals of architecture echoed the international scene and spread to the various agents involved in the building of the city.

One such architectural debate of the late nineteenth and early twentieth centuries will be discussed here, through a study of the opinions expressed and positions adopted in news items and in articles by Montreal architects published in specialized journals, in the minutes of meetings of the Montreal-based Province of Quebec Association of Architects (PQAA), and in the training programs of the city's various schools of architecture.

FORUMS OF DEBATE

The modernization of architecture, both in the organization of the profession and in the emergence of a specialized press, took place relatively late in Canada as compared to other industrialized countries. The launch of *The Canadian Architect and Builder, a Journal of Modern Construction Methods* (1888–1908; *CAB*) came almost half a century after the appearance of the pioneer publications *Architectural Magazine* (1834–39) in London and *Revue générale de l'architecture* (1840–88) in Paris.[2] Produced in Toronto, *CAB* was edited by C.H. Mortimer, a one-time newspaper journalist whose career took a new direction under the impetus, it appears, of the vitality of the construction industry in the late 1880s.[3] In both form and content, the *CAB* was similar to the many regional architectural periodicals then being started across the United States, all modelled on Boston's *American Architect and Building News* (1876–1938), the first American architectural journal to achieve a lasting presence.[4] The result of new developments in printing and communications, journal publishing eased the dissemination of architectural ideas, thanks to the regularity of issues, the breaking-up of material into articles, and the participation of many authors. Hitherto, the main sources of knowledge in Quebec had been architectural treatises and, after 1840 especially, pattern books.[5]

Defending architects' interests was not the only objective of the *CAB*. As its subtitle indicated, this illustrated monthly was aimed also at civil and sanitary engineers, as well as plumbers, decorators, contractors, manufacturers, and merchants working in the construction industry.[6] Moreover, its editorial content was interspersed with numerous advertisements for building materials. Its appearance in January 1888 shortly preceded the formation of Canada's first professional architectural organizations, of which it became the official mouthpiece: the Ontario Association of Architects (OAA), founded in 1889, and the PQAA, founded the following year. Based in Toronto, the journal maintained a correspondent in Montreal, and in 1893 announced the opening of a permanent office in the Temple Building,[7] the St. James Street home of several architectural firms. The journal's Montreal content, however, remained minimal, consisting mostly of regular letters, news and annual reports of the PQAA, the rare illustration of plans or built projects, and the texts of lectures given by Montreal architects. Most of these contributions were unsigned, and identifying their authors today is difficult. From 1901 on, however, the regular contributors were mentioned by name: the director of McGill University's school of architecture

Stewart H. Capper, his successor Percy E. Nobbs, the architect Alexander F. Dunlop, and the landscape architect Frederick G. Todd.[8] Publication ceased in 1908 a few months after the journal was sold,[9] a demise that may have been pressured by competition from *Construction* (1907–34), a new Toronto periodical whose editorial approach and extensive illustration were perhaps designed somewhat more with the architect in mind. The technical content of the *CAB* was picked up by *The Canadian Contract Record*, later renamed *The Contract Record and Engineering Review* (1890–1985).

Toronto was also the home of the Royal Architectural Institute of Canada, formed in 1908 to defend the interests of architects across the country. It would eventually found *The Journal of the Royal Architectural Institute of Canada* (1924–59), which included news of interest to the profession, both provincial and national, and also documented Canadian architectural production, for the most part with no attempt at criticism. Only a few members of the PQAA contributed; most of Quebec's architects seemed reluctant to put pen to paper. Among the exceptions were Ramsay Traquair and Percy E. Nobbs, both already well known for their contributions to various general and specialized publications. Nobbs, a well-rounded professional who was at once practitioner, educator, and theorist, wrote for Canada's two town-planning journals: *Town Planning and Conservation of Life* (1914–21) and *The Journal of the Town Planning Institute of Canada* (1921–31). Traquair was a regular contributor to Quebec's emerging art press.

Le Nigog (1918), published in Montreal over a period of only a few months, was among the province's first art journals. One of the review's founders was an architecture graduate from Montreal's École Polytechnique in 1911. An enthusiastic francophile from an established family, Fernand Préfontaine – like the publication's other editors, musician Léo-Pol Morin and writer Robert de Roquebrune – had experienced the artistic exuberance of pre-war Paris.[10] In the library of his Westmount home, the young architect gathered around him a small group of artists and intellectuals from which the review's contributors would come. Several architects were among this first multidisciplinary salon: Jean-Charles Drouin and Aristide Beaugrand-Champagne (also from the École Polytechnique's first graduating class), Scottish-born Montrealer John Roxborough Smith, and Professor Traquair.[11] The enthusiasm of this small circle contrasted sharply with the standstill that had been reached, after several years of war in Europe, in construction activity and architects' associations, both in Quebec and nationally.

In the first decades of its existence, the professional association served not only as a mechanism for defending architects' interests, but also as a forum and a tribune. Indeed, the 1890 *Act to Incorporate the Province of Quebec Association of Architects* characterized its main goal in the following terms: "the acquirement and interchange of professional knowledge amongst its members, and more particularly the acquisition of that species of knowledge which shall promote the artistic, scientific, and practical efficiency of the profession of architecture."[12] Members of the PQAA met at regular meetings of an often very sociable nature. Specialized committees were formed, some for purely professional purposes, others aimed at encouraging the exchange between Association members of ideas and knowledge, and also at promoting a particular conception of architecture and architects with the general public and political authorities. The PQAA organized public events of various kinds, from 1894 mounting annual exhibitions of drawings and photographs of built or planned architectural projects at the city's most important cultural institution, the Montreal Art Association Gallery.

The PQAA maintained close ties with the architecture departments of McGill University and the École Polytechnique, both of which had been created at its instigation. Most of the directors of the two schools and many of their teachers were very active within the Association. The basic operation of the Association was entrusted to a handful of the faithful working under an annually elected president, who came generally from the group's more highly esteemed members. Not designed solely to advance the architectural knowledge of the membership, the PQAA's public and educational activities were also intended to reinforce the authority and prestige of the architect in the eyes of the public, and of building patrons in particular. Although some PQAA board members complained of poor participation in organized gatherings, many were delighted with the new solidarity and spirit of emulation that such events occasioned.[13] Questions about the fundamental nature of architecture and the status of the architect were now central issues of debate.

ARCHITECTURE AS A PROFESSION

The act that in December 1890 legally constituted the PQAA broadly marked the boundaries of the territory of architecture ("the erection of public and private buildings") and specified the profession's threefold "artistic, scientific, and practical" nature,[14] but unlike the draft document submitted by the PQAA

in October of that year, it said nothing about the role of the architect.[15] While these definitions reconciled the interests and viewpoints of various members of the construction industry, it did not address the social utility and ideals of architecture. These outstanding issues, which the profession itself strove to resolve – explicitly through formal discourse and implicitly through collective practice – were the focus of a discussion that began to reverberate within the PQAA, soon to be echoed in the pages of the professional press.

The educational program drawn up by the PQAA is revealing: as described by Alexander C. Hutchison, a member of the education committee, at a board meeting held in October 1891, it consisted of courses, lectures, and occasional tours of important buildings.[16] None of these measures, however, could take the place of the proper training program that Hutchison hoped to see established within a university context.[17] In response to the growing need for training, a number of architects began to share their expertise and knowledge with colleagues both young and old. In 1892, weekly talks on architectural styles and classes in pen-and-ink drawing began.[18] In addition, lectures were given during the Association's monthly and annual meetings, some of which were published in the *CAB*.

In the first of those published texts, which appeared in 1892, Montreal architect John Rhind maintained that every member of the profession should be a businessman first, a practical man second, and finally an artist. Rhind nevertheless stressed that it was the third quality that distinguished the architect from the engineer and the contractor, and while artistry was a gift that could not be taught, it might be developed by exposure to the fundamental, "pure" source of art, the Old Masters of Europe.[19] Andrew T. Taylor shared Rhind's opinion, later noting that architecture was one of the fine arts.[20] Taylor was one of the most vocal members of the PQAA in its early years, and this much-admired Scottish architect spoke frequently of the principles underlying the art of architecture, stressing the importance of artistic authenticity, harmonious proportions, and truth in construction. He also shared his extensive knowledge of historical works, expressing an appreciation of Westminster Abbey equalled only by his admiration for Christopher Wren, the greatest of England's Baroque architects. Taylor was the author of the book *Towers and Steeples Designed by Sir Christopher Wren*.[21]

Another regular lecturer at PQAA meetings was Alexander Cowper Hutchison. In 1896, recently returned from a visit to the Italian peninsula and Sicily, he conveyed his impressions of the masterpieces of Western and Oriental art he had seen there. His colleague Joseph Venne, by contrast, focused on more practical questions, such as the development of the architectural plan and the aesthetic value of mouldings.[22] The main objective of these instructional activities and lectures – mostly on archeological and occasionally on technical subjects – was to shape the image of the architect as a well-informed technician and a skilled designer, one who coupled an extensive and eclectic knowledge of artistic sources with sound technical know-how. The modern professional would be distinguished from the craftsman by his rationally acquired and carefully applied knowledge and by his adherence to an ideal of impartial service.

The World's Columbian Exposition that was held in Chicago in 1893 had an impact upon opinion both in the United States and in Canada, consolidating certain convictions and introducing new priorities. Andrew Taylor, Edward Maxwell, and probably Alexander Hutchison, as well, returned from the event dazzled by the new Beaux-Arts ideal the Exposition embodied.[23] At the annual PQAA convention held in September 1893, Andrew Taylor declared his admiration for the "White City," describing the Columbian Exposition as a veritable paradise in the heart of Chicago's urban chaos and marvelling at the event's positive influence on the public attitude toward architecture: "It is an undoubted triumph for architecture, and it has opened the eyes of thousands to the possibilities which lie in the work of our profession, to which they were previously blind."[24] A year later, musing about the "city of the future" and the ways in which its sanitation and external appearance could be improved, Taylor acknowledged the utility of building regulations and the need for a certain aesthetic control of urban development.[25] He thus brought to the fore two subjects that in the coming years would be the chief preoccupations of the PQAA: revision of the municipal building code and city beautification. Beside these basic issues, other more specifically professional concerns of the Association were the development of a code of ethics, the drafting of regulations for architectural competitions, and the establishment of a professional fee schedule.

THE CONTROL OF CONSTRUCTION

During the 1890s, the regulation of building in Montreal triggered an exchange of ideas that brought about the creation of the city's first true municipal building code. Those involved in the debate included not only the PQAA and municipal authorities, but others concerned with questions of public security,

hygiene, and property and real-estate values. The proceedings that led to this achievement cannot be retraced here in any detail, but the principal steps, given the architectural implications of their outcome, are worth summarizing. The PQAA had tackled the subject of building inspection from the very start, forming a committee to review construction regulations in September of 1891.[26] It was after a request from the City of Montreal, in May of 1893, that PQAA members sat to study a document prepared by municipal inspector Lacroix modifying the existing regulations, a process that demanded several meetings. In April 1895, following a second reading, the PQAA submitted a revised document, but it was not immediately taken under consideration by city council with a view to adoption.[27]

The need for such regulations, which were aimed primarily at fire prevention,[28] became particularly urgent with the serious public-health problems created by urban expansion and overcrowding, problems compounded by the dangers of an often uninformed use of new techniques and materials.[29] As in other major cities of Europe and North America, in the mid 1890s studies were conducted of the living conditions of Montreal's working-class, conditions widely denounced as unhealthy. The best-known and most rigorous of these was carried out by the industrialist Herbert Brown Ames, a leader in the municipal-reform movement. Ames published his results in 1897 in a work entitled *The City Below the Hill* [30] – a reference to the industrial neighbourhoods situated downhill from the wealthy residential area known later as the Square Mile nestled at the foot of Mount Royal. The specialized press also carried several reports of collapsed buildings and of the devastating effects of fire, especially on steel structures. Building accidents did not happen only in the big cities, where architects were more daring than in Montreal; the collapse of the 6-storey Montreal Street Railway building, for instance, was a serious blow to the career of the prominent architect John William Hopkins.[31] Frequent and often devastating fires – like the one that destroyed the Board of Trade building and some thirty other downtown structures on 23 January 1901 – continued to pose a serious threat. Only days after that event, on 4 February 1901, city council finally adopted by-law number 260, concerning construction.

In 118 articles, the new by-law laid out regulations governing the siting of buildings, construction techniques, and procedures for public control. It stipulated the creation of an independent building-inspection department within the municipal government, to be headed by an architect with at least ten years of practical experience – a position held first by Alcide Chaussée.[32]

A building-permit mechanism was also introduced that required each application to be accompanied by plans and estimates – a measure that, in theory at least, guaranteed work for members of the PQAA. Further, the by-law established categories of buildings ranked according to their capacity to withstand fire; not restricted to the stipulation of approved building materials, it specified methods of construction as well. It also limited buildings to 10 storeys, a height limit that had already won broad consensus across North America;[33] it was a measure designed to address several practical concerns, including the limited efficiency of existing fire-prevention methods and the need to protect the property values of already built structures from the effects of the shadow – both literal and figurative – cast by tall buildings.[34] The 10-storey maximum met with the approval of most PQAA members.

Though Montreal architects were generally opposed to skyscrapers, an exception was the director of McGill University's school of architecture, Stewart H. Capper, who in 1898 gave a memorable lecture in defence of the "tall building," which somewhat echoed the famous article by Louis H. Sullivan, though the architectural approach favoured by Capper was different, focusing on the technical rationality of the structure rather than on verticality.[35] The widespread opposition to height that then characterized the architectural profession was rooted in a lingering attachment to traditional monumentality. Moreover, in their plans for tall buildings architects were slow to relinquish the conventional forms of the temple, the palace, and the city hall. Another factor in this resistance was the ambivalence – a mixture of resentment and fascination – felt by many architects toward the United States, a country where technical limitations were constantly being overcome and the source of Canadian architects' main competition. In Quebec, unlike, for instance, France,[36] engineers (of whom there were relatively few in 1890) were not major rivals of architects. The initiative taken by the PQAA in establishing municipal regulations would secure for architects a substantial role in the construction industry. While the by-law, which determined building alignments, site, and height, was one major means of controlling urban form, the town plan was another. This became an issue as the specialist replaced men like John Ostell – architect, surveyor, lumber merchant, and manufacturer – the author of Montreal's master plan of 1842.[37]

CITY BEAUTIFICATION

Despite the PQAA's ongoing preoccupation after 1894 with the appearance of the city, it did not create its Municipal Improvement Committee (MIC) until 1906.[38] Composed of some of the Association's most active members, this group did not limit itself to discussion, but oversaw the production of a set of ambitious urban plans for the metropolis. Close to a number of civic organizations that advocated municipal reform in Montreal, the MIC played a role in the early development of Canadian town planning. During the 1890s, the PQAA's involvement in this area had not advanced beyond repeated requests that the municipal government set up an arts commission, along the lines of the Chicago Municipal Improvement League, to study all new proposals, projects, and models with a view to adding monuments and expanding and beautifying thoroughfares and public squares. Their efforts came to nothing, however, despite the support they had won from several influential citizens.[39] Once the MIC was established, under the chairmanship of William S. Maxwell, the idea of a comprehensive plan aimed at the aesthetic enhancement of Montreal's main thoroughfares emerged; a parks system was planned and connecting streets were proposed that linked the city centre with the outskirts.[40] Participants in these deliberations were Professor Percy E. Nobbs, Jean-Omer Marchand, Joseph Venne, and John Rawson Gardiner (little-known today, Gardiner was an architect friend of Nobbs who had a special interest in urban planning).[41] The Committee's work continued in 1907–08 and, with financial support from the city, ideas were transformed into projects.[42]

In 1908 a set of five urban plans (fig. 81) was produced with the collaboration of Rickson Outhet, a landscape architect who had worked with Frederick Law Olmsted. Placed side by side, the plans outlined a vast system of boulevards and parks ringing the south side of the mountain and reaching to the river in the west and along Sherbrooke Street in the east. The focus of the plan was Fletcher's Field (today Parc Jeanne-Mance), divided by a Park Avenue transformed into a broad mall with five rows of trees and equipped with a series of playgrounds and sports fields. To the west, a broadened Prince Arthur Street wound around the mountainside between Sherbrooke Street and Pine Avenue, connecting the park with Côte des Neiges Road. Still further west, Atwater Avenue – also widened and tree-lined – ran down to the St. Lawrence River, where it was extended by a riverfront promenade leading to a large park situated beneath Victoria Bridge. A year later in 1909, the PQAA put forward a

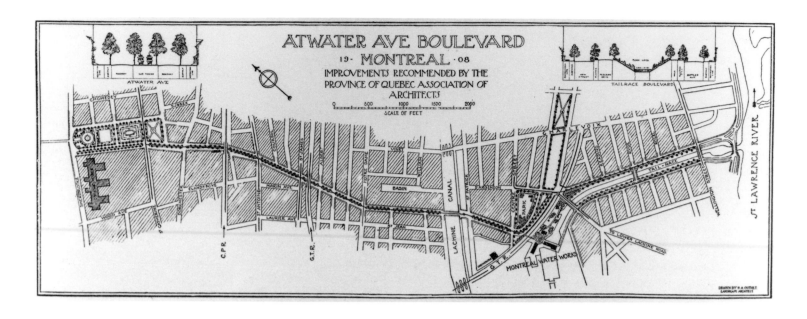

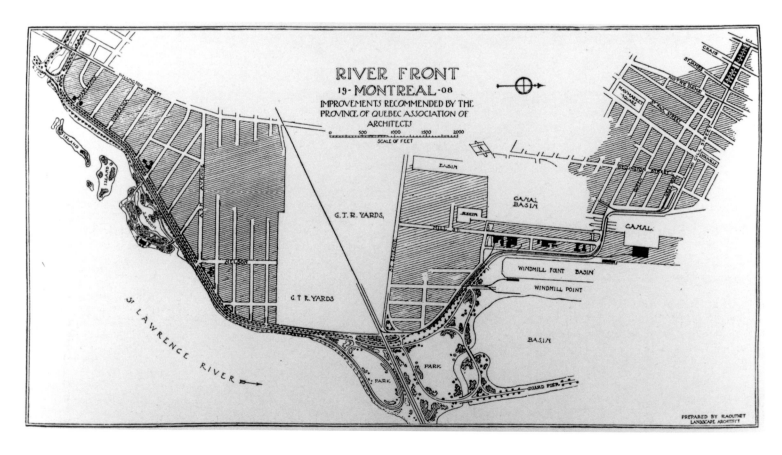

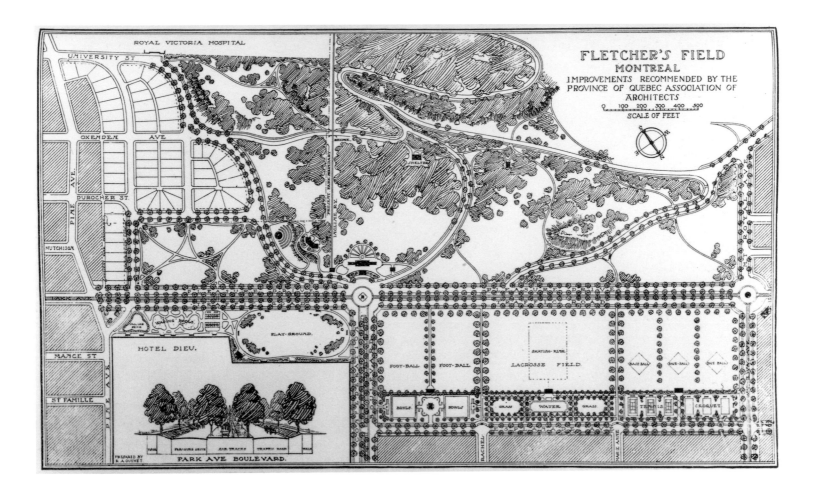

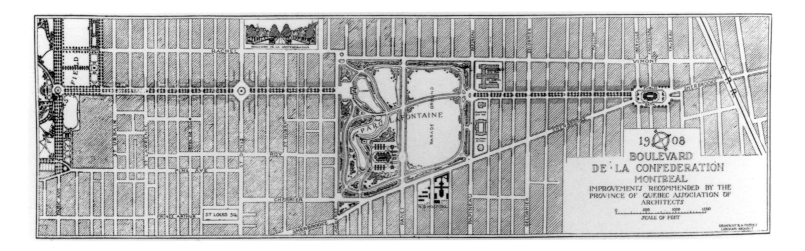

81 Four of the five development plans proposed by the PQAA in 1908. From the PQAA Yearbook, 1909–10. Cartography: R.A. Outhet.
Archives nationales du Québec, Fonds Ordre des architectes du Québec, P124 annuaire 1909–10.

further proposal (fig. 82), envisioning three avenues radiating from Victoria Square that would divide the city diagonally, joining with Sherbrooke Street in the east, Côte des Neiges Road in the west, and Victoria Bridge in the south. In 1911, when the construction of buildings for the law courts, municipal library, and city hall was discussed, the MIC, well versed in the principles of the City Beautiful movement, proposed that the mayor use this opportunity to build a civic centre worthy of "Canada's business capital" – a not altogether impartial proposal, since the suggestion included the creation of a committee of experts or the announcement of a competition for study of the project.[43]

The PQAA's push for city beautification received the support of the Montreal Parks and Playgrounds Association, organizer of activities and games for children in parks and schoolyards. Founded in 1904, it was officially directed by various eminent university professors and businessmen and gave women an important role.[44] After 1906 the beautification campaign waged by the PQAA benefitted from a newly energized reform movement led by citizens' committees formed by the powerful anglophone Board of Trade and its francophone counterpart.[45] In 1909, the PQAA presented its urban projects to the first meeting of the City Improvement League of Montreal (recently created by the organizers of the first exhibition mounted in Montreal in the fight against tuberculosis), with which it was affiliated. The goal of this federation of civic and professional groups was to promote the development of a city that was healthy, morally attractive, and aesthetically pleasing.[46] The following year, partly in response to the demands of well-to-do citizens' groups battling a bad city administration, the provincial government created the Metropolitan Parks' Commission,[47] whose role was to recommend plans and measures for creating new thoroughfares, recreational areas, public facilities (like baths), and residential neighbourhoods for the working classes.[48] The Commission, comprised of political leaders and businessmen, approached the firm of the American specialist Frederick Law Olmsted on the advice of the PQAA's Municipal Improvement Committee, still headed by William S. Maxwell.[49] One Committee member, Percy Nobbs, did not support the decision and resigned temporarily in a show of disapproval.[50]

In Montreal as in the United States, the City Beautiful movement did not gain impetus immediately after the World's Columbian Exposition of 1893. About ten years separated the Chicago fair, whose construction had been coordinated by the American architect Daniel Burnham, and the first city plans Burnham drew up for Washington, D.C. (1902), and San Francisco (1905). At the time, the ensemble of exhibition pavilions built near Lake Michigan was considered a marvel of both sanitation and aesthetics, as much a model of municipal engineering as of the unity of Neoclassical architecture, enhanced by monumental sculpture and painting. The event had the added effect of reinforcing the authority of the architect, not as builder alone but as coordinator of the many skills that had to be harnessed in the re-establishment of urban beauty and order.[51] It was a view that greatly appealed to many members of the profession in Montreal.

ARCHITECTURE AS A FINE ART

In Canada's metropolis, the leading promoter of American Beaux-Arts ideals was the brilliant young architect William Sutherland Maxwell, who had trained in both Boston and Paris. Although a PQAA colleague of the Scottish-born Percy Nobbs, the two men held opposing positions, the Americanism of the former clashing with the nationalism of the latter. While Nobbs's views on architecture were laid out in his many published articles, Maxwell's theoretical position is harder to grasp, for he wrote very little. A single text published before the war – a lecture on education given before the OAA in January 1908 – is thus an extremely valuable source.[52] Here Maxwell mentions the activities of the PQAA's Sketching Club, whose short history throws light on the gulf that separated the two men.

The PQAA Sketching Club was founded in 1905, though this was not the first initiative of its kind. Some ten years earlier the Association's student members had formed a similar group, no doubt stimulated by the enthusiasm of their young colleague Jean-Omer Marchand. "Ah! What energy, what emulation!" he wrote in the *Canadian Architect and Builder*,[53] speaking of the competitions organized in Paris by the École des Beaux-Arts, where Marchand had recently begun studies. That venture was apparently short-lived, however, like the Amateur Sketch Club that followed soon after in 1897.[54] The president of the more solidly grounded PQAA Sketching Club was the architect Cecil S. Burgess, who sat on a jury to evaluate the Club's drawings with his friend and collaborator Percy Nobbs and colleagues John S. Archibald and William Maxwell. The Sketching Club offered a wide range of activities to student members and working draftsmen, including lectures, competitions, a monthly examination of the sketches and renderings produced during evening meetings in the Association's offices, as well as the creation of measured drawings of historical buildings. This last

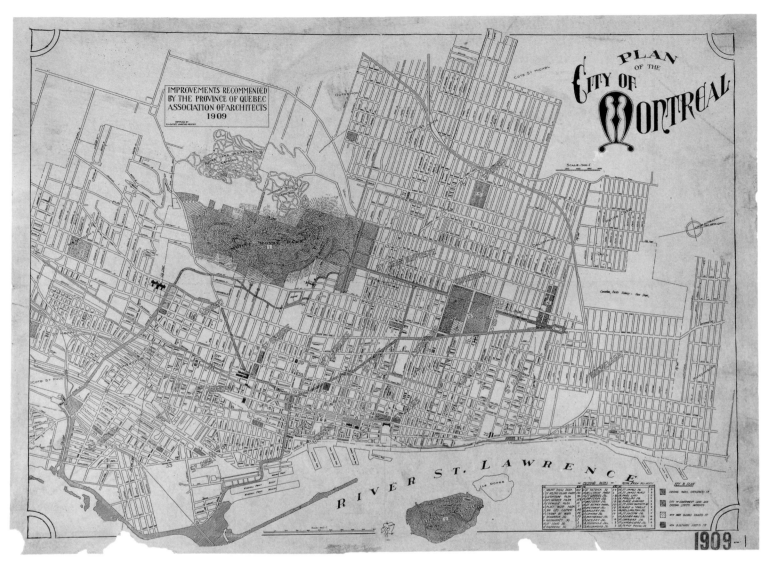

82 Plan of the City of Montreal with improvements recommended by the PQAA, 1909. Cartography: R.A. Outhet.
Lithograph mounted on paperboard, 31 x 41 cm. Ville de Montréal, gestion de documents et archives.

activity was particularly dear to Nobbs, who personally provided the funds for the prize awarded for best drawing.[55] Beaux-Arts ideals and Arts and Crafts principles were both in operation here, for the ability to design and the possession of graphic skills were valued as highly as the "intimate" knowledge of national architecture that could be gained by sketching (fig. 83). That alliance, however, would be short-lived.

After three successful years highlighted by exhibitions in the PQAA headquarters, the Sketching Club's activities dwindled.[56] In 1909, efforts focused on "the organization of a systematic study of design training" under the exclusive direction of William Maxwell.[57] By this time meetings were being held outside the Association's offices, and in 1911 the Sketching Club broke away from the professional association and aligned itself with the Society of Beaux Arts Architects based in New York,[58] becoming a studio in the purest Beaux-Arts tradition, set up by William Maxwell not far from his own architectural offices.[59] It was not the young architect's first involvement in teaching.

Maxwell had founded the Renaissance Club (fig. 84) early in 1899, a few months after returning from Boston, where he had been a regular and enthusiastic participant in the Architectural Club run by the French architect Désiré Despradelles, a professor at the Massachusetts Institute of Technology (MIT). Maxwell was then assisting his brother Edward on work for a new building for the British insurance company London and Lancashire Life, on St. James Street (fig. 92). Several young fellow-architects joined his cultural enterprise: Charles J. Saxe, who had recently left the Maxwell office; George Hyde, a final-year student at McGill; and two MIT graduates, David MacFarlane and the American David Jerome Spence.[60] Professor Capper was honorary president of the Renaissance Club and gave the inaugural lecture on the theme of Scotch Baronial Architecture. In its premises on Phillips Square, the group gave its consideration to architecture and the "sister arts" of painting and sculpture, with an eye to engaging the general public as well as the artistic community at large. A first studio soon got under way, devoted to modelling and run by George Hill, a Paris-trained sculptor who was a friend and regular collaborator of Edward Maxwell.[61] With the arrival of fine weather, excursions to the country were organized for watercolour enthusiasts. But after mention of its well-attended second annual meeting in December 1899,[62] references to the club vanish from the professional press. We can only surmise that with the departure of its founder for Paris in the summer of 1900, the group simply fizzled out. This early experiment remains, however, a clear indication of the depth

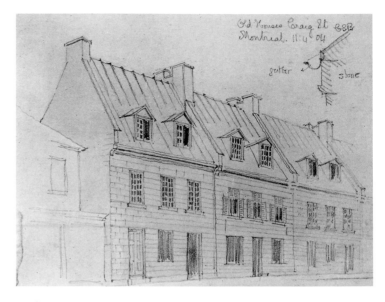

83 Cecil Burgess, draftsman, Sketch of Old Montreal; façades of typical dwellings, 1904. From *Supplement to Canadian Architect and Builder* (May 1904).

of William Maxwell's conviction that architecture belonged within the fine arts.

In a talk given to Ontario colleagues in 1908, Maxwell recalled the extraordinary sense of solidarity that had marked the meetings of the Boston Architectural Club, where, he noted, he had "first seriously realized the greatness and nobility of architecture." Citing at length the words of the Committee on Education of the American Institute of Architects, he affirmed its view of the architect "as one ranking in the class of men of culture, learning, and refinement, differentiated from the others of his class solely by his function as a creator of pure beauty, as an exponent through material forms of the ... civilization of his time, and as an organizer and director of manifold and varied industries and activities."[63] Like his colleagues involved in the American Renaissance movement, Maxwell believed in the superior social status and civic role of artists in general and the architect in particular – a position he cultivated and defended through his involvement in several specialized organizations. Closely associated with the activities of the Arts Club of Montreal, an artists' group,[64] he was also a respected and active member of the PQAA, of which he was elected president in 1914. In Maxwell's opinion, it was the architect's responsibility to manifest, in the urban environment, the power of the State and the city's new cultural institutions, to build the headquarters of society's most prosperous businesses, and to give form to the refined and individual lifestyles of its most

84 Article on the Renaissance Club. From *Canadian Architect and Builder* (March 1899).

affluent citizens: "A nation is judged, not only by the tons of steel rails produced, but by the level of cultivation which the buildings and art of the country express."[65]

ARCHITECTURE AS A NATIONAL ART

Another architect who held his profession in the highest regard was Professor Percy E. Nobbs. He viewed the architect not so much as a great artist whose fertile imagination was disciplined by reason but as a figure with an independent, even critical, mind. Speaking in 1910 at an annual meeting of the OAA, he extolled the benefits of a university education in the

formation of cultivated men, demoting the apprenticeship system and art schools to the technical and vocational level.[66] For Nobbs, education "*par le crayon,*" as he expressed it, was insufficient, although he admitted that the acquisition of drawing skills and a mastery of design were the principal aims of architectural instruction. That position was an implicit attack on the Paris École des Beaux-Arts and on all the schools that had adopted its studio-centred teaching philosophy – according to Julien Guadet, artistic education at its most necessary and sufficient.[67] Nobbs felt that study trips to the United States were only useful as a last resort, for he set little store by second-hand models. While questioning the relevance of the French-rooted Beaux-Arts tradition for Canada, he did not, however, go so far as to challenge the entire system.[68]

Nobbs revised the existing program at McGill University's Department of Architecture when he succeeded Stewart H. Capper as director in 1903, separating architectural studies from civil engineering and making the two courses distinct right from the first year of study, also introducing the specialized degree of Bachelor of Architecture.[69] While Capper, the school's first director, had seemed unable to decide whether the architect was artist or engineer – architecture was, for him, the most artistic of the sciences and the most scientific of the arts[70] – Nobbs kept the science courses to a strict minimum, for in his view they were of far less value than instruction in the arts and literature.[71] To the history and drawing classes and the architecture studio that had hitherto formed the core of the program, he added classes in aesthetics and the theory of architecture.[72] In 1909, Nobbs modified the curriculum again, the study of design was strengthened, and greater emphasis was placed on drawing as a technique of visual comprehension and conception. He also eliminated the hands-on experience with materials and execution that was advocated by the British Arts and Crafts movement,[73] which had been an integral component of architecture and civil engineering programs under Capper. Nobbs divided the study of design into three levels separate from the annually based course units and not including an additional component of architectural theory that completed the studio class. Students could now concentrate on the practical or on the theoretical in independence from each other.[74] This pedagogic structure was similar to the one employed at the École des Beaux-Arts in Paris, which Nobbs had earlier so firmly rejected. The ambivalence towards cultural traditions evident in Nobbs's pedagogy also characterized his universe of architectural references, where the Gothic co-existed with the classical.

In a talk given in 1907 to his American colleagues – for whose major Canadian projects he was full of praise – Nobbs defended the Gothic Revival, claiming that it alone could lead to renewal and an emancipation of classicism.[75] At the OAA annual meeting of 1906 (the year the PQAA formed its Municipal Improvement Committee), where he spoke on the official architecture of Europe's capitals, Nobbs had acknowledged the superiority, in urban and public architecture, of the classical style, which since its origins in Ancient Rome had been employed to evoke feelings of order, dignity, power, and pride. He emphasized, however, that classicism was not necessarily synonymous with French academicism, and, citing the examples of Berlin, Vienna, and St. Petersburg, went on to argue that the great models of papal Rome and monarchical Paris could be modified according to national tradition, whose source for Canada lay in Great Britain.[76] These ideas governed his approach in the major urban projects he executed elsewhere in the country. Analogous opportunities remained rare in Montreal, where the reform movement's support of architectural beautification projects had little concrete impact on the urban environment. Nobbs did, however, draw upon just such principles in the planning of the McGill campus (fig. 80), a highly pragmatic development given that his original mandate was simply to install a new boiler room in the engineering pavilion, under reconstruction after a fire.[77] A champion of Canadian architecture, Nobbs sought its distinct character in the confluence of British craft culture, the French Beaux-Arts tradition, and the great sobriety of the American model.

In Nobbs's view, art in general and architecture in particular were not instances of pure beauty: formal beauty did not exist in the abstract either in nature or in architecture, but was rather a function of an object's use, material, and structure.[78] Such creations were the concrete expression of human feeling, either individual or collective; in the case of architecture, the most democratic of the arts, this feeling was that of the age and the nation. In the early years of the century, Nobbs had not yet turned away from the teaching of general history, which he rejected in favour of recent history in the 1920s.[79] For him, works from the past were not so much models to be imitated as lessons in structural rationality.[80] Much of a work's significance he perceived as being rooted in the social forces that lay behind it. That belief in the collective nature of architecture made Nobbs one of the Montreal architects who dealt most successfully with the upheaval in values that would mark the 1910s.

A CITY HEALTHY AND EFFICIENT

Although the citizens' groups that supported the PQAA's urban projects were much preoccupied with city beautification, they were concerned with practical issues as well. In 1913, for example, Montreal's powerful Board of Trade denounced the anarchy of the city's development. Arguing for a more efficient and profitable traffic of goods and people, it demanded the elaboration of a comprehensive plan, tied to population growth, that would improve communication in the city through the introduction of transverse arteries.[81] On the eve of the First World War, when the urban networks were overtaxed and the living conditions of the populace, their numbers swelled by immigrants, were deteriorating steadily, social priorities were strengthening with the emergence, nationally, of an urbanist institution and the adoption of the first town-planning and housing policies.

In 1914 the role of Montreal's Metropolitan Parks' Commission, now established on a permanent basis, was extended. Responsible for the layout and creation of the thoroughfares and public spaces required for communication and recreation, it was also charged with producing an overall plan of the city's urban and suburban territory.[82] These additional powers, however, had no effect, due to the perpetual lack of City funding.[83] Equally ineffective were Quebec's first housing laws, passed by the National Assembly in 1914 and 1915 and in 1919 with a promise of financing from the federal government. Such measures did not receive absolute support. Some among the wealthy class and the intellectual and professional sector cited the problems that could be triggered by a sudden increase in post-war speculation and demonstrated concern over the rising tide of labour unrest.[84] Private builders and the Island's municipalities were reluctant to take the initiative. Though renewed prosperity postponed the housing question until the next recession, the debate over urban problems was far from over.[85]

In the 1910s, the federal government assumed an important role in the emergence of Canadian town planning by creating the Commission of Conservation of Canada, an intergovernmental advisory agency concerned with both population and mineral and agricultural resources. The first expert appointed to the new organization, Dr. Charles Hodgetts, established the close relationship between public health and housing conditions, impressed by British achievements in the area of housing and town-planning.[86] In 1914, as plans were underway for the National Housing and Town Planning Congress, the idea to invite British town planner Thomas Adams received support from several organizations including the Montreal Parks and Playgrounds Association.[87] Adams enjoyed an international reputation owing to his involvement in the creation of England's first Garden City and his subsequent work as an inspector under the pioneer Housing and Town Planning Act of 1909. A few months after the Congress was held in Ottawa in 1914, he was named as permanent advisor on town planning to the Commission of Conservation of Canada. Under his direction considerable progress was made: the legislative model for controlling urban development, which had been proposed to the provinces, was revised; the first Canadian town-planning journal – *Town Planning and Conservation of Life* – began publication; and the City Improvement League was organized at the national level.[88] At the instigation of Adams and the League, Montreal hosted its own first conference on planning in 1915.[89] Adams also served as president of the new Town Planning Institute of Canada, whose first conference, held in Ottawa in 1919, was attended by several Montreal architects: Edward Maxwell and Robert H. Macdonald, both heads of major architectural firms, Ramsay Traquair, and Percy Nobbs.[90] Nobbs, who had followed the early development of the Garden City movement in England and who had worked for the London County Council before coming to Canada in 1903, was extremely sensitive to the new issues; in the 1920s he was the architect who played the most progressive role in Quebec's town-planning movement.

In 1925, Percy Nobbs, now chairman of both the PQAA's Municipal Improvement Committee and Montreal's City Improvement League, initiated a study and public-education campaign aimed at creating a financially viable town-planning commission with a mandate to develop a master plan for the metropolis.[91] The movement was supported by a large group of energetic, long-time members of the League who came from all sectors of society: along with businessmen and activists in the women's movement were lawyers and other professionals, a substantial group of road engineers, landscape architects, and architects. Among the architects were Jules Poivert, director of the architecture department of the Montreal École des Beaux-Arts, Hugh H. Vallance, Eugène Payette, Ernest Cormier, and Charles David, plus the American-born Montrealers Hugh G. Jones and Harold Lawson.[92]

Throughout the following year the League presented lectures at McGill University and the Université de Montréal, also pub-

lishing brochures on various topics that included American developments in the field.[93] At the same time, instead of the usual presentation of architectural photographs and drawings, the PQAA's annual exhibition was devoted to the technical and community aspects of town planning, recalling similar events held in Europe a decade before in London, Ghent, and Brussels. As the architect Harold Lawson noted in his review of the exhibition, some of the works on display – all from Canada and the United States – represented major contributions towards the resolution of local town-planning problems.[94] Nobbs presented several projects for specific districts, including his McGill campus proposal (1925; fig. 80) and two residential developments – Queen Mary's Garden, for Hampstead (1925), and Belvedere Terrace, for Westmount (1925–27; fig. 85).

Other exhibits addressed the whole city: Lawson's clearly Haussmannian plan; a radical proposal for introducing a network of major boulevards into the heart of the city, signed by an engineer named Lavoie; and the traffic and zoning plan of another engineer, James Ewings, a traffic specialist who was the Montreal town-planning movement's leading spokesman in the post-war era. All of these projects gave evidence of the broader perspective that had been adopted, integrating the city into its region. The new vision was soon given concrete form in the proposal for the Jacques Cartier Bridge (1925–30; fig. 7), after studies initiated by the federal government in 1922 led to construction in 1925 by the Harbour Commission. Initially conceived primarily as an addition to the city's port facilities, this new infrastructure meant that the south shore of the St. Lawrence River could be integrated into the residential and industrial development of the metropolitan region, an important issue in the debate. The PQAA exhibition of 1926 presented the master plans of Lawson, Lavoie, and Ewings alongside the planning projects developed some fifteen years earlier at the instigation of the PQAA's Municipal Improvement Committee. As Lawson pointedly remarked, the city's traffic situation would have been vastly improved had some of those proposals been carried out. His review made no mention of aesthetic intention – another indication of the shift in priorities that had occurred since 1908. By the mid 1920s, when the metropolis was enjoying a new era of prosperity and vitality, public health and urban efficiency were very much the issues of the day.

That such values were shared by Percy Nobbs is evident from the text he wrote to introduce his Queen Mary's Garden project, a community-housing complex designed to replace

85 Proposed development of Belvedere Terrace (1925–27, Nobbs and Hyde, architects), Westmount, 1925. Ink on tracing paper, 46 x 60.5 cm. Canadian Architecture Collection, McGill University.

the traditional – in his view "inauspicious" and even "pernicious" – property-division system inherited from seigneurial days. Nobbs stressed the importance of sunlight to human well-being, as well as the various economic benefits that would follow from grouping together forty or so homes, guaranteeing from the outset better professional services in both design and construction, a more profitable land use, the reservation of a zone for community services, and a reduction in the buildings' energy-loss.[95] That project, like most of the plans featured in the PQAA's 1926 exhibition, appeared in a large special issue of

the *Revue municipale* in December 1927 – published by the Committee on Town Planning of the City Improvement League, of which Nobbs was president. In their introduction, the editors identified traffic, unsanitary housing, and suburban sprawl as the three most urgent planning issues. Their proposed solution lay in the creation of a municipal town-planning commission and the establishment of a rational plan governed by the principle of zoning.[96] Just as these tools for controlling urban development were being contemplated, the building code once again came into question.

BUILDING REGULATIONS
AND THE CONTROL OF URBAN FORM

The question of building heights resurfaced as the construction industry geared up again with the end of the First World War. In 1920, the city administration contravened article 23 of the *Montreal Building By-law* by issuing a permit for the construction of a 16-storey hotel near Dominion Square:[97] the Mount Royal (fig. 106), commissioned from the firm of Ross and Macdonald by an American hotel chain. The decision provoked strong reactions from several members of the profession. The PQAA, still very active in such debates, was concerned to modify the 1901 building code following the introduction of a series of amendments. At the annual meeting on 17 January 1920, the Association endorsed a report submitted by the architect John R. Gardiner denouncing the departure from the norm. The wide distribution it gave that document, sent to all interested public bodies, is undoubtedly a measure of the PQAA's extreme disapproval.[98] Although the protest did have some impact, the issue of maximum building heights had evolved since 1916, when the New York Zoning Resolution was adopted in New York City, spatially classifying the city's main functions (establishing residential, commercial, and industrial zones) and lifting restrictions on highrise construction (though limiting this to five city districts).[99] One event in particular illustrates the attitude of Montreal architects to tall buildings.

In 1923, at its first annual meeting since the war, the PQAA hosted an exhibition of the designs submitted in the famous competition organized by the *Chicago Tribune*. That this presentation was not a wholehearted sanctioning of tall-building construction was manifest in the choice of principal lecturer, the American architect Egerton Swartwout, a fierce opponent of the skyscraper, condemned by Swartwout as an ugly generator of urban congestion.[100] Nevertheless, in April 1924 Montreal amended article 23 of by-law 260 so as to permit the construction of buildings above 10 stories, while imposing the use of setbacks for buildings of 12 floors and higher and limiting total square footage according to the size of the lot. That modification may have been the result of criticism levelled in 1923 by members of the Board of Trade, which had argued that the by-law was out-of-date and confused.[101] Whatever its cause, the new regulation did not meet with unanimous approval, for only a few months later the amendment to by-law 260 was revised. The principle remained untouched, but the wording was altered to make the 12-storey limit the rule and higher buildings the

exception[102] – a revision that in fact had little effect on actual practice. Within only a few years, however, the debate was opened up yet again.

By the end of the decade work had begun on the new head offices of the Royal Bank of Canada (1927–28; figs. 114 and 115) on St. James Street and the Bell Telephone Co. Building (1927–29; fig. 116) on Beaver Hall Hill. The contribution of these two towers, rising up some 20 stories, to the Montreal skyline made the subject of building heights considerably more concrete, and gave both the public and municipal authorities a real idea of the city-wide impact of any future proliferation of skyscrapers. The special town-planning issue of the *Revue municipale* denounced the "canyon street," rejected for reasons of fire prevention and public health and considered a barrier to the diffusion of natural light.[103] In 1927 the PQAA – then under the presidency of Jean-Omer Marchand – set up a special committee led by Percy Nobbs to develop a new regulation linking building heights to street widths, a formula that was accepted by city council in 1929.[104] This approach was in accordance with the then-prevailing conception of the city, in which issues of hygiene overrode aesthetic ones. Yet while the construction regulations established in the 1920s tended to preserve traditional urban forms, they contained the germ of a new aesthetic involving the break-up of classical frontality: the conception of the building as a three-dimensional object. Moreover, like the New York Zoning Resolution, the new regulations offered an unprecedented degree of control – beneficial as well as restrictive – over building shape and urban form.[105] For the moment, however, those measures remained superfluous, for the Depression would choke the life out of Montreal's building sector for some years to come, at the same time encouraging a form of regionalism very different from the one promoted by Nobbs since the beginning of the century.

ARCHITECTURAL MODERNITY SUSPENDED

The interest in early local architecture demonstrated by Percy Nobbs, who was now deeply involved in the debate on the city, was taken up in the 1920s by Nobbs's McGill colleague Ramsay Traquair, director of the school of architecture since 1913. Both looked upon architecture as a form of emotional expression – hardly surprising, given their common intellectual background. In 1920, Traquair revived the graphic study of the province's architectural heritage initiated some fifteen years earlier by the Sketching Club. His defence of early Quebec architecture contributed to the emergence in the 1930s of French-Canadian architectural regionalism, a trend that must be looked at in relation to the cultural modernism that had found its first champions among the editors of *Le Nigog* just after the war.

Documenting the province's historical architecture was an issue first raised within the PQAA at the end of the nineteenth century.[106] At the annual meeting of 1899, incoming president Stewart H. Capper proposed the publication of a book illustrating the colonial buildings of Quebec, an early sign of what was to become the heritage movement.[107] More than ten years later, in 1912, the Association moved further toward a documentation project with plans to establish an archive and organize a photography competition among its members – but the outcome of these plans is unknown.[108] The idea was taken up again in 1917 at McGill University.[109] Traquair used his position as a professor to complete a study of Canadian, and more particularly Quebec, architecture, requiring his students to make measured drawings of early buildings and encouraging the PQAA to provide a travel grant, offered for the first time in 1920.[110]

In 1924, these drawings and various other documents were presented in an exhibition in the galleries of the Montreal Art Association that was co-organized with the Dominion Archives, the National McCord Museum, and a number of private collectors. Traquair reviewed the event in the *Journal of the Royal Architectural Institute of Canada,* that article being the first in a long series on the results of the historical and archaeological studies he was conducting with various colleagues: his faithful assistant Gordon A. Neilson, the anthropologist Marius Barbeau, and a McGill colleague, the historian E.R. Adair.[111] Despite the effort that had gone into assembling a wide range of documents testifying to the richness of Quebec's vernacular architecture and decorative arts, the exhibition appears to have had little contemporary impact.[112] During the 1920s, however, graduates from the McGill school drew upon this heritage in their residential designs: Harold Edgar Shorey, Harold Lea Fetherstonhaugh, and Alexander Tilloch Galt Durnford, for example, built a number of houses of French-Canadian inspiration in the city's West End (figs. 86 and 87). But it was not until the mid 1930s that Traquair's message got through to the architectural community as a whole, both French-speaking and English-speaking alike.

In 1934, Professor Traquair gave a highly successful lecture organized by the Association canadienne-française pour l'avancement des sciences. The francophone press applauded this Scottish Canadian who had revealed to French Canadians the artistic value of their old churches and who believed that the province's architecture and domestic arts should maintain their links with tradition.[113] Traquair thus became the champion of a French-Canadian renaissance that shunned the city and took as its ideal model for architecture (suburban and urban) the ancestral French home, "these structures that rise from the earth like noble stone trees and that are shaped with a view to fulfilling a certain function, reproducing a certain order, and demonstrating a certain goodness."[114] This regionalism emptied of the rationalist element, which was transmitted throughout Quebec society in the period between the wars, can be seen as a resistance to modernity. By contrast, the regionalism advocated early in the century by Nobbs contributed somewhat to the arrival of modernity.[115]

Traquair, however, had been part of the *Nigog* circle, Quebec's embryonic avant-garde, in 1918. Its members, all concerned with the future of various artistic disciplines in a backward-looking society, did not, however, share a common cultural viewpoint. It was not Traquair but the young architect Fernand Préfontaine who used the journal's pages to defend early local architecture – the only real national tradition – and to recommend that students record that heritage in measured drawings.[116] Indeed, it was Préfontaine who penned most of the items published in the *Nigog* on architecture and the decorative arts, two artistic realms whose kinship he saw as rooted in their shared utilitarian function. In other articles Préfontaine did not hesitate to denounce regionalism in painting, the local academicism that subordinated art to the imperatives of ethnicity and religion. In the name of autonomy of form and freedom of subject, he outlined a set of fundamentally modernist views, arguing for internationalism and the appeal to a cultivated public.[117] It was a position that differed somewhat from Traquair's, in which the artist was a bringer of emotion to ordinary people.[118] While the traditional solid, sober, and comfortable stone houses were the only Montreal architecture Préfontaine could approve of, these were to be used not as models but as sources of inspiration,[119] a distinction advanced earlier by Nobbs. For Préfontaine, art was creation and progress, while the spirit of modernity, marked by innovation and logic, had existed all through time. In the eyes of both Préfontaine and Paul Cointe (a specialist in industrial technology and a teacher at the Polytechnique),[120] the real works of art being produced in the contemporary world were the creations of engineers. Cointe had been especially impressed by Victoria Bridge and Grain Elevator no. 2 (fig. 88),[121] the latter having also been noted by various members of Europe's avant-garde.[122] For the first time in Quebec's history, the architect's

86 A.J. Nesbitt House (Shorey and Ritchie, architects), Priests' Farm, Westmount; principal elevation, 1926. Blueline print, 45 x 79 cm. City of Westmount Archives.

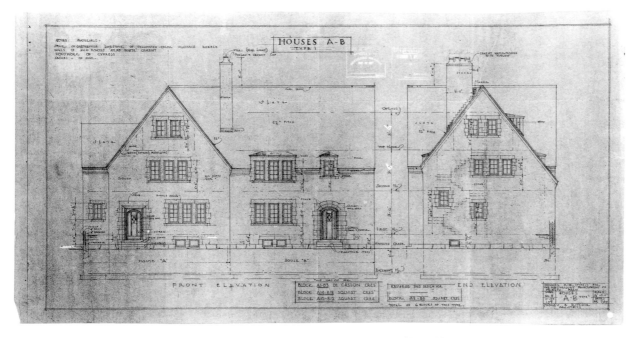

87 Houses for the Westmount Development Co. (Shorey and Ritchie, architects), Priests' Farm, Westmount; front and side elevations of houses A and B, type 1, 1927. Blueline print, 46 x 89 cm. City of Westmount Archives.

88 Grain Elevator no. 2 (1910–12, John S. Metcalf Co. Ltd., engineers), Montreal Harbour, 1912.
Unknown photographer. Archives du port de Montréal.

references were other than historical, although several *Nigog* contributors continued to praise contemporary works that drew upon the past. Jean-Charles Drouin, for example, wrote a review of the Bank of Montreal Annex (fig. 76), which he regarded as a structure inspired "by the purest classical works," its beauty derived equally from soundness of proportion and expression of utility.[123] Not all of its contributors were equally "daring," however, according to an article that appeared in the École Polytechnique's *Revue trimestrielle* after the demise of *Le Nigog*, which was denounced for its "really dangerous tendencies."[124]

Le Nigog's impact on the Montreal milieu is difficult to assess. The fact that its writers on architecture came mostly from the École Polytechnique and that an article deploring the journal's closure was published in the school's *Revue Trimestrielle* indicate something of the close relation between the review and an institution whose teaching remained on the whole quite traditional. The structure of the Polytechnique's program, established under the direction of the French architect Max Doumic, was similar to that offered by the École des Beaux-Arts in Paris: the architecture division comprised three successive classes where the work done in drafting and design was graded by competition and where courses focusing on the theory of architecture were supplemented by a few in applied sciences.[125] When in 1922 the division became part of Montreal's newly opened École des Beaux-Arts, the science courses were replaced by additional drafting classes and a course in the history of architecture.[126] Under the direction of Charles Maillard, the École des Beaux-Arts became a stronghold of artistic nationalism.[127] But the ideas defended by *Le Nigog* were not entirely forgotten: several of the last graduates of the Polytechnique's architecture division followed its architect-editor's opinion that Paris was still the best place to obtain a thorough grounding in architectural theory.[128] Among those who went there were Antoine Monette, René Rodolphe Tourville, Émile Venne, and Marcel Parizeau, who joined the ranks of the many French-speaking artists and scholars (such as Jean-Omer Marchand and Ernest Cormier) who had flocked to the City of Light since the end of the nineteenth century. This time, however, several were supported by European grants offered by the Taschereau government. These young men were to become leading figures in the architectural scene of the 1930s and 1940s, once again raising the issue of architectural modernity.

DURING THIS HALF CENTURY OF DEBATE IN MONTREAL, architectural ideals changed, as did the profile of the architect. While the early members of the PQAA had accepted the challenge of promoting the competence and integrity of the architect, they had seen their profession as art, science, and service, and nourished their eclectic practice with references to many historical periods. Their successors, led by William S. Maxwell, further emphasized the ties that bound architecture to the fine arts and the great academic tradition. At the same time, they broadened their range of activities, making the city as a whole and its overall beautification an issue of concern to architects. In the United States, this new movement had been spurred by the self-confidence and pride of a large and prosperous nation, rapidly gaining in international power. Across Canada, and in the metropolis especially, that movement was fuelled by the tremendous economic boom of the early twentieth century, coupled with an emerging national confidence. But faced with these contemporary challenges, Percy Nobbs, a newly arrived disciple of the English Arts and Crafts movement, took another stance, becoming a tireless defender of a uniquely Canadian architecture rooted in the traditions on which the country had been built. Upon his return from the war, his social consciousness and rationalism placed him at the head of a movement that advocated a healthier, more efficient city in a sphere of activity where architects now competed with engineers. While his efforts to promote early Quebec architecture were taken up by his colleague Ramsay Traquair, Nobbs nonetheless remained a pivotal figure, one who provided the link – at least theoretically – between tradition and modernity. In 1930, this champion of a rational and socially-oriented contemporary architecture turned the trail first blazed by *Le Nigog*[129] into a road that would be further travelled by the younger graduates of Montreal's École Polytechnique.

89 Proposed Canadian National Railway complex (Hugh Griffith Jones, architect), c. 1929.
Graphite and wax crayon on paper, 40 x 60 cm. Canadian Architecture Collection, McGill University.

GIGANTISM IN DOWNTOWN MONTREAL

Isabelle Gournay

SEVERAL MAJOR THEMES EMERGE IN THIS BOOK: the dialectical relationship between economic vitality on the one hand and architectural practice and debate on the other; the existence of major commissions for which Montreal and American architects engaged in a stimulating competition; the quest for a metropolitan identity; and the interest shown in American modernity – all features that contributed to the rise and development of commercial gigantism. These various socio-economic, urban, and architectural factors were reflected in the changing scale of office buildings and in the advent of loft-type buildings, permanent and temporary housing, and places for mass consumption and leisure, all programs which achieved a truly metropolitan character (the addition of large apartment buildings to purely commercial programs being justified by the essentially speculative and depersonalized nature of this new type of residential commission).

This change of scale and densification – a phenomenon linked to concepts of progress and urban rationalization and generated by rising consumerism, real-estate speculation, and an increasingly abstract commission process – was particularly apparent on Place d'Armes and Dominion Square. Thus, in a process that began around 1840, Old Montreal was transformed into an administrative and financial centre and, even more spectacularly, a new downtown core arose several blocks further west. Montreal was being rebuilt and growing denser as certain older activities gave way to more profitable ventures. The spatio-temporal analysis of commercial gigantism that follows aims to identify the socio-economic mechanisms and formal manifestations that were specific to downtown Montreal. Two major periods of change become apparent: the first ended with the 1913 recession and was limited by a 1901 by-law imposing a maximum building height of 130 feet (40 m); the second paralleled the construction boom of the 1920s, a phase marked by the appearance of huge buildings occupying entire city blocks and Montreal's first skyscrapers, built after height restrictions were eased in 1924.

It is important to situate commercial gigantism – a manifestation of the economic and social power of big business and the Anglo-Protestant upper class – among other forms of gigantism already present in Montreal. An examination of the international context is also necessary, particularly in the three countries most closely linked with Quebec: France, Great Britain, and the United States. In Montreal, monumentality traditionally symbolized the authority of religious and political powers, and its earliest and most forceful manifestations were linked with the Catholic Church. Downtown, the "benchmarks" that the first skyscrapers needed to surpass were the Church of Notre Dame (1824–29; fig. 2) on Place d'Armes and the Cathedral of St. James the Great (1870–94; fig. 71) just off Dominion Square.[1] Between 1880 and 1930, construction by the Catholic Church occurred mainly in Montreal's peripheral neighbourhoods and municipalities. The Church commissioned work on St. Joseph's Oratory (fig. 44) and several imposing convents and schools (its role in the erection of the main pavilion of the Université de Montreal is noteworthy), and it dotted the city with large parish complexes for the French-speaking working-class neighbourhoods.

Secular authorities – municipal, provincial, and federal – affirmed their presence in buildings such as City Hall (1876–78) and the main Post Office on St. James Street (1874–76), designed by Henri-Maurice Perrault. The public buildings constructed between 1880 and 1930 – in particular the Customs House (1912–16, E.L. Horwood), the City Hall Annex (1912–13, Marchand and Haskell), and the Court House Annex (1920–26, Ernest Cormier in collaboration with Louis-A. Amos and Charles J. Saxe; fig. 47) – were not located in the heart of Old Montreal. The administrative district that developed east of Place d'Armes lacked the homogeneity of a true civic centre. The numerous cultural facilities spread across the city – museums, libraries, secondary schools, and establishments of higher learning – were too scattered to form a monumental entity.[2] Among financial institutions, the reconstructed dome of the Bank of Montreal Head Office on Place d'Armes and the impressive colonnades of the new head offices of the Canadian Bank of Commerce (1907, Darling and Pearson of Toronto; fig. 58) and the Royal Bank of Canada (1907, Howard C. Stone; figs. 114 and 115) on St. James Street stood as important symbols of success and power. However, the presence of the two most prestigious semi-public financial buildings built between 1880

and 1918 – the Stock Exchange (fig. 61) and the Bank of Montreal Head Office (figs. 75–77) – did not surpass that of the imposing office structures adjacent to them. Industrial gigantism arrived in advance of commercial gigantism in facilities for the production, transportation, and storage of consumer goods, exemplified first by the Victoria Bridge (1854–60) and the warehouses of the Religious Hospitallers of St. Joseph (1861, Victor Bourgeau; 1874, Henri-Maurice Perrault and Albert Mesnard), and then by the harbour's impressive grain elevators (fig. 88), the Angus Shops (1903–04), the factories of Maisonneuve, and the vast Northern Electric Co. Factory, built in 1913 and considerably extended in the late 1920s.[3] The expansion of Windsor Station was another part of this phenomenon. Throughout our period of study, these two sources of gigantism – industrial and commercial – remained complementary aspects.

In the late nineteenth and early twentieth centuries, commercial gigantism took different forms in the major capitals and cities of Europe and North America. The skyward trend that is most frequently studied (in terms of style, technology, and economics) occurred essentially in New York City and Chicago, but was far from the only manifestation of gigantism.[4] The rivalry among the big and "ever-bigger" European capitals – Paris, London, Vienna, and Berlin – expressed both their desire for economic modernization and their quest for a political power imbued with nationalist, if not imperialist, overtones. In Paris, where height regulations were even more restrictive than in Montreal, gigantism worked hand in hand with the Hausmannism of wide boulevards and the classical tradition of *ordonnancement*. Hence the creation of large residential blocks, both formally and socially homogeneous, and the establishment along the *grands boulevards* of "banking palaces," department stores, and imposing head offices.[5] In London, the most spectacular display of commercial gigantism was the Kingsway, where the construction of office buildings, theatres, and hotels reached a peak between 1905 and 1920.[6] In Britain, monumentality showed up in the business districts of regional centres as well, Glasgow and Liverpool being two examples.[7]

In New York City, several architects who also worked in Montreal built commercial structures characterized not by their great height but by their formidable footprint. George B. Post, for instance, built the Produce Exchange (1881–84, demolished) and also the Mills Building (1881–83, demolished), an office complex whose U-shaped configuration eliminated inner courtyards, which were deemed unhealthy. Also notable are two buildings by Henry Janeway Hardenbergh: the Dakota

Apartments (1880–84), occupying an entire city block on Central Park West, and the Waldorf-Astoria Hotel (1891–93, 1895–97, demolished), which covered nearly 70,000 square feet of land (6,500 square m) and numbered 1,000 rooms. Chicago, however, would not be outdone: Adler and Sullivan's Auditorium Building (1887) was the first of the huge hybrid buildings,[8] and Daniel Burnham remains the true father of both civic and commercial gigantism.

From the early 1890s, regional centres in the United States began to fall in step with New York and Chicago. Buffalo, with a population even smaller than Montreal's, prided itself on Adler and Sullivan's Guaranty Building (1896) and boasted the largest office building in the world: Elicott Square (1906), designed by Burnham after the Rookery Building (1885–87) he had built in Chicago. In Cleveland, a city comparable in size to Montreal, George B. Post and Sons completed the 1,000-room Statler Hotel in 1912. Five years later Burnham's successors, Graham Anderson Probst and White, broke ground for the first building in the Terminal Group, constructed in phases until 1930. Centred above a railway junction, that distinctive complex united a skyscraper with lower comb-shaped buildings – complementary types to be encountered again in Montreal.[9] In terms of building height, Toronto was considerably ahead of Montreal, starting with the 14-storey tower of the Traders' Bank of Canada (1905, Carrère and Hastings). It was in Toronto, in fact, that Montreal architects first showed their boldness, as in the 20-storey Royal Bank of Canada Building completed there by Ross and Macdonald in 1915.[10] Though gigantism in North America's regional cities resulted in buildings whose size or height was relatively modest by comparison with the Chrysler Building or Merchandise Mart, the phenomenon was just as pronounced in the regional centres as it was in New York or Chicago. Even if confined to just a few pockets of the urban fabric, the relative jump in scale was as powerful and unmistakeable in these cities as it was in the largest metropolises.

OBSTACLES AND RESERVATIONS

In Montreal, commercial gigantism arrived somewhat more slowly than in other North American cities of equal size, as it faced significant physical, economic, legislative, and cultural barriers. The fabric of Old Montreal was particularly dense. Land subdivision in the new downtown area, originally drawn up for single-family homes, was scarcely more favourable to a change in scale; here city blocks were generally quite deep, street widths

varied considerably, and there were numerous alleys, mostly running east–west. Public authorities missed the chance to develop a concerted land-use policy that would encourage a more rational densification. In the downtown core, unlike the peripheral neighbourhoods, little was done to alter the street network, a task thought prohibitively expensive and complex. After a serious fire in Old Montreal in 1901, for instance, buildings were constructed of a much larger size than had previously been built there, yet the narrow, weaving network of streets north of Youville Square was restored, and the Board of Trade Building was simply rebuilt on its old foundations.

While real-estate pressures, the population explosion, and topographical constraints (concentrating commercial activities within an area bounded by the river and the mountain) were certainly significant, they were not so absolute that building upward became a necessity. Indeed, it was feared that uncontrolled building heights would lower property values. The dominant financial and transportation corporations felt no compulsion to exploit the symbolic and advertising potential of towering head offices with the aggressiveness seen in other cities, where the economic interests of newspapers and department-store chains, for example, were more directly dependent upon a consumer base.

Montrealers accustomed to the hierarchy of traditional monumental building types felt a certain discomfort as they watched, in the somewhat exaggerated charge of *Canadian Architect and Builder,* "the colossal premises of the New York Life Insurance building completely dwarf the towers of the French parish church."[11] Even as American architects claimed significant commissions in Montreal and their local colleagues became increasingly attuned to developments in the United States, the skyscraper remained a special case, crystallizing fantasies and antagonisms far outside the realm of architectural criticism. Until the early 1890s the skyscraper seemed to be exclusively "the product of conditions specific to New York and Chicago."[12] *Canadian Architect and Builder* reflected the reservations expressed by Montreal's architectural community – shared also by George B. Post and a significant number of his New York colleagues. In 1896, architect W.E. Doran stated that "greed and the desire to make the most use of land regardless of the right of neighbors to light and air called into existence the monstrosities of seventeen and twenty stories, now promising to reach out to thirty."[13] A short note also denounced the 14-storey building project planned for the site of the St. Lawrence Hall Hotel on St. James Street. "The unsatisfactory experience of our American

90 Prominent buildings on Place d'Armes: from left to right, the Royal Insurance Co., Post Office, Bank of Montreal, Canadian Bank of Commerce, Life Association of Scotland, Banque du Peuple, New York Life Insurance Co., Banque Jacques-Cartier, and Evan Muir Co., c. 1900. Ville de Montréal, gestion de documents and archives.

neighbors in this direction, coupled with the lower land values in Canadian cities, would seem to render inadvisable the erection of structures exceeding say six or eight stories in height."[14]

A year later Stuart Henbest Capper of McGill University delivered his impressions of New York in an address to his colleagues in the Province of Quebec Association of Architects (PQAA). Capper declared that it was time to accept the skyscraper as a new building type dictated by the ever-increasing cost of land, and to see it as an architectural achievement and not purely a feat of engineering. Anticipating the by-laws of 1920, Capper recommended that tall buildings "surround themselves with shorter neighbours" and be "designed as only the central portions of a larger, lower block." As isolated objects, each of their façades would produce a beautiful effect unlike the St. Paul Building designed by George B. Post, whose construction site Capper had seen in New York. Capper advocated terracotta as a cladding material for metal-frame construction – much more honest than stone or brick – and condemned the excessive ornamentation he had seen used by American architects. He favoured emphasizing major horizontal divisions instead of verticality, and while he took no position on the validity of skyscrapers in Montreal, he rejected their export to Europe.[15]

Capper's presentation aroused a response reported in the pages of *Canadian Architect and Builder*. Joseph Venne contrasted New York's skyscrapers unfavourably with the "architectural masterpieces in European cities;" Alexander Hutchison described them as "monstrous and gigantic boxes," declaring that tall-building construction was still in an "experimental phase." Andrew Taylor, loyal to Montreal's lithic tradition, was concerned about how a steel frame would age.[16] What obsessed architects most was the rough brick blind walls that would be exposed by height differences. Such reactions were not unrelated

91 Left to right, buildings of the Royal Insurance Co., Liverpool and London and Globe Insurance Co., Bank of Montreal, and Imperial Assurance Life Co., c. 1907. Unknown photographer. From *Montreal: The Commercial Metropolis of Canada* (September 1907).

to the adoption of Montreal's first height by-laws, included in the 1901 building code with a view to harmonizing the urban landscape: "no building, in any street in the City, shall exceed 10 storeys in height above the sidewalk or street level, or be more than 130 feet [40 m] from level of sidewalk to the roof."[17] As the twentieth century dawned in Montreal, the height permitted by the code had still not been reached in Canada's metropolis.

THE EVOLUTION OF THE OFFICE BUILDING

Canadian Architect and Builder indicates that Montreal architects were nevertheless responsive to the faith in progress so prevalent in the business world – a corollary of its undeniable dynamism – and kept up with technical innovations relative to highrise construction in the United States. Backed by a strong network of American and Canadian contractors and manufacturers of construction materials, architects adopted new foundation techniques (designed to support heavy loads without affecting the stability of adjacent structures) and fire-protection equipment (particularly sprinklers and fire-resistant materials) that made it possible to build taller and larger buildings.

The logic of capitalism, along with a certain desire to flaunt success, transformed the scale and architecture of office buildings, which in the late nineteenth century had not spread beyond the confines of Old Montreal. Insurance companies led the way in this development. For these businesses, real-estate investment held out two advantages. Not only would a building present

an image of success and stability reassuring to present and future policyholders, but, the spatial needs of an insurance company being limited (at the time, only one or two floors were needed for their own operations), office space could be leased profitably to other services like accounting or law firms.[18]

On Place d'Armes (fig. 90), the erection of the New York Life Insurance Co. Building (1887–88, Babb Cook and Willard; fig. 2) triggered in buildings on the square not demolition and rebuilding but expansion and the addition of floors – from a financial and symbolic point of view, a less risky option than reconstruction. Renovation of this type was frequently seen in New York City and Chicago, where it was carried out even by major architects;[19] the additional floors, usually added only a few years after initial construction, were rarely envisioned in the original drawings. In 1888, the Imperial Assurance Life Co. asked New York architect Charles Clinton to double the height of the building next to the Bank of Montreal (fig. 91), which it had purchased from the Consolidated Bank (it had previously housed the offices of the Canadian Pacific Railway, now located at Windsor Station).[20] Right next door to the New York Life building, the Banque Jacques-Cartier added two floors and a turret to its building. On the west side of Place d'Armes, the Royal Insurance Co. increased the height of its branch office and subsequently expanded the building, while the Liverpool and London and Globe Insurance Co. acquired and demolished two buildings to erect its new offices (1901–03, Hutchison and Wood).[21] In 1909, the Life Association of Scotland Building

92 London and Lancashire Life Assurance Co. Building (1899, Edward Maxwell, architect); detail of St. James Street pavilion. Pen and ink on drafting cloth, 67 x 90 cm. Canadian Architecture Collection, McGill University.

(1870, Hopkins and Wily), on the northwest corner of the square, gained another three stories and was thoroughly renovated by Marchand and Haskell. Within two decades, this gradual change in scale radically transformed the character of Place d'Armes.

On St. James Street, where the completion of the Standard Life Assurance Co. Building in 1885 accelerated the densification and specialization of the service sector, new construction dominated. Façade types changed rapidly here, and clearly indicate the formal difficulties faced by late nineteenth-century architects when composing the elevations of tall buildings. The façades of the Nordheimer Building (1888, John James Brown), anchored by a central gabled pavilion, and of the Temple Building (1889–90, Alexander Dunlop; fig. 20; demolished in 1906 to make way for the Canadian Bank of Commerce) are related to contemporary Chicago buildings in their plasticity and the design of their doors

and windows. On this relatively narrow but very prestigious street, which Montrealers liked to compare to Wall Street, insurance companies vied to outdo each other in decorative excess. An abundance of sculpted relief – work of the highest quality by Henri Beaumont – characterized the Canada Life Insurance Co. Building (1894–96, Richard Waite; fig. 58), whose façade was harshly criticized in *Canadian Architect and Builder*:

In the upper stories, there are faults violating the most elementary rules of art, as, for instance, the idea of superimposing two rows of columns on top of one another, with the lower row much thinner and weaker in construction, and more delicate in design than the above one. The mouldings, although good enough in profile, are so placed and arranged as to make the building appear to have been erected in sections, and the parts present no relations to one another. The doorway is also too low for a building of such importance.[22]

93 Dominion Express Co. Building (1910–12, Edward and W.S. Maxwell, architects), 1912. Photograph: William Notman. Notman Photographic Archives, McCord Museum of Canadian History, Montreal.

94 Transportation Building (1911–12, Carrère and Hastings, architects; Eustace G. Bird, partner; Ross and MacFarlane, supervising architects), 1912. Photograph: William Notman. Notman Photographic Archives, McCord Museum of Canadian History, Montreal.

The building of the London and Lancashire Life Assurance Co. (1899, Edward Maxwell; fig. 92), some of whose drawings were signed by the young William Maxwell, emphasized "distinction" and cosmopolitanism with its tall roofs, neo-Baroque details, and wrought-iron balconies then so popular in Paris, London, and New York City.[23]

In response to the trend to wider façades and the imposed height limit of 130 feet (40 m), the new construction cycle which occurred in the early 1910s introduced two types of tripartite composition. The first emphasized the vertical lines of the middle register; the steel frame was clad in a terracotta whose whiteness and reflective properties made a striking contrast with the city's older structures. Two such buildings on opposite corners at St. James and St. François Xavier streets, both completed in 1912, exemplified this trend. In one, designed

for the Dominion Express Co., an affiliate of Canadian Pacific (fig. 93), the Maxwell brothers sustained their fondness for eclectic ornamentation in strong relief in a building that featured large windows and a continuous balcony on the ninth floor (justified by the presence of the posh Montreal Club). In the Transportation Building (Carrère and Hastings and Eustace G. Bird; Ross and MacFarlane, supervising architects; fig. 94), a rental property, the exterior decoration was more fully integrated into the structure.

The second type of tripartite composition stressed the major horizontal divisions, as advocated by Stewart Capper. Clad in stone, the intermediate register features uniformly spaced windows of modest size; the crowning on the top two or three floors alternated columns or pilasters (single or double) with either straight or arcaded windows. One of these was the New

95 Royal Trust Building (1912–13, McKim Mead and White, architects; Daniel T. Webster, supervising architect), c. 1915. Unknown photographer. Collection Canadian Centre for Architecture, Montréal. Ernest Isbell Barott Archive.

Birks Building on Phillips Square designed by Nobbs and Hyde for jeweller Henry Birks (1911–12; fig. 43), the first office building erected in the new downtown area. Simpler and more monumental than the preliminary scheme (dated February 1911), the building is reminiscent of the Gorham Building (1903–06) designed by McKim Mead and White for the New York jeweller Gorham. The same New York firm conceived the Royal Trust Building on Place d'Armes (1912–13; fig. 95), within view of St. James Street, as a complement and foil for the Bank of Montreal building next door, one of whose subsidiaries it housed. Here the firm proceeded with a skilful "collage" of earlier projects: both the entrance register, imbued with a more civic than commercial character, and the treatment of the corners in the upper floors were reminiscent of the apartment building McKim Mead and White had just

designed for 998 Fifth Avenue in New York (1910–14), while the crowning is derivative of the Gorham Building, although with a less-prominent cornice.[24]

This introduction of American Beaux-Arts classicism to the commercial sector reflected, as it did in the United States, the business community's concern to appear less aggressive and rapacious; it was part of an attempt to sway a public increasingly critical of freewheeling capitalism.[25] Classical details and relief were emphasized on buildings celebrating a company name – like the Canada Cement Co. Building on Phillips Square (1921–22; fig. 43), by the firm of Barott Blackader and Webster (who had supervised the construction of the Royal Trust Building). In office buildings designed as rental spaces, such details were minimized or eliminated altogether. Architects favoured a formula that was easily adaptable in both width and height, and the limiting of choices and aesthetic risks allowed them to focus on the plans and the rationalization of the construction site. The type introduced with the New Birks and Royal Trust buildings was perfectly suited to façades of 12 to 15 stories. Both classical in its vocabulary and modern in its adaptability, it would have a significant impact – far more than neo-Tudor and Art Deco – on the office-building landscape of Montreal up to the very end of our period of study.

AMENITIES FOR THE MODERN METROPOLIS

To the northwest of Old Montreal, new types of commercial buildings reflected changes in social behaviour brought about by the rise of consumer and mass culture. In the 1890s, St. Catherine Street began to attract competing department stores. On Phillips Square the Henry Morgan & Co. Ltd. store (1890–91, John Pearce Hill; fig. 28) contained nearly 9,000 square metres of floor space, as much as the New York Life Building on Place d'Armes. At the same time, and very near this main artery, large performance halls were built, such as Her Majesty's Theatre (1898, John Bailey McElfatrick) and the Imperial Theatre (1913, Albert Westover and Ulric Asselin, site architect), the latter seating nearly 2,000 people.

New developments on Sherbrooke Street were described in *Canadian Architect and Builder:* "the new buildings are big flats and other expensive works which prefer to dispense with gardens and trees of their own. The place is thus rapidly becoming a boulevard, and probably will be a magnificent one."[26] Beginning in 1905, the Square Mile and the streets immediately east of the McGill University campus saw the construction of a growing

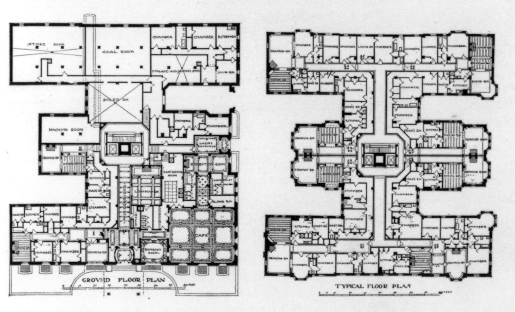

"THE LINTON," SHERBROOKE ST., MONTREAL, CANADA.—FINLEY & SPENCE, ARCHITECTS.

APARTMENT-HOUSES.—20.

The American Architect and Building News.
International Edition.

Volume XCI., Number 1619.
January 5, 1907.

96 The Linton Apartments (1906–07, Finley and Spence, architects); perspective, ground-floor plan, and typical floor plan. From *American Architect and Building News* (January 1907).

number of apartment buildings designed for the Anglo-Protestant upper class, an alternative to the private home whose maintenance had become quite costly. Some of these buildings, like the Bishop Court (1904–05, Saxe and Archibald) at the corner of Bishop and Burnside (today Boulevard de Maisonneuve) and the Grosvenor (1905, Finley and Spence) at the corner of Sherbrooke and Guy, were 3 or 4 stories high, and displayed a clearly British character. Others were 10 stories high, the maximum allowable, and were designed in the spirit of the great residential apartment buildings of New York City. The largest and most luxurious of these, the Linton on Sherbrooke Street (1906–07, Finley and Spence), was included in an international panorama published in *American Architect and Building News* (fig. 96).[27] The Linton brought a new degree of service and comfort to Montreal, offering a ground-floor café, "which will easily accommodate one hundred and fifty guests," with a "ladies' entrance" on Simpson Street. On the top floor a few single rooms with bath were at the disposal of tenants who might, on occasion, require greater bedroom accommodations than their own apartments provided, as was a "ladies' tea-room" reserved for tenants and their guests. As in the New York apartment hotels, some of the units had no kitchens. The construction of luxury apartments became a profitable business as a greater number of Montreal residents embraced this lifestyle. Even Edward Maxwell was tempted, both designing and financing the Maxwelton (1914) on Sherbrooke Street.

Also in the new downtown core but at the opposite end from the apartment district, light manufacturing activities began to predominate in the years after 1910.[28] The loft-type buildings that arose here could also reach 10 stories (some had a total floor-space of more than 20,000 square m), and were built with stronger floors, longer spans, higher ceilings, and sturdier elevators than those found in conventional office buildings. The Read Building (1912–13, Ross and MacFarlane)[29] and the Unity Building (1912–13, David J. Spence), both on St. Alexander Street (fig. 97), and the Belgo Building on St. Catherine Street (1911–12, Finley and Spence; fig. 30) were all designed by well-known architects who made use of the opportunity to experiment with simplified façades.

Loft buildings were often designed to hold both offices and light-manufacturing workshops, a strategy intended to minimize financial risk as much as to meet business needs. The frame of the Jacobs Building on St. Catherine Street (1909–10, Mitchell and Creighton; fig. 98), then considered the "largest concrete building in Canada," was designed to support four additional floors, and behind its uniform façade were both the St. Regis Hotel and a café.[30] Some prestigious office buildings also included a large number of related services, readily accessible through multiple entrances. Progress in ventilation technology gave the basement levels of the Dominion Express Co. and the Transportation buildings (figs. 93 and 94) on St. James Street – covering slightly more area than their ground floors – a restaurant, a bar, and a barbershop, masculine domains in both function and decor. The mechanical equipment was located in the sub-basement. In the Dominion Express building, the ground floor was mostly taken up by a "public arcade" of parcel-shipment counters, wickets for the sale of train and boat tickets, and a telegraph service. Purchasers of third-class tickets were directed to a room at a lower level, entered from St. François Xavier Street as well. A vestibule separate from the public areas and containing the elevator banks leading to the upper floors was accessible from St. James Street and Fortification Lane by a secondary entrance at the basement level. The large reception rooms of the ninth-floor Montreal Club were accessed through a vaulted vestibule topped by a pergola offering "magnificent views over the hills, city, and port,"[31] which was closed and heated during the winter and opened to the balcony during the summer. Hence the club was the elitist and equally masculine counterpart to the services found in the basement.

The Transportation Building (fig. 94) had a less-complex horizontal stratification than the Dominion Express Building, since its upper floors contained only work spaces, and it successfully integrated both its public and private areas and its horizontal and vertical circulation spaces. The presence of two symmetrical banks of elevators made the subdivision of the office floors much more flexible (fig. 99), a crucial factor in the success of a purely speculative venture. Treated as an extension of the street-level sidewalks, the interior concourse (fig. 100) was accessible from equally important entrances on St. James, St. François Xavier, and Notre Dame streets; inside, a grand central staircase led not only to the basement level but also to a spacious mezzanine offering services for the general public. Because of its size – its nearly 5 acres (2 hectares) of floor space made it, as reported in *Construction*, "the largest office building in the British Empire" – and its homogeneous mass, bordered on three sides by major thoroughfares of Old Montreal, the Transportation Building marked an important turning point in the architectonic translation of a key strategy of commercial gigantism: the appropriation of the city block.[32] As noted above,

97 St. Alexander Street, showing from left to right the Southam Press, Gillette, Read, and Unity buildings, 1913. Unknown photographer. Bibliothèque nationale du Québec, fonds Massicotte, 5-26A.

98 The Jacobs Building (1909–10, Mitchell and Creighton, architects) under construction. Unknown photographer. From *Construction* (March 1910).

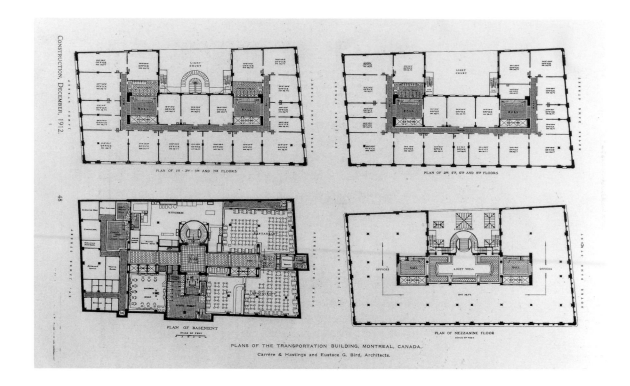

99 Transportation Building (1911–12, Carrère and Hastings, architects; Eustace G. Bird, associate; Ross and MacFarlane, supervising architects); floor plans of upper floors, basement, and mezzanine. From *Construction* (December 1912).

100 Transportation Building (1911–12, Carrère and Hastings, architects; Eustace G. Bird, associate; Ross and MacFarlane, supervising architects); main corridor. Unknown photographer. From *Construction* (December 1912).

101 Proposed buildings and station for Canadian Northern (partially realized, 1917–18, Warren and Wetmore, architects), 1913. Photograph of a lost rendering. Avery Architectural and Fine Arts Library, Columbia University in the City of New York.

vertical growth was permitted in Montreal only after 1924, making this alternative all the more important. In Old Montreal the Board of Trade Building (fig. 59) and the Grand Trunk Railway Head Office (fig. 67) already occupied their own modest-sized blocks, but these reflected a more traditional monumentality in their relatively low massing and height. In the new downtown area several large prestigious buildings almost filled the blocks they were sited on and were visible on three sides: the Windsor Hotel on Dominion Square (fig. 72), Morgan's department store on Phillips Square (fig. 102), and the Linton Apartments (fig. 96) and the Ritz-Carlton Hotel (fig. 79) on Sherbrooke Street. Full-block ownership, however, was often

difficult to achieve in Montreal, as real-estate holdings were already very fragmented. Manufacturing buildings such as the Belgo on St. Catherine Street (fig. 30) and the Read Building on St. Alexander (fig. 97) fell short of full-block occupancy, stopped by a single small lot already in other hands.

A perspective drawing by Warren and Wetmore illustrating a complex proposed for land above Canadian Northern's railway tracks at the edge of the new downtown – apparently published only once in 1913 (fig. 101) and not developed further – is an important document in the history of gigantism in Montreal. For the first time in the Canadian metropolis, vast buildings hug the boundaries of entire city blocks. Capitalism

December 26, 1923   CONTRACT RECORD AND ENGINEERING REVIEW   1243

The Henry Morgan and Co's. store in Montreal

196 Days Completed Henry Morgan Store

Speedy Erection Characterized the Recently Opened Addition to
Montreal Departmental Shop—A Building that Involved
Many Unique Construction Features

102 Addition to the Henry Morgan & Co. Ltd. Department Store (1922–23, Barott and Blackader, architects); perspective view from Union and St. Catherine streets. From *Contract Record and Engineering Review* (December 1923).

was starting to bank seriously on commercial gigantism and planning. The artist's bird's-eye view clearly reveals the form chosen for the four 10-storey revenue-generating commercial buildings: U-shaped blocks that conceal the much lower mass of the railway terminal and produce an airier interior court than was found in the Transportation Building.[33] The entire proposal invites comparison with the "Terminal City" project in which the New York Central Railroad intended to use its air rights to the space above Grand Central Terminal north of 42nd Street (a perspective drawing by designer Vernon Howe Bailey was published in *Harper's Weekly* on 12 January 1907).[34] The façades are reminiscent of both the exhibition halls (known as Grand Central Palace), which had just been completed by Warren and Wetmore, and the office buildings that were constructed for the New York Central.

THE BOOM OF THE 1920S

The financial crash of 1913 and the onset of war led to a net slowdown in commercial construction in which only movie theatres and loft buildings seem to have been spared. The construction cycle of the next decade, which reached its peak in 1928, began on a somewhat new footing. The influx of capital from financial syndicates – companies issuing "shares to collect the capital required for construction, the return on shares produced by leasing the spaces"[35] – which had previously been concentrated on a few prestigious projects (the Ritz-Carlton Hotel, the Transportation Building, and various apartment buildings), became

commonplace and played a major role in increasing real-estate pressures. The effusive titles of articles reporting on new Montreal projects published in the *Contract Record and Engineering Review* give some idea of the spirit that had infected both the building industry and a good many of its clients. Size and cost became more important factors than traditional aesthetic criteria. Considerable emphasis was also placed on speed of construction (a crucial factor due to the obstruction of increasingly dense traffic and the hardships of the winter work-site), made even more efficient with the production systems available after the war.[36] Architects too were held to the new pace of technology.

These were the years in which movie theatres became super-palaces[37] and existing department stores multiplied their surface area as new chains from Toronto moved onto St. Catherine Street. In 1922–23, the expansion of Morgan's by Barott and Blackader quadrupled the store's size (fig. 102), and construction required the moving of a 6-storey building whose owner had refused to sell: cheaper than demolishing and reconstructing it, the building was picked up and deposited 259 feet (80 m) up the block.[38] The downtown department store and movie theatre of the 1920s illustrate opposite facets of metropolitan life, the extroverted and the introverted. The former favoured a linear expanse of façade involving large surfaces of glass, inviting the ever-so-metropolitan practice of window-shopping; in an effort to reduce high land-costs and real-estate taxes, the latter projected a narrow façade out to the sidewalk, its presence maximized by garish exterior decoration and signage, while substantial square footage inside the lot was occupied by the auditorium.[39] Real-estate development and property speculation also supported a booming market for apartment buildings.[40] On Sherbrooke Street, the very discriminating Château Apartments (1924–26, Ross and Macdonald; H.L. Fethersonhaugh, associate architect; fig. 103) included 150 apartments and was built in just 11 months.[41] On Burnside, the Drummond (1919–20, Audet and Charbonneau) and the Drummond Court (1923, H.L. Fethersonhaugh) apartments together offered more than 200 units.[42]

While Old Montreal was increasingly dominated by the financial and insurance sector, the evolution of structures for the service industry in the new downtown reflected some major socio-economic changes. Specialized buildings were now designed for professionals. The Medical Arts Building, opened in 1923 on the corner of Sherbrooke and Guy (Ross and Macdonald; fig. 104), was the first in Canada to be entirely

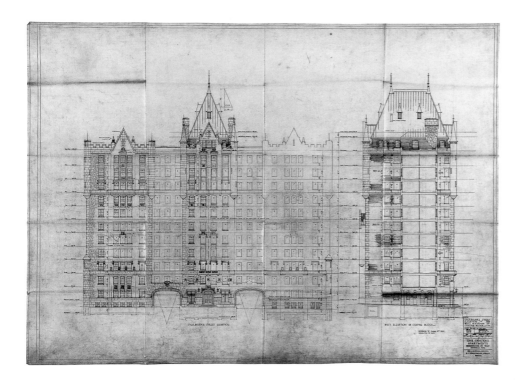

103 The Château Apartments (1924–26, Ross and Macdonald, architects; Harold Lea Fetherstonhaugh, associate architect); principal façade elevation and section-elevation of the central tower, 1925. Pen and ink on drafting cloth, 85.2 x 117.5 cm. Collection Canadian Centre for Architecture, Montréal. Ross and Macdonald Archive.

104 Medical Arts Building (1922–23, Ross and Macdonald, architects); view of the entrance, c. 1924. Photograph: S.J. Hayward Studio. Collection Canadian Centre for Architecture, Montréal. Ross and Macdonald Archive.

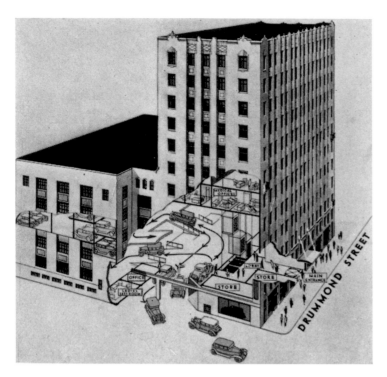

105 Drummond Medical Building (1929–30, Nobbs and Hyde, architects); perspective and section. From *Architectural Forum* (June 1930).

devoted to the practice of medicine; such a program already existed in the United States.[43] It included even operating rooms and a few private rooms for patients. On Drummond Street just north of St. Catherine, where a free-standing garage project for 400 automobiles had been declared illegal, Nobbs and Hyde combined the garage with a medical building. The Drummond Medical Building (1929–30; fig. 105) incorporated above-ground parking spaces "camouflaged" by a bay of medical offices, and one of its elevators was proportioned to accommodate a stretcher.[44] With the Architects' Building on Beaver Hall Hill (1930–32, Ross and Macdonald; figs. 54 and 55), Montreal also became the first Canadian city endowed with a structure designed primarily for professionals in the building industry.[45]

TOWARDS THE SUPERBLOCK

In the area around the intersection of St. Catherine and Peel streets – one corner of which held the first office building constructed in the western part of the new downtown, the Drummond Building (1914–15, Howard C. Stone) – two large buildings went up that spectacularly illustrated the concept of block appropriation: the Mount Royal Hotel and the

Dominion Square Building, both by Ross and Macdonald. Headlines in a trade journal in July of 1920 read "Montreal Will Build Thousand Room Hotel Costing Eight Millions."[46] The Mount Royal Hotel (fig. 106) was to be the Canadian jewel in the United Hotel Co. of America chain,[47] and was slated for the former site of Montreal High School: a block bounded by Peel, Metcalfe, and Burnside and by a specially created service alley. Construction was entrusted to the New York contracting firm Thompson Starrett, which opened a Canadian branch office for the job.

A growing awareness of the city's metropolitan identity increased the social role of its hotels. As tourism democratized and professional gatherings became common practice, the Windsor Hotel and the Ritz-Carlton could no longer handle the city's needs. Montreal therefore acquired an elegant and popular *caravanserai,* an amenity without which no metropolis could consider itself truly modern.[48] With 1,046 rooms, the Mount Royal Hotel became one of North America's largest hotel establishments and set a new record for the British Empire.[49] Only New York City's Commodore Hotel (1919, Warren and Wetmore), with 2,000 rooms, and Pennsylvania Hotel (1915–19, McKim Mead and White), with 2,200 rooms, surpassed it to any significant degree.

The massing formula of a base (hugging the contours of the lot) topped by parallel wings was imported to Montreal from the United States. It had often been employed for the construction of 10-to-20-storey buildings in regional centres like Cleveland and Detroit, where real-estate pressures were less intense than in New York and Chicago.[50] Ross and Macdonald adapted the formula that American hotel operators had come to consider the most modern and profitable. The base contained three public levels – the ground floor (fig. 107), the main floor (fig. 108), and the mezzanine – which included the main lobby (fig. 109) with the standard "palm room," boutiques, and various types of restaurant. The upper levels contained the guest rooms with, on the ninth floor, the "function rooms" (fig. 110) and another mezzanine. The ninth-floor banquet hall could accommodate 2,000 people, making Montreal Canada's "convention mecca;" on the same floor were a ballroom, a convention room, a huge kitchen, and in the north wing "helps' dormitories."[51] It was the rectangular configuration of the banquet hall and ballroom that dictated the T-shaped plan of the central wings. The Mount Royal Hotel also included a medical clinic, and thus became known as a place where "one might be born …, pass an eventful life … and shuffle off this mortal coil from the premises."[52]

106 Robert Gall Heughan, draftsman, Mount Royal Hotel (1920–22, Ross and Macdonald, architects); perspective view from Peel Street looking northeast, 1920. Reproduction on tracing paper, 69.7 x 47 cm. Collection Canadian Centre for Architecture, Montréal. Ross and Macdonald Archive.

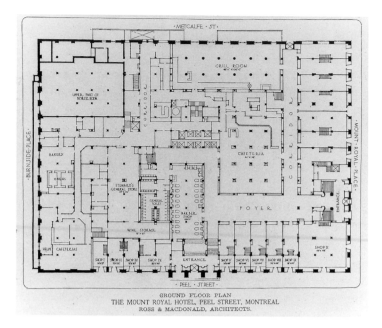

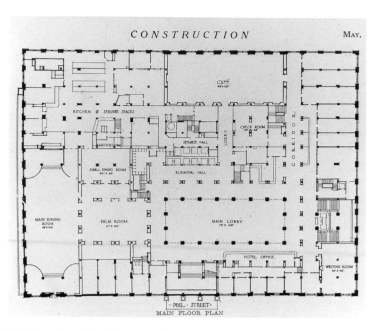

107 Mount Royal Hotel (1920–22, Ross and Macdonald, architects); ground-floor plan. From *Construction* (May 1923).

108 Mount Royal Hotel (1920–22, Ross and Macdonald, architects); main-floor plan. From *Construction* (May 1923).

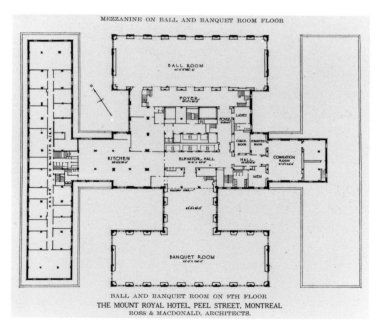

109 Mount Royal Hotel (1920–22, Ross and Macdonald, architects); main lobby, 1923. Photograph: Patent and Copyright Office.
Patent and Copyright Office, Canada/National Archives of Canada/PA-030834.

110 Mount Royal Hotel (1920–22, Ross and Macdonald, architects); 9th-floor plan. From *Construction* (May 1923).

The function of each horizontal register – public, private, semi-public – could be clearly read on the façade. The neutral and imposing mass of brick of the intermediate zone, containing the hotel rooms, was made even more colossal by the relative narrowness of the street, and visually outweighed the neo-Renaissance decor of the base and the top floor, making the ornamentation seem incidental. The tribute paid to the Equitable Building and the Pennsylvania Hotel in New York City by German architect Ludwig Hilberseimer is aptly applicable to the Mount Royal Hotel, since its mass was also designed as a "monumental organism" endowed with "inner consistency and logical cohesion."[53] The hotel's plans read somewhat like a flowchart; transitional spaces and circulation were reduced to a minimum, and full advantage was taken of any residual space.

The Mount Royal, whose main façades were erected on a sloping site, did not extend southward as far as St. Catherine Street, and so did not completely occupy a major block in the city grid. Imperfections in its plan had many rooms looking out onto semi-closed courtyards. Financed in part by American interests,[54] the Dominion Square Building (1928–30, Ross and Macdonald; figs. 111 and 112) was built on an almost flat lot, of smaller than average size for Montreal, bounded by three major streets (St. Catherine, Peel, and Metcalfe) and by the largest open space in the downtown area.[55] Its location was both prestigious and attractive, particularly for those office spaces enjoying a southern exposure and a view of Dominion Square. Twin setbacks in the façade, only the upper one strictly required by law, provided light for the offices located in the rear and enhanced the building's massing. The façades, clad uniformly in Alabama Rockwood limestone, possessed a generous, less conventional, Italianate decor that was better integrated than that of the Mount Royal Hotel. The building's arched entrance echoed the arched corbel-table (or Lombardy frieze) of its cornice, a motif that had appeared earlier in the Transportation Building. The plan (fig. 113), calling for a commercial base topped by offices in a double comb-shape, was less complex than that of the Mount Royal Hotel, but offered two additional elements. The base was the visible part of a 4-level below-ground realm that included two levels of parking for 600 cars. Whereas the Transportation Building had only a single widened corridor on the ground floor, the Dominion Square Building had a veritable indoor street paralleling St. Catherine: a T-shaped shopping arcade on two levels that also featured Montreal's first escalators. According to an advertising pamphlet, it was "an impressive concourse – the rendez-vous of a city within a city."[56]

THE FIRST SKYSCRAPERS

In 1920 an application by its owners to exempt the planned Mount Royal Hotel from the by-law limiting building height was turned down by city council, which argued that the construction of a 16-storey building would block traffic and would cost the city an additional expenditure for the provision of water and fire safety.[57] A year later the front page of *Le Devoir* quoted urban planner Thomas Adams's claim that the skyscraper was generally "not a financial success," lending support to journalist Louis Dupire, who concluded: "For goodness' sake, let Toronto copy American cities: Montreal should keep its distinctive character and personality. And, from this point of view, the spiral staircase does less harm than the skyscraper. At least the style is our own, however ugly it may be."[58] Another front page in 1921, this time in *La Patrie,* carried a conversation with French painter Albert Besnard, former director of the French Academy in Rome, under the heading "Save Us from the Skyscraper."[59]

The reactions of architects were somewhat ambiguous. Throughout the 1910s, *Construction* published spectacular photographs of skyscrapers being built in the United States alongside articles severely condemning the tall building. In 1919, a review in *Canadian Bookman* of Claude Blagdon's *Architecture and Democracy* gave Ramsay Traquair, a man certainly not known for his pro-American sentiments, the opportunity to state that "the skyscraper is the one genuine contribution of America to Architecture, and in the case notably of the Woolworth Building in New York, it has produced a monument of great beauty.... The United States is a great commercial nation, its greatest contributions to the art of Architecture are its commercial buildings."[60] Among Montreal architects, only American-born Hugh Jones took part in the *Chicago Tribune* competition of 1922, the winning designs of which were exhibited in Montreal. Probably because of Montreal's proximity to the United States, the skyscraper did not have the symbolic and fantasy role here that it acquired in Europe. However, it was impossible to ignore the debate on height regulations and the New York Zoning Resolution of 1916, which filled both the specialized and the popular American press.[61]

Two height regulations were adopted consecutively in Montreal in 1924. The second applied to "First Class Buildings" or "buildings of fire-proof construction" over 130 feet (40 m). It was now possible to build onto the central portion if it was set back at least 23 feet (7 m) from the façade and was not "more than one ground-floor and eleven stories in height, from the

III Dominion Square Building
(1928–30, Ross and Macdonald, architects);
St. Catherine Street elevation, 1929.
Pen and ink on drafting cloth,
82.7 x 105.4 cm. Collection Canadian
Centre for Architecture, Montréal.
Ross and Macdonald Archive.

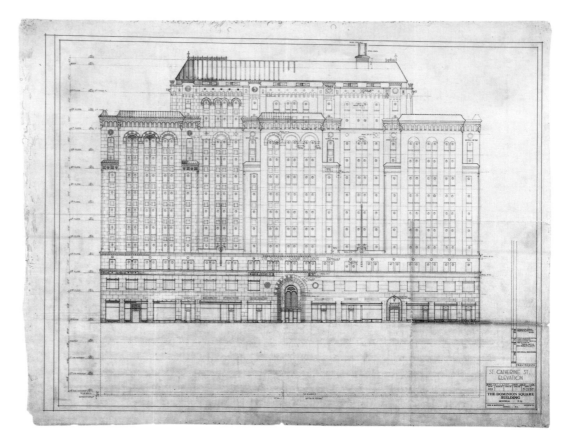

112 Dominion Square Building (1928–30,
Ross and Macdonald, architects); longi-
tudinal section, 1928. Pen and ink on
drafting cloth, 80 x 105 cm. Collection
Canadian Centre for Architecture,
Montréal. Ross and Macdonald Archive.

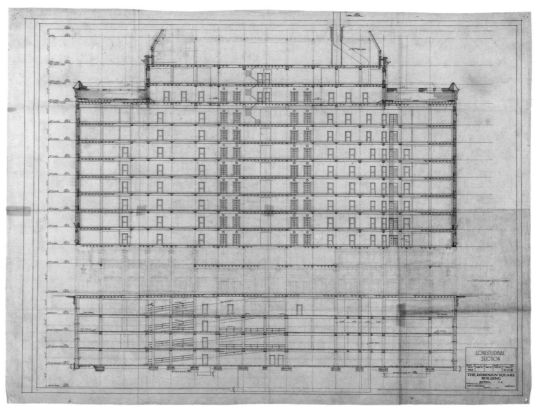

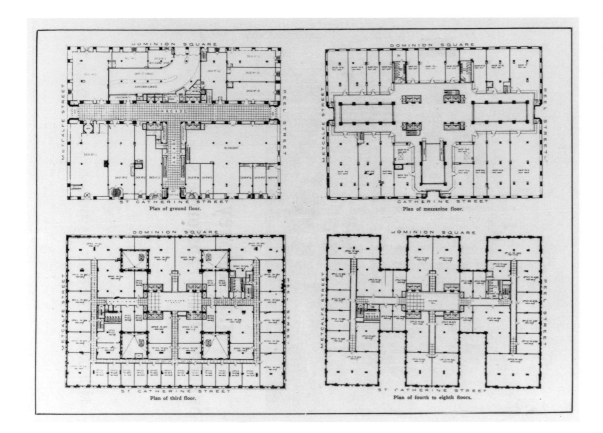

113 Dominion Square Building (1928–30, Ross and Macdonald, architects); plans of ground floor, mezzanine, 3rd floor, and upper floors. From *Contract Record and Engineering Review* (January 1930).

level of the sidewalk or of the street, to the highest point of the roof."[62] Unlike the New York resolutions, the Montreal by-laws did not zone the city according to density, height, and type of activity (housing, retail trade, offices, and light industry), and did not permit unlimited vertical construction.

However, the erection of a tower of some 20 storeys would remain exceptional, since obtaining sufficient useable area on the upper floors required a huge lot, difficult to come by in such a fragmented real-estate market. Only two skyscrapers were built while the 1924 regulation was in effect: the Royal Bank of Canada Building on St. James Street (1927–28, York and Sawyer, S.G. Davenport, associate architect; figs. 114, 115, and back cover) and the Bell Telephone Co. of Canada Head Office (1927–29, Barott and Blackader; fig. 116). Both buildings were erected on irregular lots. Initially planned in 1927, the addition of extra floors to the Sun Life Head Office (figs. 117 and 118) by Darling and Pearson did not take place until late 1929 to 1931. Despite their superior height, these three skyscrapers spread across the city were far more traditional than the Mount Royal Hotel or the Dominion Square Building. Unclassifiable – out of fashion or beyond fashion – they do not to conform to the "Jazz Age" image

of skyscrapers in the late 1920s. This difference in style was not solely a matter of taste, but was inspired by the concern for simplicity and dignity that McKim Mead and White had introduced in the Bank of Montreal and Royal Trust buildings. The towers financed by the Royal Bank, Bell Canada, and Sun Life were reserved exclusively or primarily for their own head offices. Definitely aggressive in their own markets, these companies were conservative in their corporate image, institutions that disparaged profit at any price and made it a point of honour to treat their customers royally and, as paternalistic enterprises, to ensure the well-being of their large clerical staff. Shops or underground parking lots were out of the question; however, provision was made for huge halls, cafeterias, libraries, comfortable smoking rooms, and executive offices inspired by British private clubs. The Bell building even featured a 400-seat auditorium, a small grocery store, and a medical office and infirmary. The representative function of the building outweighed its speculative strategy; in the Royal Bank Building, for instance, the axial placement of the banking hall dictated an atypical lateral position for the single elevator bank. Reviews of these buildings in professional journals and promotional pamphlets accurately reflected this spirit, in both their illustrations and their slightly moralistic comments. According to the *Journal of the Royal Architectural Institute of Canada,* the Bell Telephone Company had "decided to erect a building that would not only be ample for its many commercial requirements, but also be symbolic of the great service which it renders to the public and a monument to their progress and faith in the future of Canada."[63]

In 1907, the Royal Bank (founded in Halifax in 1869 as the Merchants' Bank of Halifax and renamed in 1901) moved its headquarters into a relatively modest, colonnaded building on St. James Street that was designed by American-born architect Howard C. Stone. While the bank did not hesitate to call on Carrère and Hastings to design its Toronto and Central American offices, the activities of its head office and its branch in Montreal were dispersed in four different buildings, two on St. James Street and two on St. François Xavier. A new lot was acquired in 1919,[64] although a building permit was not issued until December 1926. The lost time was soon made up, however, and the cornerstone of the new company headquarters was laid in April of 1927; in May of 1928 employees moved in (fig. 115). The selection of York and Sawyer, who collaborated with in-house architect S.G. Davenport, was easy to understand. What better way to challenge the Bank of Montreal than to hire McKim Mead and White's former employees and worthiest successors in the field of bank architecture?

The scheme adhered to height restrictions and York and Sawyer's Greco-Florentine style, employing a good urban and symbolic strategy. The base stayed below the maximum height to avoid overshadowing the neighbouring buildings. The tower was placed according to the compulsory 23-foot (7 m) setback, and had only one additional setback at the top to maximize floor space for rental offices. The building was topped by an unusual hipped roof and lantern (figs. 114 and back cover), bringing its total height to 392.95 feet (121 m). Here compliance with municipal by-laws resulted in simplicity and a bipartite envelope, a "collage" that with the severe and heroic exterior decoration gave the building a "modern" appearance. True to their ways, York and Sawyer brilliantly adapted a proven formula, adjusting the scale of the stone dressing and mouldings. The rusticated base is reminiscent of the sublime approach of Ledoux and Boullée. Despite the impression of an opaque mass, a mezzanine above the vast banking room is punctuated by small windows and behind the colonnade are two levels of bank offices.[65]

Bell also pursued a policy of architectural quality – in 1897, for instance, employing the Maxwell brothers for its head office,

114 St. James Street and the business district with, in the background, the Royal Bank of Canada tower, 1930. Photograph: S.J. Hayward Studio. Courtesy of the Royal Bank Corporate Archives.

a beautiful and proud structure in the spirit of Richardson. When it wished to centralize its operations in 1927, Bell called on the firm of Barott and Blackader, commissioning a skyscraper for its 2,000 employees with a branch of the Bank of Montreal on the ground floor (fig. 116). It was the first skyscraper commission to be awarded to a local firm. Soon after, in 1930–31, the same firm was asked to provide an adjacent telephone exchange, designed to be 21 stories high (though it started out with only seven). Bell's selection of Ernest Barott, a member of the McKim Mead and White "connection," was probably due to the building he had designed for Canada Cement on Phillips Square (fig. 43). Barott did not adopt the

115 Royal Bank of Canada Building (1927–28, York and Sawyer, architects; S.G. Davenport, associate architect), c. 1928. Photograph: Kenneth Clark. Courtesy of the Royal Bank Corporate Archives.

116 Beaver Hall Building of the Bell Telephone Co. of Canada (1927–29, Barott and Blackader, architects), c. 1929. Coloured pencil on photostat mounted on paperboard, 30.8 x 18.5 cm. Collection Canadian Centre for Architecture, Montréal. Ernest Isbell Barott Archive.

dichotomy between base and tower that characterized the Royal Bank Building. The Bell Telephone Co. of Canada Head Office, familiarly known as the Beaver Hall Building, was some 70 feet (21 m) lower than the tower on St. James Street, and its graduated setbacks were shallower than those of the Royal Bank. Bell Canada did not follow the example of its big brother in the United States, whose impressive "telephone buildings" in New York, St. Louis, and San Francisco were widely published and admired (fig. 57), popularizing setback profiles and the Art Deco style. True to what was still, at the time, his own world of reference, Barott appears to have taken as his starting point the Fiske Company Building in New York City (1919), a huge building of average height designed by Benjamin Wistar Morriss and Thomas Hastings. Duplicating the concept of a crowning with colossal pilasters so dear to McKim Mead and White, and topping the building with a roof evoking a flattened mausoleum of Halicarnassus, he adopted an exterior decoration which, while slightly heavier than that used on the Royal Bank Building, remained sober and appropriate to the building's scale.

The Sun Life head office was an "accidental" skyscraper whose step-by-step growth, under the direction of Darling and Pearson of Toronto, is reminiscent of that of buildings that had expanded this way on Place d'Armes in the late nineteenth century. In 1918, the Sun Life Assurance Co. moved from Old Montreal to the former site of the YMCA designed by Fuller and Wheeler on Dominion Square (fig. 71).[66] The square building erected on the corner of Dorchester and Metcalfe streets (fig. 117) was gradually expanded between 1923 and 1925 as far as Mansfield Street, and brought about the demolition of the Knox Presbyterian Church.[67] In June 1927 it was announced that work had begun on an extension that would reach 450 feet (138 m) in height (fig. 118).[68] Initially, the plan was to raise the building level by level, one register at a time – hence the "wedding-cake" look of the extension with its two colonnades. The planned addition does not seem to have been foreseen four years earlier, since it placed a burden on the existing structure, whose steel frame had to be shored up in a slow and complicated procedure – a task apparently completed without displacing the staff.[69] In December 1929, however, the decision was made to build just high enough to beat the height record set by the Royal Bank Building.[70] The result was a massive structure divided into a restricted number of registers, more horizontal than American skyscrapers, still homogeneous despite the numerous construction campaigns.[71]

117 S.H. Maw, draftsman, Sun Life Assurance Co. Building (1914–18, Darling and Pearson, architects), Dominion Square; perspective, 1927. Graphite on paper, 30 x 40 cm. Sun Life of Canada Corporate Archives.

118 S.H. Maw, draftsman. Sun Life Assurance Co. Building (1914–18, extensions 1923–25, 1929–31, Darling and Pearson, architects), after 1931. Etching on paper, 29.1 x 22.7 cm. Collection Canadian Centre for Architecture, Montreal.

A NEW HEIGHT BY-LAW

When Percy Nobbs and the PQAA campaigned to change the 1924 by-law, their aim was not just to follow more closely the example of New York, a model for legislation adopted in numerous American cities, but to "stimulate original," less traditional architectural solutions.[72] Public opinion slowly but surely rallied to the idea of the skyscraper as the symbol of North American modernity, thanks to opinions like those expressed by architect Fernand Préfontaine in *La Patrie* in April of 1926:

Our American neighbours, who influence us tremendously in many areas, have nearly succeeded in achieving an American style. The skyscrapers built recently, some of which are very beautiful, affirm the existence of a national art in the United States. The American architects, who were nearly all trained at the Paris École des Beaux-Arts, have been able to rid themselves of the habit of copying the monument of French, Italian, or English art.... They have sought logical solutions to the problems to be solved.[73]

According to the new by-law of 1929, which remained unchanged until 1948, the mandatory setback above the height of 130 feet (40 m) had to measure "one foot for every four feet additional height," thus adopting the pyramid envelope so characteristic of the New York skyscraper. And while the previous clause stating that "the total area of the floors of the building, including the ground-floor, do not exceed twelve times the area of that part of the lot which may be lawfully built upon" remained in effect, there was a major change in that this calculation did not include the area of the setback towers.[74] Downtown, the total height could not exceed two-and-a-half times the width of the street in front of the building "except on the streets less than fifty feet [15 m] in width ... where it shall be lawful to erect buildings to a maximum height of 100 feet [30 m]."[75]

A more contemporary look shaped two skyscrapers built entirely as rental spaces and with much-less imposing footprints than the head offices of Bell Canada and Sun Life: the Aldred Building on Place d'Armes (1929–31, Barott and Blackader; fig. 50) and University Tower on the corner of St. Catherine and

119 University Tower (1929–30, Harold Lea Fetherstonhaugh, architect), 1929. Pastel on diazotype mounted on paperboard, 59 x 42.9 cm (image). Collection Canadian Centre for Architecture, Montréal. Harold Lea Fetherstonhaugh Archive.

University streets (1929–30, H.L. Fetherstonhaugh; fig. 119).[76] Their setbacksilhouettes, energized by the continuous rhythm of the pilasters, broke with the then-current classicism and the trend toward horizontality. The design for the Aldred Building changed considerably, from a "mini-Bell" building to a much taller tower that sought to distance itself from the New York Life Building by opening its first setback lower down. In addition to the stylistic shift, we can see how Barott, in an attempt to take full advantage of the maximum permitted density,[77] applied a

particularly interesting clause in the 1929 by-law: "In the case of a building fronting on a square or a public park, it shall be lawful to erect a tower exceeding the heights permitted ... provided that such tower does not exceed in width and in depth 40 per cent of the width of that part of the lot which may be lawfully built upon, nor, in any case, 50 feet in width and 50 feet in depth, and that the height does not exceed the permissible heights by more than 200 feet [62 m]."[78]

The 1929 height regulation also allowed the department store of T. Eaton Co. Ltd. on St. Catherine Street to conduct a metamorphosis of its own, symbolizing, like the Aldred Building, the spirit of the times. It took advantage of a new stipulation for department stores, according to which the square footage of the floors could be up to 8 times the area of the building lot "when the building is provided with entrance and exit doors for the public on three or more streets."[79] Ross and Macdonald, working on this project with Sproatt and Rolph of Toronto, proceeded to build a second 3-storey addition in 1930–31 (fig. 120). The first, accompanied by a complete renovation of the façades of the former Goodwin's department store, had been completed less than three years earlier. To give the store a social function that was both prestigious and lucrative, French architect Jacques Carlu, a professor at MIT, was asked to design a restaurant on the ninth and top floor (fig. 121) entered through a tea-room foyer with large windows overlooking St. Catherine Street. The sophistication and originality of the whole floor serves to counterbalance the building's neutral exterior. When the Ninth Floor Restaurant and Lounge opened in 1931 it received extensive media coverage in Canada, the United States, and France.[80] There was a striking contrast between this restaurant and the other large halls built in Montreal in the 1920s, all of which were highly eclectic – particularly the neo-Tudor concert hall constructed in 1929 in Ogilvy's department store, another vertical addition executed by Ross and Macdonald.[81] At Eaton's, Carlu, a winner of the *Premier Grand Prix de Rome*, recreated the scale and elegance of the great transatlantic ocean liners; there remains, however, a notable similarity between his dining-room and the great basilican volume of the Bank of Montreal Annex designed by McKim Mead and White. Carlu related his design to Beaux-Arts gigantism while also exploring a new direction known as "Streamline Moderne." The Eaton's restaurant is undeniably one of the most beautiful public Art Deco landmarks in North America – one of those high-ceilinged spaces hovering above the city so beloved by Hollywood film-makers.

120 T. Eaton Co. Ltd. department store (1930–31, second extension; Ross and Macdonald, architects; Sproatt and Rolph, associate architects), 1930. Photograph: E.W. Bennett. Notman Photographic Archives, McCord Museum of Canadian History, Montreal.

121 Ninth Floor Restaurant and Lounge, T. Eaton Co. Ltd. (1929, Jacques Carlu, architect), c. 1931. Unknown photographer. Archives of Ontario.

122 Proposed Central Station for the Grand Trunk Railway Co.
(c. 1905, Frost and Granger, architects), version D.
Graphite, watercolour, and ink on paper.
Frost & Granger/National Archives of Canada/NMC-18486.

123 Proposed Central Station and office complex for the Canadian National
Railways, c. 1930. From *Montréal, la Métropole du Canada* (Montreal 1931).
Collection Canadian Centre for Architecture, Montréal.

124 Project for a new Windsor Station (Fellheimer and Wagner, architects). From *Canadian Pacific Railway Co., Studies for the Windsor Street Terminal Montreal* (July 1930). Canadian Pacific Archives.

THE CITY AS A WORK-IN-PROGRESS

Two structures that in retrospect represent an important milestone in commercial gigantism were the reconstruction project for Windsor Station and the land-development project of the Canadian National Railways (CNR). At the time, however, their architecture (which was delineated with less precision than their infrastructure) provoked no public debate and no reaction in the specialized press. These projects appear all the more ambitious and innovative in that Montreal lagged significantly behind most major Canadian and American cities in the field of railway architecture. For instance, the Canadian Pacific Railway (CPR) had decided to enlarge Windsor Station slowly, in stages, and the Grand Trunk Railway chose not to rebuild Bonaventure Station. Neither company could reach the sort of agreement achieved in Toronto, where a Union Station of monumental proportions was built.

The rail projects of the 1930s are related to the manifestation of commercial gigantism in this period: the transformation of the traditional railway station from a monument generating little revenue into a more profitable form of real-estate venture. In some cases a hotel was added to the terminal, as at Viger Square (fig. 69); in others the complex was completed with an office building, as in the proposed reconstruction of Bonaventure Station by Frost and Granger in 1905 (fig. 122).[82] The CNR project (fig. 123) centred on an office tower of some 25 storeys housing the company offices then scattered through 14 buildings and, below ground, a station. Over the CNR tracks was a complex of office buildings for rent to businesses; the unsigned sketches pub-lished in the media show large, tiered buildings – not true sky-scrapers – rendered in the style of New York illustrator Hugh Ferriss.[83] Drawings apparently done on his own initiative by Hugh G. Jones, the CNR's consulting architect, present a terminal tower and satellite buildings (fig. 89) that are reminis-cent of the architecture of the Dominion Square Building. It is interesting to note that the portion of McGill-College Avenue between Cathcart and St. Catherine streets was at the time lined by a taller and starker building than the one sketched by Jones: the Confederation Building (1927–28, Ross and Macdonald), financed by the Child Real Estate Company of New York City and reflecting the spirit of the Chicago Plan designed by Burnham and Bennett.

Fellheimer and Wagner proposed to connect the Windsor concourse, which was to be entirely rebuilt, to a hotel tower standing more than 50 stories high and covering an area between 200 by 300 feet (62 by 92 m) or 400 by 340 feet (123 by 105 m), according to different versions of the proposal (fig. 124). That part of Dominion Square to the south of Dorchester Street would become the *parvis* for this tower.[84] Spectacular renderings superimposed the two most innovative commercial forms of massing in use in North America: the large comb-shaped build-ing and the setback skyscraper.[85] The result was what Carol Willis has called the superblock: "a giant stepped-back tower rising over a full, or even, multiblock base."[86] It was a design formula that the CPR could have expected from Fellheimer and Wagner, architects who had already proposed it for down-town Philadelphia in 1927[87] and who had just implemented the scheme, though on a much-reduced scale, for the New York Central Railway in Buffalo.[88]

These grand architectural plans were evidently taken seriously by their backers, judging from the press campaign the CNR mounted to announce the completion, despite financial straights, of its infrastructure, and from the CPR's commission-ioning of large oil paintings illustrating their tower project. But like the projects envisioned by Canadian Northern in 1913, these schemes were both doomed to failure by the onslaught of the Depression. They remain important, however, for an understanding of the evolution of Montreal's urban landscape, as they reintroduced ideas that other architects had failed to win approval for (starting with the large signal tower that Price had wanted for Windsor Station), while foreshadowing the urban renewal that took place after the Second World War. Extending the monumental core established by the Mount Royal Hotel, the Dominion Square Building, and the Sun Life Head Office, the CNR project anticipated the transformation of Dorchester Street into a major tertiary axis. It was on this same site that Central Station (1938–43, John Schofield) and I.M. Pei's Place Ville-Marie (1958–66) would be erected. The harbinger of a new change in scale for Dominion Square, the Fellheimer and Wagner sketches were the first proposal of a large free-standing tower for a specific Montreal site, one that only a few years later would house the Château Champlain hotel.

In the 1920s and after 1930, the urban dynamics of gigantism was pursued north of the new downtown core – indeed, that trend was what led Ernest Cormier to abandon his pavilion scheme for the Université de Montréal in favour of a single structure whose plans were completed in 1927.[89] It was also implemented on the southern flank of Mount Royal, where the château-style Gleneagles (1929) and Trafalgar (1931) apartments were built. At a time when the population of metropolitan Montreal was growing beyond the million mark, architects were promoting the creation of a core of tertiary buildings that became denser and taller, but that would not expand much thereafter. In their architectural translations of economic dynamism, they applied by-laws that protected urban morphology, but also began to generate contrasts in scale that were increasingly difficult to manage. The construc-tion booms of the late 1880s and early 1910s and 1920s made it possible to constantly modernize the range of the commercial and residential facilities required for a North American city the size of Montreal, and the very end of our period saw the construction of several buildings (the Dominion Square and the Sun Life buildings, in particular) and the promotion of railway-company projects on a scale that demonstrated Montreal's intent to maintain its special status as the metropolis of Canada. While skyscrapers remained the exception, archi-tects were able to master the functional and formal charac-teristics of the large multi-purpose building.[90] With regard to the built environment, commercial gigantism – though here more technological and programmatic than stylistic in nature – remained the principal vehicle of architectural modernity in Montreal between 1880 and 1930.

NOTES

Abbreviations

AABN	*American Architect and Building News*
AAM	Art Association of Montreal
AIA	American Institute of Architects
ANQM	Archives nationales du Québec à Montréal
CAB	*Canadian Architect and Builder*
CAC	Canadian Architecture Collection, McGill University
CCA	Canadian Centre for Architecture
CHA	Canadian Historical Association
CNR	Canadian National Railways
CPR	Canadian Pacific Railway
CRER	*Contract Record and Engineering Review*
CUM	Communauté urbaine de Montréal
EBA	École des Beaux-Arts
EPM	École Polytechnique de Montréal
GRHPM	Groupe de recherche sur l'histoire du Port de Montréal
GTR	Grand Trunk Railway
JSAH	*Journal of the Society of Architectural Historians*
MIT	Massachusetts Institute of Technology
OAA	Ontario Association of Architects
PQAA	Province of Quebec Association of Architects
RAIC	Royal Architectural Institute of Canada
RCAA	Royal Canadian Academy of Arts
RIBA	Royal Institute of British Architects
SSAC	*Society for the Study of Architecture in Canada*

For holdings of the PQAA *Year Book* and Minutes, see ANQM, Fonds Ordre des Architectes.

Foreword

1 The expression "downtown" had recently entered popular speech. The *Oxford English Dictionary* notes references in the 1830s, with usage from the 1850s connoting the central and business sections of cities.

2 E.J. Hobsbawm, *On History* (London: Weidenfeld and Nicolson, 1997), 38.

3 Phyllis Lambert and Alan Stewart, eds., *Opening the Gates of Eighteenth-Century Montréal* (Montréal: CCA, 1992); Robert Fortier, ed., *Villes industrielles planifiées* (Montréal: CCA, Boréal, 1996); Rhodri Windsor Liscombe, *The New Spirit: Modern Architecture in Vancouver, 1938–1963* (Montréal: CCA; Vancouver: Douglas and McIntyre, 1997).

Montreal Metropolis

1 Mattei Dogan and John D. Kasarda, *A World of Giant Cities*, vol. 1 of *The Metropolis Era* (Beverly Hills: Sage, 1988).

2 Anthony Sutcliffe, ed., *Metropolis 1890–1940* (London: Mansell, 1984), esp. 1–66, 381–83.

3 H.W. Pleket, "Rome: A Pre-industrial Megalopolis," in *Megalopolis: The Giant City in History*, ed. Theo Barker and Anthony Sutcliffe (New York: St. Martin's Press, 1993), 14–20.

4 Donald J. Olsen, *The City as a Work of Art: London, Paris, Vienna* (New Haven and London: Yale University Press, 1986), 23.

5 For the significance of the SMSA, as defined by the Bureau of the Census, see Dennis Welland, ed., *The United States: A Companion to American Studies* (London: Methuen, 1974), 117–25.

6 See Adna F. Weber, *The Growth of Cities in the Nineteenth Century* (New York: Columbia University, 1899); Max Weber, *The City* (London: Heinemann, 1960); Louis Wirth, "Urbanism as a Way of Life," *American Journal of Sociology* 44 (1938), 1–24; Lewis Mumford, *The City in History* (London: Secker and Warburg, 1961); Le Corbusier, *The Radiant City* (London: Faber, 1967); Michael Simpson, *Thomas Adams and the Modern Town Planning Movement: Britain, Canada, and the United States, 1900–1940* (London: Mansell, 1985).

7 R. Douglas Francis et al., *Destinies: Canadian History Since Confederation* (Toronto: Holt, Rinehart, and Winston of Canada, 1988), 1–8.

8 For the development of the Atlantic trading system, see Ralph Davis, *The Rise of the Atlantic Economies* (London: Weidenfeld and Nicolson, 1973).

9 James Foreman-Peck, *A History of the World Economy: International Economic Relations Since 1850* (Brighton: Wheatsheaf Books, 1983), 104.

10 Robert C. Brown and Ramsay Cook, *Canada 1896–1921: A Nation Transformed* (Toronto: McClelland and Stewart, 1974), 1–4.

11 Jean-Claude Marsan, *Montreal in Evolution* (Montréal: McGill-Queen's University Press, 1981), 34–44.

12 Anthony Sutcliffe, "La Victoire de l'Immeuble de Rapport: Un Problème de l'Histoire des Grandes Villes Européennes au Dix-neuvième Siècle," *Histoire Sociale/Social History* 13:25 (May 1980), 215–24.

13 See Anthony Sutcliffe, *The Autumn of Central Paris: The Defeat of Town Planning, 1850–1970* (London: Edward Arnold, 1970).

14 On the building in London of a boulevard in the Parisian style, see Dirk Schubert and Anthony Sutcliffe, "The 'Haussmannisation' of London: The Planning and Construction of Kingsway-Aldwych, 1889–1935," *Planning Perspectives* 11:2 (1996), 115–44.

15 Kenneth T. Jackson, ed., *The Encyclopaedia of New York City* (New Haven and London: Yale University Press, 1995), 1288.

16 See Stephen V. Ward, ed., *The Garden City: Past, Present, and Future* (London: Spon, 1992).

17 Anthony Sutcliffe, "Britain's First Town Planning Act: A Review of the 1909 Achievement," *Town Planning Review* 59:3 (1988), 289–304.

18 Simpson [see n. 6], 76–81.

19 Simpson, 87, 112–15.

20 See Larry D. McCann, "Planning and Building the Corporate Suburb of Mount Royal, 1910–1925," *Planning Perspectives* 11:3 (1996), 259–301.

Factors in the Development of Montreal, 1880–1930

1 For many years studies of Montreal's history tended to be chronicles of events rather than systematic analyses of the factors influencing urban development. An exception was geographer Raoul Blanchard's *Montréal: Esquisse de géographie urbaine*, first published in 1947, then published in *L'Ouest du Canada français: Montréal et sa région* (Montréal: Beauchemin, 1953), and finally re-issued under its original title with an introduction by Gilles Sénécal (Montréal: VLB, 1992), 279 pp. Since the 1970s the study of Montreal's history has been profoundly changed by the blossoming of urban history and the great progress made in the analysis of economic structures, social and political forces, and the organization of urban space. This evolution is reflected in the most recent surveys, notably Paul-André Linteau, *Histoire de Montréal depuis la Confédération* (Montréal: Boréal, 1992), 613 pp.; Jean-Claude Robert, "Montréal: l'histoire," in *Montréal 1642–1992*, ed. J.-P. Duquette (Montréal: Hurtubise-HMH, 1992), 11–59; Jean-Claude Robert, *Atlas historique de Montréal* (Montréal: Libre Expression, 1994), 167 pp. For references to more specialized studies, see Joanne Burgess et al., *Clés pour l'histoire de Montréal: Bibliographie* (Montréal: Boréal, 1992), 247 pp.

2 For an account of Montreal's physical transformation, see Jean-Claude Marsan, *Montreal in Evolution* (Montréal: McGill-Queen's University Press, 1981), 456 pp. For a more general view see Harold Kalman, *A History of Canadian Architecture* (Toronto: Oxford University Press, 1994).

3 *Montreal Illustrated 1894* (Montréal: The Consolidated Illustrating Co., 1894), 37.

4 *Report of the Royal Commission on Dominion-Provincial Relations, Book 1, Canada: 1867–1939* (Ottawa 1940, reprinted 1954), 166.

5 Margaret W. Westley, *Remembrance of Grandeur: The Anglo-Protestant Elite of Montreal 1900–1950* (Montréal: Libre Expression, 1990), 311 pp.

6 William L. Marr and Donald G. Paterson, *Canada: An Economic History* (Toronto: Gage, 1980), 265–301; Paul-André Linteau, René Durocher, and Jean-Claude Robert, *Quebec: A History, 1867–1929* (Toronto: Lorimer, 1983), 59 61, 335–39.

7 Herbert Marshall, Frank Southard, Jr., and Kenneth W. Taylor, *Cana-dian-American Industry* (Toronto: McClelland and Stewart, 1976), 220–22; Gerald Bloomfield et al., "The Changing Structure of Manufacturing," in *Historical Atlas of Canada, III, Addressing the Twentieth Century 1891–1961*, ed. D. Kerr and D.W. Holdsworth (Toronto: University of Toronto Press, 1990), plate 7.

8 French-speaking public-health doctors, for example, belonged to the American Public Health Association and participated in conferences in the United States. Claudine Pierre-Deschênes, "Santé publique et organisation de la profession médicale au Québec, 1870–1918," *Revue d'histoire de l'Amérique française* 35:3 (December 1981), 372–73.

9 Warren Magnusson stresses that Canadian municipal reformers were inspired more by the American than the British model. See his "Introduction: The Development of Canadian Urban Government," in *City Politics in Canada,* ed. W. Magnusson and A. Sancton (Toronto: University of Toronto Press, 1983), 13–20.

10 Christopher Armstrong and H.V. Nelles, *Monopoly's Moment: The Organization and Regulation of Canadian Utilities, 1830–1930* (Philadelphia: Temple University Press, 1986), 144.

11 Charles N. Glaab and A. Theodore Brown, *A History of Urban America* (New York: Macmillan, 1976), 179–80.

12 A good example is the footwear industry, very strong in Montreal. Production equipment was provided by an American monopoly, the United Shoe Machinery Co., which in 1899 established a Canadian branch with its Montreal factory, moving in 1911 to new premises in Maisonneuve. See Jacques Ferland, "Not For Sale – American Technology and Canadian Shoe Factories: The United Shoe Machinery Company of Canada, 1899–1912," *American Review of Canadian Studies* 18:1 (spring 1988), 59–82.

13 The British approach to railway construction required heavy initial investment, for example the building of stone bridges; the Americans, with so much more territory to cover, preferred less-expensive methods and structures, such as wooden or iron bridges.

14 See for example Clarence Hogue, André Bolduc, and Daniel Larouche, *Québec, un siècle d'électricité* (Montréal: Libre Expression, 1979), 61; Claire Poitras, "Sûreté, salubrité et monolithisme: l'introduction du béton armé à Montréal, de 1905 à 1922," *Urban History Review/Revue d'histoire urbaine* 25:1 (October 1996), 19–35.

15 Gerald J.J. Tulchinsky, *The River Barons: Montreal Businessmen and the Growth of Industry and Transportation 1837–53* (Toronto: University of Toronto Press, 1977), 310 pp.

16 Huet Massue, *Financial and Economic Situation of Montreal Compared with That of Toronto* (Montréal: Shawinigan Water and Power Co., 1940); George A. Nader, *Theoretical, Historical, and Planning Perspectives,* vol. 1 of *Cities of Canada* (Toronto: Macmillan, 1975), 214–24; Benjamin Higgins, *The Rise and Fall? of Montreal: A Case Study of Urban Growth, Regional Economic Expansion, and National Development* (Moncton: Institut canadien de recherche sur le développement régional, 1986), 32–52.

17 Nader, 224–32.

18 Paul-André Linteau and Sylvie Taschereau, "The Industrial Development of Montréal," in *Historical Atlas of Canada,* vol. 3, plate 14.

19 Paul-André Linteau, "La montée du cosmopolitisme montréalais," *Questions de culture* 2 (1982), 23–53.

20 Benoît Brouillette, "Le port et les transports," in *Montréal économique,* ed. E. Minville (Montréal: Fides-HEC, 1943), 126–67; Pierre Brouillard, "Le développement du port de Montréal, 1850–1896" (Master's thesis, History, Université du Québec à Montréal, 1977), 73–85; Paul-André Linteau, "Le développement du port de

Montréal au début du xxᵉ siècle," in *Historical Papers 1972* (Ottawa: CHA, 1974), 181–205; Pauline Desjardins and Louise Pothier, *Étude du potentiel archéologique du Vieux-Port de Montréal*, Cahier 1, *Rapport synthèse* (Montréal: Le Vieux-Port de Montréal, 1990), 159 pp.

21 Raoul Blanchard, *Montréal: esquisse de géographie urbaine* (Montréal: VLB, 1992), 147–58, 180–93; Linteau, *Histoire de Montréal*, 24–29, 148–50, 299–303.

22 Gunter Gad, William Code, Neil Quigley, "Financial Institutions," in *Historical Atlas of Canada*, vol. 3, plate 9.

23 Linteau, *Histoire de Montréal*, 283–312, 375–84.

24 Paul-André Linteau, *The Promoters' City: Building the Industrial Town of Maisonneuve, 1883–1918* (Toronto: Lorimer, 1985), 225 pp.; Jean-Pierre Collin, *Histoire de l'urbanisation de la paroisse de Montréal, 1851–1941* (Montréal: INRS-Urbanisation, 1984), 175 pp.; Jean-Pierre Collin, "La Cité sur mesure: Spécialisation sociale de l'espace et autonomie municipale dans la banlieue montréalaise, 1875–1920," *Urban History Review/Revue d'histoire urbaine* 13:1 (June 1984), 19–34; Walter van Nus, "The Role of Suburban Government in the City Building Process: The Case of Notre Dame de Grâces, Québec, 1876–1910," *Urban History Review/Revue d'histoire urbaine* 13:2 (October 1984), 91–103.

25 "A Brief History of the Montreal Street Railway Company from 1861 to 1910," *Annual Report of the Montreal Street Railway Company for the Fiscal Year Ended 30th September 1910*, 25–42; Richard M. Binns, *Montreal's Electric Streetcars: An Illustrated History of the Tramway Era, 1892 to 1959* (Montréal 1973), 152 pp.; Paul-André Linteau, "Urban Mass Transit," in *Building Canada: A History of Public Works*, ed. Norman R. Ball (Toronto: University of Toronto Press, 1988), 59–72.

26 The expression "Old Montreal" was already in use before 1930, although the term became an official name only later. On the fortified town, see Phyllis Lambert and Alan Stewart, eds., *Opening the Gates of Eighteenth-Century Montréal* (Montréal: CCA, 1992), 93 pp.

27 Madeleine Forget, *Les gratte-ciel de Montréal* (Montréal: Méridien, 1990), 164 pp.

28 Linteau and Taschereau, plate 14; J.-C. Robert, *Atlas historique de Montréal*, 130–31, 140–41.

29 Michèle Benoît and Roger Gratton, *Pignon sur rue: Les quartiers de Montréal* (Montréal: Guérin, 1991), 393 pp.

30 David B. Hanna, "Montreal: A City Built by Small Builders, 1867–1880" (Ph.D. diss., Dept. of Geography, McGill University, 1986), 303 pp.; Réjean Legault, "Architecture et forme urbaine: l'exemple du triplex à Montréal de 1870 à 1914," *Urban History Review/Revue d'histoire urbaine* 18:1 (June 1989), 1–10.

31 Bettina Bradbury, *Working Families: Age, Gender, and Daily Survival in Industrializing Montreal* (Toronto: McClelland and Stewart, 1993), 310 pp.

32 See, for example, Olivier Zunz, *The Changing Face of Inequality: Urbanization, Industrial Development, and Immigrants in Detroit, 1880–1920* (Chicago: University of Chicago Press, 1982).

33 R. Blanchard, *Montréal: esquisse de géographie urbaine*, 163–70; Linteau, "La montée du cosmopolitisme montréalais," 23–53; Claire McNicoll, *Montréal: Une société multiculturelle* (Paris: Belin, 1993), 131–55.

34 Linteau, *Histoire de Montréal*, 55–73, 166–85, 333–46.

35 Fernande Roy, *Progrès, harmonie, liberté: Le libéralisme des milieux d'affaires francophones à Montréal au tournant du siècle* (Montréal: Boréal, 1988), 301 pp.; *Un siècle à entreprendre: La Chambre de commerce de Montréal, 1887–1987* (Montréal: Libre Expression, 1987), 191 pp.

36 Michael Gauvin, "The Municipal Reform Movement in Montreal 1896–1914" (Master's thesis, Dept. of History, University of Ottawa, 1972); Michel Gauvin, "The Reformer and the Machine: Montreal Civic Politics from Raymond Préfontaine to Mederic Martin," *Journal of Canadian Studies* 13:2 (summer 1978), 16–26; D.J. Russell, "H.B. Ames as Municipal Reformer" (Master's thesis, Dept. of History, McGill University, 1971), 147 pp.; Francine Nagant, "La politique municipale à Montréal, de 1910 à 1914: l'échec des réformistes et le triomphe de Médéric Martin" (Master's thesis, History, Université de Montréal, 1982).

37 Michèle Dagenais, "Vie culturelle et pouvoirs publics locaux: La fondation de la bibliothèque municipale de Montréal," *Urban History Review/Revue d'histoire urbaine* 24:2 (March 1996), 40–56.

38 Linteau, *Histoire de Montréal*, 258–62, 411–13; Honoré Parent, "L'administration municipale," in *Montréal économique*, 363–67.

39 Linteau, *The Promoters' City*; Paul-André Linteau, "Le contrôle de l'espace et du bâti dans la banlieue montréalaise (1840–1914)," in *Habiter la ville, XIXᵉ–XXᵉ siècles*, ed. M. Garden and Y. Lequin (Lyon: Presses Universitaires de Lyon, 1984), 153–74; W. van Nus, "The Role of Suburban Government in the City Building Process," 91–103; Larry D. McCann, "Planning and Building the Corporate Suburb of Mount Royal, 1910–1925," *Planning Perspectives* 11:4 (October 1996), 259–301.

40 *Répertoire d'architecture traditionnelle sur le territoire de la communauté urbaine de Montréal: Architecture industrielle* (Montréal: CUM, 1982), 322 pp.

41 Joseph Schull, *The Century of the Sun: The First Hundred Years of Sun Life* (Toronto: Macmillan of Canada, 1971); Graham S. Lowe, *Women in the Administrative Revolution* (Toronto: University of Toronto Press, 1987), 30–32.

42 *Le diocèse de Montréal à la fin du dix-neuvième siècle* (Montréal: Eusèbe Sénécal, 1900), 799 pp.; *Répertoire d'architecture traditionnelle sur le territoire de la communauté urbaine de Montréal: Les Églises* (Montréal: CUM, 1981), 490 pp.; *Répertoire d'architecture traditionnelle sur le territoire de la communauté urbaine de Montréal: Les Couvents* (Montréal: CUM, 1984), 391 pp.

43 Isabelle Gournay, ed., *Ernest Cormier and the Université de Montréal* (Montréal: CCA, 1990), 179 pp.

An Age Rich in Miracles

1 A. Leblond de Brumath, *Histoire populaire de Montréal*, 3rd ed. (Montréal: Librairie Beauchemin, 1926), 292.

2 Margaret W. Westley, *Remembrance of Grandeur: The Anglo-Protestant Elite of Montreal 1900–1959* (Montréal: Libre Expression, 1990), 334 pp.

3 Everett C. Hughes, *Rencontre de deux mondes: la crise d'industrialisation du Canada français* (Montréal: Parizeau, 1944), 388 pp.

4 Jean-Charles Falardeau, "Existe-t-il une culture canadienne-française définitive ou en voie de disparition?," *L'Action nationale* 12:3 (March 1941), 206.

5 The inventor of the gramophone, Emile Berliner, obtained a Canadian patent in 1899 and moved to Montreal. His first record was produced in Montreal by the Berliner Gram-O-Phone Co. in 1900. Gramophones quickly became popular as a result of advertising and appeared in the Eaton's and Simpson's catalogues from 1901.

6 Elzéar Lavoie, "La constitution d'une modernité culturelle populaire dans les médias au Québec (1900–1950)," in *L'avènement de la modernité culturelle au Québec*, ed. Yvan Lamonde and Esther Trépanier (Quebec City: Institut québécois de recherche sur la culture, 1986), 257.

7 Lavoie, 257. Illiteracy was on the decrease: among the adult population it fell from 33 percent in 1861 to 15 percent in 1901.

8 Pierre de Grandpré, *Histoire de*

la littérature française du Québec (Montréal: Librairie Beauchemin, 1971), vol. 2 (1900–1930), 149.

9 Between the late nineteenth century and the Second World War there were several ways of participating in literary and intellectual life, for instance as a member of the clergy or by joining one of the liberal professions such as law or medicine. Other means soon opened up, however. Among writers born between 1850 and 1920, 28.3 percent worked in teaching and journalism and 17.8 percent in the provincial or federal public service. See Marcel Fournier, "Portraits d'un groupe," *Possibles* 10:2 (winter 1986), 129–44.

10 Bernard K. Sandwell, "Review of the Musical and Dramatic Life in Montreal" (1915), cited by Mireille Barrière in "Montréal, microcosme du théâtre lyrique nord-américain (1893–1913)," in *Québécois et Américains: La culture québécoise aux XIXᵉ et XXᵉ siècles,* ed. Yvan Lamonde (Montréal: Fides, 1995), 382.

11 We should also mention Queen's Hall (1880) and Windsor Hall (1890), which held 1,150 and 1,300 seats respectively. Then there were venues for "shows and curiosities": the Éden Musée and the Gaiety Museum and Theatorium, established in 1891 on St. Lawrence Street.

12 That is to say, 2,113 performances out of a total of 3,436. Barrière, 173.

13 *La Presse*, 10 September 1903, 7, and 17 November 1903, 8. Cited by Barrière, 178.

14 See John E. Hare, "Le théâtre professionnel à Montréal de 1898 à 1937," in *Le théâtre canadien-français: évolution, témoignages, bibliographie,* vol. 5 of *Archives des Lettres canadiennes,* ed. Paul Wyczynski, Bernard Julien, and Hélène Beauchamp-Rank (Montréal: Fides, 1976), 239–48.

15 Germain Lacasse, *Histoire de scopes: Le Cinéma du Québec* (Montréal: Cinémathèque québécoise, 1988), 15.

16 Lacasse, 15–38; Yvan Lamonde and Pierre François Hébert, *Le cinéma*

au Québec, essai de statistiques historiques (1896 à nos jours) (Quebec City: IQRC, 1981), 173–76; Jocelyne Martineau, *Les salles de cinéma construites avant 1940 sur le territoire de la communauté urbaine de Montréal* (Montréal: Ministère des Affaires culturelles, Direction du patrimoine de Montréal, 1987–88), 2 t. in 6 vols. The astonishing proliferation of theatres can be judged from the following partial list: the Théâtroscope (1896), the Odéon (1897), the Mutoscope (1904), the American Noveltyscope (1906), the Gymnastoscope (1906), the Cynematograph Albani (1906), Le Cercle (1906), the Kenetoscope (1906), the Rochonoscope (1906), the Olivascope (1906), the Supérioscope (1906), the Vitoscope (1906), the Ladébauchoscope (1906), the Nationscope (1907), the Crystal Palace (1908), the Dreamland (1908), the Variety (1908), the Wonderland Moving Pictures (1908), the King Edward Moving Pictures (1910), the Frindland Cinematograph (1910), the Ludger Leroux (1910), the Maple Leaf Palace (1910), the Crowland (1911), the Gem (1911), the Atlantic Palace (1912), the Globe Theatre (1912), and the Midway Photoplay (1913).

17 City council passed a by-law for this purpose that was contested by theatre operators. See Paul-André Linteau, *Histoire de Montréal depuis la Confédération* (Montréal: Boréal, 1992), 250, and Germain Lacasse, "Le dimanche: Montréal va aux vues ou la ville aux vues animées," in *Montréal, ville de cinéma,* ed. Pierre Véronneau (Montréal: Cinémathèque québécoise/Musée du cinéma, 1992), 5–12.

18 Marcel Jean, "Un siècle de cinéma à Montréal," in *Montréal, 1642–1992,* ed. Jean-Pierre Duquette (LaSalle: Hurtubise-HMH, 1992), 107.

19 Marcel Jean, *Le cinéma québécois* (Montréal: Boréal, 1991), 11.

20 On Sunday, 9 January 1927, the Laurier Palace cinema on St. Catherine Street went up in flames,

full of children despite a regulation prohibiting attendance by those under 15; 78 people died from smoke inhalation in the crush to escape. Véronneau, 10.

21 "The insecure republic of letters that opens our twentieth century...." Jacques Allard, "La novation dans la narrativité romanesque au Québec (1900–1960)," in Lamonde and Trépanier, 45.

22 Other new publications included the *Bulletin de la Société de géographie de Québec* (1880); the *Canada français* (1888), a periodical produced by professors at the Université Laval; and the *Parler français* (1902), published under the auspices of the Société du bon parler. E.-Z. Massicotte founded two poetry reviews in Lévis: *Le Recueil littéraire* (1889) and *Le Petit Recueil littéraire* (1889). See Andrée Fortin, *Passage de la Modernité: Les intellectuels québécois et leurs revues* (Quebec City: Presses de l'Université Laval, 1993), 406 pp.

23 The average per decade between 1900 and 1940 was 1.5 per year (1900–10), 2.5 (1910–20), 8.6 (1920–30), and 14.4 (1930–40). See Allard, "La novation dans la narrativité," 47.

24 These were *Florence* (1900), *Marie Calumet* (1904), *Rédemption* (1906), and *L'Algonquine* (1910).

25 Founded in 1908, the Société pour l'avancement des sciences, des lettres et des arts du Canada succeeded in presenting several lectures with the participation of French professors. One of the founding members was J.-B. Lagacé, professor of aesthetics and the history of art.

26 The Librairie Déom, founded in 1896, was located near the Université Laval in Montreal at the corner of St. Catherine and Cadieux (now de Bullion) streets. See Robert Lahaise, *Guy Delahaye et la modernité littéraire* (Montréal: Hurtubise-HMH, 1987), 130.

27 Thirteen new magazines and periodicals were founded in the decade 1870–80, 27 in 1880–90, and 26 in 1890–1900. See Fortin.

28 Jacques Blais, "Poètes québécois

d'avant 1940 en quête de modernité," in Lamonde and Trépanier, 37.

29 Robert de Roquebrune, "Hommage à Nelligan," *Le Nigog,* cited by Lahaise, 291.

30 Louvigny de Montigny was a poet and journalist; a lawyer by training, he became a translator for the Canadian Senate after 1910. Jean Charbonneau, poet, literary critic, and playwright, was also trained as a lawyer and became a translator for the Quebec Legislative Assembly. Another member of the École littéraire was E.-Z. Massicotte; a great admirer of Verlaine, he authored several volumes of poetry and also worked in journalism, as a columnist for *L'Étendard* and editor of *Le Monde illustré.*

31 Charles Gill, "Notre revue," *Le Terroir* (January 1909), 5. The editorial secretary was Germain Beaulieu; Jean Charbonneau and Albert Ferland were on the editorial board.

32 Louis Dantin, preface to *Émile Nelligan et son œuvre* (Montréal: Librairie Beauchemin, 1903), iv.

33 While living in Paris Marcel Dugas wrote, "Montreal is crap." Marcel Dugas to Alice Courteau, 14 April 1914, in *Études françaises* 7:3 (August 1971), 282, cited in Lahaise, 229.

34 Turc (Victor Barbeau), "Une dernière plume," *La Presse,* 16 June 1919, 2.

35 For an in-depth analysis of the image of Montreal in literature, see Pierre Nepveu and Gilles Marcotte, eds., *Montréal imaginaire: ville et littérature* (Montréal: Fides, 1992), 424 pp.

36 Marcel Dugas, *Approches* (Quebec City: Éditions du Chien d'or, 1942), 27.

37 Paul Wyczynski, François Gallays, and Sylvain Simard, *Archives des Lettres canadiennes,* vol. 7, *Le Nigog* (Montréal: Fides, 1987), 390 pp.

38 P.P. Le Cointe, "L'esthétique de l'ingénieur," *Le Nigog* 5 (March 1918), 144; Esther Trépanier, "L'émergence d'un discours de la modernité dans la critique d'art (Montréal 1918–1938)," in

Lamonde and Trépanier, 69–112.

39 Jean-René Ostiguy, *Adrien Hébert, premier interprète de la modernité québécoise* (Saint-Laurent: Éditions du Trécarré, 1986), 133 pp.; Trépanier, "L'émergence d'un discours," 69–112.

40 Rodolphe Duguay, *Carnets intimes* (Montréal: Boréal Express, 1978), 98.

41 Alfred Laliberté, *Mes souvenirs* (Montréal: Boréal Express, 1978), 168.

42 Laurier Lacroix, ed., *Peindre à Montréal 1915–1930: Les peintres de la Montée Saint-Michel et leurs contemporains* (Montréal: Galerie de l'UQAM et Musée du Québec, 1996), 144 pp.

43 See William Watson, *Retrospective: Recollections of a Montreal Dealer* (Toronto: University of Toronto Press, 1974), 11.

44 To this list could be added the Hebrew Public Library (begun in 1888), a less ambitious undertaking that was to become the Jewish Public Library in 1914. In 1881 the Jewish community of Quebec, mostly settled in Montreal, comprised less than a thousand people. The arrival of Yiddish-speaking Eastern European Jews brought the population in Montreal up to almost 30,000 people by 1911, creating a community with its own schools, synagogues, and newspapers. See Ira Robinson, Pierre Anctil, and Marvin Butovsky, eds., *An Everyday Miracle: Yiddish Culture in Montreal* (Montréal: Vehicule Press, 1990), 169 pp.

45 See Yvan Lamonde, "Social Origins of the Public Library in Montreal," *Canadian Library Journal* 38:6 (1981), 363–70; Yvan Lamonde, *Les bibliothèques de collectivités à Montréal (17e–19e siècles)* (Montréal: Bibliothèque nationale du Québec, 1979), 139 pp.

46 Janet M. Brooke, *Le Goût de l'art: Les collectionneurs montréalais 1880–1920* (Montréal: The Montréal Museum of Fine Arts, 1989), 254 pp.

47 Leblond de Brumath, 292.

48 The Dominion College of Music (1894–1940), affiliated with

Bishop's University after 1895, was originally established to administer practical and theoretical examinations, but between 1896 and 1899 also offered music classes. The Institut Nazareth was widely regarded as Montreal's first conservatory: a mixed school for blind students founded in Montreal in 1861 by Benjamin-Victor Rousselot and the Grey Nuns, it also incorporated a school of music organized by Paul Letondal and Rosalie Euvrard. In 1917 the Université Laval granted the Institut Nazareth the status of an affiliated school of music, and in 1920 the Université de Montréal made it one of its affiliated music schools (an association that ended in 1967). The Institut Nazareth merged with the Institut Braille in 1975. The Royal Victoria College for Women, founded in 1896, opened its department of music in 1899 and became part of McGill University in 1904. Free courses were offered by the Société artistique canadienne (1894–1901), which was also dedicated to developing musical taste and encouraging artists. A plan by its members to create a Quebec conservatory of music came to an end when the federal government banned lotteries, the source of its funding, forcing the Société to close. Lastly, the Trafalgar Institute, which became the Trafalgar School for Girls after 1887, was affiliated with McGill University in 1911.

49 On the vicissitudes of the history of the Montreal Symphony Orchestra, see Helmut Kallmann, Gilles Potvin, and Kenneth Winters, eds., *Encyclopedia of Music in Canada*, 2nd ed. (Toronto: University of Toronto Press, 1992), 879–82.

50 Linteau, 168–69.

51 Marcel Fournier, *L'entrée dans la Modernité: Sciences, culture et société au Québec* (Montréal: Éditions Saint-Martin, 1986), 239 pp.

52 André Lavallée, *Québec contre Montréal: La querelle universitaire 1876–1891* (Montréal: Presses de l'Université de Montréal, 1974), 259 pp.

53 Marcel Fournier, "Tradition and Modernism: The Construction of the Université de Montréal," in *Ernest Cormier and the Université de Montréal,* ed. Isabelle Gournay (Montréal: CCA, 1990), 43–62.

54 Marcel Fournier, "Le frère Marie-Victorin et les petites sciences," in Fournier, *L'entrée dans la Modernité,* 75–115; Luc Chartrand, Raymond Duchesne, and Yves Gingras, *Histoire des sciences au Québec* (Montréal: Boréal, 1987), 487 pp.

55 Jean-René Ostiguy, *Modernism in Quebec Art, 1916–1946* (Ottawa: National Gallery of Canada, 1982), 28.

56 Carl E. Schorske, *Fin-de-siècle Vienna, Politics and Culture* (New York: Knopf, 1980), 378 pp.; David S. Luft, *Robert Musil and the Crisis of European Culture, 1880–1942* (Berkeley: University of California Press, 1980), 323 pp.

57 Fournier, *L'entrée dans la Modernité.*

The Importance of Transportation Infrastructure

1 David B. Hanna, "The New Town of Montreal" (Master's diss., Dept. of Geography, University of Toronto, 1977), 95–99; see also Jean-Claude Marsan, *Montreal in Evolution* (Montréal: McGill-Queen's University Press, 1981), chapters 7–9 and 11. For contemporaneous illustrations see Luc d'Iberville-Moreau, *Lost Montreal* (Toronto: Oxford University Press, 1975).

2 For fuller details on the canal enlargement, hydraulic lots, and resulting industrial development, see General Railroad Committee, Grand Trunk Railway, *Montreal in 1856* (Montréal 1856).

3 *Semi-Centennial Report of the Montreal Board of Trade* (Montréal: The Gazette Printing Co., 1893), 47, 88, 121; Sherry H. Olson, *Baltimore, The Building of an American City* (Baltimore: Johns Hopkins University Press, 1980), 157; Ralph K. Andrist, *The Erie Canal*

(New York: American Heritage Publishing, 1964), 33, 143.

4 Stanley Triggs, "The Bridge," in *Victoria Bridge: A Vital Link,* Stanley Triggs et al. (Montréal: McCord Museum of Canadian History, 1992), 32–73.

5 W.T. Easterbrook and H.G. Aitken, *Canadian Economic History* (Toronto: Macmillan Co., 1958), 307–14; Mark C. Carnes and John A. Garraty, "Toward a National Railway Network: Fragmentation and Standardization," in *Mapping America's Past: A Historical Atlas* (New York: Henry Holt and Co., 1996), 128–29.

6 William J. Wilgus, *The Railway Interrelations of the United States and Canada* (New York: Russell and Russell, 1937); Easterbrook and Aitken, 314.

7 *Timetables of the Grand Trunk Railway of Canada and Connecting Lines,* May 1881.

8 McKim Mead and White, *A Monograph of the Works of McKim, Mead, and White, 1879–1915* (1915; New York: Arno Press, 1977), 70; Alan Burnham, ed., *New York Landmarks* (Middletown, Conn.: Wesleyan University Press, 1963), 368.

9 "CPR," *Railroad Gazette* (New York) 26 (3 November 1882), 683. The predecessor railway, the Quebec Montreal Ottawa & Occidental, had laid plans in 1879 to extend its line into the city along present-day Boulevard de Maisonneuve to Avenue Papineau, but had never actually carried them to completion. See "QMO & O," *Railroad Gazette* (New York) 23 (8 August 1879), 433, and Henry W. Hopkins, *Atlas of the City and Island of Montreal* (Montréal: Provincial Surveying and Publishing Co., 1879).

10 For fuller details, see David B. Hanna, "Stratégies ferroviaires: emprises et terminus de Montréal," in *Montréal portuaire et ferroviaire,* Actes du 5e Congrès de l'Association québécoise pour le patrimoine industriel, Montréal, 8 et 9 mai 1992 (Montréal 1993), 43–46; G.R. Stevens, *Canadian National Railways,* vol. 1, *Sixty Years of Trial and*

Error, 1836–1896 (Toronto: Clarke, Irwin, and Co., 1960), 342–54.

11 D'Iberville-Moreau, 107; "Montreal," *CAB* 2:1 (January 1889), 9.

12 Carroll L.V. Meeks, *The Railroad Station, an Architectural History* (New Haven: Yale University Press, 1956), 105–06 and figs. 129, 133, 135.

13 P.B. Motley, "Double Tracking of the Canadian Pacific Railway's St. Lawrence River Bridge," *Canadian Railway and Marine World* 17 (April 1914), 150, documents the entire history of the original CPR bridge.

14 Douglas Smith, "Windsor Station," *Passenger Train Journal* (June 1993), 28–29; Omer Lavallée, "Windsor Station 1889–1914," *Canadian Rail* 152 (February 1964), 27–32.

15 Meeks, 105–06 and figs. 131, 134.

16 *CAB* 10:2 (February 1897); Robert Rumilly, *Histoire de Montréal*, vol. 3 (Montréal: Fides, 1972), 291.

17 G.R. Stevens, *Canadian National Railways*, vol. 2, *Towards the Inevitable, 1896–1922* (Toronto: Clarke, Irwin, and Co., 1962), 236.

18 *The Gazette* (Montréal), 3 June 1902.

19 Robert Lemire, ed., *The Architecture of Edward and W.S. Maxwell* (Montréal: Montreal Museum of Fine Arts, 1991), 85; Smith, 31; and Lavallée, 32–35.

20 Harry W. Desmond, "The Work of Frost and Granger," *Architectural Record* 18:2 (August 1905), 136–37, features the 6-storey design, while drawings for the 3-storey and 8-storey designs may be found in the National Archives of Canada in Ottawa, under the title "Sketch for Proposed Terminal Station for the Grand Trunk Railway Co., Montreal, Canada."

21 On the Pittsburgh and Washington railway stations, see Meeks, 24, 89, 110, 116, 121, 124, 131 and figs. 159, 161–63.

22 Easterbrook and Aitken, 438–40.

23 Stevens, *Canadian National Railways*, vol. 2, 246, 253; *The Railroad Age Gazette* (New York) 45:3 (19 June 1908), 180–82.

24 "The Angus Shops of the Canadian Pacific Railway," *The Railway Age* (Chicago) 38 (9 December 1904), 814–20, 854–60.

25 Linteau, *Histoire de Montréal*, 148, 204.

26 The project is described in *La Patrie*, 10 June 1911.

27 See full plans and description in Frederick H. Moody, "Steel Passenger and Freight Car Shop, Angus Shops, Canadian Pacific Railway, Montreal," *Canadian Railway and Marine World* 17 (June 1914), 245–48, and "Locomotive Shop Addition, Angus Shops, Canadian Pacific Railway, Montreal," 17 (October 1914), 445–47.

28 See full plans and description of the project in Motley [see n. 13], 149–56.

29 After a new system patented by Lincoln Bush in 1904 and first used on the Delaware Lackawanna & Western terminal at Hoboken across from New York City (1904–05). Meeks, 122 and fig. 160.

30 Meeks, 116 and figs. 147–48.

31 See the following articles in *Canadian Railway and Marine World*: "Windsor Street Station and Terminal Yards, Canadian Pacific Railway," 16 (November 1913), 527; "The Canadian Pacific Railway's Windsor Street Station, Montreal," 17 (January 1914), 9; "Trainshed at Windsor St. Station, Montreal, Canadian Pacific Railway," 17 (July 1914), 317–19. See also Smith, 30–32.

32 Lavallée, 37–38.

33 On the death of C.M. Hays, see Rumilly, 455; on the Bonaventure Station fire, see "Bonaventure Station, Montreal, Destroyed by Fire," *Canadian Railway and Marine World* 19 (April 1916), 141.

34 Smith, 32–33; Hanna, "Stratégies ferroviaires," 48; *Historical Sketch of Rutland Railroad Company, 1849–1949* (Rutland Railroad 1949).

35 Stevens, *Canadian National Railways*, vol. 2, 351–54; see also Hanna, "Stratégies ferroviaires," 49.

36 For fuller description, see T.D. Regehr, *The Canadian Northern Railway: Pioneer Road of the Northern Prairies, 1895–1918* (Toronto: MacMillan, 1976), 126–56; Stevens, *Canadian National Railways*, vol. 2, 343–47.

37 Regehr, 320–21.

38 Regehr, 321–22.

39 L.D. McCann, "Planning and Building the Corporate Suburb of Mount Royal, 1910–1925," *Planning Perspectives* 11 (1996), 265–66, 268–71.

40 *The Mount Royal Tunnel* (Toronto: Canadian Northern Railway, 1913), 7–8; "Canadian Northern Railway, Construction Betterments, Etc.," *Canadian Railway and Marine World* 16 (May 1913), 227.

41 Meeks, 131, fig. 172.

42 Documented in several issues of *Canadian Railway and Marine World*: S.P. Brown, "Canadian Northern Railway Mount Royal Tunnel," 16 (August 1913), 359–62; Henry K. Wicksteed, "The Canadian Northern Montreal–Port Arthur Line," 16 (September 1913), 407; "Electrification of the Mount Royal Tunnel, Canadian Northern Railway," 16 (November 1913), 530.

43 See *Canadian Railway and Marine World*: "Canadian Northern Railway, Construction Betterments, Etc.," 17 (October 1914), 467; "The Canadian Northern Railway's Station in Montreal," 20 (July 1917), 257–59.

44 "New Terminals at Montreal for Canadian National Railways," *Canadian Railway and Marine World* 32 (July 1929), 415–18.

45 A set of six exterior perspective drawings in graphite, 40 x 60 cm and 80 x 60 cm, at McGill University, CAC, 19 1001003/1–6.

46 *La Revue Populaire* (January 1931), 11–14.

47 Alfred Fellheimer and Steward Wagner, *Studies for the Windsor Street Terminal Facilities* (New York 1930), Canadian Pacific Corporate Archives.

48 Linda O. Stanford, "Railway Designs by Fellheimer and Wagner, New York to Cincinnati," *Queen City Heritage* (Cincinnati Historical Society) 43:53 (autumn 1985), 11.

49 *Construction* (Toronto) 25:3 (March 1932), 57; see also *Canadian Railway and Marine World*: "Canadian Pacific Railway Station for North End of Montréal," 34 (February 1931), 82; "Station Built at Park Avenue, Montréal, by Canadian Pacific Railway," 34 (December 1931), 745–47.

50 All details and maps pertaining to wharfage development during this period are described in detail in GRHPM, *Travaux d'aménagement du Havre de Montréal 1830–1850* (Montréal: Société du Port de Montréal, 1982).

51 GRHPM, *Construction des élévateurs à grain du Port de Montréal 1885–1970* (Montréal: Société du Port de Montréal, 1981), 15.

52 J.E. Laurin, *Histoire économique de Montréal et des cités et villes du Québec* (Ottawa: Laurin, 1942), 19; Kathleen Jenkins, *Montreal, Island City of the St. Lawrence* (New York: Doubleday, 1966), 340. See also Ernest J. Chambers, *The Book of Montreal* (Montréal: Book of Montreal Co., 1903), 83–85.

53 Chambers, 108; GRHPM, *Construction des élévateurs*, 16–17.

54 Linteau, *Histoire de Montréal*, 136; Rumilly, 124; *Semi-Centennial Report of the Montreal Board of Trade*, 69.

55 GRHPM, *Construction des élévateurs*, 15.

56 An excellent isometric drawing for the identical CPR grain elevators at Fort William (under Charles E. Goad, *Canadian Pacific Railway Elevators, Fort William, Ontario*, Special Survey No. 104, December 1891), complete with technical data, is in the McGill University Rare Books Library.

57 Henry-Russell Hitchcock, "Buffalo Architecture in 1940," in Buffalo Architectural Guidebook Corp., *Buffalo Architecture: A Guide* (Cambridge, Mass.: MIT Press, 1981), 29–31.

58 *Semi-Centennial Report of the Montreal Board of Trade*, 68–69; Marsan, 170.

59 Marsan, 170; Paul-André Linteau, "Le développement du port de Montréal au début du 20e siècle," in CHA/SHC, *Historical Papers/Communications historiques* (1972), 181–205.

60 Rumilly, 317–323.

61 Linteau, *Histoire de Montréal*, 147.

62 Linteau, *Histoire de Montréal*, 145–47; A.R. Pinsoneault, *Atlas of the Island and City of Montreal and Ile Bizard* (Montréal: The Atlas Publishing Co. Ltd., n.d. [c. 1907]).

63 Rumilly, 329; GRHPM, *Construction des élévateurs*, 17–24.

64 Pauline Desjardins, "Les équipements du Port et leur évolution," in *Montréal portuaire et ferroviaire*, 19–21; "New Grain Elevator for the Montreal Harbor Commissioners," *Engineering Record* (5 October 1912), 383–85.

65 Desjardins, 19–20; Rumilly, 370–71; GRHPM, *Construction des élévateurs*, 25–26.

66 Rumilly, 320.

67 John S. Metcalf Co. Ltd., *Grain Elevators* (Montréal: Librairie Beauchemin, 1926).

68 "New Grain Elevator for the Montreal Harbor Commissioners," 383–85.

69 See Reyner Banham, *A Concrete Atlantis: U.S. Industrial Building and European Modern Architecture* (Cambridge, Mass.: MIT Press, 1986); also Lisa Mahar-Keplinger, *Grain Elevators* (New York: Princeton Architectural Press, 1965).

70 Linteau, *Histoire de Montréal*, 147.

71 GRHPM, *Construction des élévateurs*, 26.

72 G.P. Glazebrook, *A History of Transportation in Canada* (originally published 1938; Toronto: McClelland and Stewart, 1964), vol. 2, 227.

73 CRER 38:2 (1924); GRHPM, *Construction des élévateurs*, 59–68.

74 *The Tramway and Railway World* (18 December 1924), 322–24.

75 Linteau, *Histoire de Montréal*, 290.

76 See Melvin Charney, "The Grain Elevator Revisited," *Architectural Design* 37 (July 1967), 328–31.

77 George Musk, *Canadian Pacific Afloat 1883–1968* (Warrington, England: Canadian Pacific, 1968), 13.

78 William W. Kratville, *Steam, Steel, and Limiteds* (Omaha: Kratville Publications, 1967), 60–61, 64–67; also CPR timetable (September 1930),

79 Kratville, 60–65; CPR timetable

80 Kratville, 401, 405, 408; CPR timetable (September 1930).

81 Meeks, 158–59 and figs. 224–25.

82 Leonard L. Knott, *La Place* (Montréal: Rolph, Clark, Stone, Benallack, 1962).

83 Julie Harris, "Les aéroports," in *Bâtir un pays: Histoire des travaux publics au Canada,* ed. N. Ball (Montréal: Boréal, 1988), 313.

84 Glazebrook, vol. 2, 259.

85 Edwin C. Guillet, *The Story of Canadian Roads* (Toronto: University of Toronto Press, 1966).

86 L.R. Wilson, *The Montreal–South Shore Bridge: Fabrication and Erection of the Superstructure of the Montreal–South Shore Bridge* (Montréal: Dominion Bridge Co., 1930), 7.

A Community of Communities

1 Paul-André Linteau, *Histoire de Montréal depuis la Confédération* (Montréal: Boréal, 1992), 39–40, 160.

2 Jean-Pierre Collin, "Pouvoir municipal et enjeux politiques locaux dans la Paroisse de Montréal, de 1871 à 1921" (M.A. thesis, Département de sciences politique, UQAM, 1982), 23.

3 From 2,549 to 13,053 hectares. Jean-Pierre Collin, *Histoire de l'urbanisation de la Paroisse de Montréal, 1851–1941* (Montréal: INRS-Urbanisation, 1984), 30.

4 The proportion would increase to 18.5 percent by 1931 and remain almost static until 1945. See Table 12.1 in Linteau, *Histoire de Montréal*, 314.

5 From 1907, however, Montreal could schedule the suburb's referendum on the City's own terms of union. *Statutes of Quebec*, 7 Edw. 7, 1907, c. 63.

6 *Census of Canada*, 1881 and 1901.

7 Collin, "Pouvoir municipal," 152, 172–75.

8 For instance, Victor Hudon's textile mill and Macdonald Tobacco. Paul-André Linteau, *The Promoters' City: Building the Industrial Town of Maisonneuve,*

1883–1918, transl. Robert Chodos (Toronto: Lorimer, 1985), 85–87.

9 *Statutes of Quebec*, 1 Geo. 5, 1910, c. 63; Ville de Montréal-Est, *Cinquantième anniversaire de la Ville de Montréal-Est* (1960), unpaginated [9, 23, 25, 76, 80, and maps facing back cover].

10 Calculated from the Town's 1959 census, summarized in Ville de Montréal-Est, *Cinquantième anniversaire*, [80].

11 Julien Déziel, *Histoire de Verdun, 1665, 1876–1976* (Verdun: Comité du Centenaire, 1976), 84–85, 89, 96, 107, 111, 129, 157–70. Further improvements were made in 1904 and 1915.

12 Collin, *Histoire de l'urbanisation*, 135; Linteau, *Histoire de Montréal*, 214–17.

13 David B. Hanna, "Montreal: A City Built by Small Builders, 1867–1880" (Ph.D. diss., Dept. of Geography, McGill University, 1986), ch. 5.

14 Élie-J. Auclair, *Saint-Henri des Tanneries de Montréal* (Montréal: Imprimerie de-la-Salle, 1942), 63, 85.

15 Michelle Benoît and Roger Gratton, *Les villages du "Plateau": Le patrimoine de Montréal, Quartiers du Plateau Mont-Royal,* Collection "Pignon sur rue" no. 6 (Montréal: CIDEM-Communications, n.d.), 6, 40; Collin, *Histoire de l'urbanisation*, 94–98.

16 Linteau, *The Promoters' City*, 55–78, 123, 128.

17 Benoît and Gratton, *Le rêve industriel: Le patrimoine de Montréal, Quartiers Hochelaga, Maisonneuve et Préfontaine,* Collection "Pignon sur rue" no. 5 (Montréal: CIDEM-Communications, n.d.), 18, 22.

18 Linteau, *The Promoters' City*, 144–69.

19 Terry Copp, *The Anatomy of Poverty: The Condition of the Working Class in Montreal, 1897–1929* (Toronto: McClelland and Stewart, 1974), ch. 2.

20 Lloyd G. Reynolds, *The British Immigrant: His Social and Economic Adjustment in Canada* (Toronto: Oxford University Press, 1935), 128–29.

21 Claude LaRivière, *Crise économique*

et contrôle social: le cas de Montréal (1929–1937) (Montréal: Éditions coopératives Albert Saint-Martin, 1977), 152.

22 John S. Bryce, "The Making of Westmount, Quebec, 1870–1929: A Study of Landscape and Community Construction" (M.A. thesis, Dept. of Geography, McGill University, 1990), 10.

23 Françoise Ricour, "Outremont: monographie urbaine" (predoctoral diss., Faculté des lettres, Université de Montréal, 1962), 6.

24 The words of Armstrong and Cook, the principal developers of Montreal West, in their advertisement in *The Montreal Star,* 10 February 1912.

25 For example in the "Dufferin District," south of present-day Place-des-Arts. Collin, "Pouvoir municipal," 106.

26 A copy of the deed of sale is in the possession of Dr. Frederick Bode of 75 Columbia Avenue.

27 *The Montreal Star*, 17 April 1903.

28 L.D. McCann, "Planning and Building the Corporate Suburb of Mount Royal, 1910–1925," *Planning Perspectives* 11 (1996), 283 n. 99; *Statutes of Quebec*, 17 Geo. 5, 1926, c. 90.

29 Ville de Notre Dame de Grâces, *Livre des Règlements du Conseil,* Règlement 57.

30 Ville de Notre Dame de Grâces, *Livre des Minutes des Délibérations du Conseil municipal,* 30 August and 7 December 1909.

31 Ville de Notre Dame de Grâces, *Rôle d'Évaluation 1909*, vols. 4 and 5.

32 Hubert Groves, ed., *History of the City of Westmount* (Westmount: The Westmount News, n.d. [1913]), 2.

33 Town of Westmount and City of Westmount, *By-laws 136 to 246,* By-laws 190 (1909) and 229 (1911).

34 *The Westmount News*, 16 August 1912.

35 Town of Outremont, *By-laws,* vol. 2, By-laws 87 (1910) and 98 (1911).

36 Danny Fry, "A History of Hampstead, 1914–1957" (seminar research essay, Dept. of History, Concordia University, 1980), 21.

37 *The Westmount News*, 23 February 1912.

38 Westmount, *By-laws 61 to 135*, By-law 75 (1897). The failure of both the Province's Town Corporations General Clauses Act and Westmount's town charter to grant such power proved easy to remedy. The Town simply asked its member of the Quebec Legislature to oversee passage of a private member's bill that added the needed authority to the Town charter (Statutes of Quebec, 59 Victoria, 1895, ch. 54). Obtaining additional powers in this way was common practice among growing towns and cities in Quebec.

39 Westmount, *By-laws 136 to 246*, By-law 184 (1908).

40 Westmount, *By-laws 136 to 246*, By-law 190.

41 City of Westmount, *By-law Records No. 4*, By-law 266 (1913).

42 Robert Rumilly, *Histoire d'Outremont (1875–1975)* (Montréal: Leméac, 1975), 116–19, 124. The trend towards rows of duplexes and triplexes, before that use was confirmed in the 1910 Building By-law, is evident. On Durocher Avenue, for instance, 17 existed before 1910. Calculated from Pierre-Richard Bisson et Associés, "Le Patrimoine Architectural d'Outremont: Inventaire photographique" (Outremont: City Clerk's Office, 1990), vol. 9.

43 Town of Outremont, *By-laws*, vol. 1, By-law 63 (1905); vol. 2, By-law 87 (1910).

44 Westmount, *By-law Records No. 4*, By-law 413; Outremont, *By-laws*, vol. 4, By-law 232.

45 Linteau, *Histoire de Montréal*, 354.

46 Robert Fishman, *Bourgeois Utopias: The Rise and Fall of Suburbia* (New York: Basic Books, 1987), 53–54.

47 Westmount began to establish its "building lines" in 1898 and had regulated most of the town by 1912. The required depths ranged, tellingly, from 8 feet (2.4 m) along Bruce Avenue (adjacent to the CPR) to 25 feet (3.7 m) on the north side of The Boulevard. By 1911, Outremont had placed setbacks of 10 feet (3 m) along

most plebeian streets, of 20 feet (6.1 m) along most others, and of 30 feet (9.1 m) along the finest ones, like Côte St. Catherine Road. Westmount, *By-laws 61–135*, By-law 103 (1902); *By-law Records No. 4*, By-law 251 (1912); Outremont, *By-laws*, vol. 2, By-laws 87 (1910) and 94 (1911).

48 Outremont, *By-laws*, vol. 2, By-law 87 (1910), sec. 14; vol. 4, By-law 181 (1925).

49 Westmount, *By-laws 61 to 135*, By-law 103 (1899); *By-laws 136–246*, By-law 224 (1910); *The Westmount News*, 10 and 24 March 1911.

50 Westmount, *By-law Records No. 4*, By-law 318. Applicants were granted the right of appeal to Council.

51 Town of Mount Royal, *Minute Books*, 4 May 1921; McCann, 286.

52 Fry, 20–21.

53 Outremont, *By-laws*, vol. 5, By-law 223.

54 *The Westmount News*, 1 July 1910.

55 Collin, "Pouvoir municipal," 170–71; W.D. Lighthall, "Westmount: A Municipal Illustration," *University of Toronto Studies in History and Economics* 2 (1907), 31; Westmount, *By-laws 136–246*, By-law 221 (1910); *The Westmount News*, 16 December 1910, 26 May 1911.

56 Ricour, 20.

57 Collin, *Histoire d'urbanisation*, 136.

58 Déziel, 71, 140.

59 Collin, "Pouvoir municipal," 163.

60 Town of Côte Saint-Antoine, *Book of By-laws*, By-law 13 (1877).

61 See letter from Alderman Hyde, *The Westmount News*, 25 November 1910.

62 *The Westmount News*, 16 February 1912.

63 Ricour, 26.

64 Outremont, *By-laws*, vol. 1, By-law 23 (1888); Rumilly, 205.

65 *The Westmount News*, 23 June 1911.

66 Westmount, *By-laws 61–135*, By-law 82 (1897); *The Westmount News*, 27 June 1908.

67 *The Westmount News*, 13 August 1909, 14 November 1910.

68 *The Westmount News*, 23 November 1907, 26 June 1909; Lighthall, 28.

69 Westmount, *By-laws 61–135*, By-law 69 (1896); *By-laws 136–246*,

By-laws 198 (1909) and 246 (1911).

70 *The Westmount News*, 12 June 1909; 19 November 1909.

71 *The Westmount News*, 26 June 1909.

72 *The Westmount News*, 14 April 1911; Rumilly, 188–89.

73 Westmount, *By-laws 136–246*, By-law 184.

74 Collin, *Histoire d'urbanisation*, 147.

75 See the advertisement for the building, in Collin, *Histoire d'urbanisation*, facing 148.

76 In 1910–11 Outremont restricted apartment construction to specified streets in the eastern section, requiring all apartments over three storeys to be of First Class construction. In 1913, Westmount rescinded its ban on apartment construction but restricted it to five small areas (all south of Sherbrooke) plus the entire lengths of Atwater Avenue and St. Catherine and Sherbrooke streets. None might exceed a height of 50 feet (15.2 m) and all must be of First Class construction. Outremont, *By-laws*, By-laws 87 (1910) and 94 (1911); Westmount, *By-law Records No. 4*, By-law 266 (1913). (By-law 339 [1919] did allow 3-storey apartments to be of Second Class construction.)

77 This was the case from the outset of our period: already in 1881, 90 percent of Montreal's population east of St. Lawrence Boulevard was of French origin, compared to only 30 percent west of that line. Linteau, *Histoire de Montréal*, 47.

78 Town of Mount Royal Archives, *Minute Books*, 12 May 1926, 7 July 1926.

79 Linteau, *The Promoters' City*, 42.

80 Rumilly, 52–55, 58, 68, 74, 76, 158, 116–19, 127–28.

81 Rumilly, 143, 172–73, 192.

82 Marc J. Levine, *The Reconquest of Montreal: Language Policy and Social Change in a Bilingual City* (Philadelphia: Temple University Press, 1990), 13.

83 Bryce, 59.

84 William Westfall, *Two Worlds: The Protestant Culture of Nineteenth-Century Ontario* (Montréal: McGill-Queen's University Press, 1989), 130–34, 139.

85 Aline Gubbay and Sally Hooff, *Montreal's Little Mountain: A Portrait of Westmount* (Westmount: Trillium Books, 1979), 14, 96; *The Westmount News*, 24 June 1910, 21 March 1913.

86 A list of these buildings giving the total cost of each appears in Groves, 31.

87 *The Westmount News*, 29 February 1908.

88 The extent to which subdividers determined the street layouts of older suburbs should not be exaggerated. While the location of side streets was often controlled by developers, surveyors working for suburban governments would make plans showing the future routes of principal arteries, and the towns would homologate such plans in Superior Court well in advance of actual construction, so that abutting proprietors could not build on the rights-of-way and later claim compensation. Quebec municipalities had enjoyed this power since at least 1870 (*Statutes of Quebec*, 34 Vict., c. 68). Westmount, for example, homologated the route for Sherbrooke Street in 1880 but did not begin construction west of Clarke Avenue until 1892. Westmount, *By-laws 1–60*, By-law 20 (1892).

89 An exclusive neighbourhood with curving streets in Outremont, laid out before the First World War, is the Maplewood Avenue area (next to Mount Royal Cemetery). In Westmount, in 1910, Herbert Holt and partners commissioned a curvilinear street plan for their "West Crescent Heights" development north of The Boulevard, and in the late 1920s the "Priests' Farm" project (on land bought from the Sulpicians) was designed with curved lanes by the architectural firm of Shorey and Ritchie. Westmount, *By-laws 136–246*, By-law 222 (1910); Gubbay and Hooff, 117–18. It should be added that, having followed ancient Amerindian trails, a few old roads like Côte St. Antoine in Westmount and Côte St. Catherine in Outremont had become curving

thoroughfares without benefit of modern planning.

90 McCann, 276–79.

91 Fry, 1–2.

92 *The Westmount News*, 16 November 1907.

93 Bryce, 88.

94 While Westmount was first to begin the conversion (1909), Outremont became the first town in Canada to have its streetlight network powered by underground cables (December 1914). *The Westmount News*, 17 July 1909; Outremont, *By-laws*, vol. 2, By-law 108 (1913); Rumilly, 171, 178, 183–84

95 *The Westmount News*, 25 April 1913; Rumilly, 202.

96 Rumilly, 148, 197–99; Déziel, 125, 137; *The Westmount News*, 18 and 25 November 1910.

Montreal Architects and the Challenge of Commissions

1 "Construction: Montreal," *CAB* 1:1 (January 1888), 6.

2 Raymonde Landry-Gauthier, "Victor Bourgeau et l'architecture religieuse et conventuelle dans le diocèse de Montréal" (Ph.D. diss. in arts, Université Laval, 1983).

3 The historical data in this chapter is drawn from research for this book and also from a study of the architectural profession in Quebec (1890–1939) funded by the Conseil de recherches en sciences humaines. Documentation of the architects and their careers was carried out with the collaboration of Michèle Picard and David Rose. Assistance with regard to professional organizations and architectural training was also provided by Réjean Legault and Guy Besner. General information on the architects is drawn from Robert Hill, *Biographical Dictionary of Architects in Canada 1800–1950* (June 1986).

4 Hugh G. Jones, in collaboration with Edmund Dyonnet, "History of the Royal Canadian Academy of Arts," manuscript, 1934, 2.4.

5 Barrington Kaye, *The Development of the Architectural Profession in Britain: A Sociological Study* (London: George Allen and Unwin Ltd., 1960), 41, 82; Andrew Saint, "The Architect as Professional: Britain in the Nineteenth Century," in *The Image of the Architect* (New Haven: Yale University Press, 1985), 61, 62; Howard Colvin, "The Beginnings of the Architectural Profession in Scotland," *Architectural History: Journal of the Society of Architectural Historians of Great Britain* 29 (1986), 178–79.

6 Jean-Pierre Epron, Bertrand Lemoine, and Jacques Rosen, Preface to *Architecture Architectes: Enseignement, institution, profession, Anthologie 1790–1948*, ed. J.-P. Epron, B. Lemoine, J. Rosen, and F. Coulamy (Paris: Institut français d'architecture, 1981), 28–33; Paul R. Baker, *Richard Morris Hunt* (Cambridge, Mass.: MIT Press, 1980), 108–17.

7 The architectural community lacked critical mass, as was noted by architect and engineer Charles Baillairgé in his "Organization of the Province of Quebec Association of Architects," *CAB* 3:10 (October 1890), 114.

8 Kelly Crossman, *Architecture in Transition: From Art to Practice, 1885–1906* (Montréal and Kingston: McGill-Queen's University Press, 1987), 9–27.

9 "Montreal: A Prophet Hath Honor Save in His Own Country," *CAB* 2:8 (August 1889), 91.

10 "Quebec," *CAB* 3:3 (March 1890), 30–31.

11 "Quebec Architects Organizing," *CAB* 3:5 (May 1890), 53.

12 Baillargé, 112–14.

13 *An Act to Incorporate The Province of Quebec Association of Architects* s.q. 54 Vict., 1890, c. 59, 101.

14 *L'œuvre d'un siècle: les Frères des Écoles Chrétiennes du Canada* (Montréal: Les Frères des Écoles Chrétiennes du Canada, 1937), 315.

15 Courses given in high schools by practising architects focused mainly on religious architecture, as Norbert Schoenauer remarks in *Stewart Henbest Capper, First Macdonald Professor of Architecture* (Montréal: McGill University Press, 1996), 5.

16 The expression "mechanic" referred to anyone paid for manual labour, according to Pierre Leduc in "Notes sur les origines et la première phase de développement du mouvement des Mechanics' Institutions en Grande-Bretagne," *Recherches sociographiques* 16:2 (1975), 256–60. Ruby Heap, "Un chapitre dans l'histoire de l'éducation des adultes au Québec: les écoles du soir, 1889–1892," *Revue d'histoire de l'Amérique française* 34:4 (March 1981), 598–99. Two architects were chairmen of the Mechanics' Institute of Montreal: David Brown in 1844 and John Ostell in 1846. Ralph Mackay, *The Mechanics' Institute of Montreal/Atwater Library Archive Holding* (Montréal: Mechanics' Institute, 1994), n.p.

17 Jean-Pierre Charland, *L'enseignement spécialisé au Québec: 1867 à 1982* (Quebec City: Institut québécois de recherche sur la culture, 1982), 74.

18 Nikolaus Pevsner, *Academies of Art, Past and Present* (Cambridge: The University Press, 1940), 243–49.

19 Description of the architectural drafting courses at the Conseil des arts et manufactures de la Province de Québec, "Règlements des classes de dessin industriel du soir, École de Montréal, 1893–1894," 6, ANQM, Fonds Conseil des Arts et Manufactures, microfilm 1641.

20 James Philip Noffsinger, *The Influence of the Ecole des Beaux-Arts on the Architects of the United States* (Washington: Catholic University of America Press, 1955), plate 1, 24.

21 In his speech at the inaugural banquet, the architect Andrew Taylor recounted his several attempts to create a Chair of Architecture at McGill University: "Organization of the Province of Quebec Association of Architects," *CAB* 3:10 (October 1890), 116; see also the letter sent by the secretary to the governor of McGill College, "Montreal, May 3, 1893, Assemblée mensuelle régulière du Conseil ...," Minute Book of the PQAA, vol. 1, 315. At the annual general meeting in September 1893, the debate on the election of a new chairman centred on this question. See Charles Baillairgé, "Plaidoyer en faveur d'une école canadienne d'architecture," *CAB* 6:9 (September 1893), 104–10; the discussion of a newspaper campaign in favour of setting up a Canadian School of Architecture, in the bound manuscript of the Record of Meetings of the PQAA, vol. 2, 19; and the letter from McGill University thanking the PQAA for its support in the creation of the Chair of Architecture, December 1896, "Échange épistolaire entre l'AAPQ et Macdonald, le fondateur de la chaire d'architecture," Record of Meetings of the PQAA, vol. 3, 37, 51, 53.

22 As proposed by Schoenauer, 5.

23 An attitude emphasized by D.C. Masters, "The Scottish Tradition in Higher Education," in *The Scottish Tradition in Canada*, ed. Stanford W. Reid (Toronto: McClelland and Stewart, 1976), 259.

24 Stanley Brice Frost, *McGill University for the Advancement of Learning 1895–1971* (Montréal and Kingston: McGill-Queen's University Press, 1984), vol. 2, 5–6, 13–14.

25 Robert Gagnon, *Histoire de l'École Polytechnique de Montréal* (Montréal: Boréal, 1991), 137.

26 Stanford W. Reid, "The Scottish Background," in *The Scottish Tradition in Canada*, 9.

27 Schoenauer, 9; John Bland, "Ramsay Traquair: Biography," in *Ramsay Traquair and His Successors: Guide to the Archives/ Ramsay Traquair et ses successeurs: Guide du fonds*, ed. Irena Murray (Montréal: CAC, 1987), vol. 1, 10. William Peterson stayed in close touch with his native land; see Frost, 7.

28 Norbert Schoenauer, "McGill's School of Architecture: A Retrospection," *McGill Schools of Architecture and Urban Planning, Prospectus* (Montréal: McGill Schools of Architecture and Urban Planning, 1987), 4, 5.

29 Founded in 1892, the Edinburgh College of Art taught architecture and crafts in the true spirit of the Arts and Crafts movement; in 1907 it merged with the city's art college. Alan Powers, "Architectural Education and the Arts and Crafts Movements in England," *Architectural Education* 3 (1983), 49. In 1904 Traquair became a teacher at the college, and when a department of architecture was established was appointed its head. Bland, 9; see also Isabelle Gournay, "The First Leaders of McGill's School of Architecture: Stewart Henbest Capper, Percy Nobbs, and Ramsay Traquair," *SSAC Bulletin SEAC* 21:3 (September 1996), 60–64.

30 Susan Wagg, *Percy Erskine Nobbs: Architect, Artist, Craftsman* (Montréal and Kingston: McGill-Queen's University Press, 1982), 21.

31 Bland, 9, 10.

32 During its difficult early days the École could not bring in qualified professors of engineering directly from France, but a number of the first instructors were Canadians of French birth. Gagnon, 55–63.

33 In 1882 the government of Quebec preceded its federal counterpart in appointing a representative to Paris to promote French investment in Quebec. At the turn of the century many university students and young artists went to finish their training in Paris. Bernard Pénisson, "Le Commissariat canadien à Paris," *Revue d'histoire de l'Amérique française* 34:3 (December 1890), 369.

34 Hébrard's refusal resulted in the appointment of the French painter Edmond Dyonnet as professor of drawing. Robert Gagnon and Armand J. Ross, "La montée des ingénieurs francophones," in *Histoire de l'École Polytechnique de Montréal*, 137. Dyonnet, who came to Canada in 1875, became professor of drawing at the Montreal school of the Conseil des arts et manufactures in the early 1890s. "Montreal (Correspondence of the *CAB*)," *CAB* 2:1 (January 1889), 10;

"Montreal," *CAB* 7:11 (November 1894), 142.

35 Pierre-Richard Bisson, "Anniversaires: Max Doumic (1863–1914)," *ARQ* 38 (August 1987), 32–33.

36 Francine Couture and Suzanne Lemerise, "Insertion sociale de l'École des beaux-arts de Montréal: 1923–1969," in "L'enseignement des arts au Québec" (manuscript; Montréal: Université du Québec à Montréal, 1980), 4.

37 *An Act to Incorporate the PQAA*, 1890, c. 163–64; *An Act Respecting the Association of Architects*, R.S.Q. 1925, c. 220, 2701–13.

38 *An Act to Amend the Act Incorporating the Province of Quebec Association of Architects*, S.Q. 61 Vict., 1898, c. 33, 58–59; *An Act to Amend the Architects' Act*, R.S.Q. 19 Geo. 5, 1929, c. 67, 195–96.

39 In Great Britain debate over the restriction of the profession through registration raged for several decades. In 1877 the RIBA gave its support to the establishment of an examination, and in 1886 a bill was drafted to register architects, but the *Architects Registration Act* was not passed until 1931 and imposed relatively few restrictions. Barrington Kaye, *The Development of the Profession in Britain: A Sociological Study* (London: George Allen and Unwin Ltd., 1960), 98–100, 129, 147–53; Andrew Saint, *The Image of the Architect*, 92–94. In the United States the first bill controlling the practice was passed in Illinois in 1897, but in the country as a whole the process was not completed until 1951. Richard Levy, "The Professionalization of American Architects and Civil Engineers, 1865–1917" (Ph.D. diss., Architecture, University of California, Berkeley, 1980), 132–38. In France, the law of 1940 creating the Ordre des Architectes established titular protection without imposing a monopoly. Jean-Pierre Epron, *Architecture, une anthologie: Les architectes et le projet* (Brussels and Liège: Mardaga, 1992), vol. 2, 295.

40 David B. Hanna, "The New Town of Montreal" (Master's thesis,

Dept. of Geography, University of Toronto, 1977).

41 Guy Pinard, *Montréal, son histoire, son architecture* (Montréal: Les Éditions La Presse, 1988), vol. 2, 174.

42 The architect of Bonaventure Station was Thomas S. Scott, according to "Montreal," *CAB* 2:1 (January 1889), 9; Mathilde Brosseau, "Le pittoresque et le revivalisme architecturaux au Canada et leur application aux gares du Grand Tronc et du Canadien Pacifique" (Ph.D. diss. in art history, Université de Montréal, 1975).

43 Total derived from the members of the PQAA and the 36 architects in 26 offices who advertised in *Lovell's Directory* of 1890–91.

44 "Montreal," *CAB* 7:5 (May 1894), 66.

45 Baillairgé, "Organization of the Province," 112; "An Act to Incorporate the Province of Quebec Association of Architects," *CAB* 4:4 (March 1891), 35.

46 *An Act to Incorporate the PQAA*, c. 101–68; *An Act to Amend the Act Incorporating the PQAA*, c. 59–60.

47 The use of steel reinforcement became widespread in Canadian building around the middle of the decade, this structure being one of its first appearances in Montreal. Crossman, 74, 78, n. 37.

48 According to *The Metropolis of Canada Illustrated* (Montréal 1894), Hutchison was "one of the most widely and favorably known architects in Montreal."

49 "Mr. A.C. Hutchison, R.C.A.," *CAB* 8:10 (October 1895), 117. He also took courses at a private school. Julia Gersovitz, "Montreal Architects and Their Works, 1870–1914" (Master's thesis, Architecture, Columbia University, 1980), 44.

50 Hutchison explained his stand on training at the inaugural lunch of the PQAA; Baillairgé, "Organization of the Province." He would soon head the PQAA education committee set up in 1891.

51 Ernest John Chambers, *The Book of Montreal: A Souvenir of Canada's Commercial Metropolis* (Montréal: Congress of the Chambers of

Commerce of the British Empire, 5th, 1903).

52 This dynasty of architects sprang from a line of craftsmen in the building trade, in business since French rule in Quebec. Landry-Gauthier, 202.

53 Olivier Maurault, "The University of Montreal," *JRAIC* 3:1 (January–February 1926), 6–7.

54 Landry-Gauthier, 204–07; André Laberge, "Transcender le style et la fonction: l'architecture religieuse de Viau et Venne (1898–1938)" (Ph.D. diss. in humanities, Université Laval, 1990), 42–43.

55 Jacques Lachapelle, "Monument national," in *Les chemins de la mémoire: Monuments et sites historiques du Québec* (Quebec City: Les Publications du Québec, 1991), vol. 2, 84.

56 Robert Rumilly, *Histoire d'Outremont, 1875–1975* (Montréal: Léméac, 1975), 110.

57 *The Montreal Herald*, cited by Stephen Robinson, "An Architect Discovered: The Work of A.F. Dunlop" (Master's thesis, Dept. of Art History, Concordia University, 1992), vol. 1, 6.

58 His Scots-born parents settled in Montreal in the 1840s. Robinson, 8–16.

59 Robinson, 18–22.

60 Knox, Elliott, and Jarvis, "Sun Life Assurance Co. Building Competition – Experts' Report," *CAB* 3:1 (January 1890), 5.

61 Hazel Power, "Robert Findlay and the Macaulay Family Architecture" (Master's thesis, Dept. of Art History, Concordia University, April 1993), 52–86.

62 Crossman, 23.

63 John Bland, "Edward Maxwell: Biography," *Guide to the Archives, Edward and W.S. Maxwell* (Montréal: CAC, 1986), 3.

64 John Bland, "The Importance of the Maxwells in Canadian Architecture," in *The Architecture of Edward and W.S. Maxwell*, ed. Robert Lemire (Montréal: Montreal Museum of Fine Arts, 1991), 18; Robert Sweeny, "Building for Power: The Maxwell Practice and the Montreal Business

Community," in *The Architecture of Edward and W.S. Maxwell*, 35–38.

65 Ellen James, "H. Vincent Meredith House," in *The Architecture of Edward and W.S. Maxwell*, 104–07.

66 Robert Lemire, "Henry Birks and Sons Store and Office Building," in *The Architecture of Edward and W.S. Maxwell*, 71.

67 J.B. Forbes, "Shepley, Bulfinch, Richardson & Abbott: An Introduction," *JSAH* 17:3 (autumn 1958), 23.

68 Robert Lemire, "London & Lancashire Life Assurance Company Building," in *The Architecture of Edward and W.S. Maxwell*, 75.

69 Rosalind M. Pepall, *Construction d'un musée Beaux-Arts, Montréal 1912/Building a Beaux-Arts Museum* (Montréal: Montreal Museum of Fine Arts, 1986), 23. Taylor's rise to prominence is described by Peter F. McNally, "Dignified and Picturesque: Redpath Library in 1893," *Fontanus* 6 (1993), 73.

70 "Mr. A.T. Taylor, F.R.I.B.A.," *CAB* 9:11 (November 1896), 174.

71 In 1892 Taylor was, with architect and OAA chairman W.S. Curry, one of the two experts engaged in organizing the competition for the legislative building of British Columbia in Victoria. Anthony A. Barret and Rhodri Windsor Liscombe, *Francis Rattenbury and British Columbia: Architecture and Challenge in the Imperial Age* (Vancouver: University of British Columbia, 1983), 31.

72 Stanley Brice Frost, *McGill University for the Advancement of Learning, 1801–1895* (Montréal and Kingston: McGill-Queen's University Press, 1980), vol. 1, 273–75; vol. 2, 11–14.

73 John Bland, "McGill's Late Great Victorian Architect, Sir Andrew Taylor," *The Fifth Column* (fall 1981), 32–34.

74 A.T. Taylor, "The Function of Truth in Art," *CAB* 5:12 (December 1892), 120–21.

75 From 1903 onwards Vanier was a member of the Board, sitting for many years as secretary and becoming chairman in 1921. Archives

and year books of the PQAA.

76 "Canada's Largest Concrete Building," *Construction* 3:4 (March 1910), 57–65.

77 Claire Poitras, "Les architectes et l'introduction du béton armé à Montréal de 1900 à 1930" (Master's thesis in art history, Université de Montréal, 1989), 65–66, 88–91, 96–97. The author notes that the Kahn brothers opened a branch in Montreal in 1906 and that the first major construction in reinforced concrete was the American Tobacco Co. Building (1906) in Hochelaga, a state-of-the-art industrial complex built according to the Hennebique system.

78 Jean-René Lassonde, *La bibliothèque Saint-Sulpice, 1910–1931* (Montréal: Bibliothèque nationale du Québec, 1986), 26–27.

79 City of Westmount, *Council Minutes* (6 March 1917), 129.

80 PQAA *Year Book, 1911*, 10–15.

81 *Lovell's Directory* (1911–12).

82 *Directory of Graduates, 1890–1965* (Montréal: McGill University, 1965).

83 In 1898 the PQAA moved from its St. James Street premises to St. Catherine Street in the centre of town. "Province of Quebec Association of Architects," *CAB* 11:3 (March 1898), 49.

84 Henry B. Yates, "The Lives of Edward and William S. Maxwell," in R. Lemire, *The Architecture of Edward and W.S. Maxwell*, 22.

85 In 1907 the Maxwell brothers won competitions for both the Ministry of Justice in Ottawa (unrealized) and the Regina Legislative Building.

86 Some architects took exception to both the competition formula and the selection of candidates (which included David Brown, Hugh Vallance, and Percy E. Nobbs), accusing the Art Association's construction committee of nepotism. Pepall, 33–50.

87 Founded in 1907, the University of Saskatchewan at Saskatoon commissioned Brown and Vallance to devise a master plan for the campus and design several pavilions. *Historic Architecture*

of Saskatchewan (Regina: Saskatchewan Association of Architects, 1986), 151–52.

88 Robert Lemire, "Tudor Gothic in Downtown Montreal 1900–1929," *SSAC Bulletin* 12:1 (March 1987), 16.

89 Canon George-Marie Lepailleur, chairman of the Church committee organizing the religious celebrations of 1910, encouraged Venne to collaborate with Dalbé Viau in the design of the head office for the association of Artisans canadiens-français, and the two became partners in 1912. Their joint career is recounted by Laberge [see n. 54], 45–63.

90 An in-depth study by André Laberge illuminates Venne's early career. His main patrons were the parish priest of Saint-Enfant-Jésus-du-Mile End and its curate, Honoré-Euclide Chagnon, who had become priest of the new parish of Saint-Anselme, and also Brother André of the Congrégation de Sainte-Croix. Laberge, 74–75.

91 Laberge, 119.

92 Wagg [see n. 30], 21.

93 In 1907 Nobbs had organized the competition for the design of the Legislative Building in Regina, Saskatchewan. In 1912 the Nobbs and Hyde firm would design the Arts Building of the University of Alberta, Edmonton.

94 Percy E. Nobbs, "The Styles of Architecture and Style in Architecture," *CAB* 16:11 (November 1903), 185.

95 Robert Rumilly, *Histoire de l'École des Hautes Études Commerciales de Montréal, 1907–1967* (Montréal: Beauchemin, 1967), 33–37.

96 Irène Puchalski, "An Analysis of Four Building Types by John S. Archibald, Architect (1872–1934)" (Master's thesis, Dept. of Art History, Concordia University, 1991), 60–61.

97 Irène Puchalski, "John S. Archibald, Architect (1872–1934)," *The Journal of Canadian Art History* 14:2 (1991), 94–113.

98 Lassonde [see n. 78], 51–70.

99 Paul-André Linteau, *The*

Promoters' City: Building the Industrial Town of Maisonneuve, 1883–1918 (Toronto: Lorimer, 1985), 145–46.

100 Yearbook of the Boston Architectural Club, *The Petit Trianon* (New York: The Architectural Book Publishing Company, 1913), 200 pp.

101 The first of these, John M. Lyle, born in Ontario, studied in Paris from 1892 to 1896, attending the *atelier préparatoire* of Jules Godefroy and Jacques Freynet and in his second year Paul Blondel's *atelier* at the École des Beaux-Arts. Geoffrey Hunt, *John M. Lyle, Toward a Canadian Architecture* (Kingston: Agnes Etherington Art Centre, Queen's University, 1982), 12–17. Lyle does not seem to have received a *diplôme* from the French government.

102 Marchand took a course there in modelling and sculpture. *List of Former Pupils*, Montreal School, Mechanical Class, ANQM, Fonds Conseil des Arts et Manufactures, microfilm 1641.

103 Marchand won the *Prix Chapelin* and received eight medals according to the application form he submitted to the Société des Architectes Diplômés par le Gouvernement, 3 July 1902.

104 Hélène Pelletier-Baillargeon, *Olivar Asselin et son temps* (Montréal: Fides, 1996), 176. Pelletier-Baillargeon provides an overview of the milieux in which Marchand developed in Paris and Montreal. He was a brother-in-law by marriage of the journalist Olivar Asselin and of the French architect Jules Poivert.

105 Pierre-Richard Bisson, "Un monument de classe internationale," *ARQ* 31 (June 1986), 14–17.

106 Lassonde, 68.

107 Enjoying special status, they studied for two years at MIT instead of four, without obtaining a diploma. Jacques Lachapelle, *L'architecture des grands immeubles de Ross et Macdonald, du pragmatisme au fantasme métropolitain* (Quebec City: Université

Laval, 1994), vol. 1, 27, 34, 37.

108 David Rose has begun to clarify the situation, stressing the importance of the competition between railway companies and also between American and Canadian architects, Hays justified his about-face as a demonstration of respect for the profession in Canada. But Rose does not note that the initial architects for another great Grand Trunk railway station, Union Station in Toronto, were the former employers of MacFarlane and Carrère and Hastings, a collaboration that dated to 1906 and may explain the recourse to a young Montreal firm that on the whole had had little experience by 1908. David Rose, "The Hotel Architecture of Ross and MacFarlane/Ross and Macdonald" (Master's thesis, Dept. of Art History, Concordia University, 1992), 28–34.

109 In the 1910s the two firms constructed many buildings along the transcontinental railway lines. For the CPR the Maxwell brothers built the station (1904–05) and Royal Alexandra Hotel (1904–06) at Winnipeg, and the Palliser Hotel (1911–14) at Calgary – buildings that followed those they had done for the CPR in the previous decade. The Ross and MacFarlane/Ross and Macdonald firm built the Fort Garry Hotel (1910–14) at Winnipeg, the Macdonald Hotel (1912–14) at Edmonton, the Qu'Appelle Hotel (1913–14) at Regina, and Union Station (1914–21) at Toronto, in association with Hugh G. Jones and with the collaboration of John M. Lyle.

110 Madeleine Forget, *Gratte-ciel de Montréal* (Montréal: Méridien, 1990), 93.

111 Lachapelle, *L'architecture des grands immeubles*, 68.

112 Their major projects were as follows: in Ottawa the Château Laurier hotel and Union Station (1909–12), in Winnipeg the Fort Garry Hotel (1910–14), in Edmonton the Macdonald Hotel (1912–15), in Toronto the Central Technical School (1912–16), the 20-storey Royal Bank Building (1913–15), and Union Station (1914–21), and in Halifax a vast program of housing reconstruction following the great explosion of 1917.

113 Vancouver Terminal Station (1913–15) and the Credit Foncier Building (1913–14) in Vancouver, the Bank of British North America (1912–14) in Saint John, and the Algonquin Hotel (1914–15) in Saint Andrews-by-the-Sea, New Brunswick. See Susan Wagg, "Selected List of Works," *Ernest Isbell Barott, architecte: Une introduction/Ernest Isbell Barott, architect: An Introduction* (Montréal: CCA, 1985), 36.

114 As designer in chief on the large-scale project for the expansion of Windsor Station. Wagg, *Ernest Isbell Barott*, 6.

115 Sinaiticus, "The Drummond Medical Building," *Construction* 23:9 (September 1930), 297–306.

116 "Annual Report," 14, and "List of Members," PQAA *Year Book, 1928.*

117 *Directory of Graduates, 1890–1965* (Montréal: The Graduates' Society of McGill University, 1965); *Liste des diplômés de Polytechnique, 1877–1945* (Montréal: Association des Diplômés de Polytechnique, 1946; 1972), 121–23; François Giraldeau, "L'enseignement de l'architecture à l'École des beaux-arts de Montréal, de 1923 à 1957" (Master's thesis in planning, Université de Montréal, 1981), vol. 2, 58.

118 "Housing Development – Priests' Farm, Westmount, and Montreal, P.Q.," *JRAIC* 7:12 (December 1930), 445–50.

119 Laberge, 160.

120 Laberge, 176.

121 The historic Royal Bank of Canada Building (1927–28) has a floor space of 41,192 square metres and is 119.5 metres high; the Beaver Hall building of the Bell Telephone Company of Canada (1927–29) covers 25,256 square metres and is 98 metres high. *Répertoire d'architecture traditionnelle sur le territoire de la communauté urbaine de Montréal: les banques* (Montréal: CUM, 1991), 44, and (1983), 157.

122 Abbé Charles Perrier, "Allocution," in *La mission de l'université,* ed. Georges Gauthier (Montréal: Bibliothèque de l'Action française, 1920), 29; cited by Marcel Fournier, "Tradition and Modernism: The Construction of the Université de Montréal," in *Ernest Cormier and the Université de Montréal,* ed. Isabelle Gournay (Montréal: CCA, 1990), 44.

123 Phyllis Lambert, "Architecture Where Cultures Meet," in *Ernest Cormier and the Université de Montréal,* 25.

124 It should not be forgotten that Marchand was one of the architects chosen for the reconstruction of the Parliament Buildings in Ottawa.

125 The members were the architects Louis-A. Amos and Eugène Payette and the engineers Paul Béique, S.A. Baulne (professor at the École Polytechnique), and Augustin Frigon (director of the École). Fournier, 49.

126 Isabelle Gournay, "The Work of Ernest Cormier at the Université de Montréal," in *Ernest Cormier and the Université de Montréal,* ed. Isabelle Gournay (Montréal: CCA, 1990), 76.

127 Grattan D. Thompson, "The Canada Cement Company's Building, Montreal," *Construction* 15:9 (September 1922), 271.

128 Claude Bellavance, *Shawinigan Water and Power, 1898–1963; formation et déclin d'un groupe industriel* (Montréal: Boréal, 1994), 110–12.

129 Wagg, *Ernest Isbell Barott,* 15, 16 n. 37.

130 Sinaiticus, "University Tower Building, Montreal," *Construction* 23:7 (July 1930), 235–40; "Two Storey a Week on Tall Concrete Building in Montreal: Progress on University Tower," *CRER* 43:44 (30 October 1929), 1281–83.

131 *Répertoire d'architecture traditionnelle sur le territoire de la communauté urbaine de Montréal: les appartements* (Montréal: CUM, 1991), 44.

132 As is noted by Pierre-Richard Bisson et al., "Patrimoine architectural d'Outremont," unpublished study, 1.

133 "A 500-Car Garage on the Ramp System," *CRER* 39:21 (27 May 1925), 540–41.

134 Rumilly, *Histoire d'Outremont* [see note 56], 221, 230.

135 Louise Roussel and Danielle Croteau, "Visages d'Outremont: La contribution des firmes Perrault & Gadbois et René Charbonneau à l'architecture résidentielle," *Bulletin SÉAC* 15:1 (March 1990), 5–10.

136 Pierre-Richard Bisson and Suzel Perrotte, *Inventaire des travaux d'architectes à Outremont, de 1904 à 1987* (Montréal: Corporation Architecture, 1990), 13, 31–34.

137 "Building in Montreal for Architectural and Engineering Professions," *CRER* 44:24 (11 June 1930), 707–08.

138 Diana Balmori, "George B. Post: The Process of Design and the New American Architectural Office (1868–1913)," *JSAH* 46:4 (December 1987), 342–55.

139 France Vanlaethem, "Ernest Cormier, un grand professionnel," *The Journal of Canadian Art History* 13:2–14:1 (1990–91), 45–57.

140 This design had previously been published in *Architectural Forum* 39:4 (October 1923), plate 65.

Prestige and Professionalism

The author wishes to thank Annmarie Adams, Mary Beth Betts, Mosette Broderick, Anita Carrico, Paul Chénier, Robert Hill, Robert Lemire, Michael Lewis, Françoise Roux, Hilary Russell, Renata Guttman, and Tony Wrenn.

1 "Board of Trade Building," *CAB* 3:8 (August 1890), 89. The members of the Montreal Board of Trade chose to ignore the misfortune that had befallen their colleagues in Toronto. According to Angela Carr, "the Toronto Board of Trade held a competition for its new building in 1888

and the adjudicator, Professor William R. Ware of Columbia College in New York City awarded first Place to James and James of New York for their seven-story Romanesque design. Construction began in 1889, but was halted by the following February after a major collapse." *Toronto Architect Edmund Burke* (Montréal and Kingston: McGill-Queen's University Press, 1995), 110.

2 "Board of Trade Building," 89.

3 On the events surrounding the Montreal Board of Trade competition, see Kelly Crossman, *Architecture in Transition: From Art to Practice 1885–1906* (Montréal and Kingston: McGill-Queen's University Press, 1987), 23–26.

4 "By the 1890s, Hunt was the most honored American architect of his time and one of the most internationally honored Americans." Paul R. Baker, "Richard Morris Hunt," in *MacMillan Encyclopedia of Architects*, ed. Adolf Placzek (New York: MacMillan, 1982), vol. 2, 443.

5 See Jeffrey Karl Ochsner, *H.H. Richardson: Complete Architectural Works* (Cambridge, Mass.: The MIT Press, 1982), 394–99; J. William Rudd, "The Cincinnati Chamber of Commerce," *JSAH* 27:2 (May 1968), 115–23.

6 See A.W. Reinink, "American Influences on Late Nineteenth-Century Architecture in the Netherlands," *JSAH* 29:2 (May 1970), 163–74; R. Koch, "American Influence Abroad, 1886 and Later," *JSAH* 18:1 (March 1959), 66–69; Dimitri Tselos, "Richardson's Influence on European Architecture," *JSAH* 29:2 (May 1970), 156–62; Myra Dickman Orth, "The Influence of the 'American Romanesque' in Australia," *JSAH* 34:1 (March 1975), 3–18.

7 J.D. Forbes, "Shepley, Bulfinch, Richardson & Abbott, Architects: An Introduction," *JSAH* 17:3 (autumn 1958), 31.

8 "The Montreal Board of Trade Building," *CAB* 4:7 (July 1891), 71. The project is described as "merely a transcript of some of this successful firm's designs for warehouse buildings which have been published frequently in the American architectural journals – lifeless – commonplace – *artless*."

9 Montreal Board of Trade, *Board of Trade, Montreal: A Souvenir of the Opening of the New Building, One Thousand Eight Hundred and Ninety-Three* (Montréal: Sabiston Lithographic and Publishing, 1893), 62.

10 *CAB* 4:5 (May 1891), unnumbered plate.

11 See "Canada," *AABN* 652 (23 June 1888), 291–92. This periodical also denounces the "horrible" jealousy found among Montreal architects; see "Canada," *AABN* 665 (22 September 1888), 135; 678 (22 December 1888), 293; and 747 (19 April 1890), 40.

12 As can be seen from their fascinating correspondence, preserved in the CAC, Percy Nobbs and his fishing companion Bertram Goodhue enjoyed a close friendship and a fruitful exchange of ideas, although Goodhue never built in Montreal.

13 "It is just a little humiliating to the profession here that the work should go to New York. True we have no one here as great as Mr. McKim, but it is a little surprising to find the Montrealers protective instincts not manifesting themselves." The Gargoyle (Percy Nobbs), "Montreal Letter No. III," *CAB* 17:6 (June 1904), 98 (regarding the Mount Royal Club).

14 At the Mount Royal Club the specifications submitted by McKim Mead and White were found too costly by the construction committee, who believed the costs had been inflated by local contractors not accustomed to the strict standards demanded by the architects. Associate architect Alexander C. Hutchison complained of not having been paid by McKim Mead and White when he came to rewrite the specifications.

15 Mention should be made also of Robert E. Bostrom (settled in Montreal in 1910), Harold Lawson (1911), and Harry Edward Prindle (1914).

16 The archives of American architects working in Montreal, like those of their clients, are mostly incomplete and difficult to locate. This research is based primarily on the perusal of specialized periodicals.

17 Projects that never came to fruition aroused no reaction, whether from Montreal's professionals or from the general public. Some of these projects, such as Frank Lloyd Wright's design for the Thaxter house in Westmount, are difficult to document. According to Howard Shubert, in 1906 Wright designed a house for C.T. Shaw, co-founder of the Anglo-Canadian Leather Co., to be built in Westmount between Mountain Avenue and Cedar Avenue. In view of the project's excessively high cost, he finally proposed to renovate his client's residence at 466 Peel Street, just north of Sherbrooke Street. It has never been possible "to establish the precise extent to which these planned renovations were carried out." Howard Shubert, "Frank Lloyd Wright et le Québec," *ARQ* 91 (June 1996), 34. According to Harold Kalman, Wright's only completed project in Canada before 1931 was the leisure centre in Banff (1911–13); *A History of Canadian Architecture* (Toronto, New York, Oxford: Oxford University Press, 1994), vol. 2, 750–51.

18 Earlier, George B. Post, who held a degree in civil engineering from New York University, was called in to help after the collapse of the Montreal Street Railway Building by J.W. and E.C. Hopkins. "Building in Canada in 1894," *CAB* 8:1 (January 1895), 8. On Post, see Winston Weisman, "The Commercial Architecture of George B. Post," *JSAH* 31:3 (October 1972), 176–203; Diana Balmori, "George B. Post: The Process of Design and the New American Architectural Office," *JSAH* 46:4 (December 1987), 342–55; and Lisa B. Mausolf, "A Catalog of the Work of George B. Post, Architect" (Master's thesis, Historic Preservation, Columbia University, 1983).

19 Thomas Hastings and Charles Allerton Coolidge were appointed *Chevaliers* of the Ordre de la Légion d'Honneur in 1901, Charles McKim received the gold medal of the RIBA in 1903, and Whitney Warren was elected a corresponding member of the Académie des Beaux-Arts de l'Institut de France in 1905 and foreign associate in 1909.

20 In Toronto, Carrère and Hastings built, among other projects, the Royal Alexandra Theatre (1904–06, in association with John Lyle, once their employee), the Traders' Bank of Canada (1905–07, in association with Francis S. Baker; now Morgan Bank), the Bank of Toronto (1912, in association with Eustace C. Bird; now demolished); the banking hall of the Toronto branch of the Royal Bank (1913–15, in association with Eustace C. Bird and Ross and MacDonald, the architects of the building; now the Guardian Realty Building). They built branches of the Bank of Toronto at Gananoque and Petrolia, branches of the Dominion Bank in Windsor (1904), Vancouver (1905 and 1911), and Victoria (1913), and branches of the Royal Bank in Winnipeg (1905), San Juan, Puerto Rico (1911), William Street, New York (1911), and Port of Spain, Trinidad (1912). See "The Work of Messrs Carrère and Hastings," *The Architectural Record* 27:1 (January 1910), 1–120; Curtis Channing Blake, "The Architecture of Carrère and Hastings" (Ph.D. diss., Architecture, Columbia University, 1976). The condescending attitude taken by Bird, a Canadian who headed Carrère and Hastings's Toronto office, gave rise to impassioned debate in the Canadian architectural press, described by Angela Carr (see note 1), 132–35. On Bird, see Eric Arthur and Stephen A. Otto, *Toronto: No Mean City* (Toronto: University of Toronto Press, 1986), 242.

21 "Precautions against fire have been made to accord with the requirements of the New York fire

department, which are said to be the most stringent in the world." "Montreal (Correspondence of the *CAB*)," *CAB* 11:8 (August 1898), 138. See also Dane Lanken, *Montreal Movie Palaces* (Waterloo: Penumbra Press, 1993), 34–35. John Bailey McElfatrick figures among Hardenbergh, McKim, Mead, Post, Price, and White as one of *King's Notable New Yorkers of 1896–1899* (New York: Moses King, 1899). David Byrne Blackwood, "The Theaters of J.B. McElfatrick and Sons 1855–1922" (Ph.D. diss., History, University of Texas, 1966), does not mention the theatre in Montreal.

22 Lanken, 74–81. According to Hilary Russell, Lamb's job book records over 60 projects, some probably not realized, in Canada (22 in Montreal), including some 16 new cinemas and the renovation of 3 others. "An Architect's Progress: Thomas White Lamb," *Marquee* 21:1 (1989), 24–25. In Toronto, Lamb built the multi-storey Loew's on Yonge Street (1913, with 2,149 seats) and the Winter Garden (1914), the Regent (1916), His Majesty's (1916), the Loew's Uptown (1920), and Pantages Theater (1920) which, with its 3,626 seats, was the largest cinema ever built in Canada. Lamb also built in Ontario (notably in Brantford, Hamilton, London, Windsor, and Ottawa) and in Western Canada (Vancouver, Victoria, Calgary, and Winnipeg). The Montreal Loew's was the first Canadian example of Lamb's Adam-revival style, which was followed by a more flamboyant Baroque approach. Lamb also produced theatres in London, England, the Caribbean, Central and South America, Egypt, Australia, South Africa, and India. According to D. Lanken (*Montreal Movie Palaces*, 90), Lamb had very little to do with the Capitol project, which was carried out by his Toronto office probably with the participation of L.-J.-T. Décary.

23 Lanken, 54–59.

24 Lanken, 99–100.

25 Philip Dombowsky, "Theaters of the 1996 Conclave," *Marquee* 28:1

(1996), 13–14.

26 *The Inland Architect and News Record* 13:5 (May 1889), unnumbered plate.

27 *CAB* 5:5 (May 1892), plate 5.

28 We should also mention the Stanley Stanger house (1928), designed by the New York architect Ernest Flagg (1857–1947), illustrated in "Simplicity After the English Manner: The Home of Stanley Stanger, Esq., Queen Mary Road, Montreal," *Canadian Homes and Gardens* 5:8 (August 1928), 23. Few mail-order house designs, sold by catalogue, appear to have been imported from the United States. A notable exception was the Jane Lucretia house (1906) on Côte St. Catherine Road in Outremont, attributed to the architectural firm of Jacob H. Daverman and Son of Grand Rapids, Michigan, whose advertisements for house designs often appeared in American interior-design magazines. Charles Platt (1861–1933) served as consultant on the expansion and renovation of the Jeffrey Hale Burland house (1924–26) on Pine Avenue.

29 The attribution to Badgley of the Methodist Church on Coursol at the corner of Canning Street (1890) and the Methodist Church in Point St. Charles on Wellington at the corner of Charron (1891; now demolished) is based on a study of the inventory of building permits listed in the *Prix Courant* archived at the CCA Library. The first of these attributions is also supported by Sidney Rose Badgley's *An Architectural Souvenir, Consisting of Some of the Work Done During Twenty Years by S.R. Badgley* (Cleveland: The Cleveland Prtg. and Publ. Co., 1896), which carries a reproduction of the Coursol Street church captioned the "Centenary Methodist Church." Numerous modifications made to the upper part of this church were carried out by D. Jerome Spence, according to the *Répertoire d'architecture traditionnelle sur le territoire de la Communauté urbaine de Montréal: Architecture religieuse – Les églises* (Montréal: CUM, 1981),

84. Two handsome churches built by Badgley in Cleveland – the Epworth Memorial Methodist Church (1891–94) and the Pilgrim Congregational Church (1894) – are described and illustrated in Eric Johannesen, *Cleveland Architecture, 1876–1976* (Cleveland: The Western Reserve Historical Society, 1979), 23, 28. See "Architect Sidney Rose Badgley: His Disbelief in Competitions," *Ohio Architect and Builder* (August 1908), 23–28.

30 See Clifton Chin, "A Report on the Church of the Ascension in Westmount" (student paper, Blackader-Lauterman Library of Art and Architecture, McGill University, 1967).

31 The American company Lockwood Greene, which specialized in building textile factories, maintained an office in Montreal between 1913 and 1925. It built many factories, chiefly in the metropolis (the Montreal Shirt and Overall Co., Canadian Consolidated Rubber Co.) but also across Quebec (the Dominion Rubber Co. and Canadian Consolidated Rubber Co. Dam, Saint-Jérôme; the Granby Rubber Co.; the Canadian Shoe Manufacturing Co., Drummondville) and in Ontario and New Brunswick. Lockwood Greene built factories in China and Norway and offices for the All American Cables company in Lima, Peru, and Santa Elena, Ecuador. See Lockwood, Greene, and Company, *Industrial Plants Illustrating Building with Foresight* (Boston: The Company, [1921]); Samuel Bicknell Lincoln, *Lockwood Greene: The History of an Engineering Business 1832–1958* (Brattleboro: Stephen Greene Press, 1960).

32 "Où L'Hygeia rencontre le Bouddha: La Science Moderne s'unit à l'Art Oriental dans le Nouvel Hôtel des Thés SALADA," *Le Prix Courant* 34:44 (2 November 1921), 17–18.

33 According to Gerald Bloomfield, Kahn built assembly-line factories on the same model in Toronto (1915) and Winnipeg (1916), and built a factory in Montreal (undated in his article) for the Cana-

dian Consolidated Rubber Co. "Albert Kahn and Canadian Industrial Architecture," SSAC *Bulletin SEAC* 10:4 (December 1985), 10.

34 "New Central Y.M.C.A. Building, Montreal," *Construction* 6:7 (July 1913), 252–54.

35 On the Ross Pavilion, see Edward F. Stevens, "The American Hospital Development: Part II," *The Architectural Record* 39:1 (January 1916), 82–83; Edward F. Stevens, "Ross Pavilion of the Royal Victoria Hospital," *Construction* 10:6 (June 1917), 189–95; Edward F. Stevens, "Ross Pavilion of the Royal Victoria Hospital, Montreal," *The Modern Hospital* 12:5 (May 1919), 311–15 (Stevens was co-author of *Modern Hospitals* [New York: The American Architect, 1912] and author of *The American Hospital of the Twentieth Century* [New York: Dodge Corporation, first published in 1918]); Harold H. Smith, "Royal Victoria Montreal Maternity Hospital," *Construction* 19:8 (August 1926), 238–49.

36 It should be noted that the competition entries for the Fraser Institute by the architects T.M. Clark and Ware and Van Brunt of Boston were published along with that of Geo. Keller of Hartford in the *AABN* 1:26 (August 1876). According to L.B. Mausolf, Post had submitted a design for the Canadian Bank of Commerce in 1881. Mausolf [see n. 18], 26.

37 "Building of the Standard Life Assurance Association, Montreal, P.Q.," *AABN* 619 (5 November 1887). The building is illustrated in Crossman [see n. 3], fig. 9.

38 "Montreal," *CAB* 9:1 (January 1896), 3.

39 "Montreal," *CAB* 11:9 (September 1898), 170.

40 H.R. Ives and Company, "The Advantages (?) of Employing an American Architect," *CAB* 3:6 (July 1890), 75.

41 Crossman, 13–19.

42 "Montreal," *CAB* 7:3 (March 1894), 42. Waite had already built head offices for the Canada Life Insurance Co. in Hamilton in 1882 and in Toronto in 1888.

43 "Montreal," *CAB* 8:10 (August 1895), 117.

44 Richard A. Waite, "Grand Trunk Betterments," *The Railway and Shipping World* (November 1898), 237. The Grand Trunk head office resembled those built by Waite for the Canadian Imperial Bank of Commerce (1889–1890) in Toronto and for Sun Life (1898) in Hamilton.

45 "Address by Prof. Percy E. Nobbs," in *Proceedings of the Forty-First Annual Convention of the AIA*, ed. Alfred Stone (Washington, D.C.: AIA, 1907), 150.

46 "La Nouvelle Installation du Grand Tronc," *Le Prix Courant* 33:23 (6 June 1902), 5.

47 Price's work in Canada was singled out for praise in articles and obituaries published in the United States; see for example "Bruce Price," *Brickbuilder* 12:6 (June 1903), 112. See also Samuel Gaybrill, Jr., "Bruce Price, American Architect, 1845–1903" (Ph.D. diss., Art History, Yale University, 1957).

48 In Quebec City, the quest for a local style based on French Renaissance traditions had resulted in the beautification projects supported by Lord Dufferin in 1875, and had inspired Eugène-Étienne Taché (1836–1912). See Georges Drolet, "The Mighty Empire of the Past: Lord Dufferin's Proposals for Quebec City," *SSAC Bulletin SEAC* 21:1 (March 1996), 18–24; Émilie de Thonel d'Orgeix, "Eugène-Étienne Taché, architecte (1836–1912): l'influence française à Québec durant la seconde moitié du dix-neuvième siècle" (Master's thesis, History of art, Université Toulouse-le-Mirail, 1989).

49 Barr Ferree, "A Talk with Bruce Price," *The Architectural Record*, Great American Series, no. 5 (June 1899), 83: "originally the gables were stepped in the Scottish castellated style, and the building set off with turrets that fitted into the roof design in a most picturesque manner." For reasons of cost, the size of the building was reduced and some detailing was omitted.

50 On the subject of this tendency towards the picturesque, see Carol L.V. Meeks, *The Railroad Station* (New Haven: Yale University Press, 1956), 100–08.

51 Harold Kalman, *The Railway Hotels and the Development of the Château Style in Canada* (Victoria: University of Victoria Maltwood Museum, 1968), 8.

52 Ferree, 69.

53 Ferree, 81.

54 Kalman, *Railway Hotels*, 8.

55 Ferree, 83.

56 Ferree, 83.

57 "Canada," *AABN* 699 (18 May 1889), 235.

58 Harold C. Cross, *One Hundred Years of Service with Youth: The Story of the Montreal YMCA* (Montréal: YMCA, 1951), 164–73. The main façade and the three storeys of the Montreal YMCA building (which included a gymnasium 13 m by 19 m, two bowling alleys, a small swimming pool 5 m by 12 m, and a 500-seat auditorium) were published in Albert W. Fuller and W. Arthur Wheeler, *Artistic Homes in City and Country, with Other Examples of Domestic Architecture* (Boston: Ticknor and Company, 1891), plates 67 and 68. The building was described by William Douw Lighthall as being faced with "rich colored pressed brick with ample facing of grey cut stone … the interior is handsome, having a first class hall, a completely equipped gymnasium, a magnificent swimming bath and accessories, a bright reading room, library and other departments;" *Sights and Shrines of Montreal* (Montréal: F.E. Grafton, 1903), 50.

59 Albert W. Fuller, *Artistic Homes in City and Country* (Boston: J.R. Osgood, 1882); Albert W. Fuller, *Artistic Homes in City and Country: A Selection of Sketches Prepared in the Routine of Office-Work and Now Amplified and Enlarged* (Boston: J.R. Osgood, 1884; and Boston: Ticknor, 1886).

60 In Washington in 1886 Fuller and Wheeler built the "Green Door" house (the Denamm-Werlich house), reproduced in *AABN* 547 (19 June 1886). See *Albany Architects* (Albany: Historic Albany Foundation, 1978), 17; Diana S. Waite, ed., *Albany Architecture* (Albany: Mount Ida Press, 1993).

61 "The Collapse of the YMCA Building," *Dominion Illustrated* 144 (4 April 1891), 315.

62 "Canada – Fall of the Floors of the Young Men's Christian Association Building, Montreal," *AABN* 32:799 (18 April 1891), 44: "there is a general opinion that the plans did not provide for sufficiently strong walls." See also "Accident to the Y.M.C.A. Building, Montreal," *CAB* 4:4 (April 1891), 50. The Montreal incident did not prevent Fuller and Wheeler from building YMCAs in Hartford, Connecticut (1892), and in Oakland, California, nor from acting as consultants for the Paris YMCA.

63 "Hardenbergh was the pioneer hotel builder, the first to develop the esthetic problem of hotel design and the mechanical problem of hotel planning for safety and convenience." Richard F. Bach, "Henry Janeway Hardenbergh," *The Architectural Record* 44:1 (July 1918), 91–93.

64 See "Recent Works of H.J. Hardenbergh," *The New York Architect* 4:12 (December 1910); "Addition to the Windsor Hotel," *The Architectural Record* 19:5 (May 1906), 394.

65 "Montreal Notes," *CAB* 19:3 (March 1906), 41. According to Harold Kalman, in 1907 Gilbert was the designer of the first plans for the Château Laurier hotel in Ottawa, which anticipated in a number of ways the hotel built by Ross and MacFarlane between 1909 and 1912; *Railway Hotels*, 19. See in this regard "Architectural Ethics: The Case of the Ottawa Terminal Station and Hotel," *The Architectural Record* 24:4 (October 1908), 293–99.

66 According to Lawrence F. Abbott, New York Life bought a building in Paris in 1884 and built others in Berlin (1885), Vienna (1887), Amsterdam (1891), and Budapest (1894): "All these buildings were large, commodious and of an attractive architectural design which gave … an impression of solidity and permanency." *The Story of NYLIC* (New York: The Company, 1930), 118.

67 Both now demolished. The St. Paul branch, with very ornate Dutch-style gables, and the Minneapolis building, with its remarkable double staircase, are analyzed by the distinguished critic Montgomery Schuyler in *American Architecture* (New York: Harper and Brothers, 1892), 196–201.

68 Babb Cook and Willard's competition entry for the Kansas City branch is illustrated in *AABN* 620 (12 November 1887).

69 According to Mosette Broderick, Babb "had a profound effect on the young William R. Mead and Charles Follen McKim. The young Stanford White, who may have known Babb from the Sturgis days, also held Babb in high esteem." "Babb, Cook & Willard," in *Long Island Country Houses and Their Architects, 1860–1940*, ed. Roberta Mackay, Anthony Baker, and Carol Traynor (New York: W. Norton, 1997), 58.

70 See *CAB* 1:2 (February 1888), 2, plate 2; *AABN* 26:711 (10 August 1889), unnumbered plate; *The Architectural Review* (Boston) 1:8 (1894), plate 60; *The Dominion Illustrated* 3:69 (26 October 1889), 269, unnumbered plate.

71 Advertising brochure, unpaginated photocopy in the archives of the New York Life Insurance Co., New York.

72 See Russell Sturgis, "The Warehouse and the Factory in Architecture," *The Architectural Record* 15:1 (January 1904), 1–9; Sarah Bradford Landau, "The Tall Office Building Artistically Reconsidered: Arcaded Buildings of the New York School, c. 1870–1890," in *In Search of Modern Architecture*, ed. Helen Searing (Cambridge, Mass.: MIT Press, 1982), 136–64.

73 *Special Number of the Dominion Illustrated Devoted to Montreal, the Commercial Metropolis of Canada* (Montréal: Sabiston Lithographic and Pub. Co., 1891), 185.

74 See "Plan of the Bank of Montreal, Canada," *AABN* 589 (9 April 1887), 174–75; *CAB* 2:7 (July 1889), 76, unnumbered plate.

75 According to Andrew Taylor, "Correspondence: Review of Exhibits of Dominion and Colonial Architecture," *Journal of the Royal Institute of British Architects* 34:2 (20 November 1926), 64 (letter from Andrew T. Taylor). Referred to by Susan Wagg, *Money Matters: A Critical Look at Bank Architecture* (New York: McGraw-Hill, 1990), 271.

76 The part played by McKim is stressed by both Alfred Hoyt Granger, *Charles Follen McKim: A Study of His Life and Work* (Boston: Houghton Mifflin Company, 1913), 46–47, and Leland Roth, *McKim, Mead, and White Architects* (New York: Harper and Row, 1983), 298–301. Most of the designs were drawn up under the direction of one of the firm's young "partners," William Symmes Richardson. However, in "Correspondence: Review of Exhibits" (64), Andrew Taylor states: "Mr. Mead and I collaborated on this building, sharing the remuneration equal, and our relations all through were the happiest."

77 "Recent Bank Buildings of the United States," *The Architectural Record* 25:1 (January 1909), 9.

78 A very relevant analysis of the tectonic qualities of the Bank of Montreal is offered by Edward R. Ford, *The Details of Modern Architecture* (Cambridge, Mass.: MIT Press, 1982), vol. 1, 78–85. The dome is illustrated in an advertising brochure of R. Guastavino Co. reproduced in Janet Parks and Alan G. Neumann, *The Old World Builds the New: The Guastavino Company and the Technology of the Catalan Vault, 1885–1962* (New York: Avery Architectural and Fine Arts Library and Ira D. Wallach Art Gallery, Columbia University, 1996), 42.

79 Howard Shubert, "The Development of the Banking Hall in Canada" (Master's thesis, Art History, University of Toronto, 1983), 43.

80 Letter from the chairman of Norcross Brothers to J.-P. Anglin, supervisor for the Bank of Montreal, 19 November 1904 (New York Historical Society, Box 608): "Being desirous of showing every consideration for the Bank of Montreal that we could, we endeavored to arrange all of the work that we could with Montreal parties, which course proved very disastrous to us, as we found their methods and workmanship far inferior to that which we have been accustomed to by the owners of buildings for which we have contracts…. We were harassed by Mr. Taylor."

81 The Bank of Montreal Annex is illustrated in Egerton Swartwout, "Our Semi-Public Buildings and Their Development in the Last Thirty Years," *The Architectural Review* (Boston) 5:11 (November 1917), 247.

82 The only American banking hall built before the publication of this article that could be compared with the Bank of Montreal was that of the National City Bank, also by McKim Mead and White; see the comparative plate in Philip Sawyer, "The Planning of Banks," *The Architectural Forum* 38:6 (June 1923), 269.

83 "Recent Bank Buildings of the United States," 9.

84 Jean-Charles Drouin, "La Banque de Montréal," *Le Nigog* 1:1 (January 1918), 12.

85 Philip Turner, "The Development of Architecture in the Province of Quebec Since Confederation," *Construction* 20:6 (June 1927), 193.

86 The Gargoyle (Percy Nobbs), "Montreal Letter No. III," 98, regarding the Mount Royal Club. The expression "rarefied classic" is also found in the "Address by Prof. Percy E. Nobbs," in *Proceedings of the Forty-First Annual Convention* [see n. 45], 149.

87 See "The Ritz Carlton Hotel, New York," *American Architect* 1832 (1 February 1911), 47–52; Robert A.M. Stern, Gregory Gilmartin, and John Montague Massengale, *New York 1900* (New York: Rizzoli, 1983), 262.

88 See "Ritz-Carlton Hotel, Montreal," *Construction* 6:2 (February 1913), 47–55; "Ritz-Carlton Hotel, Montreal," *Brickbuilder* 22:3 (March 1913), plates 33 and 34; "Ritz-Carlton Hotel, Montreal," *The Architectural Review* (Boston) 2:4 (April 1913), 111–13.

89 Charles D. Wetmore, "The Development of the Modern Hotel," *The Architectural Review* (Boston) 2:4 (April 1913), 38.

Beautification versus Modernization

1 Gordon Fulton, "Canadian Architectural Periodicals," *SSAC* 19:2 (June 1994), 48–53.

2 Frank Jenkins, "Nineteenth-Century Architectural Periodicals," in *Concerning Architecture: Essays on Architectural Writers and Writing Presented to Nikolaus Pevsner,* ed. John Summerson (London: Allen Lane and Penguin Press, 1968), 153–60. The first monthly publication on the subject, *The Canadian Builder and Mechanics Magazine,* appeared in 1869; Stephen A. Otto, "Letters," *SSAC* 19:3 (September 1994), 75.

3 Kelly Crossman, *Architecture in Transition: From Art to Practice, 1885–1906* (Kingston and Montreal: McGill-Queen's University Press, 1987), 31–32.

4 David Van Zanten and Mary Woods, "La presse architecturale aux États-Unis," *Revue de l'art* 89 (1990), 24–25.

5 Raymonde Landry-Gauthier, "Victor Bourgeau et l'architecture religieuse et conventuelle dans le diocèse de Montréal" (Ph.D. diss., Laval University, 1983), 236–38.

6 Two versions were published, the more-richly-illustrated one intended for architects.

7 "Our Montreal Office," *CAB* 3:5 (May 1890), 48.

8 "Special Contributors," *CAB* 3:1 (January 1890), 1.

9 "Change of Ownership," *CAB* 20:11 (November 1907), n.p.

10 His mother was Hermantine Rolland, daughter of the founder of the Rolland paper mill, and his father was Liberal M.P. Joseph-Raymond Préfontaine, who served as both mayor of Montreal (1898–1902) and as a federal minister (1902–05). Bernadette Guilmette, "Fernand Préfontaine," Archives des Lettres canadiennes, *Le Nigog* (Montréal: Fides, 1987), 150.

11 Armand Guilmette, "De Paris à Montréal," Archives des Lettres canadiennes, *Le Nigog* (Montréal: Fides, 1987), 32–36.

12 *An Act to Incorporate The Province of Quebec Association of Architects* S.Q. 54 Vict. (1890), c. 59, 11–12.

13 As reports in the *CAB* make clear, the PQAA members who spoke at the first annual banquets were full of praise for this result of the Association's activities.

14 *An Act to Incorporate the PQAA*, 101.

15 "Organization of the Province of Quebec Association of Architects," *CAB* 3:10 (October 1890), 112–13.

16 "Compte-rendu d'assemblée ajournée," 27 October 1891, PQAA, "Minute Book," vol. 1, 181–83.

17 Alexander C. Hutchison, "Architectural Training," *CAB* 4:11 (November 1891), 97–98.

18 As noted in the report on the annual meeting held in September 1892, "Province of Quebec Association of Architects," *CAB* 5:10 (October 1892), 97.

19 J.R. Rhind, "The Architect as a Business Man and Artist," *CAB* 5:11 (November 1892), 111.

20 Andrew T. Taylor, "Some Notes on the Relation and Application of the Sister Arts, Painting and Sculpture, to Architecture," *CAB* 6:10 (October 1893), 112–13.

21 Andrew T. Taylor, *Towers and Steeples Designed by Sir Christopher Wren* (London: B.T. Bratsford High Holborn, 1881).

22 Joseph Venne, "Esthetic Value of Moulding and Profile," *CAB* 10:11 (November 1897), 207.

23 As mentioned in "Montreal," *CAB* 6:12 (December 1893), 103, Hutchison gave a lecture on the world's fair.

24 His "Brief Notes on the Architecture of the World's Fair" appear

in the "Province of Quebec Association of Architects: Proceedings of the Annual Convention," *CAB* 6:10 (October 1893), 104, 105.

25 Taylor gave the talk "Notes on Some Aspects of the City of the Future," published in the report of the "Annual Meeting of the Province of Quebec Association of Architects," *CAB* 7:10 (October 1894), 130–31.

26 PQAA, "Minutes of Special Council Meeting Decided at the Annual Meeting," Quebec City, September 1891, 175.

27 Minutes of the fourth and fifth annual meetings held 4 October 1894 and 2 October 1895, *1893–1896 PQAA*, vol. 2, 75, 177. In subsequent years, the PQAA repeatedly noted at its annual meetings that the City had so far failed to adopt the recommendations of its municipal-regulations reform committee.

28 The by-law in force at the close of the century was the *Règlement pour régler la construction des bâtiments et pour prévenir les accidents par le feu, no. 107, Passé le 6 avril 1877, Et tel qu'amendé par les règlements subséquents*, Ville de Montréal. By this law, a building inspector under the control and supervision of the Fire Committee was to inspect each site and ensure that newly erected or altered buildings on city territory conformed to regulations before issuing a permit.

29 "Accident to the Y.M.C.A. Building, Montreal," *CAB* 4:4 (April 1891), 50.

30 Herbert Brown Ames, *The City Below the Hill: A Sociological Study of a Portion of the City of Montreal, Canada* (Montréal: Bishop Engraving and Print Co., 1897).

31 Julia Gersovitz, "Montreal Architects and their Works, 1870–1914" (Master's thesis, School of Architecture, Columbia University, 1980), 43.

32 "Montreal: The New City Inspector," *CAB* 13:5 (May 1900), 112.

33 A news item reported Alcide Chaussée's attendance at the conference of American municipalities held in Minneapolis and noted the "consensus of opinion" concerning the 10-storey limit. "Notes," *CAB*

16:11 (November 1903), x.

34 The professional press reported that an article published in Montreal's *Finance and Insurance Chronicle* stated that the construction by-law was inadequate in the area of fire prevention and noted that the inspector was working on a new set of regulations modelled on those in force in major American cities. "Montreal," *CAB* 7:9 (September 1894), 112; a few years later, the *Real Estate Owners' Association* asked the city to standardize the height of buildings on new streets so as to prevent their financial depreciation; see "Montreal," *CAB* 11:12 (December 1898), 209.

35 S.H. Capper, "The American Tall Building," *CAB* 11:1 (January 1898), 5–7; Louis H. Sullivan, "The Tall Building Artistically Considered, First Published in *Lippincott's*, March 1896," *Kindergarten Chats and Other Writings* (New York: Dover, 1979), 202–13.

36 Raymonde Moulin, "Esquisse historique," in *Les architectes*, ed. Raymonde Moulin et al. (Paris: Calmann-Lévy, 1973), 13–36.

37 Ellen James, *John Ostell, Architect, Surveyor* (Montréal: McCord Museum, 1985), 5–6.

38 "Sixteenth Annual Report, 1906," PQAA *Year Book, 1907*, 16.

39 Despite the reference to the Chicago League, Taylor made it clear that his goals for Montreal were more modest; see *CAB* 7:12 (December 1894), 150, 160. The PQAA submitted a first petition to the City in December 1894; Record of Meetings of the PQAA, vol. 2, 115. Later annual reports made frequent mention of the City's lack of action, notwithstanding the PQAA's manifest interest and frequent reminders.

40 Edward Maxwell and John Gardiner, "Report of the Municipal Improvement Committee," PQAA *Year Book, 1906*. The author of the plan was almost certainly William S. Maxwell, chairman of the Municipal Improvement Committee.

41 In 1900, Gardiner published an article in the *London Building News*

in which he drew some salutary lessons from the fire that had struck the Home Life Insurance Building in New York City; see "Montreal," *CAB* 13:9 (October 1900), 176. In 1914 he collaborated with Nobbs in designing the offices of the Liverpool and London and Globe Insurance Co. on Dorchester Street. Gardiner was also a leading figure in the building-height debate in 1920.

42 "Seventeenth Annual Report, 1907," PQAA *Year Book, 1908*, 16.

43 The set of five plans was published in PQAA *Year Book, 1909–1910*, n.p., and "21st Annual Report," PQAA *Year Book, 1912*, 25.

44 See Jeanne M. Wolfe and Grace Strachan, "Practical Idealism: Women in Urban Reform, Julia Drummond and the Montreal Parks and Playgrounds Association," in *Life Spaces: Gender, Household, Employment*, ed. Caroline Andrew and Beth Moore Milroy (Vancouver: University of British Columbia Press, 1988), 65–80.

45 Paul-André Linteau, *Histoire de Montréal depuis la Confédération* (Montréal: Boréal, 1992), 258–59. Shortly after the committee's creation in 1906, Nobbs chaired a meeting attended by the most influential members of the Board of Trade. "Montreal Notes," *CAB* 19:6 (June 1906), 88.

46 W.H. Atherton, "The City Improvement League of Montreal," *Revue Municipale Édition spéciale d'urbanisme* 5 (December 1927), 30–31.

47 *An act for the appointment of a commission to consider the best means of establishing a system of parks on the Island of Montreal and Isle Jesus*, s.Q. 1 Geo. 5 (1910), c. 6, 37–38.

48 Jeanne Wolfe and Peter Jacobs, "City Planning and Urban Beautification," in *The Architecture of Edward and W.S. Maxwell*, ed. Robert Lemire (Montréal: The Montreal Museum of Fine Arts, 1991), 51–52.

49 The text of the report was published in "Report of Mr. F.L. Olmsted to the Metropolitan Parks

Commission," PQAA *Year Book, 1911*, 71–83.

50 Wolfe and Jacobs, 52.

51 William H. Wilson, "The Columbian Exposition and the City Beautiful Movement," in *The City Beautiful Movement* (Baltimore and London: Johns Hopkins University Press, 1989), 53–74.

52 William Maxwell, "Architectural Education," *CAB* 21:1 (January 1908), 21, 23. This text was republished in "Condensed Proceedings of the O.A. of A. Convention," *Construction* 1:4 (February 1908), 50–52.

53 "Ah! quel entrain et quelle émulation!" Cited by J.-O. Marchand in "Sketching Competitions in the Second Class of the School of Fine Arts, Paris," *CAB* 9:4 (March 1896), 52.

54 The origins of the first club date back to the annual meeting of October 1895, at which it was proposed that the PQAA's Montreal and Quebec City chapters organize sketching classes for the members' own personal development and to encourage a spirit of fraternity; "Province of Quebec Association of Architects," *CAB* 8:10 (October 1895), 119. In February 1896 a group of student members expressed their intent to set up a small sketching club, and monthly competitions were soon organized. Record of Meetings of the PQAA, vol. 2, 233; "Montreal," *CAB* 9:5 (May 1896), 64. However, there is not a single subsequent reference to the club's activities either in the PQAA reports or in the specialized press. The evening classes organized earlier by the PQAA had met with little success; Record of Meetings of the PQAA, vol. 2, 9. A new, private initiative nevertheless got underway in 1897; "Montreal: Amateur Sketch Club," *CAB* 10:9 (October 1897), 170.

55 "The Sketch Club, P.Q.A.A.," *CAB* 18:10 (October 1905), 157.

56 Émile Vanier and D.R. Brown, "Eighteenth Annual Report, 1908," PQAA *Year Book, 1909–10*, 19.

57 Émile Vanier and D.R. Brown, "Nineteenth Annual Report, 1909,"

PQAA *Year Book, 1909–10*, 29.

58 Émile J. Vanier and J.R. Gardiner, "21st Annual Report," PQAA *Year Book, 1911*, 26.

59 John Bland, "William Sutherland Maxwell: Biography," in *Guide to the Archives, Edward and W.S. Maxwell* (Montréal: CAC, 1986), 14–15.

60 "The Renaissance Club," *CAB* 12:3 (March 1899), 64. The year 1899 was a particularly active one for architectural clubs, of which there were a number in the United States. In June, a first architectural conference, held in Cleveland, was attended by delegates from thirteen such groups. The newly formed Toronto Architectural Club was represented, but the Renaissance Club was not. Nonetheless, this new solidarity must have encouraged the development of the two Canadian clubs, although the Ontario group was opposed by the province's professional association, a tension that does not seem to have existed in Quebec.

61 Rosalind Pepall, "Craftsmen and Decorative Artists," in *The Architecture of Edward and W.S. Maxwell* [see n. 48], 43–44.

62 "Montreal: The Renaissance Club," *CAB* 13:1 (January 1900), 6.

63 W. Maxwell [see n. 52], 21–23. In his lecture, Maxwell expressed scepticism about the value of making measured drawings of historical buildings, remarking that an understanding of structural logic can be achieved mentally and adding that such an exercise could only be of value if the drawings were coloured and shaded to bring out the architecture's plasticity. Nevertheless, in his comments on the evening gatherings of the Boston Architectural Club, Maxwell stressed the importance of drawing from nature and painting (both of which he practised himself).

64 William Maxwell was a founding member and the architect of the building that housed this club of architects, artists, craftsmen, and art-lovers created in 1912.

Rosalind Pepall, "Arts Club (alterations)," in *The Architecture of Edward and W.S. Maxwell* [see n. 48], 160–61. The club grew out of the life classes offered Saturday afternoons by the painter Maurice Cullen; Bland, 15.

65 W. Maxwell, 25.

66 Percy E. Nobbs, "Architectural Education in Canada," *Proceedings, OAA 1910*, 81–82.

67 "All the classes could disappear, and the École des Beaux-Arts would still be the École des Beaux-Arts: but without the studio the school would be inconceivable," wrote Julien Guadet, *Éléments et théorie de l'architecture* (Paris: Librairie de la construction moderne, n.d.), 78.

68 Percy E. Nobbs, "State Aid to Art Education in Canada," *Construction* 1:6 (April 1908), 44–47.

69 McGill University, *Annual Calendar for Session 1904–1905* (Montréal 1904), 153.

70 S.H. Capper, "Architecture in the University," *CAB* 9:11 (November 1896), 179–82.

71 Nobbs, "Architectural Education in Canada," 84.

72 A comparison of the programs being offered in 1902–03 and 1904–05 shows that while first-year physics classes kept the same number of hours, second-year practical studio work (focusing on an understanding of nature and the properties of materials) was first cut by half and then eliminated altogether, as were chemistry and physics classes. McGill University, *Annual Calendar for Session 1902–1903* (Montréal 1902), 174, 233; *Annual Calendar for Session 1904–1905* (Montréal 1904), 154.

73 That approach held sway at the School of Applied Art in Edinburgh, founded in 1892, where Capper had taught. Alan Powers, "Architectural Education and the Arts and Crafts Movements in England," *Architectural Education* 3 (1984), 49.

74 McGill University, *Annual Calendar for Session 1910–1911* (Montréal 1910), 193.

75 "Address by Prof. Percy E. Nobbs," AIA, *Journal of Proceedings* (1907), 149–52.

76 Percy E. Nobbs, "The Official Architecture of European Capitals," *CAB* 19:4 (April 1906), 38–40.

77 Percy E. Nobbs, "The Sites of the University Buildings," *The McGill News* 1 (June 1901), 2–5.

78 Percy E. Nobbs, "Material and Technique in Design," *CAB* 16:12 (December 1903), 200–01.

79 "The most important chapter in the history of architecture for future architects must ever be that of the last fifty years; all else is valuable just in so far as it can serve as interpretation and explanation of that." Percy E. Nobbs, "University Education in Architecture," *JRAIC* 2:2 (March–April 1925), 71.

80 Percy E. Nobbs, "Opening Lecture of the Dept. of Architecture, McGill University," *CAB* 17:10 (October 1904), 163–64.

81 Montreal Board of Trade, *Annual Report, 1913*, 43–44.

82 *An Act to establish the Metropoltan Parks Commission*, Assented to 3rd April 1912, S.Q. 2 Geo. 5 (1912), c. 8, 55–59; *An Act to amend the Act to establish the Metropoltan Parks Commission*, Assented to 19 February 1914, S.Q. 4 Geo. 5 (1914), c. 4, 31–32.

83 W.H. Atherton, "The City Improvement League of Montreal," *Revue Municipale Édition spéciale d'urbanisme* 5 (December 1927), 30–32.

84 Marc H. Choko, *Crises du logement à Montréal, 1860–1939* (Montréal: Éditions coopératives Albert Saint-Martin, 1980), 81–96.

85 John C. Bacher, *Keeping to the Marketplace: The Evolution of Canadian Housing Policy* (Montréal and Kingston: McGill-Queen's University Press, 1993), 38.

86 Alan H. Armstrong, "Thomas Adams and the Commission of Conservation," *Plan Canada* 1:1 (1959), 17–18.

87 Armstrong, 20.

88 Armstrong, 23–29.

89 Jeanne M. Wolfe and Hannah Shostack, "The Town Planning

Movement in Montreal, 1900–1941," typescript, n.d. If any members of the PQAA did attend the 1914 conference, no mention is made of the fact in the PQAA *Year Book, 1916*.

90 "First Meeting of Town Planning Institute," *Construction* 12:7 (July 1919), 207.

91 In September 1921 another town-planning conference was held in Montreal. As noted in its 1922 *Year Book*, the PQAA was represented, but neither the architects nor their Association played a major role in this gathering, which was organized by the Civic Progress League and the Town Planning Institute of Canada. The contributors were mostly engineers, and only Vanier, Traquair, and Nobbs were mentioned in the program. "Town Planning Conference, Montreal," *Construction* 14:9 (September 1921), 270.

92 The names of the members of the Montreal City Improvement League are listed in the opening pages of the *Revue Municipale, Édition spéciale d'urbanisme/Special Town Planning Number* 5 (December 1927).

93 "Memorandum on the Town Planning Movement in Montreal Since January 1st, 1926," *Journal of the Town Planning Institute of Canada* 5:2 (April 1926), 5–6.

94 Harold Lawson, "Montreal Town-planning Exhibition," *Journal of the Town Planning Institute of Canada* 5:2 (April 1926), 6–7.

95 Percy E. Nobbs, "The Subdivision of Residential Suburban Property," *Journal of the Town Planning Institute of Canada* 5:2 (April 1926), 10–16; republished under the title *Suburban Community Planning*, Series 14, Arts and Architecture, no. 7 (Montréal: McGill University Publications, 1926), 22 pp.

96 *Revue municipale, Édition spéciale d'urbanisme/Special Town Planning Number* 5 (December 1927), 144 pp.

97 "Sixteen Storey Hotel Permitted in Montreal," *The Contract Record* 55:4 (21 January 1920), 69.

98 "29th Annual Report," PQAA *Year Book, 1920*, 11.

99 Christine Boyer, *Dreaming the Rational City: The Myth of American City Planning* (Cambridge, Mass.: MIT Press, 1983), 92–94.

100 "Montreal Architects Meet at Ritz-Carlton Hotel," *Construction* 16:4 (April 1923), 150.

101 Montreal Board of Trade, *Eighty-First of the Council of the Montreal Board of Trade Being for the Year 1923* (Montréal: Gazette Printing Co., 1924), 123; Montreal Board of Trade, *Eighty-Second of the Council of the Montreal Board of Trade Being for the Year 1924* (Montréal: Gazette Printing Co., 1925), 41.

102 *By-Law No. 851 to amend By-law No. 260, entitled "The Montreal Building By-law of 1901," as amended by subsequent by-laws*, adopted 3 April 1924, City of Montreal.

103 As reported in "Heights of Buildings," *Revue Municipale Édition spéciale d'urbanisme/Special Town Planning Number* 5 (December 1927), 10.

104 *By-Law No. 1003 to amend By-Law No. 260, entitled "The Montreal Building By-law of 1901," as amended by subsequent by-laws*, signed 18 March 1929, City of Montreal.

105 Carol Willis, "Zoning and Zeitgeist: The Skyscraper City in the 1920s," *JSAH* 45:1 (March 1986), 47–59.

106 In September 1899, a proposal was put forward to create a Commission of Historical and Artistic Monuments in the Province of Quebec, whose task it would be to survey all the province's artistic and historical monuments. Record of Meetings of the PQAA, vol. 4, 163.

107 "The P.Q.A.A.," *CAB* 12:10 (October 1899), 192; Crossman [see n. 3], 115–16.

108 "Annual Report," PQAA *Year Book, 1911,* 17–22; "21st Annual Report," PQAA *Year Book, 1912,* 19–26.

109 Janet Sader, "Chronology for Ramsay Traquair: Biographical Details and Related Events," in *Ramsay Traquair and His Successors: Guide to the Archive,* ed. Irena Murray (Montréal: CAC, 1987), vol. 1, 112.

110 During the PQAA annual meeting in January 1920, Traquair proposed "that the Council be authorized to establish one or more travelling scholarships for the study of architecture, the Council to be authorized ... to draw up regulations for their management." PQAA *Year Book, 1920,* 11. The earliest measured drawings preserved in the archives date from 1920; *Ramsay Traquair and His Successors,* vol. 2, 192 ff.

111 John Bland summarizes these studies in "Ramsay Traquair: Biography," *Ramsay Traquair and His Successors,* vol. 1, 119, noting that they provided the basis for Traquair's well-known book *The Old Architecture of Quebec* (Toronto: McMillan, 1947).

112 No articles concerning the 1924 exhibition appeared in any major publication, to judge from the archives of the Montreal Museum of Fine Arts, file 0032, "Exhibition of Early Architecture in the Province of Quebec," and the list of publications on Traquair's work in *Ramsay Traquair and His Successors,* vol. 1, 155–58.

113 Olivar Asselin, "À propos d'une conférence," *Le Canada* (27 January 1934), 2.

114 Maurice Hébert, "L'habitation canadienne-française: une véritable expression de civilisation distincte et personnelle," *Mémoires de la Société Royale du Canada,* vol. 38, section 1 (May 1944), 134.

115 France Vanlaethem, "Modernité et régionalisme dans l'architecture au Québec: Du nationalisme canadien de Percy E. Nobbs au nationalisme canadien-français des années 1940," in *Architecture, forme urbaine et identité collective,* ed. Luc Noppen (Quebec City: Septentrion, 1995), 158–77.

116 Fernand Préfontaine, "L'Architecture à Montréal," *Le Nigog* (June 1918), 191, and "L'Architecture canadienne," *Le Nigog* (July 1918), 209, 212.

117 Esther Trépanier, "L'émergence d'un discours de la modernité dans la critique d'art (Montréal 1918–1938)," in *L'avènement de la modernité culturelle au Québec,* ed. Yvan Lamonde and Esther Trépanier (Quebec City: Institut québécois de recherche sur la culture, 1986), 75–76.

118 Ramsay Traquair, "The Artist and the Public (To the Unsuccessful Artist and the Inartistic Public)," *Le Nigog* (March 1918), 70.

119 Préfontaine, "L'Architecture canadienne," 211.

120 Robert Gagnon, *Histoire de l'École Polytechnique de Montréal* (Montréal: Boréal, 1991), 137.

121 Paul Cointe, "L'esthétique de l'ingénieur," *Le Nigog* (May 1918), 142, 144.

122 A photograph of Grain Elevator no. 2 on Montreal's harbourfront first appeared in the *Jahrbuch des Deutschen Werkbundes* (Jena: Verlag bei Eugen Diederichs, 1913), an annual publication in which Walter Gropius published an article entitled "Die Entwicklung moderner Industriebaukunst." It was later republished in sources that included *L'Esprit Nouveau* 1 (October 1920), 96.

123 Jean-Charles Drouin, "La Banque de Montréal," *Le Nigog* 1 (January 1918), n.p. [5–12].

124 M.R., "Revue des périodiques: *Le Nigog,*" *Revue trimestrielle canadienne* 5 (February 1919), 430–31.

125 École Polytechnique de Montréal, *Conditions d'admission, règlements et programme de cours* (Montréal: La Patrie, n.d. [c. 1916–17]), 29–31.

126 Province de Québec, Département du Secrétaire de la Province, *École des beaux-arts de Montréal: Première exposition publique: Première proclamation des Récompenses, Vendredi 23 mai,* 16–21.

127 "Année active en vue à l'École des beaux-arts," *Le Canada* (20 October 1927); "L'Art canadien et l'école d'art canadien: Intéressants aperçus exposés par M. Charles Maillard dans sa causerie de samedi soir," *Le Devoir* (26 January 1931).

128 Préfontaine, "L'architecture canadienne," 212.

129 Percy Nobbs, "Present Tendencies Affecting Architecture in Canada, Part II: Modernity," *JRAIC* 7 (September 1930), 314–17.

Gigantism in Downtown Montreal

The author wishes to thank Guy Besner, Robert Fortier, Laurier Lacroix, Sarah Landau, Michèle Picard, and David Rose.

1 According to Franklin Toker, *The Church of Notre-Dame in Montreal: An Architectural History,* 2nd ed. (Montréal: McGill-Queen's University Press, 1991), 59: "Everything about Notre-Dame marked a first in the history of building in Canada. It was the highest building, it had the widest clear span, and it encompassed the greatest interior volume of any construction in Canada ... Certainly it was the largest church in Canada or the United States until the completion of St. Patrick's Cathedral in New York in 1879." Protestant congregations, because of their multiplicity and their Calvinist outlook, tended to build smaller churches.

2 An American critic described the Art Association Gallery as "a carefully and well executed building that, however, appears curiously deceptive in scale, as the exterior views entirely fail in suggesting anywhere its real size;" *Architectural Review* (Boston) 3:2 (February 1914), 31.

3 See "Extensive Factory Additions for Northern Electric Co. – Speedy Erection of Large Buildings," *CRER* 44:43 (22 October 1930), 1331–33.

4 Geographers rather than architectural historians have studied the dynamics that underpinned gigantism in the downtown areas of metropolises. An important theoretical text in this discussion, though focusing more on the

period following the Second World War, is Alan Colquhoun's "The Superbloc," in *Essays in Architectural Criticism: Modern Architecture and Historical Change* (Cambridge, Mass.: MIT Press, 1981), 83–109. In North America, more has been written about the upward thrust of buildings than about their increase in footprint. Among the newest approaches to the skyward issue are Carol Willis, *Form Follows Finance: Skyscrapers and Skylines in New York and Chicago* (New York: Princeton Architectural Press, 1995), emphasizing economic data; Sarah Bradford Landau and Carl W. Condit, *Rise of the New York Skyscraper, 1865–1913* (New Haven: Yale University Press, 1996), very interesting from a technical point of view; and Daniel Bluestone, in *Constructing Chicago* (New Haven: Yale University Press, 1991), adopting a more sociological and cultural viewpoint.

5 Jean-François Pinchon, *Les Palais d'Argent* (Paris: Musée d'Orsay, 1992).

6 Dirk Schubert and Anthony Sutcliffe, "The 'Haussmannisation' of London: The Planning and Construction of Kingsway-Aldwych, 1889–1935," *Planning Perspectives* 11:2 (April 1996), 115–44.

7 See, for instance, "The New Cunard Building," *The Architectural Review* 41:246 (May 1917), 86–98.

8 See Joseph Fenton, *Hybrid Buildings*, Architecture Pamphlet no. 11 (New York: Princeton Architectural Books, 1985).

9 The buildings of the Cleveland Terminal Group are the Cleveland Hotel (1917–19), the Builder's Exchange (1926–28), Highbee's Department Store (1928–30), the Medical Arts Building (1928–30), the Midland Bank (1928–30), and the Terminal Tower and Cleveland Union Station (opened 1930). See Sally A. Kitt Chappell, *Architecture and Planning of Graham, Anderson, Probst, and White, 1912–1936* (Chicago: University of Chicago Press, 1992), 36–39.

10 For two excellent studies on Toronto's tertiary sector, see Gunther Gad and Deryck W. Holdsworth, "Corporate Capitalism and the Emergence of the High-Rise Office Building," *Urban Geography* 8 (1987), 212–31, and Graham S. Lowe, "'The Enormous File': The Evolution of the Modern Office Building in Early Twentieth Century Canada," *Archivaria* 19 (winter 1985), 137–51.

11 "Montreal (Correspondence of the CAB)," *CAB* 2:1 (January 1889), 9.

12 Kelly Crossman, *Architecture in Transition: From Art to Practice, 1885–1906* (Montréal and Kingston: McGill-Queen's University Press, 1996), 81.

13 W.E. Doran, "Truth in Architecture," *CAB* 8:6 (June 1896), 86.

14 "Tall Building," *CAB* 9:12 (December 1896), 191.

15 "Province of Quebec Association of Architects: Proceedings of the Seventh Annual Convention," *CAB* 10:10 (October 1897), 192; Stewart Henbest Capper, "The American Tall Building from a European Point of View," *Engineering Magazine* (New York, 14 November 1897), 239–52; Stewart Henbest Capper, "The American Tall Building," *CAB* 11:1 (January 1898), 5–7. Charles Baillairgé also recommended horizontal divisions in "How Skyscrapers Can Be Made More Aesthetic," *CAB* 15:180 (December 1902), 144.

16 "Province of Quebec Association of Architects: Proceedings of the Seventh Annual Convention," 193.

17 City of Montreal, by-law no. 260, section 23, adopted 4 February 1901. At the time, building height was limited to 65 feet (20 m) in Paris, 77 feet (24 m) in Vienna, and 12 stories in Washington (1899) and Denver (1908; to avoid spoiling the view of the surrounding mountains). Boston imposed a limit of 155 feet (48 m) from 1904 until the late 1920s, Los Angeles a height of 150 feet (46 m) until the late 1950s (with the exception of purely ornamental towers), and Baltimore a limit of 175 feet (54 m).

18 On the subject of the early rivalry between New York insurance companies, see Kenneth Gibbs, "Insurance Rivalry and Business Architecture," in *Business Architectural Imagery in America* (Ann Arbor: UMI Research Press, 1984), 23–40. The life-insurance business in Canada began to thrive with the passing of the Canada Life Insurance Act of 1877. On the various insurance companies established on Place d'Armes, see Marc H. Choko, *The Major Squares of Montreal* (Montréal: Meridien, 1990), 40–56.

19 This was the case of the Tribune Building by Richard Morris Hunt in New York City and the Home Life Insurance Building by William Le Baron Jenney in Chicago.

20 Building permit no. 162 (July 1888), listed in the compilation of *Le Prix Courant* conserved at the CCA. This project, discussed in "Canada," *AABN* 24:657 (28 July 1888), 43, "will tower considerably over and dwarf the good proportions of the Bank;" "two monster buildings will entirely spoil the appearance of the little square." According to Landau and Condit, in 1885 Clinton had added three stories onto the Brown Brothers and Co. Banking House (Edward T. Potter, 1864–65) at 59 Wall Street in New York; *Rise of the New York Skyscraper,* 55.

21 According to *Le Prix Courant* 33:8 (21 February 1902), 42, Peabody and Stearns of Boston, winners of a closed competition for the Liverpool and London and Globe Insurance Co. Building, worked with Hutchison and Wood to prepare the plans and specifications. According to the item "Montreal," *CAB* 15:1 (January 1902), 4, the local architects who took part in the competition "were advised not to complete their designs, as the work had been given to the makers of the conditions of competition, Messrs. Peabody and Stearns, of Boston." However, the presentation drawing for the new Liverpool and London and Globe Building illustrated in *CAB* 15:11 (November 1902) credits only Hutchison and Wood.

22 "Montreal," *CAB* 8:10 (August 1895), 117.

23 In 1909 the Maxwells planned to dismantle and reassemble the roof of the London and Lancashire Life Assurance Co. Building after adding on two additional floors, but this scheme was apparently dropped; Robert Lemire, "London & Lancashire Life Assurance Company Building," in *The Architecture of Edward & W.S. Maxwell* (Montréal: Montreal Museum of Fine Arts, 1991), 75.

24 [Royal Trust Company Building], *Architect and Building* 46 (January 1914), 20–22.

25 For the United States context, see Kenneth Gibbs, "Business Architectural Imagery in the Progressive Era," in *Business Architectural Imagery in America* (Ann Arbor: UMI Research Press, 1984), 125–50.

26 Concordia Salus (Percy Nobbs), "Montreal Notes," *CAB* 18:11 (October 1905), 157.

27 "Apartment-Houses in Montreal, Canada," *AABN* 91:1619 (5 January 1907), 17–18. See also "The Linton Apartments, Montreal," *CAB* 14:4 (April 1906), 53.

28 See John Zacharias, "The Emergence of a 'Loft' District in Montreal," *Urban History Review* 19:3 (February 1991), 226–32. However, unlike Toronto and Winnipeg, Montreal did not have large warehouses used for the sale of consumer goods by mail-order.

29 "Le plus grand édifice d'affaires du Canada" [The largest business building in Canada], *La Presse,* 13 April 1912, 33.

30 "Canada's Largest Concrete Building," *Construction* 3:3 (March 1910), 57–64.

31 *Railway and Marine World* 15 (February 1911), 157; cited by Robert Lemire, "Dominion Express Building," in *The Architecture of Edward & W.S. Maxwell,* 83. See also "The Dominion Express Building, Montreal, Que.," *Construction* 5:11 (November 1912), 46–54.

32 "The Transportation Building, Montreal, Canada," *Construction* 5:12 (December 1912), 47–56.

33 See Canadian Northern, *The*

Mount Royal Tunnel (Montréal: The Canadian Northern Railway, 1913), 7, and "Proposed Union Station and Tunnel, Montreal," *Contract Record* 30:25 (21 June 1916), 621.

34 The Terminal City project was published in William D. Middleton, *Grand Central, the World's Greatest Railway Terminal* (San Marino: Golden West Books, 1977), 96. For more on the development around the Grand Central Terminal, see Deborah Nevins, *Grand Central: Architecture as a Celebration of Daily Life* (New York: Municipal Art Society, 1982).

35 Madeleine Forget, *Les gratte-ciel de Montréal* (Montréal: Méridien, 1990), 93.

36 See, for instance, "196 Days Completed Henry Morgan Store," *CRER* 37:52 (26 December 1923), 1243; "Rapid Progress Being Made in Erection of Murphy Store, Montreal," *CRER* 43:28 (10 July 1929), 815–16; "Two Storeys a Week on Tall Concrete Building in Montreal," *CRER* 43:44 (30 October 1929), 1281–83 (University Tower); "Rapid Reconstruction: A Feature of the Erection of Large Montreal Store," *CRER* 44:7 (12 February 1930), 153–56.

37 The Amherst Building (1925, Ross and MacDonald) at the corner of St. Catherine and St. Timothée featured a 1,697-seat cinema. Construction was entrusted to Howard Crane, assisted by C.D. Goodman.

38 "Large Six-Storey Building for Henry Morgan & Co. Moved 259 Feet," *CRER* 37:20 (16 May 1923), 449–53. The company that handled the move was based in Cedar Rapids, Iowa.

39 See "The New Caron Building, Montreal," *Construction* 17:8 (August 1924), 256–61, and "New Caron Building, Montreal," *Architectural Forum* 41 (September 1924), 158. There is no comparison, however, between the development of the loft-building district in Montreal and New York's extensive Garment District, on which see Robert A. Stern, Gregory Gilmartin, and Thomas Mellins,

New York 1930 (New York: Rizzoli, 1987), 516 ff. The Caron Building was equipped with a freight elevator that could accommodate a delivery truck. A similar phenomenon occurred in telephone-exchange buildings. At the corner of Ontario and St. Urbain streets, the Plateau Exchange (1915, attributed to W.J. Carmichael, architect for the Bell company) was expanded laterally by the Lancaster (or St. Urbain) Exchange (1923–25, W.J. Carmichael). Bell's long-distance exchange, on Belmont Street (1930–31, E.I. Barott), was originally intended to be 21 stories high.

40 Marc Choko, "Le 'boom' des immeubles d'appartements à Montréal de 1921 à 1951," *Urban History Review* 23:1 (November 1994), 3–18.

41 D.G. Anglin, "A 'Modern Methods' Building of Unusual Character," *CRER* 40:21 (26 May 1926), 510–13; and D.G. Anglin, "The Chateau Apartments, Montreal," *Construction* 19:9 (September 1926), 270–80.

42 "The Largest Apartment House in the Dominion of Canada," *CRER* 37:22 (30 May 1923), 127 (Drummond apartment building); and "Montreal Apartments Are Empire's Largest," *CRER* 37:52 (26 December 1923), 1237–38, 1242 (Drummond Court).

43 "A Building Exclusively for Medical Men," *CRER* 38:22 (28 May 1924), 556–59.

44 Sinaiticus, "The Drummond Medical Building, Montreal," *Construction* 23:9 (September 1930), 303–06. A perspective section of the Drummond Medical Building can be found in N.H. Owens, "Incorporating a Parking Garage in the Office Building," *Architectural Forum* 52:6 (June 1930), 902.

45 "Architects Building, Montreal," *JRAIC* 8:9 (September 1931), 325–34; "The Architects Building, Montreal," *Construction* 23:6 (June 1930), 210; "Building in Montreal for Architectural and Engineering Professions," *CRER* 44:24 (11 June 1930), 707–08; "Le gratte-ciel des

architectes," *La Presse*, 16 May 1930, 33. The Montreal building was similar to the one erected in Los Angeles and illustrated in *American Architect* 133:2545 (20 May 1928), 657. Its most notable precedent was the Architects' Building in New York City (1912–13, Ewing and Chappell), described in D. Everett Waid, "The Business Side of an Architect's Office," *Brickbuilder* 22:8 (August 1913), 179–81.

46 The title of an item in *CRER* 35:30 (28 July 1920), 709.

47 This chain already owned three Ontario hotels: the Prince Edward in Windsor, the Royal Connaught in Hamilton, and the King Edward in Toronto.

48 "The Mount-Royal Hotel, Montreal," *Construction* 15:7 (July 1922), 204–11; "The Mount-Royal Hotel, Montreal," *Construction* 16:5 (May 1923), 157–75; "The Mount Royal Hotel," *CRER* 36:26 (28 June 1922), 619–35; "Mount Royal Hotel, Montreal," *Architectural Forum*, Hotel Reference Number, 39:5 (November 1923), plates 85–88, 210, 272; David A. Rose, "The Hotel Architecture of Ross and MacFarlane/Ross and MacDonald" (M.A. thesis, Dept. of Art History, Concordia University, 1992).

49 By comparison, the Grand Hôtel du Louvre (1855) in Paris had 700 rooms while the Cecil Hotel in London (1890–96, Archer and Green) had 800.

50 An E-shaped plan had already been adopted by the Maxwell brothers for the Palliser Hotel in Calgary (1911–14), an undertaking that was considerably smaller than the Mount Royal Hotel. The best known comb-shaped building remains the General Motors head office by Albert Kahn in Detroit, which opened in 1922. At 15 stories tall, it was at the time of its construction the second-largest structure in the world in floor area, after New York's Equitable Building. Its 500-by-250-foot base (154 by 77 m) hosted commercial activities; there was also a restaurant at the top.

51 "$9,000,000 Hotel in Montreal

Is Now Assured," *CRER* 35:6 (9 February 1921), 129–30. The layout of the Mount Royal Hotel would influence that of the Roosevelt Hotel in New York (1924, George B. Post and Son), which belonged to the same chain and contained 1,100 rooms.

52 *The Montreal Star*, 16 December 1922.

53 Fritz Neumeyer, "Manhattan Transfer: The New York Myth and Berlin Architecture in the Context of Ludwig Hilberseimer's High-Rise City," *Berlin–New York: Like and Unlike* (New York: Rizzoli, 1993), 323.

54 "United States interests are said to be largely behind the project;" "Montreal to Get Modern Structure," *Construction* 21:4 (April 1928), 118.

55 "One of Canada's Largest Structures and an Outstanding Construction Achievement: The Dominion Square Building, Montreal," *CRER* 44:5 (29 January 1930), 115–26; "Canada's Largest Office Structure," *CRER* 42:31 (1 August 1928), 800; "Imposing Addition to Montreal's Business Facilities," *CRER* 44:5 (29 January 1930), 115.

56 *Dominion Square Building* (Montréal 1929), 7.

57 "Sixteen Storey Hotel Permitted in Montreal," *CRER* 35:3 (21 January 1920), 69.

58 Louis Dupire, "Le procès du gratte-ciel," *Le Devoir*, 7 June 1921, 1. See also Thomas Adams, "The Need for Town Planning," *CRER* 35:34 (24 August 1921), 766. In April 1926, when he was head of the Regional Plan of New York, Adams returned to Montreal to talk about New York's city planning at a conference lunch organized by the Town Planning Institute of Canada. Montrealers were very sensitive to the negative assessments of skyscrapers by Europeans.

59 Laurier Lacroix, *Peindre à Montréal* (Montréal: Galeries de l'UQAM, 1996), 34.

60 Ramsay Traquair, "Architecture and Democracy," *Canadian Bookman*, n.o. 114 (October 1919), 11–12.

61 See Carol Willis, "Zoning and Zeitgeist," *JSAH* 45 (March 1986), 47–59.

62 City of Montreal, By-law 260, passed by city council 29 September 1924.

63 "The Beaver Hall Building, Montreal," *JRAIC* 6:10 (October 1929), 355.

64 Clifford H. Ince, *The Royal Bank of Canada: A Chronology 1864–1969* (Montréal: Royal Bank of Canada, 1970), 42.

65 James Blomfield, "The Royal Bank of Canada," *Construction* 22:2 (February 1929), 34–60, 68; *The Royal Bank Building* (Montréal: Royal Bank of Canada, 1929); Philip Sawyer, "The Problem of Building a Bank," *Architectural Forum* 48:6 (June 1928), 791.

66 "The New Sun Life Building, Montreal, Que.," *Construction* 11:12 (December 1918), 371–92; A. Cyril Merchant, "A Great Canadian Building: The Sun Life Company's New Premises, Montreal," *Architectural Review* (London) 46:10 (September 1919), 52–55.

67 "Imposing Addition to Sun Life Building under Construction in Montreal," *CRER* 38:27 (2 July 1924), 662.

68 "A Huge Building for the Sun Life," *CRER* 41:22 (1 June 1927), 558.

69 A.H. Harkness, "Developments in Structural Design," *CRER* 43:54 (25 December 1929), 1488–90; "Difficult Structural Problems in Erecting Sun Life Building, Montreal," *CRER* 45:6 (11 February 1931), 125–26.

70 "Sun Life Building, Montreal, to be Completed in Its Entirety," *CRER* 43:51 (18 December 1929), 1455–56. For a short time the Sun Life Building was the tallest building in the British Empire, a record soon broken by the 34-storey Canadian Imperial Bank of Commerce Building in Toronto, designed by York and Sawyer and completed in 1931.

71 Its silhouette as well as the location of its second colonnade were similar to those of the Cunard Building (1921) in New York, by Thomas Hastings.

72 "It is claimed that the proposals will give greater elasticity than the present by-law and will stimulate inventive design." "Building Heights in Montreal," *CRER* 42:5 (8 February 1928), 148.

73 Fernand Préfontaine, "L'Architecture Canadienne," *La Patrie,* 3 April 1926.

74 City of Montreal, By-law 1003, section 9, passed by city council in March 1929.

75 City of Montreal, By-law 1003, section 23. See also article 5: "When a building is erected with a frontage on two streets, the permissible height shall be governed by the wider street." By-law 1002, passed 22 February 1929, stipulated a minimum height of 35 feet (11 m) for downtown, or three stories, including the ground floor.

76 According to "Sinaiticus," if a new regulation was passed to widen St. Catherine Street, the building's first row of boutiques would be turned into an arcade linked with the sidewalk. "University Tower Building, Montreal," *Construction* 23:7 (July 1930), 240.

77 John Zacharias, "La morphologie architecturale du centre-ville ou l'émergence d'un nouvel ordre spatial à Montréal" (Ph.D. diss., Université de Montréal, 1990), 81.

78 City of Montreal, By-law 1003, section 8, passed by city council in March 1929.

79 City of Montreal, By-law 1003, section 14, passed by city council in March 1929.

80 For a complete bibliography, see Isabelle Gournay, "Le restaurant Eaton," *Continuité* 42 (winter 1989), 20–23. Note that at the same time Ross and MacDonald were building a skyscraper for Eaton's in Toronto.

81 "The Ogilvy Store," *Construction* 22:5 (May 1929), 164–66, 169.

82 To our knowledge, the first major station–office-building complex was Reading Terminal in Philadelphia (1891–93, Kimball and Wilson Brothers). Another good example, which includes a 16-storey office building, is the Michigan Central Railroad Station in Detroit (1913, Reed and Stem, Warren and Wetmore).

83 C.B. Brown, "Immense Benefits to Montreal from $50,000 Terminal Project," *CRER* 44:37 (10 September 1930), 1087; "La Gare Centrale du Canadien National à Montréal," *La Revue Populaire* (January 1931), 11–14; Sir Henry Thornton, "The Canadian National Terminal in Montreal," *McGill News* (1931), 11–14 (a description of the infrastructure only), unattributed perspective drawing on page 11. Contrary to what has been written, the dates indicate that there could not have been any influence from Rockefeller Center.

84 Alfred Fellheimer, Steward Wagner, and O.S. Payzant Associate, "Studies for the Determination of Basic Principles, Policies, and Construction Methods for the Future Improvement and Enlargement of the Windsor Street Terminal Facilities of the Canadian Pacific Railway Company, Montreal, Canada, July 1930, New York, Prepared by Alfred Fellheimer and Steward Wagner, Architects and Engineers" (CCA collection). The Fellheimer project was given one illustration in Choko, *Les grandes places,* 177.

85 The profile of the Fellheimer and Wagner towers was strongly inspired by the hotel planned by Eliel Saarinen for construction over the suburban lakefront lines in Chicago, illustrated in Eliel Saarinen, "Project for Lake Front Development of the City of Chicago," *American Architect* 124:2434 (5 December 1923), 502.

86 Willis, "Zoning and Zeitgeist," 48. Willis, however, does not cite the use of this term in the literature of the time. In the late 1920s, the term superblock seems to have been used mainly to describe very large blocks formed by residential clusters, on dead-end streets, that were criss-crossed by walkways following the formula popularized in Radburn.

87 The Philadelphia project is illustrated in Linda Oliphant Stanford, "Railway Designs by Fellheimer and Wagner, New York to Cincinnati," *Queen City Heritage* (Cincinnati Historical Society) 43:53 (fall 1985), 11. On p. 9, Stanford reproduces a study for Chicago done in 1921 by Alfred Fellheimer for Illinois Central and Michigan Central, proposing the construction of large buildings and a tower over the railway tracks along Grant Park, as well as the pyramid tower scheme for which Fellheimer and Wagner won honourable mention in the *Chicago Tribune* competition of 1922. A parallel can also be drawn between the Montreal project and that of the 75-storey Chicago Tower (1928, Walter B. Ahlschlager), built on the air rights of the Illinois and Michigan Central on the promontory where the Chicago River empties into Lake Michigan; published in W.A. Starrett, *Skyscrapers and the Men Who Build Them* (New York: Charles Scribner's Sons, 1928), 103, and analyzed by Carol Krinsky, "Sister Cities," in *Chicago and New York: Architectural Interactions* (Chicago: The Art Institute of Chicago, 1984), 67–68.

88 Alfred Fellheimer, "Passenger Station at Buffalo, New York, for the New York Central Railroad," *American Architect* 131 (1927), 481–86.

89 Isabelle Gournay, ed., *Ernest Cormier and the Université de Montréal* (Montréal: CCA, 1990).

90 Reyner Banham, "Megacity Montreal," *Megastructure: Urban Futures of the Recent Past* (New York and London: Harper and Row, 1976), 105–29.

APPENDICES

ARCHITECTS ACTIVE IN MONTREAL, 1880–1930

Montreal Architects

Amos, Louis-Auguste
(Montreal 1869–Montreal 1948). Studied engineering at Royal Military College, Kingston, Ontario, 1886–90; apprenticed to E.P. Hannaford, chief engineer of GTR, 1890–92; in Europe 1892; in partnership with Alfred Arthur Cox (Great Britain 1860–Great Britain 1944), Cox and Amos, Architects (1892–1910); own firm 1910–26; in partnership with son Pierre-Charles Amos (Montreal 1897–Montreal 1976), L.-A. et P.-C. Amos, Architectes (1926–35). Fellow of RIBA (1892; associate member and member of the Engineering Institute of Canada 1915); member of PQAA (1898); member (1909) and Fellow of RAIC.

Archibald, John Smith
(Inverness, Scotland, 1872–Montreal 1934). Apprenticed to John William MacIntosh, Inverness, 1887–93; moved to Montreal 1893 and worked for Edward Maxwell; in partnership with Charles Jewett Saxe (Saint Albans, Vermont, 1870–Montreal 1943), Saxe and Archibald, Architects (1897–1915); own firm 1915–34. Member and president of PQAA (1898, 1905); member, president, and Fellow of RAIC (1909, 1924–26, 1930).

Barott, Ernest Isbell (Canastota, N.Y., 1884–Montreal 1966). Studied architecture at the University of Syracuse 1902–05; further studies and travels in Europe 1906; worked for McKim Mead and White, New York City, 1905–11; moved to Montreal 1911; in partnership with Gordon H. Blackader and Daniel T. Webster, Barott Blackader and Webster, Architects (1912–17); partner in Barott and Blackader, Architects (1917–35). Member of PQAA and of RAIC (1912); Fellow of RAIC (1930); president of PQAA (1931); Fellow of RIBA (1932).

Beaugrand-Champagne, Aristide
(Saint-Anicet, Quebec, 1876–Outremont 1950). Diploma in architecture from EPM 1911; taught in Montreal at EPM from 1908 and at EBA from 1923; own firm 1902–30. Member of PQAA and of RAIC (1913).

Blackader, Gordon Home (Montreal 1885–Ypres, Belgium, 1916). B.Arch., McGill University 1906; worked for McKim Mead and White, New York City, 1907–08; studied at EBA, Paris, in studio of Laloux-Chifflot 1909–12; partner in Barott Blackader and Webster, Architects (1912–16). Member of PQAA and of RAIC (1912).

Brown, David Robertson (Montreal 1869–Montreal 1946). Apprenticed to A.F. Dunlop 1885, then Hutchison and Steele; worked for Shepley Rutan and Coolidge, Boston; returned to Montreal and opened own firm 1892; partner in Brown MacVicar and Heriot, Architects (1895–98), Brown and Miller, Architects (1898), and Brown and Vallance, Architects (1905–19); opened own firm 1919. Member and president of PQAA (1893, 1908); member (1909), Fellow, and president of RAIC (1920–22); Fellow of RIBA.

Burgess, Cecil Scott (Bombay, India, 1870–Edmonton, Alberta, 1971). Apprenticed to Sir G. Washington Browne, Edinburgh, 1887–91, then Peddie and Washington Browne 1891–95; in Europe 1900; moved to Montreal 1903; president of PQAA Sketching Club 1905; assistant professor, Dept. of Architecture, McGill University 1906–11; taught at University of Alberta 1913–40 while serving as consulting architect for Alberta government. Member of RIBA (1896), of PQAA (1903), and of RAIC (1909).

Capper, Stewart Henbest
(London 1859–Cairo 1925). M.A., University of Edinburgh 1880; tutor and private secretary to a British diplomat, Lisbon and Madrid, 1879–84; studied at EBA, Paris, in studio of Jean-Louis Pascal and travelled in France and Italy 1884–87; worked for Sir G. Washington Browne and F.W. Simon, Edinburgh, until 1891; own firm 1891–96; taught at School of Applied Art and at University of Edinburgh; moved to Montreal to become first Macdonald Professor of Architecture, McGill University, 1896–1903; returned to Great Britain 1903. Member of RIBA (1891) and of PQAA (1896); member of RCAA (1898); president of PQAA (1899–1900).

Charbonneau, René (St. Henri, Quebec, 1881–Montreal 1969). Business College diploma 1900; draftsman for architect Joseph Sawyer; opened own firm 1909; in partnership with Louis-Napoléon Audet (Lambton, Quebec, 1881–Sherbrooke 1971), Audet et Charbonneau, Architectes (1913–18). Member of PQAA (1907) and of RAIC (1909).

Cormier, Ernest (Montreal 1885–Montreal 1980). Engineering diploma, EPM, 1906; structural engineer, Dominion Bridge Co., Montreal, 1906–08; correspondence course with École du Bâtiment, Paris, 1907; entered studio of Godefroy and Freynet, Paris, 1908; studied at EBA, Paris, in studio of Jean-Louis Pascal 1909–14; French government diploma (DPLG) 1917; worked for Pierre Patout, Paris, 1912; in Rome on RIBA-sponsored Jarvis scholarship 1914–17; worked for Considère Pelnard et Caquot, Paris, 1917; returned to Montreal and opened own firm, Ernest Cormier, Architecte et Ingénieur (1918–74); design assistant, Dept. of Architecture, McGill University, 1919 and 1920; in partnership with Jean-Omer Marchand 1919–23; lecturer, EPM, 1925–54. Member of PQAA, of RAIC (1918), and of Corporation des ingénieurs professionnels du Québec (1920); president of PQAA (1929); Fellow of RIBA (1929) and of RAIC (1930); member of RCAA (1932).

Doumic, Julien-Maxime-Stéphane
(Paris 1863–Sillery-Bellevue, France,
1914). Apprenticed to the architect
Bonnier, Paris; studied at EBA, Paris,
in studios of Douillard and Deglane,
André and Laloux, 1883–93; French
government diploma (DPLG) 1893;
in Italy; opened own firm in Paris
1894–98; head of architects' division,
EPM, 1907; returned to France 1909.
Member of PQAA (1907).

Dufort, Cajetan (Montreal 1868–
Montreal 1936). Apprenticed in
Montreal 1887–89; studied architecture
at MIT 1893; returned to Montreal
1895; opened own firm 1895; in part-
nership with Louis-Joseph-Théophile
Décary (Saint-Jérôme 1882–? 1952),
Dufort et Décary, Architectes (1912–
14). Member of PQAA (1895) and of
RAIC (1909).

Dufresne, Marius (Pointe-du-Lac,
Quebec, 1883–Sainte-Rose, Quebec,
1945). Engineering diploma, EPM,
1905; municipal engineer for Town
of Maisonneuve 1910–18; founded
Dufresne Construction Ltd. 1922.
Member of Corporation des
ingénieurs professionnels du Québec
(1917), of PQAA, and of RAIC (1917).

Dunlop, Alexander Francis
(Montreal 1842–Montreal 1923).
Apprenticed to George and John
James Brown; practiced in Detroit
1871–74; returned to Montreal and
opened own firm (1874–1923); in
partnership with John Charles Allison
Heriot (Montreal 1862–Montreal
1921), Dunlop and Heriot, Architects
(1893–95); contributed to CAB. Member of RCAA (1890); founding member
and president of PQAA (1890, 1907);
founding member and first president
of RAIC (1907, 1907–10).

Fetherstonhaugh, Harold Lea
(Montreal 1887–Montreal 1971).
B.Arch., McGill University, 1909;
worked for the Maxwell brothers
1910–11; worked and studied in Europe
1911–13; in partnership with James
Cecil McDougall (Trois-Rivières
1886–Montreal 1959), Fetherstonhaugh
and McDougall, Architects (1913–23);
opened own firm 1923. Member of

PQAA, of RAIC, of Corporation des
ingénieurs professionnels du Québec,
of Engineering Institute of Canada;
associate of RIBA (1914).

Findlay, Robert (Inverness, Scotland,
1859–Montreal 1951). Apprenticed
to John Rhind, Inverness, 1876–81;
worked in firm of Sir John James
Burnet, Glasgow, 1881–85; moved to
Montreal 1885; worked in firms of
several architects including A.F.
Dunlop 1885–90; opened own firm
(1890–1912); in partnership with
son Francis Robert Findlay (Montreal
1888–Montreal 1977), Robert and
F.R. Findlay, Architects (1913–41).
Founding member of PQAA (1890);
member of RAIC (1909).

Gauthier, Louis-Zéphirin (? 1842–?
1922). In partnership with Victor Roy
(1837–1922), Roy et Gauthier, Architectes (1890–96) then with Joseph-
Égilde-Césaire Daoust (? 1881–? 1946),
Gauthier et Daoust, Architectes
(1904–22). Founding member of
PQAA (1890); member of RAIC (1909).

Hopkins, John William (Liverpool
1825–Montreal 1905). Apprenticed in
England; moved to Montreal 1852;
partner in Hopkins and Nelson,
Architects (1853–55) then Hopkins
Lawford and Nelson, Architects
(1855–59); own firm 1862–68; in partnership with Daniel Wily, Hopkins
and Wily, Architects (1869–79) and
with son Edward C. Hopkins
(Montreal 1857–? ?), J.W. and E.C.
Hopkins, Architects (1879–96); own
firm 1896–1904. Member of RCAA
(1880); founding member and first
president of PQAA (1890, 1891).

Hutchison, Alexander Cowper
(Montreal 1838–Montreal 1922).
Apprenticed to his building-
contractor father from 1850; courses
at Mechanics' Institute; practiced
as stonecutter; taught drafting
at Mechanics' Institute; established
as architect c. 1865; in partnership
with Alexander Denton Steele
(Great Britain 1841–Great Britain
1890), Hutchison and Steele, Architects (1876–90), then with son William
Burnet Hutchison (Montreal 1865–

Montreal 1959) and son-in-law and
former employee George Winks
Wood (Montreal 1863–Montreal 1941),
Hutchison and Wood, Architects
(1898–1909), then with John Melville
Miller (Montreal 1875–Montreal 1948),
Hutchison Wood and Miller, Architects (1909–19). Member of RCAA
(1882); founding member and president of PQAA (1890, 1895–96);
member of RAIC (1909).

Jones, Hugh Griffith (Randolph,
Wisconsin, 1872–Montreal 1947).
Studied at University of Minnesota;
apprenticed to George E. Bertrand,
Minneapolis; draftsman for Brite
and Bacon and for Ernest Flagg, New
York City; moved to Montreal and
became assistant to chief architect
of CPR 1908; opened own firm 1911;
entered *Chicago Tribune* competition
1922. Member of PQAA and of RAIC
(1923); Fellow of RIBA (1921); member
of RCAA (1926).

Lemieux, Ludger (Farnham,
Quebec, 1872–Montreal 1953). In
partnership with Joseph Honoré
Macduff (Longueuil 1868–Montreal
1918), Macduff et Lemieux, Architectes (1897–1918); opened own firm
1918–31, working with his son Paul
M. Lemieux. Member of PQAA (1897)
and of RAIC (1909).

Macdonald, Robert Henry
(Melbourne, Australia, 1875–Montreal
1942). Studied surveying, architecture,
and construction at Technical College,
Melbourne, 1891–94; apprenticed
to Richard B. Whitaker, Melbourne,
1890–94; acquired architectural
experience with several firms including that of cousin Robert Findlay,
Montreal, 1895–1900, 1901–03,
of George B. Post, 1903–04, and of
W.W. Bosworth, New York City;
travelled in 1900; moved to Montreal
and worked for Ross and MacFarlane
from 1907; partner in Ross and
Macdonald, Architects (1913–42).
Member of PQAA (1898) and of
RAIC (1909); Fellow of RIBA (1930).

MacFarlane, David Huron (Montreal
1875–Saint-Hilaire, Quebec, 1950).
Studied at MIT 1897, 1898; worked in

Montreal for Edward Maxwell
1898–1901 and for Hutchison and
Wood, Architects, 1901–03; studied
in Paris and travelled in Europe 1903,
1904; partner in Ross and MacFarlane,
Architects (1905–12); own firm 1912–
25; retired 1925. Member of PQAA
(1903) and of RAIC (1909).

Marchand, Jean-Omer (Montreal
1872–Montreal 1936). Apprenticed
to Perrault et Mesnard, Architectes,
1889–92; studied at École du Conseil
des Arts et Manufactures, Montreal,
1893; studied at EBA, Paris, in studio
of Gaston Redon 1893–1902; French
government diploma (DPLG) 1902;
returned to Montreal; in partnership
with Samuel Stevens Haskell (? 1871–?
1913) in the firms Marchand and
Haskell, New York City (1903–06)
and Marchand and Haskell, Architects, Montreal (1903–13); lecturer in
architecture at EPM 1904–10; own
firm in Montreal 1914–36; in partnership with Ernest Cormier 1919–23;
architectural consultant to City
of Montreal 1927. Member of PQAA
(1902) and of RAIC (1909); president
of Conseil supérieur des Beaux-Arts
du Québec (1924); Chevalier, Ordre
de la Légion d'honneur (1926);
member of RCAA (1926); president of
PQAA (1927); Fellow of RIBA (1928).

Maxwell, Edward (Montreal 1867–
Montreal 1923). Apprenticed to
A.F. Dunlop 1886; moved to Boston
c. 1886; draftsman for Shepley Rutan
and Coolidge 1888–91; returned
to Montreal 1891; opened own firm
1892; in Europe 1895, 1896; created
firm (1899–1902) with George Cutler
Shattuck (? 1864–? 1923), former
colleague at Shepley Rutan and
Coolidge; travelled to New York City,
London, and Paris 1901; in partnership
with brother William Sutherland
Maxwell in Edward and W.S. Maxwell,
Architects (1902–23). Member of
PQAA (1891), of RCAA (1908), and
of RAIC (1909).

Maxwell, William Sutherland
(Montreal 1874–Montreal 1952).
Worked in firm of his brother Edward
1892, 1898–99, 1900–02; apprenticed
to Winslow and Wetherell, Boston,

1895–98; evening classes at Boston Architectural Club; studied at EBA, Paris, in studio of Jean-Louis Pascal 1899–1900; in partnership with brother Edward in Edward and W.S. Maxwell, Architects (1902–23); in Europe 1925. Member of PQAA (1898) and of RCAA (1912); president of PQAA (1914); Fellow of RIBA (1928).

Nobbs, Percy Erskine (Haddington, Scotland, 1875–Montreal 1964). Drawing courses at Heriot Watt College, School of Art, and School of Applied Art, Edinburgh, 1889–96; M.A., University of Edinburgh, 1896; apprenticed to Robert Lorimer 1896–1900; received Tite prize from RIBA 1900; in Europe 1900; worked for London County Council 1901; received Owen Jones scholarship from RIBA and worked for Alfred Hessell Tiltman 1902; worked in various London offices 1903; moved to Montreal 1903; second Macdonald Professor of Architecture, McGill University, 1903–11; in practice with several colleagues and in partnership with George Taylor Hyde (Montreal 1879–Montreal 1944), Nobbs and Hyde, Architects (1910–44); professor of design, Dept. of Architecture, McGill University, 1911–39. Associate member of RIBA (1900); member of PQAA (1903) and of RAIC (1909); Fellow of RIBA (1910); member of RCAA (1919); president of PQAA (1924), of Town Planning Institute of Canada (1928–29), and of RAIC (1929–32).

Painter, Walter Scott (? 1877–? 1957). Studied in Pennsylvania and in Michigan; moved to Montreal 1901; partner in Brown and Painter, Architects (Toronto; 1904–05); chief architect, CPR, 1905–11; opened own firm 1911. Member of PQAA and of RAIC (1909).

Payette, Eugène (Montreal 1874–Montreal 1959). Apprenticed to William McLea Walbank 1889–93; worked for Joseph Venne 1896–1902; in partnership with Joseph E. Huot, Huot et Payette, Architectes (1902–07); own firm 1907–47. Member and president of PQAA (1896, 1922); member of RAIC (1909); Fellow of RIBA (1928).

Perrault, Jean-Julien (Montreal 1893–Montreal 1970). B.Arch., McGill University, 1915; studied at Columbia University and New York Institute of Design 1915; draftsman for Warren and Wetmore, New York City, c. 1916, then for Donn Barber and for Francis Y. Joannes; returned to Montreal and worked with architect father Joseph-Ovide Perrault (? 1866–Montreal 1923), brother of Maurice Perrault; in partnership with Joseph-Roméo Gadbois (? 1890–? 1959), Perrault et Gadbois, Architectes (1923–32). Member of PQAA and of RAIC (1915).

Perrault, Maurice (Montreal 1857–? 1909). Apprenticed to his father Henri-Maurice Perrault (Montreal 1828–? 1903) succeeding him in 1880; in partnership with architect and sculptor Albert Mesnard (? 1845–? 1909), a former employee of his father, in firm Perrault et Mesnard, Architectes (1880–92), which became Perrault Mesnard et Venne, Architectes (1892–95) with the arrival of Joseph Venne. Founding member of PQAA (1890).

Poivert, Jules (Bordeaux 1867–Montreal 1955). Studied at EBA, Paris, in studios of Blanquier and Laloux from 1886; French government diploma (DPLG) 1905; practiced in Paris, in particular with Victor Laloux; Inspecteur, Exposition Universelle, Paris, 1900; moved to Montreal; professor and head of architecture division, EPM, 1909–23; professor and head of department of architecture, EBA, Montreal, from 1923. Member of PQAA and of RAIC (1910).

Préfontaine, Fernand (Montreal 1888–Montreal, 1949). Diploma in architecture, EPM, 1911; frequent trips to Paris; a founder of the review *Le Nigog*, 1918.

Resther, Jean-Baptiste (Montreal 1830–Montreal 1896). Worked with his contractor father 1847–49; contractor, St. Hyacinthe; opened own firm in Montreal 1867; in partnership with son Jean-Zéphyrin Resther, J.-B. Resther et Fils, Architectes (1878–81, 1893–1904), which became Resther et Vanier, Architectes (1881–93)

with the arrival of J.-É. Vanier. Founding member of PQAA (1890).

Resther, Jean-Zéphyrin (St. Hyacinthe, Quebec, 1857–Montreal 1910). Apprenticed to George Browne then Victor Roy 1876, 1877; worked in engineering division, Compagnie de navigation Ontario Richelieu, and for CPR; in partnership with his father Jean-Baptiste Resther 1878–96; opened own firm 1896. Founding member and president of PQAA (1890, 1909); member of RAIC (1909).

Ross, George Allen (Montreal 1878–Montreal 1946). Draftsman for GTR 1900; studied at MIT 1900–02; worked for Parker and Thomas, Boston, and Carrère and Hastings, New York City, 1903–04; studied at EBA, Paris, in studio of Gaston Redon 1904–05; partner in Ross and MacFarlane, Architects (1905–12) then Ross and Macdonald, Architects (1913–42). Fellow of RIBA (1904); member of PQAA (1905) and of RAIC (1909).

Shorey, Harold Edgar (Montreal 1886–? 1971). B.Arch., McGill University, 1907; worked in New York City for Warren and Wetmore and for George B. Post and Sons; in Europe 1912; opened own firm 1913; in partnership with Samuel Douglas Ritchie (? 1887–? 1959), Shorey and Ritchie, Architects (1919–47).

Spence, David Jerome (Louisville, Kentucky, 1873–Montreal 1955). Studied architecture at MIT, 1896; studied in Paris; practiced in Boston with Chapman and Frazer and with Ball and Dabney; arrived in Montreal 1901; in partnership with former fellow MIT student Samuel Arnold Finley (Montreal 1873–Monte-Carlo 1933), Finley and Spence, Architects (1901–12); own firm 1912–37. Member of PQAA (1901); member (1909) and Fellow of RAIC.

Stone, Howard Colton (Northampton, Mass., ?–Montreal 1918). Practiced in New York City; arrived in Montreal 1896; opened own firm 1901. Member of PQAA (1901) and of RAIC (1909).

Taylor, Sir Andrew Thomas (Edinburgh 1850–London 1937). Apprenticed in Edinburgh with the firms Frederick Thomas Pinkington and John Bell 1864–69; worked for William Smith, architect for the City of Aberdeen, 1870, 1871; studied at Royal Academy, London, 1874–78; worked in firm of Joseph Clarke, architect for the diocese of Canterbury, 1872–78; received second prize in competition for Glasgow Municipal Building; in partnership with George William Hamilton Gordon (London 1854–London 1906) in London firm Taylor and Gordon (1882–88); moved to Montreal 1883; partner in Taylor Gordon and Bousfield, Architects (1884–88), Taylor and Gordon, Architects (1888–1903), and Taylor Hogle and Davis, Architects (1903–09) with two former apprentices Huntly Ward Davis (Montreal 1875–Montreal 1952) and Morley W. Hogle (Phillipsburg, Quebec, 1870–Phillipsburg 1920); taught architecture at Montreal Presbyterian College; returned to London c. 1904. RIBA medal (1874, 1881); member and Fellow of RIBA (1878, 1889); founding member and president of PQAA (1890, 1896–97); member of RCAA (1890).

Traquair, Ramsay (Edinburgh 1874–Guysborough, Nova Scotia, 1952). Studied at University of Edinburgh 1891; apprenticed to S.H. Capper 1891–94; studied at University of Bonn 1895 and School of Applied Art, Edinburgh, 1896; scholarship from National Art Survey of Scotland 1896–97; worked for Sir G. Washington Browne 1897 then for Robert Lorimer and Sydney Mitchell 1899–1904; travelled in Europe with P.E. Nobbs and Cecil S. Burgess 1900; taught at Edinburgh College of Art 1904–13, directing architectural program in 1908; opened own firm in Edinburgh (1905–13); bursary from British School of Archeology, Athens, 1905; scholarship from Byzantine Research Fund 1909; moved to Montreal 1913; professor of architecture and third Macdonald Professor of Architecture, McGill University, 1913–38. Associate of RIBA (1900); member of PQAA and of RAIC (1915); Fellow of RIBA (1921) and of RAIC.

Vallance, Hugh (Hamilton, Ontario, 1866–Montreal? 1947). Worked for Charles W. Mulligan, Hamilton, 1883; studied at MIT and in Paris 1883–1900; chief draftsman with Hartwill Richardson and Driver, Boston, 1900–07; vice-president, Boston Architectural Club, 1905; moved to Montreal 1907; in partnership with David Robertson Brown, Brown and Vallance, Architects (1907–19); own firm 1919–37. Member and president of PQAA (1907, 1917); member of RAIC (1909) and of RCAA (1926); Fellow of RIBA (1928).

Vanier, Joseph-Émile (Terrebonne, Quebec, 1858–Montreal 1934). Engineering diploma, EPM, 1877; worked in Los Angeles 1878, 1879; returned to Montreal and directed public works in several municipalities; professor, EPM, 1880–96; partner in Resther Resther et Vanier, Architectes (1881–93). Member of Corporation des ingénieurs professionnels du Québec; member and president of PQAA (1898, 1921); member of Engineering Institute of Canada; member of RAIC (1909).

Venne, Joseph (Montreal 1859–Montreal 1925). Chief draftsman, Perrault et Mesnard, Architectes, 1891, 1892; partner in Perrault Mesnard et Venne, Architectes (1892–95); own firm 1896–1910; in partnership with Louis Labelle, Venne et Labelle, Architectes (1911–23). Founding member (1890) and president of PQAA (1901–02, 1912); member of RAIC (1909).

Venne, Louis-Alphonse (Montreal 1875–Montreal 1934). Studied at École du Conseil des Arts et Manufactures, Montreal; apprenticed to Perrault Mesnard et Venne, Architectes, 1893–95; chief draftsman, Maurice Perrault, Architecte 1896–1909; own firm (1903–11); drawing instructor, École du Conseil des Arts et Manufactures, 1902–09, 1910–12; in partnership with Joseph-Dalbé Viau (Ste. Anne de Bellevue, Quebec, 1881–Lachine? 1938), Viau et Venne, Architectes (1912–34). Member of PQAA (1898) and of RAIC (1909).

American Firms

Babb Cook and Willard
New York City, 1884–c. 1900
Babb, George Fletcher (New York City 1836–Holden, Mass., 1915). Apprenticed to T.R. Jackson, New York City, c. 1852–59; in partnership with Nathaniel G. Foster (1859–65); worked for Russell Sturgis 1865–68; in partnership with Walter Cook (1877–84) then Daniel W. Willard, Babb Cook and Willard (1884–1900).
Cook, Walter (Buffalo 1846–New York City 1916). B.A. and M.A., Harvard University, 1869, 1872; studied at Polytechnikum, Munich, 1872–74; studied at EBA, Paris, in studio of Émile Vaudremer 1874–77; returned to New York City 1877; in partnership with George F. Babb (1877–84) then Daniel W. Willard, Babb Cook and Willard. Fellow and president of AIA (1891, 1912–13); member of National Society of Arts and Letters.
Willard, Daniel Wheelock (Brookline, Mass., 1849–California, after 1902). Bachelor of mechanical engineering, MIT, 1870; partner in Babb Cook and Willard.

Badgley, Sidney Rose (Ernestown, Ontario, 1850–Cleveland 1917). Apprenticed to Richard Cunningham Windeyer, Toronto, c. 1871–75; opened own firm in Saint Catharines, Ontario, 1876; moved to and opened firm in Cleveland, Ohio, 1887; in partnership with William H. Nicklas c. 1896.

Carrère and Hastings
New York City, 1885–1911, 1911–29
Carrère, John Merven (Rio de Janeiro 1858–New York City 1911). Studied at EBA, Paris, in studios of Ruprich and Robert, Lainé and Ginain, 1878–82; moved to New York City 1882; worked for McKim Mead and White 1883–85; in partnership with Thomas Hastings; chief architect, Pan American Fair, Buffalo, 1901. Fellow of AIA (1891); member of National Academy of Design (1910).
Hastings, Thomas (New York City 1860–New York City 1929). Worked for Herter Brothers and Charles Atwood, New York City; studied architecture at Columbia University, New York City,

1878–80; studied at EBA, Paris, in studios of André and Laloux 1880–82; worked for McKim Mead and White 1883–85; in partnership with J.M. Carrère. Fellow of AIA (1892); member of the jury, Exposition Universelle, Paris, 1900; Chevalier, Ordre de la Légion d'honneur (1901); member of National Academy of Design; Gold Medal, RIBA (1922); Membre étranger associé, Académie des Beaux-Arts, Paris (1926); member of PQAA.

Clinton, Charles William (New York City 1838–New York City 1910). Apprenticed to and worked for Richard Upjohn, c. 1854–57; opened firm of Clinton and McDonald (1857–62), in partnership with Edward T. Potter (1863–94); in partnership with William H. Russell, of Clinton and Russell (1894–1907); own firm 1907–10. Fellow of AIA (1864).

Crane, Charles Howard (Hartford, Conn., 1885–London 1952). Worked for Bailey and Goodrich, Hartford; worked for Albert Kahn, for Finch Hinchmans and Grill, and for Gustave A. Mueller, Detroit; opened own firm in Detroit 1909; opened firm in Windsor, Ontario; worked in Milan 1934; moved to Great Britain 1935.

Densmore and Leclear
Boston, c. 1905–25
Densmore, Edward Dana (Sommerville, Mass., 1871–? 1925). Studied mechanical engineering at MIT; in partnership with Clifford Leclear.

Fellheimer and Wagner
New York City, 1923–c. 1958
Fellheimer, Alfred T. (Chicago 1875–New York City 1959). B.Arch., University of Illinois, 1895; worked for Frost and Granger, Chicago, c. 1898–1902 then for Reed and Stem, Saint Paul, 1903–11; in partnership with Allen H. Stem (1911–14); opened firms of Fellheimer and Long and Allen Stem Associated, New York City (1914–22), and Fellheimer and Wagner (1923–c. 1958); in Europe 1927. Fellow of AIA (1935).
Wagner, Steward (Marlin, Texas, 1886–New York City 1958). Worked for

Allan Jacobs, New York City, 1907–09; studied at Columbia University 1907–09 and in studio of Henry Hornbostel, New York City, 1907–10; worked for Architectural Dept., Board of Education, Newark, 1909, 1910; worked in New York City for Henry Van Buren Magonigle 1910–12 then Tracy and Swartwout 1912–14; opened own firm, New York City (1915–21); in partnership with Alfred T. Fellheimer, Fellheimer and Wagner. Fellow of AIA (1936).

Frost and Granger
Chicago, 1898–1910
Frost, Charles Sumner (Lewiston, Maine, 1856–Chicago 1931). B.Sc., MIT, 1876; worked for Peabody and Stearns, Boston, 1879–81; moved to Chicago and formed partnership with Henry Ives Cobb (1882–89); own firm 1890–97; in partnership with A.H. Granger. Fellow of AIA (1889); member of PQAA (1903).
Granger, Alfred Hoyt (Zanesville, Ohio, 1867–Roxbury, Conn., 1939). B.A., Kenyon College, 1887; studied at MIT 1887; studied at EBA, Paris, in studio of Jean-Louis Pascal 1887–89; worked for Shepley Rutan and Coolidge, Boston, c. 1889–93 then for Jenney and Mundie, Chicago, 1893; opened own firm (1893–95); in partnership with Frank B. Meade, Cleveland (1895–98) then Charles S. Frost, Chicago (1898–1910); moved to Philadelphia 1910; partner in Granger Lowe and Bollenbacher (1910–30). Fellow of AIA (1926).

Fuller and Wheeler
Albany, N.Y., 1883–97
Fuller, Albert W. (Clinton, N.Y., 1854–Albany 1934). Worked for Ogden and Wright, Albany, 1873–79; opened own firm 1880; in partnership with William Arthur Wheeler, Fuller and Wheeler; publication of first version of *Artistic Homes in City and Country*, 1882; own firm 1898–1910; partner in Fuller and Robinson (1910–34).

Gilbert, Bradford Lee (Watertown, N.Y., 1853–New York City 1911). Apprenticed to J. Cleveland Cady; opened own firm, New York City, 1882; published *Sketch Portfolio of Railroad*

Stations 1895; Supervised International and Cotton States Exposition, Atlanta, 1895 and South Carolina Interstate and West Indian Exposition, Charleston, 1901.

Hardenbergh, Henry Janeway (New Brunswick, N.J., 1847–New York City 1918). Apprenticed to Detlef Lienau, New York City (1865–70); opened own firm 1870. Fellow of AIA (1887); president of Architectural League of New York (1901–02); member of PQAA (1907); associate member of National Academy of Design (1910).

Jackson and Rosencrans
New York City, c. 1905–20
Jackson, John F. (New Brunswick, N.J., 1867–Passaic, N.J., 1948). Worked for Green and Wicks, Buffalo, 1893; moved to New York City 1901; partner in Jackson Rosencrans and Canfield then Jackson and Rosencrans.

Lamb, Thomas White (Dundee, Scotland, 1871–New York City 1942). Emigrated to the United States 1883; opened own firm in New York City 1892; building inspector and plan examiner, Bureau of Buildings, New York City, 1892–97; B.Sc., Cooper Union, 1898; partnership with businessman Marcus Loew 1908–26; opened subsidiary in Toronto c. 1913.

Lockwood Greene and Co.
Boston, 1832–1958
Montreal branch, 1913–25.

Maginnis and Walsh
Boston, 1906–34, 1934–55
Maginnis, Charles Donah (Londonderry, Northern Ireland, 1867–Brookline, Mass., 1955). Studied at South Kensington Museum School of Art, London; moved to Toronto 1884; in Boston 1885; worked for William P. Wentworth 1886–88; chief draftsman, Edmund Wheelwright, 1888–96; in partnership with Timothy F. Walsh; publication of *Pen Drawing*, 1898. Fellow of AIA (1906); president of Liturgical Arts Society; president of AIA (1937–39); Knight of Malta (1945); Gold Medal, AIA (1948).
Walsh, Timothy Francis (Cambridge, Mass., 1868–North Scituate, Mass.,

1934). Apprenticed to and worked for Peabody and Stearns 1887–97; in Paris 1894. Fellow of AIA (1925).

J.B. McElfatrick and Sons
Brooklyn, N.Y., 1886–1906, 1906–22
McElfatrick, John Bailey (Middletown, Pennsylvania, 1828–New York City 1906). Own practice, Fort Wayne (Indiana), Louisville, and Saint Louis; moved to New York City 1886; opened with sons John M. and William H. firm of J.B. McElfatrick and Sons.
McElfatrick, John Morgan (Fort Wayne, Indiana, 1853–? 1891)
McElfatrick, William H. (Fort Wayne, Indiana, 1854–Brooklyn, N.Y., 1922). Apprenticed to and worked for his father, with whom he became partner.

McKim Mead and White
New York City, 1879–1906, 1906–09, 1909–19
McKim, Charles Follen (Isabelle Furnace, Pennsylvania, 1847–Saint James, N.Y., 1909). Studied civil engineering, Lawrence Scientific School, Harvard University, 1866, 1867; apprenticed to Russell Sturgis, New York City, 1867; studied at EBA, Paris, in studio of Daumet 1868–70; worked for Gambrill and Richardson 1870–72; in partnership with William R. Mead (1872–77); partner in McKim Mead and Bigelow (1877–79), which became McKim Mead and White. Fellow of AIA (1877); founder of American Academy, Rome (1894); member of Senate Park Commission, Washington, D.C. (1901–02); president of AIA (1902–03); Gold Medal, RIBA (1903); member of PQAA (1905) and of National Academy of Design (1907); Gold Medal, AIA (1909).
Mead, William Rutherford (Brattleboro, Vermont, 1846–Paris 1928). B.A., Amherst College, 1867; apprenticed to Russell Sturgis, New York City, 1870, 1871; in Florence 1871, 1872; partner in McKim Mead and White. Fellow of AIA (1902); member of PQAA (1905).
White, Stanford (New York City 1853–New York City 1906). Worked for Gambrill and Richardson 1872–78; in Europe 1878, 1879; partner in McKim Mead and White (1879–1906). Fellow of AIA (1886).

George B. Post
New York City, 1868–1904
Post, George Browne (New York City 1837–Bernardsville, N.J., 1913). Bachelor of civil engineering, New York University, 1858; apprenticed to Richard Morriss Hunt 1858–60; partner in Post and Gambrill (1860–61, 1864–66); own firm 1868–1904. Fellow of AIA (1864); president of Architectural League of New York (1893–97); president of AIA (1896–98); director of Municipal Art Society, New York City (1901–09); member and honorary correspondent of RIBA (1907); member of National Academy of Design (1908); Gold Medal, AIA (1911).

Price, Bruce (Cumberland, Maryland, 1845–Paris 1903). Studied at Princeton University 1862; apprenticed to Niernsee and Neilson, Baltimore, 1864–68; in Europe 1868; in partnership with Ephraim Francis Baldwin, Baltimore (1869–73); in Europe 1873; own firm in Wilkes-Barre, Pennsylvania, 1873–77; moved to New York City 1877; published *A Large Country Home* 1887. Fellow of AIA (1889); president of Architectural League of New York (1897–99).

Rotch and Tilden
Boston, 1881–94
Rotch, Arthur (Boston 1850–Beverly, Mass., 1894). B.A., Harvard University, 1871; studied at MIT 1871–73; studied at EBA, Paris, in studio of Émile Vaudremer 1874–80; worked for George T. Tilden, with whom he became partner. Fellow of AIA (1883).
Tilden, George Thomas (Concord, N.H., 1845–Milton, Mass., 1919). Apprenticed to Ware and Van Brunt, Boston; studied at Lowell Institute; studied at EBA, Paris, in studio of Émile Vaudremer; opened own firm in Boston 1880; in partnership with A. Rotch; own firm 1894–1915. Fellow of AIA (1889).

Shepley Rutan and Coolidge
Boston, Chicago, 1886–1903, 1903–14
Shepley, George Forter (Saint Louis, Missouri, 1858–Promontonio, Switzerland, 1903). B.A., Washington

University, Saint Louis, 1880; studied architecture at MIT 1882; worked for Henry Hobson Richardson 1882–86, marrying Richardson's daughter 1886; partner in Shepley Rutan and Coolidge. Fellow of AIA (1889).
Coolidge, Charles Allerton (Boston 1858–Locust Valley, Long Island, N.Y., 1936). B.A., Harvard University, 1881; studied architecture at MIT 1881–83; worked for Ware and Van Brunt, then Henry Hobson Richardson 1883–86; partner in Shepley Rutan and Coolidge, directing its Chicago branch 1892–97. Fellow of AIA (1891); member of American delegation to Exposition Universelle, Paris (1900); Chevalier, Ordre de la Légion d'honneur (1901); doctorate in arts, Harvard University (1906); member of U.S. Commission of Fine Arts; member of Academy of Arts and Sciences; director of American Federation of the Arts.
Rutan, Charles Hercules (Newark, N.J., 1851–Brookline, Mass., 1914). Studied engineering; worked for Henry Hobson Richardson 1869–86; partner in Shepley Rutan and Coolidge. Fellow of AIA (1889).

Stevens and Lee
Boston and Toronto, 1912–33
Stevens, Edward Fletcher (Dunstable, Mass., 1860–Newton, Mass., 1946). Studied architecture at MIT 1883; worked for Allen and Kenway, Boston, and for McKim Mead and White, 1889, 1890; opened firms Kendall and Stevens (1890–95), Kendall Taylor and Stevens (1895–1909), Kendall Stevens and Lee (1909–12), and Stevens and Lee; publication of *The American Hospital of the Twentieth Century*, 1910. Civilian consultant, U.S. Army Corps of Engineers (1917–18). Fellow of AIA (1923); member of PQAA (1914).
Lee, Frederick Clare (Chicago 1874–? ?). Studied at Yale University; studied at EBA, Paris, 1897–1902; opened firms of Kendall Stevens and Lee (1909–12) and Stevens and Lee.

Waite, Richard Alfred (London 1848–New York City 1911). Emigrated to New York City 1857; moved to Buffalo c. 1860; studied mechanical engineering; apprenticed to John Kellum, New York City, c. 1865; studied mathematics and sculpture at Cooper Union; returned to Buffalo 1870; opened own firm 1871; in partnership with his brother, R.A. and W.T. Waite (1901–06); moved to New York City 1906.

Warren and Wetmore
New York City, 1896–1931
Warren, Whitney (New York City 1864–New York City 1943). Studied mining at Columbia University 1882, 1883; moved to France 1883; studied at EBA, Paris, in studios of Daumet and Girault 1887–91; returned to New York City 1896; partner in Warren and Wetmore. Membre étranger associé of Académie des Beaux-Arts, Paris (1905, 1909); member of PQAA (1911); Officier, Ordre de la Légion d'honneur (1918).
Wetmore, Charles Delevan (Elmira, N.Y., 1867–New York City 1941). B.A., 1889, and law diploma, 1892, Harvard University 1880s; partner in Warren and Wetmore. Fellow of AIA (1907).

Westover, Albert E.
Philadelphia, 1901–19.

York and Sawyer
New York City 1898–1928
York, Edward Palmer (Wellsville, N.Y., 1865–New York City, 1928). Studied architecture, Cornell University, 1887–89; worked for McKim Mead and White 1890–98; opened firm of York and Sawyer. Fellow of AIA (1926).
Sawyer, Philip (New London, Conn., 1868–New York City 1949). Studied civil engineering; worked for U.S. Geological Survey, New Mexico, 1888; Worked for McKim Mead and White 1891–98; studied architecture, Columbia University, c. 1891; studied at EBA, Paris, in studio of Godefroy 1892; opened firm of York and Sawyer.

PROFILES OF INSTITUTIONS

Province of Quebec Association of Architects
Founded in October 1890 by some 30 architects from Montreal and Quebec City in order to raise the professional standards of its members and to gain control of architectural practice. On 30 December 1890 Quebec's Legislative Assembly voted into law the *Act to Incorporate the Province of Quebec Association of Architects*, which protected the designation "registered" architect, a qualification elimated in its first amendment in 1898, a change that at least in principle would give the PQAA a monopoly in the practice of architecture in Quebec. A further amendment of 1905 increased penalties in the case of illegalities; another of 1929 limited the access of foreign architects to commissions. In the interests of its membership the PQAA formed many internal committees and framed regulations. It adopted its first fee schedule in 1896, its first code of ethics in 1900, and its first code for competitions in 1905. The PQAA favoured the formation of the Dominion Association of Architects in 1896. It was fully involved in the foundation of the Royal Architectural Institute of Canada, which was incorporated in June 1908 to become a federation of provincial organizations under the name Royal Institute of Architecture of Canada. *Canadian Architect and Builder* (Toronto, 1888–1908) became the official publication of the PQAA, focused on professional news – information that would later be published in the *Journal of the Royal Architectural Institute of Canada* (Toronto, 1924–59). From 1905 onward, the PQAA published an annual report. By 1930 the PQAA had 248 members throughout the province.
Sources: Fonds OAQ, ANQM.

Department of Architecture, McGill University, Montreal
In 1896, through the generosity of one of the richest men in metropolitan Montreal, William C. Macdonald, a department of architecture was created within the Faculty of Engineering at McGill University, founded in 1871. The new four-year course led to a Bachelor of Applied Science (architecture) degree. Students had common first-year courses, then diversified into specialties. The architecture program gained autonomy in 1903, after which graduates earned a Bachelor of Architecture degree. The program was extended to five years in 1914. The first three department heads were all architects originally from Scotland: Stewart H. Capper from 1896, Percy E. Nobbs from 1903, and Ramsay Traquair from 1913.

Section d'architecture, École Polytechnique de Montréal
In 1907 an architectural division was created within the École Polytechnique de Montréal, which had been founded by the Quebec government and the Commission des écoles catholiques de Montréal in 1873 and formally incorporated in 1894. Architecture was taught in two sections over four years. The first division heads were the French architects Max Doumic, in 1907, and Jules Poivert, in 1909. The division and its teaching staff were absorbed by the École des Beaux-Arts de Montréal when the latter was created in 1922.

Section d'architecture, École des Beaux-Arts de Montréal
The École des Beaux-Arts in Montreal and in Quebec City were both founded in March 1922, at the prompting of the Provincial Secretary Athanase David. The Montreal school opened its doors the following year. The initiative was part of a complex of cultural institutions that included a museum and a commission of historical monuments and archives. Under the direction of Jules Poivert, the Section d'architecture at the new school, based on that of the old École Polytechnique, offered a five-year program that led to a Bachelor of Architecture degree.

CONTRIBUTORS

Marcel Fournier is Professor in the Département de sociologie at the Université de Montréal.

Isabelle Gournay is Associate Professor in the School of Architecture at the University of Maryland.

David B. Hanna is Professor in the Département d'études urbaines at the Université du Québec à Montréal.

Paul-André Linteau is Professor in the Département d'histoire at the Université du Québec à Montréal.

Véronique Rodriguez is completing a doctorate in sociology at the Université de Montréal.

Anthony Sutcliffe is Professor in the Department of Economic and Social History at the University of Leicester, England.

France Vanlaethem is Professor in the Département de design at the Université du Québec à Montréal.

Walter van Nus is Associate Professor in the Department of History at Concordia University in Montréal.

LIST OF ILLUSTRATIONS

38 **Maisonneuve Public Baths**, 1914
(1914–16, Marius Dufresne, architect).

39 **Police and Fire Station, Maisonneuve**, 1914
(1914–15, Marius Dufresne, architect).

40 **Mother house of the Sisters of the Congregation of Notre Dame**, 1905
(1904–08, Marchand and Haskell, architects).

41 **Project for the Bibliothèque Saint-Sulpice competition**, 1911
(Jean-Omer Marchand).

42 **Bank of British North America**, 1914
(1912–14, Barott Blackader and Webster, architects).

43 **Phillips Square**, c. 1930, showing
the **Dubrule Building**
(1919–21, Ernest Cormier and Jean-Omer Marchand, architects),
the **Canada Cement Building**
(1921–22, Barott and Blackader, architects),
and the **New Birks Building**
(1911–12, Nobbs and Hyde, architects).

44 **St. Joseph's Oratory**, phase I, 1927
(1910–30, Viau and Venne, architects).

45 **Mother house of the Sœurs des Saints Noms de Jésus et de Marie, Outremont**, 1924
(1923–25, Viau and Venne, architects).

46 **Dubrule Building**, c. 1920
(1919–21, Ernest Cormier and Jean-Omer Marchand, architects).

47 **Court House Annex**, c. 1927
(1920–26, Ernest Cormier with L.A. Amos and C.J. Saxe, architects).

48 **Main pavilion of the Université de Montréal**, 1930
(1928–43, Ernest Cormier, architect).

49 **Castle Building**, c. 1928
(1926, Ross and Macdonald, architects).

50 **Aldred Building**, final version, 1934
(1929–31, Barott and Blackader, architects).

51 **Apartments for Bernard Street, Outremont**, 1922
(1922–23, Perrault and Gadbois, architects).

52 **Apartments for Bernard Street, Outremont**, 1922
(1922–23, Perrault and Gadbois, architects).

53 **Outremont Theatre**, 1928
(1928–29, René Charbonneau, architect).

54 **Architects' Building**, 1931
(1930–32, Ross and Macdonald, architects),
plan showing offices for Ross and Macdonald.

55 **Architects' Building**, 1930
(1930–32, Ross and Macdonald, architects), elevation.

56 **Banque du Peuple Building**, c. 1895
(1893, Perrault Mesnard and Venne, architects),
plan of offices for Perrault Mesnard and Venne.

57 **Crane Building, Montreal**,
(1923, Hugh Vallance, architect),
Telephone Building, San Francisco,
(1924, J.R. Miller and T.L. Pflueger, architects),
and project for a building in concrete
(Hugh Ferris, architect).

58 **Canada Life Insurance Co. Building**
(1894–96, Richard Waite, architect)
and **Canadian Bank of Commerce Building**
(1907, Darling and Pearson, architects), 1914.

59 **Board of Trade Building**
(1891–93, Shepley Rutan and Coolidge, architects;
Edward Maxwell, supervising architect).

60 **Board of Trade Building**
(1891–93, Shepley Rutan and Coolidge, architects;
Edward Maxwell, supervising architect), entrance.

61 **Montreal Stock Exchange**, 1903
(1903–04, George B. Post, architect,
Edward and W.S. Maxwell, supervising architects).

62 **Mount Royal Club**, 1904
(1904–06, McKim Mead and White, architects;
Hutchison and Wood, associate architects).

63 **Loew's Theatre**, 1916
(1917, Thomas Lamb, architect).

64 **James Ross house**, c. 1900
(1890–92, Bruce Price, architect).

65 **Central Branch of the YMCA**, 1912
(1909–12, Jackson and Rosencrans, architects;
Ross and MacFarlane, associate architects), elevation.

66 **Central Branch of the YMCA**
(1909–12, Jackson and Rosencrans architects;
Ross and MacFarlane, associate architects), section, 1910, revised 1926.

67 **Grand Trunk Railway Head Office**, c. 1900–25
(1899–1902, Richard Waite, architect).

68 **Windsor Station**, 1889
(1888–89, Bruce Price, architect).

69 **Viger Station-Hotel**, c. 1901
(1896–98, Bruce Price, architect).

70 **Windsor Station**, 1886
(Bruce Price, architect), proposed elevation.

71 **Dominion Square with the YMCA Building**, c. 1894
(1889–91, Fuller and Wheeler, architects)
and **St. James's Cathedral**.

72 **Windsor Hotel**, c. 1906
(1876–78, William W. Boyington;
annex, 1905–07, Bradford Lee Gilbert and
Henry Janeway Hardenbergh, architects).

73 **New York Life Insurance Co. Building**, c. 1890
(1887–88, Babb Cook and Willard, architects).

74 **Bank of Montreal**, c. 1885
(1889, Andrew T. Taylor, architect in chief, renovation),
alteration plans.

75 **Bank of Montreal**, 1904
(1901–05, McKim Mead and White, architects;
Andrew T. Taylor, associate architect), ground-floor plan.

76 **Bank of Montreal**
(1901–05, McKim Mead and White, architects;
Andrew T. Taylor, associate architect), vestibule.

77 **Bank of Montreal**, 1906
(1901–05, McKim Mead and White, architects;
Andrew T. Taylor, associate architect), Craig Street façade.

78 **Ritz-Carlton Hotel, New York City**, 1911
(1910, Warren and Wetmore, architects).

79 **Ritz-Carlton Hotel, Montreal**, 1915
(1911–12, Warren and Wetmore, architects).

80 **Project for the development of McGill University campus**, 1920
(Nobbs and Hyde, architects).

81 **Development plans proposed by the PQAA**, 1908.

82 **Plan of the City of Montreal with improvements
recommended by the PQAA**, 1909.

83 **Typical dwellings of Old Montreal**, 1904
(Cecil Burgess, draftsman).

INDEX